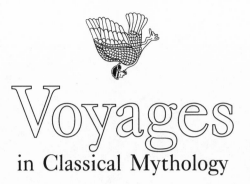

Voyages

in Classical Mythology

Voyages

in Classical Mythology

Mary Ellen Snodgrass

ABC-CLIO
Santa Barbara, California
Denver, Colorado
Oxford, England

Library of Congress Cataloging-in-Publication Data

Snodgrass, Mary Ellen.
    Voyages in classical mythology / Mary Ellen Snodgrass.
        p.   cm. — (Mythology and religion)
    Includes bibliographical references and index.
    1. Mythology, Classical.   2. Voyages and travels—Mythology.
    I. Title. II. Series.
    BL727.S66 1994 291.1'3—dc20   94-21167

ISBN 0-87436-734-4 (alk. paper)

00 99 98 97 96 95 94   10 9 8 7 6 5 4 3 2 1

ABC-CLIO, Inc.
130 Cremona Drive, P.O. Box 1911
Santa Barbara, California 93116-1911

This book is printed on acid-free paper ∞.
Manufactured in the United States of America

To Penelope, his wife, Odysseus, the radiant voyager,
spoke of all the pain he had caused others,
and also recalled the wretchedness of his worst days at sea.
Gazing with worship at her husband,
she devoured with her eyes his whole story.

Homer's *Odyssey*,
Book 23, 306–309

Contents

Author's Note

Re-creating the circumstance of a mythological voyage is like sailing the classical literary world alone in a teacup. There is so much to see, so much to comprehend, that the viewer, hampered by a limited point of view, paddles hard, spins round, and stares at a dizzying panorama while trying to take it all in. For the student of mythology, there are few polestars. The stories of the strongman Herakles, Theseus the Minotaur-killer, and the wanderer Odysseus vary from province to province. In search of aggrandizement, little communities tried to ennoble themselves by identifying a local maiden who won the voyager's love. After his departure, she remained in port to bear the offspring who sported a bit of godly or heroic genetics for local peasants to revere and to create the beginnings of new myths.

Around the Mediterranean world, there are colonnades, temples, shrines, grottoes, and rock piles that link neighborhood worship ceremonies to reverence for Dionysus, who probably passed that way at some point in his bigger-than-life journeys about the known world. Likewise, genealogies from as far east as the Black Sea, as far west as Spain and Morocco, as far north as the British Isles, and as far south as Egypt and Ethiopia boast kinship with the daring Jason and his Argonauts, with Menelaus and Helen, with Aeneas and Odysseus, and even with the obscure pilot Canopus. Such a disorderly peddler's bag of claims suggests a human need to stake out a connection of any size and significance with the grandeur of classical mythology.

A second consideration in explaining mythology involves the analysis of different eras. The stories of the gods reflect the times in which the deity ruled. Ocean or Oceanus was a Titan, the son of Uranus (Heaven) and Gaea (Earth), all names for the earliest, mightiest, and least civilized panoply of heavenly beings. Such divinities resemble metaphors for nature rather than full-blown characters. More humanized than Ocean is Poseidon, one of the Olympian gods who sprang from Cronus, Ocean's brother. Poseidon's union with earthly women reflects a lordly, yet anthropomorphic relationship with humankind. Thus, both Poseidon and Ocean represent power over the sea and, to some degree, over the weather, but the times in which they were worshiped varied by hundreds of years. By the latter portion of classical literature, the Romans, who inherited the conundrum of Greek lore, renamed the sea god Neptune and attached a whole new series of qualities and human relationships to his name.

Author's Note

As an outgrowth of a more civilized time and place, the god moved farther from the cosmically powerful, unfeeling Titans to the less capricious, more humane deities with whom Romans identified.

The conclusion the reader draws is immediately obtrusive: mythology is not tidy. In view of these far-flung, loose connections, the audience should not be surprised to find mythological beings out of chronology, out of place, and out of character. A useful example is the mixture of information about Helen of Troy. The obscure story of Menelaus in Egypt reflects a loving husband who is happy to recover his real wife and to acknowledge that the scorned Helen, whose seduction and abduction were the precipitating factors in the Trojan War, was only a *ka,* an Egyptian mirage, playing the part of self-absorbed trollop. In contrast to the tawdry Helen of Homer and the Greek tragedians, the Egyptian Helen claims a sinless decade apart from her husband as she waits for the war to end and her king to reinstall her as Sparta's queen.

With so many incarnations of mythological characters and actions, the reader is left to wonder which stories are true and which propaganda. Perhaps mythology begs the question of detail with its overriding query: What is truth? Where should tedious alignments of fact give place to a holistic perception of order in the world? And most pressing of all concerns, what is the reader's part in internalizing the themes that ancient writers selected for the edification of their readers? In short, there is no orthodox answer—only stories, wonderful stories, that capture and exemplify the facets of human nature—greed and generosity, humility and pride, savagery and compassion.

However unmanageable or amorphous, the enduring classic narratives remain as a legacy of Western lore. Some, like pot shards, preserve only a glimmer or profile of a thought; others are as detailed as the complex arrangement of tesserae into mosaics. Each myth is one small increment of human knowledge. Timeless and timely, mythology affords the reader the same challenge as the sea grants the voyager, a taste of what life offers to those who dare. (Regarding quotes throughout this book, where ancient texts violate the idioms and rhythms of current speech, I provided my own translations as a means of returning the reader to familiar territory. Where errors appear, I claim them as my own.)

Introduction

To the early Greek, listening to a travel story was an evening well spent. The soft strum of the lyre and the hypnotic chant of the poet swelled hearts with pride in ancient ancestries and filled imaginations with pictures: of an enchanted isle, where a buxom nymph could ensnare a zealous warrior with her wiles and change his men into pigs; of the silent boatman, poling his launch across the fearsome, chill waters that encircled Hades as he carried a pair of dread-filled passengers to the throne of the Underworld; of a distant realm, where a bewitching princess, infatuated with a handsome ship captain, would abandon her family and follow the crew back to Greece, sacrificing in their wake the dismembered remains of her brother. For the audience, the setting of these lyric, suspenseful retellings of mythic lore required the basic elements of hospitality—comrades, a fireside, banquet, table, full cup, and full belly. Anxieties and worries slipped away as half-lidded eyes gazed beyond trenchers to the spume of the deep, where pointed prows sliced through the waves and rocked to the rhythm of creaking ropes and wind on sail.

Much like people of modern times, dwellers of the ancient Mediterranean world maintained an inherent interest in their neighbors and in wandering. Voyagers and adventurers made distinguished forays into distant lands, often as a matter of personal or national business and sometimes out of curiosity. The vitae of voyagers include some of the great moments in mythology, particularly Jason's search for the Golden Fleece, a trip that took him east from Greece through the Hellespont into the distant waters of the Sea of Marmara and the Black Sea. In the lair of a scaly monster, Jason snatched his treasure from a tree limb, gathered up the king's daughter, and slapped oars against wave in a dash toward home. Likewise, Herakles, who was dispatched from Argos to satisfy the whims of a malevolent king, accomplished difficult quests in his twelve labors and on later treks. Ultimately, the total route took him about the Peloponnesus and beyond Greek territory as far west as the Pillars of Herakles, which marked the separation between Spain and Morocco, and into the Underworld to steal a dog more terrifying than Jason's dragon. Orpheus also followed the shadowy way downward to Persephone's throne, where he sang his solemn ballad and begged for the return of his bride. Unlike Herakles and Jason, however, he bore no prizes and enjoyed no homecoming.

Not all mythical quests reflect so singular an effort. The Trojan War saga depicts human agents acting in unison to carry out divine instructions. Like draftees from all times and places, the warriors who shipped east across the Aegean Sea had no say in their own destinies but followed the iron decree of gods and goddesses who demanded recompense for a contrived debacle. The sufferings of two nations—Greece and Troy—hinged on the questionable fortune of Paris, an outcast royal son turned shepherd, whom Olympian gods selected for a trivial task, the judging of a beauty contest. For his role in picking the fairest goddess, Paris won an appropriate reward: the Spartan queen, who was considered the world's most delectable woman. When Paris sailed west and claimed his winnings, he committed a crime that rocked the Mediterranean periphery: he accepted hospitality from a Spartan king, then violated the king's trust by seducing and abducting Helen. Paris's actions caused a chain of events that implicated an extensive cast of characters: Agamemnon lied to his wife so that he could sacrifice their daughter so that the ships could depart the harbor at Aulis safely; Epeius built a wooden horse so that the army could burn Troy and Menelaus could return Helen to his throne and his bed. Along the way, Agamemnon's warriors shanghaied Odysseus and Achilles and drew them into the maw of international warfare, a conflict that ended in death for Paris and Achilles and lengthy wanderings for Menelaus and Odysseus, extending ten years of war with a meandering sojourn far from home. On the Trojan side, Aeneas, extracted from a losing situation, was forced onto the Mediterranean Sea to search out a place on which to house Troy's gods. Thus Troy, founded again on the banks of Italy's Tiber River, got a new beginning from members of the ragtag band who managed to survive their goddess-cursed leader's repeated false starts.

Not all voyages were dominated by male questers like Agamemnon, Achilles, and Aeneas. After the war, Andromache, a thrice-married widow, found love and welcome in a fourth liaison, which took her far from Troy, the fallen city left behind in ash and grievous memory. So, too, did the Danaides of Egypt flee a miserable matrimony and search out a better life in Argos, and Helen abandoned a makeshift refuge among Egyptians and returned with her husband to Sparta. One may well wonder whether the women were as successful as the men. Did these women turn potential disaster into happiness, as did Jason, Odysseus, and Aeneas? In mythology, happiness is too fleeting a term to apply so indiscriminately. Perhaps the words *contentment* or *wisdom* better describe their compromise with fate, which classed women as the rewards of aggression and the pawns of the winners. In contrast to these human voyagers was Dionysus, the divinity-to-be who moved freely about the ancient world as far east as the Tigris and Ganges rivers, back through Thrace, and south into central Greece as he accrued an ecstatic following, decked with ivy, the symbol of eternity. From this protracted voyage—which changed a pirate schooner into a fantastical throne—evolved a worship so filled with joy and enthusiasm that it inspired Greek festivals based on the growing and harvesting of the grape vine. Dionysus himself, voyager and deity, gathered a cult so intense that he developed an entire new system of devotion based on hymns and chants, which became theater, one of Greece's most lasting gifts to humanity. From theater came re-creations of the voyages of humankind, commemorating the trips of those who learned the hard way that attempting too much is deadly fare.

The story of Dionysus was only part of mythology's rovings about inviting island clusters and stormy beachheads. So widespread was the ancient world's interest in travel, so deeply instilled the wonder of far places and mysteries that Western literature has become a shrine to the voyager, an altar to the quest. The varied names of Diomedes, Bellerophon, Leto, Dardanus, Icarus, Palinurus, Arion, and Alcaeus raise memories of fearful difficulties preceding noble and often vaunted ambitions. Dardanus's one-man skin raft reflects the determination of the wanderer to seek an unknown goal; Palinurus's fate, the antithesis of so fanciful a chase, echoes the gods' rejoinder that not all seekers, however dutiful, will succeed. Some, including Bellerophon and Icarus, died not far from home; others, such as Arion, escaped a watery death only by the benevolence of a passing sea deity. Similar to the modern urge to test the limits and touch the surface of distant stars, the ancient voyager's impulses led to murky climes and ravenous monsters and satisfied an inner drive to push beyond the sunset—to find a place not marked on maps. The price to the journeyer varied: for Daedalus, a flight curving above the Cyclades cost him a son; for Ariadne, a voyage from Crete brought brief passion with the god-like Theseus, abandonment on a distant isle, and the dizzying rebirth of passion with the god Dionysus. So it goes throughout mythology—the taking of risks and the fulfillment of the quest. And so it goes with the poet, whose job it is to tell the tale.

Voyages
in Classical Mythology

Achilles

[uh kihl' eez]

Genealogy and Background

Fated to surpass his father and to become Greek literature's thin-skinned lionheart, Achilles was the auburn-haired, bright-eyed, comely child of Thetis, the silver-footed Nereid or sea goddess, and Peleus, king of Phthia, in Thessaly in Greece's northeastern heartland bordering the Aegean Sea. Humiliated by so lowly a match, Thetis, who was once pursued by Zeus, eluded her mortal mate by changing herself into fire, water, serpent, and lion. Peleus finally overcame Thetis's trickery and impregnated her seven times; Achilles was conceived the last time.

In boyhood, Achilles was named Ligyron, which means "whining," and was alternately referred to as Peleides or son of Peleus, and as Aeacides, grandson of Aeacus, who was king of Aegina and great-grandson of Zeus. As an infant, Achilles was nearly incinerated by his mother as she tried to singe away human elements from her immortal child. Quick-witted Peleus stayed her actions and saved the boy from a fiery death, and Thetis then oiled him with healing ambrosia. Nevertheless, after Achilles was treated for a burned foot and charred lips, he enjoyed a normal two-parent upbringing until his father left with Jason and his Argonauts on the voyage to the Black Sea.

Calchas, the prophet, foretold that Achilles, then nine years of age, would someday conquer Troy. To assure his readiness, his parents had him tutored by Phoenix, the Boeotian prince who was blinded and then had his sight restored by Chiron, a wise Centaur, who also served as Achilles's tutor. As Peleus requested, Phoenix shaped his protege into an orator and warrior. Growing up swift and cunning, Achilles, noted for his commanding voice, epitomized *arete*—the quest for excellence. He learned to tame horses and wrestle, to outsmart wild prey, and even to practice medicine and debate fine points of philosophy. With the help of the muse Calliope, Achilles learned to play the panpipes and sing verses to the accompaniment of the lyre to amuse friends at banquets and to lighten his private moments of depression.

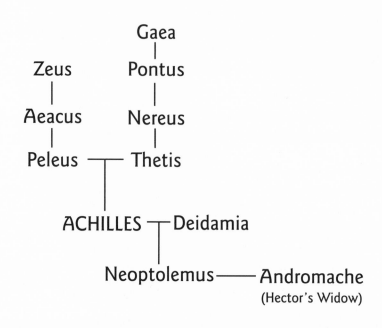

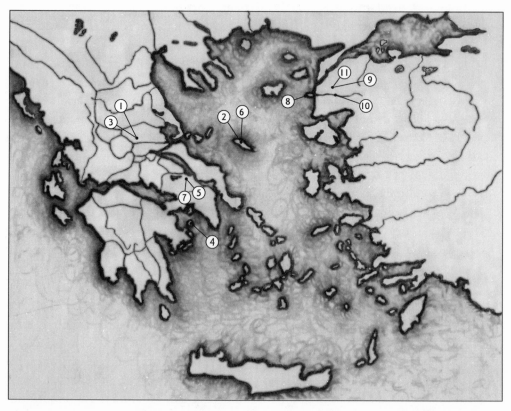

1. Phthia 2. Scyros 3. Phthia 4. Aegina 5. Aulis 6. Scyros 7. Aulis 8. Tenedos
9. Troy 10. Scamander River 11. Troy

At the end of his rigorous preparation for manhood, Achilles returned to his ancestral home, where his mother hovered over him.

Journey Warned by his mother that he had to choose between a long, mundane life or a short, illustrious one, Achilles opted for military glory, even if it brought death at an early age. Although younger than the men who had courted Helen, Achilles—at the urging of Odysseus, Nestor, and Patroclus, his second cousin who was slightly older and who had grown up in Peleus's court—agreed to accompany the Greeks to Troy and to lead his forces, the Myrmidons of the island of Aegina. As admiral of his troops' fifty ships, fifteen-year-old Achilles set sail eastward with the knowledge that his life would be shortened by the war.

The family's parting was both poignant and futile. His father, determined to assure his son's return, offered a gift of Achilles's hair to the river god, Spercheus. Thetis, far more practical in her parting moments, stood on the docks of Aulis, her hands laden with Peleus's magnificent wedding armor, which was crafted by Hephaestus, the god of fire and metalwork. She also provided Achilles with two sturdy war steeds, Xanthus and Balius, selected by Poseidon, god of the sea. Thetis's final gift to her son was a companion, whose sole job was to prevent Achilles from killing Apollo's son, the unthinkable deed for which prophecy had already condemned him.

Achilles's forces departed from Aulis, the Boeotian port across the promontory from Athens. The crew mistook Mysia, the area north of Lydia, for Troy. In Mysia, Achilles attacked Prince Telephus and pierced his thigh with a lance as the boy fled the scene. A second setback to the expedition was a storm that drove Achilles west toward the island of Scyros—nearly back to his starting point—where he again encountered Telephus. As an act of contrition, Achilles cured his victim by rubbing rust from his weapon and sprinkling it on Telephus's wound. Once the fleet returned to Aulis, it was held in port by slack winds and awaited the intervention of the priest Calchas.

Calchas called for the sacrifice of Iphigenia, the beloved daughter of Agamemnon and Clytemnestra, who was supposedly pledged as Achilles's bride. Outraged by such savagery toward an innocent maid, Achilles, the embodiment of *ate* or blind rage, attempted to rescue the hapless girl and received a rain of stones from the bloodthirsty Greeks for his trouble. The naive girl, overcome by the solemnity of the moment, gave herself willingly on the altar, and proclaiming herself savior of Greece, she predicted that her name would be blessed and honored and bid the Greeks to follow and take Troy.

With this gory sacrifice behind them, the Greek fleet moved relentlessly toward the Troad in modern-day Turkey. At Tenedos, an island off the army's intended beachhead, Achilles, noted for an ungoverned temper and conceit, quarreled with Agamemnon, his commander-in-chief. After he menaced Apollo's daughter, Hemithea, whom the earth swallowed up, Achilles caused his third bloodletting by killing Hemithea's protector, her brother, Tenes, the son of Apollo. As the oracle foretold, Achilles had sealed his fate.

For nine years, the war raged. Among Achilles's illustrious battles were the following lesser victories:

- The defeat and strangling of Cycnus, a Trojan warrior who tried to prevent the Greeks from landing, whom Achilles dispatched by strangling him with the chinstraps of his helmet.
- The killing of Andromache's father, King Eetion, and of her seven brothers, and the apprehension of the queen, who was ransomed.
- The capture of Aeneas's oxen from Mount Ida.
- The murder of Troilus, prince of Troy.
- The capture of Troilus's brothers, Lycaon, Isus, and Antiphus, acceptance of ransom for the trio, then the later slaughter of the royal brothers in battle.
- The killing of Memnon, the Ethiopian king who had bested Antilochus, Nestor's son.
- The capture of twelve neighboring towns and some islands.
- The lethal battle with Penthesilea, leader of the Amazons.

This last romanticized story describes how Achilles, pulling the face guard from the dying queen, was so drawn to her loveliness that the contemptuous Thersites, the Greeks' bow-legged bully, derided him for necrophilia. Because Thersites defaced the young woman's corpse by ripping her eyes with his lance, Achilles bashed him to the ground, shattering his teeth and killing him with his fists. For this outrage on a Greek, Achilles had to do penance on Lesbos, an island south of the Troad, before he could again command his forces.

More crucial to Homer's *Iliad* was the tenth year of the war and Achilles's boundless anger, which is the focus of the opening line of Book 1, "Sing, Goddess, the wrath of Achilles." After a successful battle against the Trojan supporter Mynes in Lyrnessos, Achilles destroyed Mynes's ancestral home and provoked Brises's suicide by abducting his daughter, Hippodameia, commonly called Briseis, who was wife of Mynes. Achilles was so taken with his war prize that he added her to his harem. In order to end a plague among his troops, Agamemnon acceded to pressure from Achilles to return Chryseis, his own war prize, who was daughter of Apollo's priest. In retaliation, Agamemnon demanded that Achilles forfeit Briseis to his commander-in-chief. Angered by such kingly highhandedness toward the Greeks' best fighter, Achilles, a victim of the deadly sin of *hubris,* or unbridled arrogance, was tempted to strike Agamemnon with his sword, but Athena, the goddess of wisdom and arts, pulled on his hair to steady his ruinous ire.

Instead, the aggrandized, self-absorbed Achilles gathered his supporters and withdrew to his tent to pluck the strings of the lyre and sing paeans to ancient heroes.

He avoided war councils and wallowed in self-pity. However much Achilles longed to return to the fray, he debated whether he should pull out permanently and return home. Weeping at the ocean's edge, he called to his mother, who came to soothe his smarting pride. Thetis, ever ready to direct her son's adult life, reminded him that the mayhem resulting from his absence might be the proper inducement to Agamemnon to return Briseis. Not content with manipulating her son, Thetis inveigled Zeus to allow the Trojans to pummel the Greeks and kill them by the hundreds to demonstrate her son's value to the army.

The ruse proved successful. Nestor, aware of the seriousness of the Greek position, urged the commander to acknowledge his insult to Achilles. Agamemnon, who could hardly deny Achilles's role as Greek strongman, made a gesture of conciliation by sending Ajax the Great, Odysseus, and Phoenix, who was Achilles's teacher and guardian, with horses, gold, tripods, and cauldrons, six gifted seamstresses—and Briseis—the focus of their quarrel. In addition, Agamemnon promised Achilles fabulous wealth, twenty Trojan women, seven rich cities, and the honor of marrying three of his own daughters.

Achilles displayed traditional courtesy to his guests by welcoming them to his tent and making them comfortable. Not so eager to yield the psychological advantage, he refused to be bribed, even with all the riches in Egypt, and pondered his choice between a short life of glory or a normal lifespan uncrowned by victories. Even though the fatherly Phoenix counseled otherwise, Achilles spurned Agamemnon's generosity with cold, spiteful words. He dawdled aboard his ship and gloated over the whipping the Trojans were dealing the Greeks. After the Trojans pushed all the way to the Greek fleet and incinerated one ship, Achilles's companion and lover, Patroclus, offered to raise morale by posing in Achilles's armor and leading Achilles's loyal Myrmidons in a drive against the Trojan advance. Achilles agreed, but warned Patroclus to return swiftly after he had achieved that one goal. The deception did indeed inspire the dispirited Greeks, who gloried in what they believed to be their invincible leader. However, Achilles failed to anticipate a fatal flaw in the deception—that Apollo would intervene and Patroclus would be killed.

Weighed down by grief and self-reproach, Achilles cried out in anguish as Hector stripped the gorgeous armor from Patroclus's corpse. Achilles was so frenzied with grief that he rolled in dust and ash and threatened to slit his own throat. For the next morning's battle against Hector, Thetis, never far from her son, rushed to Mount Etna and requisitioned a new suit of armor from Hephaestus, which he inlaid with magnificent scenes from mythic lore. In the meantime, Achilles, distraught beyond reason, led his men in funeral hymns, drove his chariot around Patroclus's bier, and vowed to accept neither food nor wine until he avenged his companion.

Distracted from his show of *hubris,* Achilles turned his attention toward a more maudlin obsession—assuaging his grief for Patroclus. Near the shore, Achilles shed copious tears for his lover until he fell asleep from exhaustion. Patroclus's spirit approached and scolded him for neglecting proper funeral rites so that Patroclus could

cross the river Styx on his final journey to Hades. Before withdrawing into the mist, the spirit directed Achilles to expect his own death and to arrange for their bones to lie intermingled in the double-handled urn provided by Thetis.

Achilles ordered nine days' celebration to honor Patroclus. Book 23 of Homer's *Iliad* details the elaborate preparations and costly sacrifices, including horses, sheep, oxen, dogs, and a dozen Trojan youths. At the end of the ritual burning, Patroclus's bones were laid aside to be mingled with those of Achilles. The rite ended with chariot racing, boxing, wrestling, footracing, archery, the discus and javelin throw, and dueling. For the winner of the chariot race, the host offered "a woman skilled in fair handiwork." During this period, Achilles insisted that Hector's corpse lie unburied and unhonored.

With his dear mate slain because of Achilles's vanity, one epic battle remained: Achilles had to atone for his wrongdoings by facing Hector, Troy's star military man and Patroclus's slayer. Achilles pushed aside his epic feud with Agamemnon and the proffered bribes. Once Agamemnon and Achilles patched up their differences by reinstalling Briseis in Achilles's tent, the great Greek warrior redirected his attention to battle and plunged unarmed into the fray, routing the enemy by his frenzied shrieks for vengeance until Thetis convinced him of the recklessness of his behavior. He recognized that time was limited in the foreshortened, but glorious life he preferred. Even his doughty warhorse Xanthus spoke human words prophesying that Achilles could not elude the fate allotted him.

Distracted by an abortive battle against Aeneas, Achilles crossed the Scamander River and, driven by epic anger, captured twenty Trojan warriors, intending to slaughter them on Patroclus's grave. Strutting in unmanly vainglory, as Homer's *Iliad* reports, he taunted the fallen Trojan Lycaon, who postured like a suppliant:

> What would you vainly weeping? Patroclus died, who was far
> better than you. Look upon me! Am I not beautiful and tall,
> and sprung of a good father, and a goddess the mother that bare
> me? Yet, lo, Death is over me, and the mighty hand of Doom.

His grandiose speech completed, Achilles lustily speared the Trojan in the neck and tossed his remains to the river. Choked with gore, the river god, Spercheus, attempted to halt the bloodbath. The god Hephaestus, who had previously taken Achilles's side, overruled Spercheus. However, before Achilles could continue his savage desecration of the Scamander River, Apollo diverted him.

The final confrontation with Hector still lay tantalizingly close at hand. Undaunted by Achilles's savagery, the valiant Trojan stood ready at the Scaean gate. Achilles, as magnificent and terrifying as Ares, the god of war, in his frenzy, directed his chariot over bodies and weapons of fallen warriors and the corpses of horses in his eagerness to dispatch Hector. Fear gripped Hector at the last moment, who ran around the city's walls three times in a futile attempt to evade Achilles's wrath. Achilles, taunt-ing and cruel, pursued and mocked Hector's cowardice.

Absorbed by the magnitude of the face-off between two military giants, the Olym-pian deities became involved. Zeus weighed the outcome and found in favor of Achil-les. Athena, assuming the likeness of Hector's brother, Deiphobus, goaded the victim to the inevitable confrontation.

Hand to hand, Achilles and Hector played out their fates. Before the fatal blow, Hector requested an oath of honor for the body of the victim; Achilles, still smarting with self-reproach for Patroclus's death, refused to negotiate and struck his prey a deathblow to the unprotected soft tissue of his neck with a bronze-tipped spear. In a last utterance, Hector predicted that Achilles would himself die soon at the Scaean gate, far from Phthia, and, out of respect for King Priam, Hector asked that his own body be returned to camp for the appropriate ceremonial honors.

Uncontrollably angered, Achilles rejected his noble opponent's proposition, then rejoiced in his victim's agonizing death, wishing that he could cannibalize the body. Driven by inhuman emotions, he laced the corpse at the ankles with thongs and, for twelve days, dragged it about the city behind his chariot in sight of Hector's mourners, threatening Hector's parents and wife Andromache that he intended to hurl the re-mains to the dogs and ravening birds. Again, the gods intervened at this monstrous show of disrespect. Thetis, bearer of Zeus's ultimatum, prevailed.

Under cover of darkness, Priam, the king of Troy and Hector's father, guided by Hermes, humbly drove a cart bearing gold equaling Hector's weight toward Achilles's camp to exchange for his son's battered corpse. Impressed by the aged man's courage, Achilles's anger subsided in nostalgia for Peleus. Greeting old Priam with empathetic tears, he allowed the grieving royal father possession of the corpse. Achilles also agreed to an eleven-day truce to conduct appropriate rites for a princely warrior. Nonetheless, the ever-present urge to wreak vengeance lurked in Achilles's thoughts, causing him to quell an urge to strike the aged king.

The end of the great Greek superwarrior, implied but not mentioned in Homer's *Iliad,* seems like a literary afterthought. Having driven the Trojans to their city walls, Achilles continued to menace the enemy. Apollo, taking the Trojan side, commanded him to desist. Refusing to yield to the god, Achilles pressed on to the Scaean gate and died with poetic justice: Apollo, the archer god, aimed an arrow into Achilles's right heel, the only spot left vulnerable after his baptism in the Styx River. Achilles was killed instantly and, so, *nemesis* or retribution ended his brief, but memorable career.

Even in death, Achilles's life was a storm center. Trojans and Greeks fought over his corpse until Odysseus rescued it. Traditional Greek rites honored his importance. His mother, assisted by weeping sea nymphs and lyric Muses, oversaw the ceremony. Athena embalmed the body in ambrosia and the Greeks burned the remains. Outside the walls of Troy, a continent away from his birthplace, Achilles's bones were interred as he had wanted—alongside Patroclus. In heroic style, funeral games were held in Achilles's honor and his armaments awarded to Odysseus, the leader whose reputation

among the enemy had rivaled Achilles. So grieved was Ajax at the loss of his comrade's armor that he went raving mad, despoiled livestock, and committed suicide.

Later, during Odysseus's sojourn in the Underworld, he spoke at length with Agamemnon. Achilles, accompanied by his comrades Antilochus and Ajax and his beloved Patroclus, joined their conversation. Odysseus greeted his old comrade-in-arms and reported that the Greeks maintained their respect for his godlike prowess in war. At first unimpressed by notoriety, Achilles repined that he would rather walk among the living, even as a common servant, than be dead. His first questions were about his father and his son, Neoptolemus; he seemed pleased that Neoptolemus gave a good account in Troy's fiery last days. With his fears relieved, Achilles strode out into a meadow of asphodel, content with his untarnished reputation.

Alternately worshiped and despised for his martial spirit, Achilles inspired a cult radiating from Greece to Asia. In Achilleum outside Troy, a temple honored his memory; as far west as Elis on the Ionian side of the Peloponnesus, women bewailed his loss as they circled his monument. Other worship centers sprang up at Sparta and Sigeum on the Hellespont. King Pyrrhus of Epirus, while facing a Roman troop, proudly boasted he was Achilles's descendant. On Leuce, a Black Sea island facing the Danube River, offerings were left in Achilles's memory and games were held to honor his strength. Sailors clung to the ghost story that claimed that his voice, rising above the roll of the surf, continued to recite Homeric accounts of bravery. Adopted as a role model by Alexander the Great, who sought to emulate Achilles's prowess, the poignantly human warrior was elevated to godhood.

| Alternate Versions | In an alternate telling of Achilles's biography, Philomela, a princess of Athens, was his mother until Chiron urged |

Peleus to marry Thetis and have her raise Philomela's son as her own. In more familiar lore, Thetis was his mother. Some accounts refer to him as her seventh and only surviving son; others as her only child. She earned lasting fame for dipping her infant son in the river Styx to make him invincible. Because she clung to her squirming babe by his heel, she neglected to remove the mortal curse from that small part of his body.

An unlikely setting describes how Arce relinquished her wings to Thetis as a wedding present and how the wings were attached to Achilles's feet, leading to the sobriquet Podarces or "swift-footed." As a child, Achilles came under the tutelage of Chiron, the noted Centaur pedagogue who taught Jason, Actaeon, and Asclepius and who doctored Achilles's burns by installing the metatarsus from the corpse of Damysus, a fleet-footed giant. Armed with knowledge that her son would be an essential participant—and victim—of the Trojan War, Thetis attempted to save her nine-year-old by hiding him from public scrutiny.

Because of her overmothering, Thetis quarreled with her husband and deserted her family. Peleus chose to leave the motherless Achilles on Mount Pelion in the care of the wise Chiron, Chiron's mother, Philyra, and his wife, Chariclo, who was the daughter of Apollo, god of prophecy. There the boy, renamed Achilles, grew strong on honey, the marrow of bear bones, and the organ meat of lions, all of which blended to form a balanced nature that was both persuasive and manly. He became so cunning and swift that legend claims he was able to outrun a deer. When the boy was still young and malleable, he returned to the palace and studied under Phoenix.

Additional alterations in the story of Achilles describe Peleus's foreknowledge that Achilles would die at Troy's gates. Thetis, in an effort to spare her favorite, hid him away among the women of Lycomedes's household on the island of Scyros, dressed the fifteen-year-old in skirts and heavy veils to conceal his budding manhood, and encouraged womanish ways by suppressing his natural bent for weapons and bravado. After nine years of transvestism under the alias of Pyrrha or "golden-haired," the boy's manhood asserted itself. He mated with Princess Deidamia and fathered his famous son Neoptolemus, also named Pyrrhus after Achilles's female alias. At the end of the Trojan War, this child, a loyal, but savage offspring, tossed Hector's son Astyanax over the walls of Troy and murdered Princess Polyxena over King Priam's grave in retaliation for Achilles's death.

A necessary part of the Greeks' war strategy, the youthful Achilles was sought by numerous messengers, but remained concealed on Scyros. Then he failed a test devised by the brainy Odysseus: disguised as a peddler, the wily Ithacan offered Achilles a choice between baubles, yard goods, sewing thread and needles, and an archery set. After Odysseus sounded a call to arms, Achilles's immediate selection of weapons revealed his identity. As might be expected, Achilles was the only "girl" of Lycomedes's harem who stood his ground in manly fashion. Either by force or persuasion, Odysseus recruited him for the war effort.

Many versions connect Achilles's name with a variety of women:

- On the way to war, he is reported to have married Deidamia at Scyros and sired a son, Oneirus.
- At Eleuthera, Achilles is reported to have attacked the city and to have abducted Stratonice.
- During a raid on Methymna, an island south of Troy off the shores of Asia Minor, Achilles is said to have fallen in love with Peisidice, the king's daughter. He agreed through secret message to marry her, and followed his men through open gates, where he had Peisidice stoned to death for treachery.
- After quarreling with Agamemnon, he is described in one account to have kidnapped Diomede from the island of Lesbos and forced her to share his tent along with Patroclus and his lover Iphis.

- In another short glimpse, Achilles fell in love with Helen, who gazed on his manful exertion in a battle near the Trojan walls and, like a strumpet, encouraged his sheep's eyes.
- The least believable account of Achilles's romantic exploits is the assertion that he rescued Iphigenia from her father's knife, seduced her, and fathered Neoptolemus.
- Also bizarre is the assertion that Achilles fathered Caystrius, Penthesilea's son, and that Penthesilea killed Achilles, but that Thetis persuaded Zeus to restore him to life.
- Achilles's lore describes a marriage with Iphigenia on Leuce, where the warrior attained cult status.
- In one romantic variation of the death of Achilles, he fell in love with the Trojan princess Polyxena, who threw her jewels over the battlements as a ransom for Hector's corpse. Another tale describes how she accompanied Andromache and Priam to the Greek camp to reclaim Hector's body. Moved by Polyxena's surpassing beauty and by her promise to be his slave in exchange for her brother's body, Achilles agreed to relinquish his war trophy, tried to negotiate an end to the hostilities so that he could wed the princess, and even implied that he would defect to Troy if he might marry Polyxena and if Helen were returned to Menelaus. Priam countered with a compromise: Achilles could have Polyxena only if the Greeks departed and left Helen behind.
- Polyxena, according to some accounts, only pretended to love Achilles. Her guile was directed toward learning his vulnerable spot so that her brother Deiphobus could avenge Hector. During a hasty betrothal rite outside the Trojan walls, Achilles, walking barefoot, was fatally wounded in the heel by a poisoned arrow. He collapsed in the arms of his friends Odysseus, Diomedes, and Ajax, who followed in secret because they suspected treachery. Achilles's dying wish was that Polyxena be sacrificed on his tomb.
- Another version casts a more martial purpose on Achilles's meetings with the Trojans. While Achilles was conducting secret talks in Apollo's temple at Thymbria, Paris, lurking behind a statue, shot at the famous Greek, clumsily missing his vital organs and striking Achilles's foot. Ironically, the inexpert warrior managed to kill the most powerful Greek soldier without being seen or endangering himself. Alternate tellings record two variations: that Apollo directed the arrow toward Achilles's weakest point and that the bone that Chiron had grafted onto Achilles's body in boyhood failed him at the crucial moment by separating from his foot. On a desolate plain outside the city, Polyxena, the inconsolable bride-to-be, threw herself on a sword over his tomb.
- In another version, Odysseus instructed Neoptolemus to slaughter Polyxena on Achilles's tomb in his honor as a means of assuring speedy passage home

for Greek vessels. Other tellings picture Achilles's spirit, clothed in shining armor, goading Neoptolemus to savage the princess Polyxena as an appeasement to his bloodlust. In one setting, the Greeks sail to Thrace, encounter calm winds, and stab Polyxena as a means of resurrecting favorable winds. In the Underworld, Achilles was said to have taken a wife, alternately identified as Helen, Iphigenia, Medea, or Polyxena. A later tale placed Achilles with his favorite warriors—Patroclus, Ajax, and Antilochus—forever on Leuce in the Black Sea, where he married Medea.

Symbolism

The *Iliad,* much beloved by the "new Achilles," Alexander the Great, whose ancestry Pyrrhus traced to the Greek hero on his mother's side, preserves a familiar motif: the vicarious satisfaction achieved by a short-lived son eager for classic vainglory to satisfy an ambitious mother, even if he must sacrifice the entire Greek army to his *hubris.* As Alexander performed the funeral ritual over Achilles's tomb at Troy, he heaped garlands and processed naked around the spot, chanting to Achilles and testifying that he had so faithful a friend in Patroclus and, after Achilles's death, the poet Homer immortalized him in verse. In honor of the noble Greek, Alexander, his Macedonian counterpart, promised to continue the Greek war against Asia and, when his men refused a foray beyond the Ganges River, even sulked in his quarters just as Achilles had done over Agamemnon's insult to his manhood. After the death of Hephaestion, Alexander's long-term lover, Alexander, mesmerized by the myth, felt that he, like Achilles after the loss of Patroclus, must take the event as an omen.

Ironically, Achilles, the Greeks' embodiment of superlatives—handsomest, boldest, swiftest, and deadliest—and the epitome of the hero who meets death during a pivotal, self-sacrificing act, suffered his deathblow in his heel. Thus, the Achilles's heel, the vulnerable point in an otherwise invulnerable body, became a symbol of mortal contact with earthly danger. Other terms attached to his life are the Achilles tendon, which binds the bone of the heel to the muscles of the calf of the leg, and *Achillea millefolium,* the botanical name for yarrow, the ferny-leafed plant that Achilles used to cure his comrades' wounds.

The Greek hero is depicted in a variety of artistic works. Cups, urns, plates, friezes, and personal adornments featuring Achilles's beauty and courage are housed in notable world museums. One anonymous vase painter of the fifth century B.C. became known as the "Achilles painter" for his depiction of Achilles and Briseis. A mural by Sosias shows Achilles dressing a wound on Patroclus's arm. A Pompeian frieze pictures Achilles, flanked by Patroclus, glowering at Agamemnon, who stands ready to accept the surrender of Briseis. In later times, Maria Luigi Cherubini wrote an opera, *Achille,* and nineteenth-century French painter Eugene Delacroix created his *Education of*

Achilles, an idealistic behind-the-scenes glimpse of the boy Achilles learning from the Centaur Chiron.

Two minor symbols attached to Achilles's lore are the spur, representative of human force protecting a vulnerable zone, and toys, items of temptation that divulge his true identity and precipitate his involvement in a fateful war. Worshiped throughout Hellas for centuries, Achilles was memorialized as a judge in the Underworld and later, alongside Agamemnon, Hector, Priam, Menelaus, Antilochus, Aeneas, Anchises, Troilus, Nestor, and Patroclus, as the first of an asteroid group known as the Trojan planets, which was discovered by Max Wolf in 1906. Not all symbols of Achilles denote honor: on Tenedos, Achilles's name remained cursed in the temple because of his crude treatment of Tenes and Hemithea.

Later poets and playwrights adorned their verse with Achilles's exploits. Geoffrey Chaucer, father of the English language, holds a literary record for referring to the noblest Greek warrior most frequently, as evidenced in *The Book of the Duchess, The House of Fame, The Parliament of Fowls, Troilus and Criseyde, The Nun's Priest's Tale, The Man of Law's Tale,* and *The Squire's Tale.* During the Renaissance, Christopher Marlowe mentions Achilles in *Tamburlaine* and William Shakespeare made six citations in *Troilus and Cressida* alone.

Other English poets used Achilles to their advantage: John Milton described Achilles in Book 9 of *Paradise Lost,* Andrew Marvell wrote an extensive retelling in *Elegy on the Death of Lord Villiers,* Alexander Pope gave a brief comment in his *Dunciad,* and Edmund Spenser, also influenced by Achilles's strengths, featured him in *Hymn in Honour of Love* and *Ruins of Time.* The English romanticists followed this pattern with homage to Achilles in Abraham Cowley's *Pindaric Ode,* Samuel Coleridge's *Recantations* and *To a Friend,* John Keats's *Hyperion,* and Lord Byron's *Childe Harold.* The Victorians, too, preserved Achilles's splendor and might, as displayed in Matthew Arnold's *Empedocles on Etna,* and Elizabeth Barrett Browning's *The Fourfold Aspect.* The tradition continued in the twentieth century with W. H. Auden's *The Shield of Achilles,* and John Masefield's *The Spearman.*

❦ See Also

Aeneas, Ajax the Great, Andromache, Helen, Jason and Medea, Odysseus.

❦ Ancient Sources

Agias of Troezen's *Returns of Heroes,* Antoninus Liberalis's *Metamorphoses;* Apollodorus's *Epitome;* Apollonius of Rhodes's *Argonautica;* Arctinus of Miletus's *Aethiopis* and *Sack of Troy;* Dares of Phrygia's *Trojan War;* Dictys Cretensis's *Trojan War Diary;* Euripides's *Andromache, Hecuba, Iphigenia in Aulis,* and *Iphigenia in Tauris;* Eustathius on Homer's *Iliad;* Hesiod's *Histories;* Homer's *Iliad* and *Odyssey;* Hyginus's *Fables;* Lesches's *Little Iliad;* Lycophron's *Cassandreis;* Ovid's *Heroides* and *Metamorphoses;* Parthenius's *Love Stories;* Pausanias's *Description of Greece;* Philostratus's *Heroica;* Photius's *Library;* Plutarch's *Greek Questions;* Ptolemy Hephaestion on Homer's *Iliad;* Quintus Smyrnaeus's *Post-Homerica;* Stasinus of Cyprus's *Cypria;* Statius's *Achilleid;* Tryphiodorus's *Sack of Troy;* Johannes Tzetzes's *On Lycophron;* Virgil's *Aeneid.*

Acrisius

[uh kree' see uhs]

Genealogy and Background

Born to Abas, king of Argos, and Aglaia or Ocaleia, Acrisius was the grandson of Lynceus, an Argonaut, and Hypermestra, one of the Danaides, and the twin of Proetus. Even before birth, the jealous pair warred in their mother's womb. At the death of Abas, the youths fought viciously over their father's kingdom, which extended over prime land on a northeastern peninsula of the Peloponnesus. Acrisius, a brooding, evil-tempered man famed for ill luck, succeeded in ousting Proetus, then made amends with him by ceding him the adjacent land of Tiryns, east of Argos.

Acrisius's wife, Eurydice, daughter of Lacedaemon, gave birth to a daughter, Danae, a disappointment to Acrisius, who wanted a son. Also called Acrisione after her royal father, she grew to be a slender, free-spirited princess, full of laughter and joy in nature. As the age for her betrothal drew near, Acrisius consulted the Pythian oracle and discovered that his daughter was destined to bear him a grandson who would slaughter him. Acrisius became so distraught at this news that he decapitated the messenger.

Acrisius then took action to avoid the foretelling. He rejected the idea of murdering his child, in fear of retribution from the gods, and chose to imprison Danae, who was a *parthenos* or "virgin," in a subterranean brass cell and to wait for death to take her. So foul was his temper and so irate his demeanor that no citizen of Argos dared to question his bizarre solution. Later, ravished by Zeus, who entered her body through gold dust (or sunlight) sprinkled through the grate, Danae bore a son, named him Perseus, meaning "avenger," and nursed him in secret.

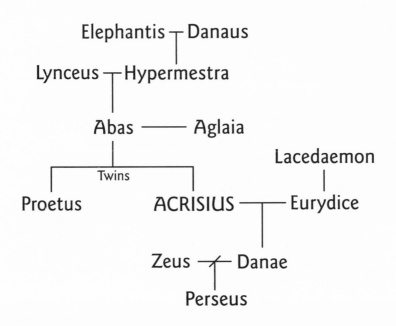

Elephantis ─┬─ Danaus

Lynceus ─┬─ Hypermestra

Abas ─── Aglaia

Twins

Proetus   ACRISIUS ─┬─ Eurydice

Lacedaemon

Zeus ─┬─ Danae

Perseus

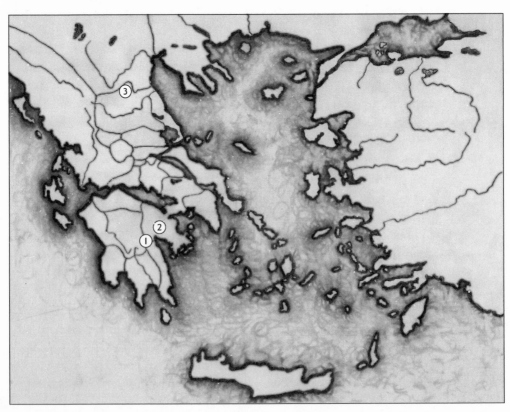

1. Argos 2. Tiryns 3. Larissa

Journey At length, the infant cried out loud enough to be heard by his grandfather, who ordered the guards to break down the brass walls and reveal the child. Acrisius was enraged and killed Danae's nurse, whom he suspected of allowing his daughter access to a suitor. Fearful that Apollo would punish him if he killed the child to avoid the prophecy, the king placed Danae and her infant in a sturdy, brass-edged wooden chest and set them afloat in the sea without food, water, or light. Zeus intervened, causing the chest to float to the island of Seriphos, where Dictys, a fisherman, netted the floating box and freed mother and son from their awful plight.

Later, Dionysus approached Argos and found that the surly old Acrisius had shut the city's gates to him and his clattering horde of Bacchantes and Satyrs. Acrisius escaped punishment for his sacrilege, but later rued his inhospitable act after Dionysus's Maenads wreaked havoc in his kingdom. In later years, after Perseus, under the protection of Zeus, was rescued and grew to manhood, he achieved hero stature and returned to Argos to visit his grandfather, who fled in terror.

To escape Perseus and certain death, Acrisius headed due north up the isthmus of Greece to Larissa in Thessaly. Perseus followed to reassure him and prepared to compete in the welcoming games held by King Teutamas, also known as Teutamides. Perseus hurled the discus; met by an unforeseen wind, the deadly revolving stone accidentally struck Acrisius's head, killing the king and fullfilling the oracle's predictions. Perseus, who bore no guilt for the act in the eyes of the gods, buried his grandfather Acrisius outside the city walls. Perseus was so grieved by the mishap that he refused to rule the kingdom of Argos, which passed into the hands of his cousin Megapenthes, the son of Proetus and ruler of Tiryns, through an exchange of the two kingdoms.

Alternate Versions An alternate telling of Acrisius's story names Aganippe rather than Eurydice as Danae's mother and claims that Euarete was Acrisius's second daughter and the mother of Leucippus, Hippodamus, Dysponteus, and Hippodameia. Acrisius is depicted imprisoning Danae for a year in a doorless tower surrounded by guard dogs, spiked walls, and sentries. There, her uncle Proetus, in order to avenge himself on Acrisius for disinheriting him, impregnated her. Acrisius, to avoid the prophecy, set her and her infant adrift in a boat without a sail, which found its way to the island of Seriphos, one of the Cyclades southeast of Attica.

After Proetus evicted Acrisius, the hapless king fled north to escape the celebrated return of his heroic grandson, Perseus. Some tellings depict Perseus as following his grandfather and others show him participating in the games without recognizing that his grandfather sat in the audience. Another version credits Acrisius with following Perseus to the island of Seriphos, where the two settled old scores. Acrisius's death scene is sometimes set at the funeral games held in honor of Polydectes on Seriphos.

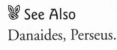
Symbolism

Acrisius, a twin, represents a common theme in ancient literature: the schism of the human spirit into good and evil. He epitomizes the darker side of human nature, as is evident by his uncontrollable temper and his plot to outwit the gods. In addition, the names Acrisius, or "darkness," and Danae, or "dawn," reflect opposites. Both were residents of Argos or "brightness." Light symbolism continues in Perseus's conception from a shower of gold, possibly a symbol of a bribe to a servant or guard. Also, Danae's child was said to be blond and is referred to as "golden-haired."

Claustrophobic images of the brass prison or tower and the floating box perpetuate the struggle between the forces of light and darkness. Acrisius's flight to Larissa suggests his attempts to avoid the coming of the light or his *nemesis*. Ultimately, Perseus, the avenger of wrongs done to his mother Danae, triumphs over darkness, but the deed is carried out by an oracular plan rather than a conscious scheme of revenge.

The term *danaeifolius* refers to laurel leaves named for Acrisius's daughter Danae. Her moving story was immortalized in paintings by Titian, Correggio, Rembrandt, and Tintoretto and in Richard Strauss's opera *Die Liebe der Danae*.

Other poetic references occur in the following works: Thomas Carew's *Mediocrity in Love* and *A Rapture;* George Chapman's *Hero and Leander;* Edmund Spenser's *Faerie Queene;* Michael Drayton's *Endymion and Phoebe;* Christopher Marlowe's *Edward II* and *Hero and Leander;* Thomas Suckling's *The Metamorphosis;* Andrew Marvell's *Mourning;* Matthew Prior's *Cupid and Ganymede* and *The Padlock;* Thomas Moore's *Intolerance;* John Keats's *Endymion;* Lord Byron's *English Bards and Scots Reviewers;* Elizabeth Barrett Browning's *A Vision of Poets;* Dante Gabriel Rossetti's *Jenny;* William Butler Yeats's *The Herne's Egg;* D. H. Lawrence's *Tommies in the Train;* Ben Jonson's *The Alchemist* (Jonson was also the only English playwright to note Acrisius's myth—in Act V of *Volpone).*

See Also

Danaides, Perseus.

❦ Ancient Sources

Apollodorus's *Epitome;* Apollonius of Rhode's *Argonautica;* Diodorus Siculus's *Library of History;* Hesiod's *Histories;* Homer's *Iliad;* Horace's *Odes;* Hyginus's *Fables* and *Poetic Astronomy;* Ovid's *Metamorphoses;* Pausanias's *Description of Greece;* Pindar's *Pythian Odes;* Scholiast on Euripides's *Orestes;* Simonides of Ceos's *Verse;* Virgil's *Aeneid.*

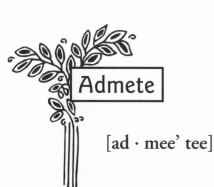

Admete

[ad · mee' tee]

Genealogy and Background

Admete was the attendant of the goddess Hera, Zeus's wife, at Argos, a city on the northeastern Peloponnesus. She was the daughter of Antimache and Eurystheus, a Mycenaean king. Admete, a respected member of an old royal family, came from good stock. Noteworthy relatives include great-grandfathers Perseus and Lycurgus, and second cousin, Herakles. Part of Admete's lore suggests that she had great influence over her royal father, who doted on her enough to insist that Herakles perform a ninth labor—to procure for her the belt of Hippolyta, the Amazon queen.

Journey

Princess Admete accompanied Herakles on his voyage to Hippolyta's court and took refuge on Samos, an island off the shore of Lydia in Asia Minor. Bearing the statue of Hera, she reopened a neglected shrine, which the nymphs and Leleges, a tribe inhabiting the Troad, had founded to honor Hera. Setting the statue in place, Admete felt that her task was complete. Later, mercenaries paid with Argive money snatched the idol and carried it to their ship. Because Hera forbade the brigands to sail away from Samos, their ship would not budge from the harbor. To appease Hera, they honored the idol on the beach, then abandoned it.

Residents discovered the idol's disappearance and deduced that the goddess herself had chosen a new spot for her worship. To assure the statue's safety, they bound it to a tree with woven rushes. However, Admete discovered the theft, unleashed the idol, anointed it anew, and returned it to its shrine.

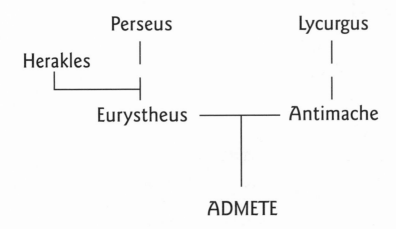

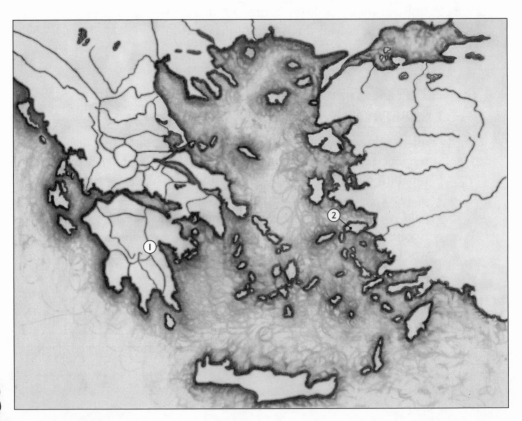

1. Argos   2. Samos

Alternate Versions One variation claims that Admete's mother was also named Admete, a sea nymph and one of the Oceanides, or daughters of Oceanus and Tethys, two early Titan deities. Another telling claims that the Argonauts carried the statue to Samos.

Symbolism The name Admete, meaning "untamed," suggests the challenge she presented Herakles. The significance of her girdle is sexual, denoting the hero's struggle for her sexual favors. Some twists to the original tale describe Admete's wily metamorphoses into a hydra, serpent, crab, deer, mare, and cloud. Another clue to the importance of Admete's myth is the fact that her name is synonymous with Athena. Because of the significance of the statue of Hera to the Samians, it became the center of Tonea, an annual feast day, during which local people presented offerings to both Hera and her devoted priestess. More recent re-creations of Admete's lore exist in artistic expressions. Geoffrey Chaucer introduced the myth of Admete to English literature in *Troilus and Criseyde;* Georg Friedrich Handel wrote an opera, *Admete.*

See Also
Herakles.

Ancient Sources
Apollodorus's *Epitome;* Athenaeus's *The Learned Banquet;* Euripides's *Ion* and *The Mad Herakles;* Justin's *Apology;* Pausanias's *Description of Greece;* Philochorus's *Atthis;* Pindar's *Nemean Odes;* Plutarch's *Greek Questions;* Scholiast on Pindar's *Nemean Odes;* Johannes Tzetzes's *On Lycophron.*

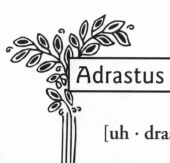

Adrastus

[uh · dras' tuhs]

Genealogy and Background

Adrastus was the son of Talaus, a minor Argive king and a distinguished member of the Argonauts, and Lysimache or Lysianassa. He married his niece, Amphithea, fathered four daughters and two sons, and became famous for his own exploits as well as those of his son-in-law, Diomedes, who fought on the Greek side at Troy. Adrastus also earned a reputation as a winner of horse races through the swiftness of his winged steed Arion, a gift from Herakles. Accompanied by his mother, sister, and four brothers, Adrastus had to flee for his life after his father died in an uprising led by his cousin, the prophet Amphiaraus.

Traveling north to Sicyon in the northeastern section of the Peloponnesus near Corinth, Adrastus inherited the realm of Polybus, who died without a male successor. Adrastus smoothed over ill feelings with Amphiaraus by pledging him his sister, Eriphyle, who bore him four children. Thus stemming a potential feud, Adrastus returned to Argos and, with Amphiaraus, ruled the Argives.

Adrastus was awakened one night by the rowdy behavior of two seekers of asylum, Tydeus of Thebes and Polynices of Calydon, the son of Oedipus, as they quarreled over the right of way. Realizing that the two men fit the description of the lion and boar whom his daughters were fated to marry, he betrothed Argia to Polynices and Deipyle to Tydeus. In Euripides's *Suppliants,* Theseus forces Adrastus to admit that his choice of sons-in-law was hasty. Nonetheless, Adrastus set out to right the wrongs that drove the two warriors from Thebes.

Journey

Known as the Seven against Thebes, the virulent conflict that arose immediately after Oedipus's death, the turf war joined Adrastus and his sons-in-law with the prophet Amphiaraus, Capaneus, Hippomedon, and Parthenopaeus, to win back co-rule in

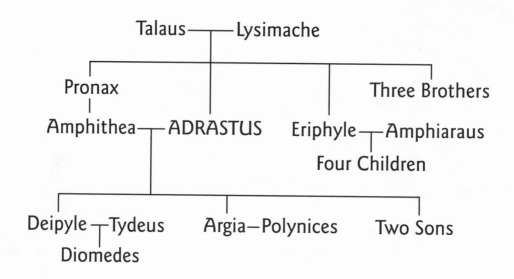

Talaus——Lysimache

Pronax   Three Brothers

Amphithea——ADRASTUS   Eriphyle——Amphiaraus

Four Children

Deipyle—Tydeus   Argia—Polynices   Two Sons

Diomedes

1. Argos 2. Sicyon 3. Argos 4. Nemea 5. Thebes 6. Eleusis 7. Megara

Thebes for Polynices, Oedipus's son and heir, who shared the throne with his brother Eteocles. These seven raised a mighty fighting force and set out for Thebes, the capital of Boeotia, which lay northeast of the Peloponnesus. The siege of Thebes began inauspiciously after Polynices bribed Eriphyle with an heirloom necklace to intercede and convince her husband and brother to help him capture the throne that rightfully belonged to him. To do so required an act of faith that Polynices and his Argive band could defeat the grasping Creon, uncle and guardian of Oedipus's four orphaned children.

On the way from the Peloponnese northeast across the narrow neck that connects the peninsula with the mainland, the band marched through Nemea, outside Corinth. While requesting directions to a spring for cool water for refreshment and bathing, they consulted the royal nurse, the priestess Hypsipyle. She settled Opheltes, the infant son of King Lycurgus and Queen Amphithea of Nemea, on an herb bed and turned to point the way. As was warned by an oracle, the child was never to touch the ground. The oracle came true when Opheltes was suffocated in the coils of the guardian serpent of the sacred grove. According to Hyginus's *Fables,* the child was buried under the name Archemorus, which means "beginning of doom," an omen of the siege that lay ahead. The warriors felt honor-bound to stop long enough to institute the first of the Nemean games held every five years in honor of Opheltes. As a reward for athletic prowess, winning athletes received coronas plaited from fragrant herbs.

Prophecy on both sides freighted the long-awaited battle with challenges to the warriors' commitment. Creon, no less concerned at the outcome, had to weigh the pronouncement of Teiresias, who warned that victory for the incumbent would require sacrifice of his only son, Menoeceus. Creon tried to evade destiny by dispatching Menoeceus from the hazards of battle. Untried with sword and spear, but eager to defend his patrimony, Menoeceus disobeyed his father and fell in the first wave. Creon took no time to mourn and redoubled his efforts to stanch the invaders. Split into siege parties against the city's seven gates, the warriors launched the seven-year expedition and, as Amphiaraus foretold, were all killed except Adrastus, who escaped on his faithful horse, Arion.

One of the most unsettling aspects of the war on Thebes was the vengeful decision of Creon, the king of Thebes, to deny the dead warriors a ritual burial. Adrastus galloped southeast to Athens, where he petitioned Theseus to allow rites for the victims of the Theban war. Theseus's mother, Aethra, spoke up and encouraged her son to allow burials. Theseus heeded her supplication and, against the orders of King Creon, marched on Thebes.

After routing Creon's soldiers, Theseus ordered the bodies of those killed in the war returned so they could be buried with honors at nearby Eleusis. When the pyre for the dead warriors was ready, Adrastus, in the presence of the mourning mothers, walked past the mangled, decaying corpses, calling them by name: Capaneus, Eteoclus, Hippomedon, Parthenopaeus, and Tydeus. As the sons of the warriors stared into the flames, a desire for vengeance was kindled in their spirits.

Euripides's version of the event dwells on drama. Adrastus singled out Capaneus's remains for special treatment. As the women crooned dirges, Evadne, Capaneus's wife, pulled away and leaped to her death on her husband's pyre. At the meeting of three roads on the isthmus, Theseus formally presented the funeral urns to the gathered families. The goddess Athena forced Adrastus to pledge that, on the pain of losing Argos, he would never lead forces against Athens. The scene ended with the sacrifice of three rams on Pythia's altar and the burial of the ritual knife in sacred soil.

Nonetheless, a decade later, Adrastus again directed an attack on Thebes, this time leading the Epigoni or "afterborn," the succeeding generation of the Seven against Thebes, in a war to avenge their fallen fathers. This second foray proved successful. Nevertheless, the loss of Adrastus's son, Aegialeus, in battle weakened the aging king. On his way south to Argos, Adrastus stopped at Megara, where he died grieving and was buried with appropriate honors.

Alternate Versions

Some accounts list Adrastus's mother as Eurynome, his wife as Demonassa, daughter of Amphiaraus, and his children as two sons, Aegialeus and Cyanippus, and three daughters, Aegialeia or Adrastine, Argeia, and Deipyle. Another son, Hipponous, receives brief mention, as does an illegitimate daughter, Eurydice, wife of Ilus, Troy's founder. A glimpse of Adrastus's realm shows a wedding between Pirithous and Adrastus's daughter Hippodamia. Other versions list Cyanippus and Aegialeia as Adrastus's grandchildren. A late version of Adrastus's elder years describes his role in the second assault on Thebes as more advisory than military. This telling describes him joining Hipponous in hurling themselves into flames to fulfill a Delphic augury.

Symbolism

Adrastus, whose names means "he who holds his position" or "the unescapable," instituted the Nemean games, established a temple to Hera at Sicyon, and was deified as a demigod in a temple in Attica and a sanctuary in Colonus and was worshipped at Sicyon and Megara. He is associated with Harma, a Boeotian town where his chariot crashed. On the Asopus River, which flows through the Peloponnesus, northeast into the Gulf of Corinth, he founded a temple to Nemesis, the goddess of retributive justice, who was called Adrasteia in his honor. The war of the Seven against Thebes prefigures the Greek siege on Troy and the destruction of the Trojan Citadel. Adrastus's story appears as the subject of Jean Racine's first play, *La Thébaide,* as well as John Skelton's *Laud and Praise,* and in brief references in Geoffrey Chaucer's *Anelida and Arcite* and Elizabeth Barrett Browning's *Queen Anelida.*

❦ See Also
Diomedes.

❦ Ancient Sources
Aeschylus's *Seven against Thebes;* Apollodorus's *Epitome;* Diodorus Siculus's *Library of History; Epigoni* (anonymous); Euripides's *Antigone, Phoenician Women,* and *Suppliants;* Homer's *Iliad* and *Odyssey;* Hyginus's *Fables;* Isocrates's *Panegyric;* Lysimadius Meursius's *On Lycophron;* Ovid's *Ibis;* Pausanias's *Description of Greece;* Pindar's *Nemean Odes;* Plutarch's *Parallel Lives;* Servius on Virgil's *Aeneid;* Scholiast on Pindar's *Nemean Odes;* Sophocles's *Antigone; Electra, Epigoni, Eriphyle,* and *Oedipus at Colonus;* Statius's *Thebaid;* Johannes Tzetzes's *On Lycophron.*

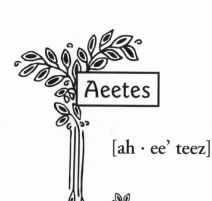

Aeetes

[ah · ee' teez]

Genealogy and Background

Although much of Aeetes's background is fraught with error and variance, he most certainly belongs to a sept known as the *Perseides,* which are named after his mother Perse or Perseis, rather than after the Heliades, a patronymic for Aeetes's father Helios, the Titan sun god. Aeetes, whose name means "man of might," "man of the land (Aea)," or "eagle," grew up with his sister Circe on the western Mediterranean island of Aeaea. The sea-washed land was sacred to Aeetes's father, who also sired Aloeus and Pasiphae.

It seemed odd that so light-adorned a parentage and home should produce so dark and moody a character as Aeetes. He was at one time king of Corinth, which his father Helios passed to him at the same time that he gave Aloeus the kingdom of Asopia. It is unclear why Aeetes grew discontent with his patrimony, left Ephyra, his Corinthian capital, to Bounus, Hermes's son, and resettled in the east. Perhaps the partially civilized land was more suited to his ruthless rule and sinister tendencies. Most of his life, Aeetes resided in Phasis, a strongly defended province of Colchis on the Phasis River, which flows into the Black Sea—the far eastern periphery of Greek mythology in what is now Turkey. Aeetes's brother, Perses, king of the Taurians, later overthrew Aeetes, snatched away the Colchian throne, and exiled Aeetes and his family.

Aeetes mated with the nymph Asterodeia, an untamed denizen of the Caucasus Mountains, and sired Chalciope. Chalciope married Phrixus and bore five sons, Argus, Melas, Phrontis, Cytissorus, and Presbon, all of whom dignified the royal line by joining Herakles's fighting force in a march on the Amazons. Aeetes and Asterodeia's most famous daughter, the sorceress Medea, suggests the genetic influence of Aeetes's family tree, which sports murky, cultish branches, suggesting the strong thread of black magic that laces together the episodes of Aeetes's history. His sister Circe, while governing the island of Aeaea, changed Odysseus's voyagers into pigs, then relented and

 33

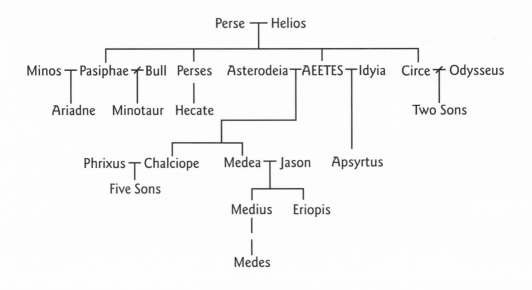

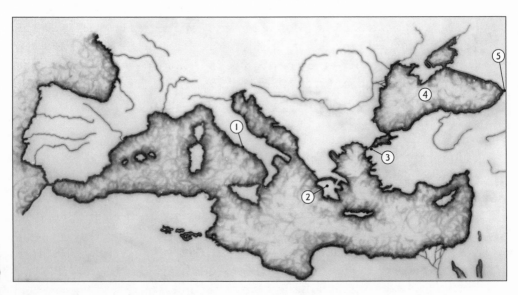

1. Aeaea 2. Corinth 3. Hellespont 4. Black Sea 5. Colchis

accepted Odysseus as lover and father of her children. Aeetes's other sister, Pasiphae, married the prestigious, fabulously wealthy Minos of Crete. Afflicted with a sexual aberration, she coupled with a bull, thus making her bestial offspring, the Minotaur, Aeetes's nephew.

After the collapse of Medea's marriage to Jason, she disguised herself, abandoned her rightful claim as Corinthian royalty, and returned to Colchis. She dispatched her eldest son Medus to kill her uncle Perses. Medea thus ended her enmity with her father by bringing him and his wife home from exile. She reestablished his rule in Colchis, possibly as a conciliatory gesture or as a means of assuring the inheritance of Medius, who founded the Medes, a major royal family in Asian history. Only Diodorus Siculus gives an account of Aeetes's death, which the Argonaut Meleager is said to have caused by stalking and murdering the king in his own palace.

Journey

Aeetes chose to journey from his realm in Greece to Colchis on the southern shores of the Black Sea. As ruler of Phasis and regent in the shining hill city of Aea, he hosted Phrixus, a Greek prince and and son of Aeetes's friend Athamas. Phrixus had escaped his stepmother Ino's plot to sacrifice him along with his sister Helle on an altar. In answer to the prayers of the children's mother, the god Hermes sent a golden-fleeced ram to save them. Phrixus sought a royal refuge by riding the ram east over the strait that separates Europe and Asia toward Aeetes's court at Aea. During this passage, Helle fell into the ocean and drowned. She is immortalized in the name of the Hellespont.

Phrixus entered unknown territory as he piloted through the air over the southeastern rim of the Black Sea, which at that time was called *Euxine* or Unfriendly Sea because of a ban on Greek adventurers. Aeetes, like other belligerent, xenophobic residents of the Black Sea coast, bore little love of Greeks or other potential usurpers from the West. Still, it was to his advantage to welcome the doughty Greek prince and give him Chalciope in marriage.

At the direction of Phrixus's mother, Phrixus and Aeetes slew the ram and dedicated it to Ares, Greek god of war. They stretched and dried the Golden Fleece, which Aeetes enshrined in an oak located in a copse sacred to Ares. To secure his treasure, Aeetes set a vigilant dragon to watch over the grove. Phrixus remained in Aeetes's debt and is said to have died of old age on Colchian soil.

When Jason, the captain of the *Argo,* came to reclaim the fleece and return it to King Pelias, he brought along Phrixus's sons, who presented an undeniable threat to Aeetes's right to the Golden Fleece. Aeetes threatened to snatch out the visitors' tongues and lop off their limbs. Then, deciding that harshness would not rid him of the Greek presence, he disarmed his visitors with hospitality, repeating his elaborate welcome of Phrixus by greeting the noble Jason with the type of courtesies found in Greek cities and other civilized ports. There was hot water for baths and a banquet table for Jason's hungry mariners before the king began questioning the reason for

their perilous mission. Jason, a straightforward man, explained that Pelias had consulted an oracle, which demanded the return of the fleece. In exchange, Jason offered to subdue the Sauromatians and add their skilled archers to Aeetes's army.

However politely Jason stated his request, Aeetes remained adamant and refused to give up his unique prize unless Jason performed the impossible—yoke Hephaestus's bronze-footed bulls, plow Ares's sacred field, and sow serpent's teeth given to Aeetes by Athena, goddess of war. Unknown to the king, his daughter Medea, a cunning, powerful magician, had fallen in love with Jason and plotted to aid his cause. With help from her sister Chalciope, Medea revealed to Jason how he could yoke the fire-breathing bulls, plow a furrow, and plant the teeth, which sprouted into warriors. As described in Book 7 of Ovid's *Metamorphoses,* Aeetes sat in royal robes with ivory scepter before his army and watched Jason attempt the impossible. Medea helped Jason overcome the warriors and complete the mission Aeetes had stipulated. As might be expected from so deceitful a man as Aeetes, he reneged on his promise and, in a rage, he schemed to burn Jason's fleet and murder captain and crew. Medea betrayed her father by escorting Jason across Ares's meadow where the fleece hung on an oak limb, and drugging the thousand-coiled serpent with a fresh bract of juniper. She stood guard while Jason stole the Golden Fleece. Together, they fled Colchis aboard the *Argo,* which was bound northwest across the Black Sea toward the mouth of the Danube River.

Loss of the fleece resulted in outrage from the priests of Ares, and a naval pursuit west, across the Black Sea led by Aeetes's son Apsyrtus or Absyrtus. Medea ended her father's hopes of capturing and reclaiming the fleece by capturing and chopping apart her brother, making a fiendish display of tossing the pieces into the waves while Aeetes watched from his own warship. The king, driven to distraction by his daughter's unspeakable act, halted to collect the parts and give them proper burial. As reported by Valerius Flaccus, he set up a peculiarly paternal howl at Medea:

> Halt your flight! and, from the distant sea,—with
> welcome and forgiveness, my daughter,—turn again.
> Why flee from your father? Steer homeward your fleet ship.
> Your friends and loving father wait to embrace you.

This speech suggests a strong link between father and daughter, however devious and wayward her treacheries against him and his kingdom. However, his words belie a vindictive heart. In private, he rained down curses on her head in the name of his son Apsyrtus.

Alternate Versions Some versions of the story list the nymph Asterodeia, Ipsia, or Idyia, daughter of Oceanus, as Aeetes's first wife, and Neaera as his second wife and mother of Apsyrtus. Hecate, the most devious witch in Greek lore, is occasionally listed as Perses's daughter and Aeetes's niece. One suspect link in the mythological genealogy suggests that Aeetes coupled with his niece Hecate to produce Medea, Circe, and Apsyrtus. Added to Circe and Pasiphae, Hecate rounds out a spectacularly dire family capable of unspeakable incantations, enchantments, and abominations. Also, a minor variant has Phrixus and Aeetes dedicating the Golden Fleece to Zeus rather than Ares. A similarly questionable rendering by Hyginus is the story of Aeetes's murder of Phrixus at the direction of the oracle. A more likely motivation for Aeetes to kill Phrixus is a desire to possess the Golden Fleece.

Aeetes's story appears in Geoffrey Chaucer's *The Legend of Good Women*. He is also a peripheral and rather poorly defined figure in versions of the epic saga of Jason and the Argonauts.

See Also

Jason and Medea.

Ancient Sources

Apollodorus's *Epitome;* Apollonius of Rhodes's *Argonautica;* Diodorus Siculus's *Library of History;* Euripedes's *Medea;* Hesiod's *Theogony;* Hesychius's *Lexicon;* Hyginus's *Fables;* Justin's *Apology;* Ovid's *Heroides* and *Metamorphoses;* Pausanias's *Description of Greece;* Pindar's *Pythian Odes;* Plutarch's *On Rivers;* Ptolemy Hephaestion's *On Homer;* Scholiast on Apollonius of Rhodes's *Argonautica;* Scholiast on Euripides's *Medea;* Scholiast on Pindar's *Pythian Odes;* Tacitus's *Annals,* Valerius Flaccus's *Argonautica.*

Aegeus

[ee' juhs]

A descendant of the noble Erechtheus and the eldest son of King Pandion II and Pylia, Aegeus, whose name means "goatlike," was prince of Megara, the capital of Megaris, the province situated on the slender neck of land connecting Attica to the Peloponnesus. Following Pandion's death, his four legitimate sons, including Aegeus, Pallas, Lycus, and Metion, divided their inheritance, with Aegeus ruling in Attica after driving out the heirs of the invidious Metion. Aegeus's illegitimate sister, the unnamed wife of Scyron, and brother, Oeneus, received nothing. Aegeus's two illegitimate sons proved their mettle in Greek mythology. Theseus, son of Aethra, killed the Minotaur, the beast that demanded annual human sacrifice; Medea's son, Medus, was the grandsire of the Medes, a powerful Asian tribe.

Journey As king of Athens, Aegeus took two queens, Meta, also called Melite, whom he divorced because she bore him no childen, then Chalciope, who also remained childless. To consult with Apollo about his lack of children, Aegeus journeyed northwest to Delphi, where the oracle warned him to keep the spout of his wineskin stoppered until he returned to the Athenian heights or else he would die grieving. Blaming Aphrodite for his misfortune, he opted to travel to the southeast of the Peloponnesus to Troezen in Argolis to discuss the oracle's meaning with the seer, Pittheus. His route took him through Corinth, where Medea implored him to rescue her from Creon in exchange for a magic spell to bring him children. He agreed to her offer and promised sanctuary.

The visit with Pittheus failed to enlighten Aegeus of the oracle's import because Pittheus deliberately hid a correct interpretation. He urged Aegeus to drink heavily and placed his daughter, Aethra, where Aegeus would be tempted. Their coupling, which took place near the

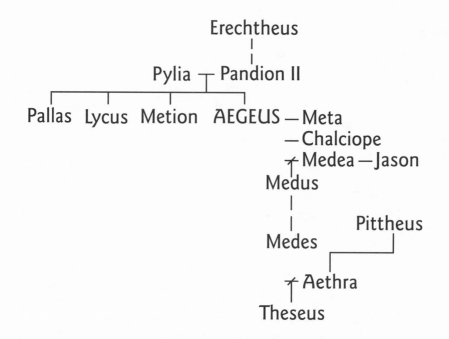

Erechtheus
|
Pylia ⊤ Pandion II
Pallas Lycus Metion AEGEUS — Meta
— Chalciope
⊤ Medea — Jason
Medus
|
|
Medes   Pittheus

⊤ Aethra
Theseus

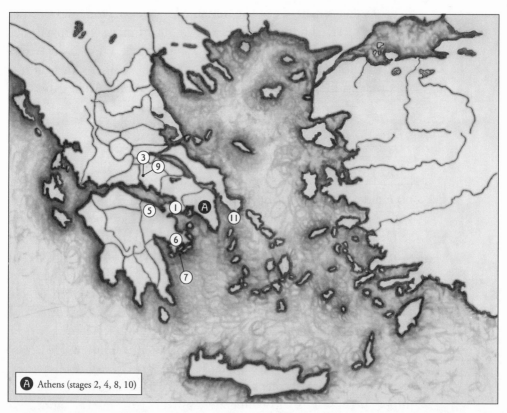

Ⓐ Athens (stages 2, 4, 8, 10)

1. Megara 2. Athens 3. Delphi 4. Athens 5. Corinth 6. Troezen 7. Sphaeria
8. Athens 9. Delphi 10. Athens 11. Aegean Sea

monument to Sphaerus, south of Troezen on the island of Sphaeria, resulted in conception. To prove paternity of the child, Aegeus left the heirloom sword of Cecrops, founder of Athens, and sandals under a boulder and instructed Aethra not to tell her son his father's name, lest jealous claimants of the Attic throne kill the boy. He ordered her to keep the child in Troezen until he was old enough to move the rock, retrieve the items, and bring them to Aegeus as tokens of identification.

Back in his Attic palace in time to celebrate the Panathenaea, Aegeus welcomed Medea, a wily enchantress who made a grand entrance in a flying chariot drawn by dragons. Taking her as wife, he fathered another son, Medus. In time, Theseus, Aegeus's sixteen-year-old son by Aethra, arrived in glory from his exploits in Corinth. Medea, spiteful and jealous of the winsome youth, poisoned Aegeus's mind against his older son. She concocted ways of endangering him, such as pitting him against a wild bull and dropping poisonous aconite in his wine during a state banquet. The boy defeated the bull, but it was Aegeus who rescued him from the deadly drink because he caught sight of the sword that he had left as a token of identity just as Theseus was raising it to slice meat.

After he banished Medea and Medus, Aegeus proclaimed Theseus heir of the Attic throne and quelled the fifty sons of Pallas, who claimed the Athenian realm. Content in his kingdom, Aegeus was nonetheless badgered by Minos of Crete, who bore a grudge against Aegeus for pitting Minos's son, Androgeus, in fatal combat against the bull of Marathon. In retaliation, Minos prayed to Zeus to bring famine and plague to Athens. Once again seeking the oracle at Delphi to save Athens, Aegeus learned that he must give in to Minos's demands for seven maids and seven youths to satisfy the blood lust of the Minotaur, a subterranean monster with the head of a bull.

Theseus volunteered for the suicide mission, which would require him and thirteen other Athenians to be devoured by the Minotaur if Theseus failed to kill him. Before letting his son depart, however, Aegeus made him promise to hoist a white sail to indicate that he had triumphed over the Minotaur. A black sail would warn the king that his son had failed. Upon Theseus's successful voyage, having forgotten his prearranged signal, he glided into the harbor under black sail. Aegeus, overcome with grief for the loss of his favorite and eager to join him in the Underworld, jumped from a tall crag to his death in the sea.

Alternate Versions

Aegeus is said to have been the real son of Scyrius and the adopted son of Pandion. Theseus's paternity is questioned in a major variation, which depicts Aethra as being ravished by Poseidon the same night she bedded with Aegeus. A different version of Aegean lore claims that Aegeus was an incarnation of Poseidon, Olympian god of the sea, but was ousted from godhood and made mortal. An alternate possibility is that Theseus had both a mortal and an immortal father. Also, Aegeus is described as marrying Aethra and abandoning her, and later, for political gain, marrying Autochthe, the daughter of Perseus and Andromeda.

Other embellishments to the story add melodrama to the meeting of Theseus and his father. One version has Aegeus accidentally upsetting the poisoned wine, spilling it on the floor where it was licked up by a dog, which immediately fell dead. An alternate version of Aegeus's death has him leaping from the roof of the shrine of Nike, the victory goddess who presides over the Acropolis.

Symbolism

A significant symbolism undergirds Aegeus's answer from the Delphic oracle. As Pittheus recognized, the wording of the injunction not to open his wineskin is twofold: he should not lose control in drunkenness and he should not bed a woman until his return to Athens. Pittheus, eager to take advantage of the child that Aegeus might father, imperiled his visitor by supplying him with drink and placing his daughter alluringly at hand. Pittheus's reward was Theseus, eventual king of Athens.

The name Theseus derives from a joining of Aegeus, from *aisso,* a verb meaning "to glide like ocean waves," and *aethra,* meaning "air." Thus, Theseus, who most likely is a mortal version of Poseidon of Aegae, combines two of the four primal elements, earth, air, fire, and water. Another aspect of the story is the age-old motif of the illegitimate son yearning to find his father and performing bold deeds to merit attention. As King Arthur wielded his lethal sword Excalibur, Theseus bore the weapon that cut through other claims to the Athenian realm, which his father gladly gave to the rightful owner.

One of the most recognizable tributes to Aegeus is the Aegean Sea, the vast expanse that separates Greece from Troy and bears his name as a memorial to his tragic demise. Also, one of the Attic tribes took the name Aegeis in his honor. Also commemorating King Aegeus were a grave in Athens, statues at both Athens and Delphi, the latter underwritten by Athenian loot from Marathon, and the altar of Zeus Sthenius near Hermione, under which Aegeus placed the sword and sandals.

Other tributes to the myth include a painting by Nicolas Poussin entitled *Theseus Finding His Father's Arms.* Writers, too, have found the story of Aegeus noteworthy. Geoffrey Chaucer refers to it in *The Knight's Tale* and *The Legend of Good Women,* Christopher Marlowe mentions it in *Tamburlaine,* and C. Day Lewis features it in *Ariadne on Naxos.* Twentieth-century writer Mary Renault turned the Aegeus saga into interlinked novels, *The King Must Die* and *The Bull from the Sea.*

 See Also

Jason and Medea, Theseus.

🌿 Ancient Sources

Apollodorus's *Epitome;* Athenaeus's *The Learned Banquet;* Bacchylides's *Choral Lyric XVIII;* Catullus's *Poems to Lesbia;* Diodorus Siculus's *Library of History;* Euripides's *Hippolytus* and *Medea;* Eustathius on Homer's *Iliad* and *Odyssey;* First Vatican Mythographer; Herodotus's *Histories;* Hesychius's *Lexicon;* Hyginus's *Fables;* Lactantius on Statius's *Thebaid;* Ovid's *Heroides* and *Metamorphoses;* Pausanias's *Description of Greece;* Pherecydes's *Heptamochos;* Plutarch's *Parallel Lives;* Scholiast on Demosthenes; Scholiast on Euripides's *Medea;* Scholiast on Sophocles's *Oedipus at Colonus;* Servius on Virgil's *Aeneid;* Simonides of Ceos's *Verse;* Strabo's *Historical Sketches;* Johannes Tzetzes's *Chiliades* and *On Lycophron.*

Aegisthus

[uh · jihs' thuhs]

Genealogy and Background

Aegisthus's doomed line, springing through Tantalus and back to Zeus and the Titan sea god, Oceanus, is one of the noblest and most violently cursed in all of classical mythology. The child of incest, Aegisthus sprang from dire, vengeful times made bloody by a family feud and international war. He was the great-grandson of Tantalus, who slaughtered his son and Aegisthus's father, Pelops, cooked his limbs, and served them to the gods. Like, Aegisthus, Tantalus earned a place among the damned and stands among the Underworld's automate who ceaselessly perform hopeless tasks. Tantalus's doom is to reach upward for fruit and down for water, both of which are just out of his grasp.

The degeneracy and greed of Aegisthus's father and uncle—Thyestes and his twin brother Atreus—confound civilized logic. Atreus and Thyestes coveted their father's throne. Thyestes, who had seduced his twin brother Atreus's wife, Aerope, and tried to cheat Atreus of his birthright, stirred murderous vengeance. In retaliation, Atreus slew three of Thyestes's sons and served them at Thyestes's table. Thyestes, wanting to wreak vengeance on Atreus, obeyed an oracle that promised him a powerful son that Thyestes had to sire by his own daughter, Pelopia. In the dark of night in Sicyon on the northeast coast of the Peloponnesus, he assaulted her and sired Aegisthus, the offspring of his sister.

To mark the shameful coupling, Pelopia stole her father/lover's sword and hid it beneath the plinth of Athena's statue. She later abandoned her son on a mountainside in Mycenae and married her uncle Atreus without revealing her kinship. They produced two of the most famous leaders in Greek history, Agamemnon and Menelaus. When war took these two leaders east to Troy, Aegisthus established an illicit liaison with Clytemnestra, Agamemnon's wife, and fathered at least two, and maybe three children—a son, Aletes, a daughter, Erigone, and possibly a second daughter, Helen. The name of the third child

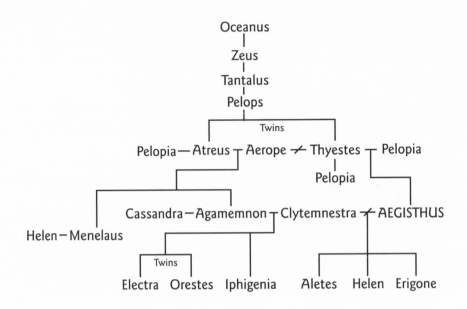

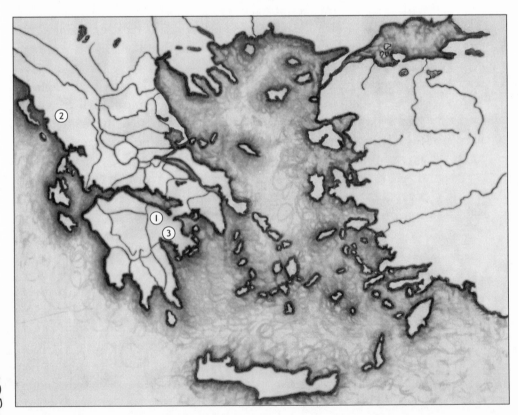

1. Sicyon 2. Thesprotia 3. Mycenae

suggests two possibilities: a namesake of her aunt Helen, or a bitter reminder that Agamemnon had sacrificed his daughter Iphigenia in his rush to return Queen Helen to Sparta.

Journey Atreus located and adopted his nephew Aegisthus, who had been rescued by shepherds from the mountainside and nurtured at the teats of a nanny goat. At an appropriate moment in his coming of age, Aegisthus was encouraged to journey far to northwest Greece to the seaside stretch known as Thesprotia to seek Thyestes. Aegisthus sought advice from the oracle, who urged him to return to Argos and bring Thyestes to justice. When the guilty father stood before his family, he recognized Aegisthus's sword, the weapon which Pelopia had stolen. Thyestes demanded a confrontation with his daughter whom he had victimized. Overcome with despair, Pelopia grasped the hilt of the sword and thrust it into her heart. Sympathizing with his father, Aegisthus retrieved the weapon from his mother's body and killed his uncle Atreus as a settlement of crimes committed against his father and brothers. Aegisthus exiled his cousins, Menelaus and Agamemnon, and reclaimed the throne of Mycenae, which he ruled in conjunction with his father Thyestes.

Aegisthus's sordid family story degenerates further during the Trojan War. Although usually characterized as a handsome, arrogant, self-serving baron of land adjacent to Agamemnon's realm, Aegisthus is often depicted as the despoiler of Clytemnestra, queen of Mycenae, the wife of his nephew and thus his niece by marriage. In Agamemnon's absence, Aegisthus, as next in line to the throne, persistently wooed Queen Clytemnestra, twin of Helen, the world's most beautiful woman. One explanation for his carnal behavior was the gossip of Nauplius, an embittered father who hated the Greek warriors for stoning his son Palamedes to death. For whatever reason, Clytemnestra willingly became Aegisthus's paramour.

To protect himself from a surprise arrival of Agamemnon's forces, Aegisthus paid spies two gold talents to watch the coastline for a year and to light signal fires all the way from Mount Ida in Troy to the Peloponnesus. As Odysseus tells it in Book 4 of the *Odyssey:*

> Then Aegisthus set his brains to work and laid a clever trap. He selected twenty of the best soldiers from the town, left them in ambush, and after ordering a banquet to be prepared in another part of the building, set out in a horse-chariot to bring home the King, with his heart full of ugly thoughts.

Upon Agamemnon's return, Aegisthus concealed his longstanding adultery and feigned welcome when the warrior king returned victorious. At a public feast held on Aegisthus's property, where Agamemnon was driven because of an ominous storm, Aegisthus fawned upon his lover's husband, then assisted her in murdering him with

a two-edged sword. Aegisthus also murdered Clytemnestra's young twins, Teledamus and Pelops, to circumvent future exactors of vengeance.

The crimes preceded a fierce battle between Aegisthus's soldiers and Agamemnon's honor guard. Every warrior died, leaving a bewildering scene of carnage as grim as Odysseus's retribution on the suitors who despoiled his palace. In the Underworld, Odysseus, unaware of the coming carnage that will mar his homecoming, heard the sordid tale from Agamemnon's ghost in Book 11 of Homer's *Odyssey:*

> It was Aegisthus with the aid of my accursed wife. He
> invited me to his house and as I feasted he killed me.
> My men too. You have seen many die in single combat or
> in battle, but never one who died as we did, by the
> wine bowl and the loaded tables in a hall where the
> floor flowed with blood.

Agamemnon recalls dying as the prophetess Cassandra's final shriek echoed in his ears. He tried to defend the Trojan princess, but Aegisthus and Clytemnestra proved triumphant, not only committing the sins of adultery and murder, but violating the sacred guest code as final fillip to their vileness.

In Aeschylus's *Oresteia,* the killer shakily rationalizes his act: he killed Agamemnon to right matters for Thyestes's children, his own brothers, whom Atreus, Agamemnon's father, murdered and served up to their father as stew. The Argive rulers remain unimpressed with Aegisthus's vituperations. In a dramatic moment of Aeschylus's play, Clytemnestra seizes the opportunity to say in their hearing, "Pay no heed to this currish howling. You and I, joint rulers, will enforce due reverence for our throne."

Nonetheless, whatever Argos's response to his crimes, Aegisthus enjoyed seven years' reign, arranged for Electra, the daughter of Agamemnon and Clytemnestra, to marry a peasant to prevent her from producing royal children, and plotted the deaths of Orestes and Electra as impediments to his lineage. Orestes, a suppliant at Delphi, returned and killed Aegisthus to avenge his father's death. In Aeschylus's *Oresteia,* the priggish Orestes, goaded by his acrimonious sister, claims that, "Aegisthus's heart is female," and that Orestes longs to "plunge a sword with lightning speed, and drop him dead."

The dramatic setting describes how Orestes, dressed in traveling cloak, disguised himself and pretended to bring news of his own demise in the form of a funeral urn. Donning false mourning, Clytemnestra, secretly delighted to be relieved of her vengeful son, summoned the wily, ambitious Aegisthus, to whom she left political matters. Orestes felled the unsuspecting usurper as he stood unguarded while sacrificing oxen on the altar of the nymphs. Aegisthus, his head already within range of Orestes's spite, recognizes too late the inauspicious omens: the calf's organs were malformed. Having invited Orestes to strike the *coup de grace,* Aegisthus found himself the victim. As Aeschylus describes the gory act:

> [Orestes] stretched up, balanced on the balls
> of his feet, and smashed a blow to his spine. The
> vertebrae of his back broke. Head down, his whole
> body convulsed, he gasped to breathe,
> writhed with a high scream, and died in his blood.

Not entirely comfortable with his role as avenger, Orestes rationalized to observers, "The man is dead. I am not guilty there. An adulterer. He had to die."

Immediately after the villain fell, Electra, Orestes's conspirator, exulted. She berated the motionless corpse and nudged his remains with her foot. Until Clytemnestra arrived for her own appointment with *nemesis,* Aegisthus's body was shoved aside. Local peasants buried him, leaving Clytemnestra to the ministrations of Menelaus and Helen.

News of Aegisthus's impiety spread throughout the Greek world. His death is mentioned in Book 1 of Homer's *Odyssey* as Zeus narrated the sorry history of Agamemnon's murderer and lamented that the gods are blamed for the impetuosity of human beings. Zeus claimed that he sent Hermes to warn Aegisthus neither to kill Agamemnon nor court Clytemnestra because Orestes, when he grew old enough, would seek revenge and reclaim the Mycenaean throne. However, Hermes could not dissuade Aegisthus. Athena replied, "Aegisthus indeed has been struck down in a death well merited. Let any other man who does thus perish as he did." Later, Odysseus, concerned for his wife, Penelope, in his long absence from home, rejoiced that he would not meet the same destiny as Agamemnon, "for surely the suitors would have plotted against me in my house as Clytemnestra and her new husband devised his death."

Aegisthus's children found no easier fate than that of their father. Erigone charged Orestes with murder, then killed herself. Aletes, destined to succeed Aegisthus, briefly ruled Mycenae. Orestes returned to Mycenae and he killed Aletes, thus ending Aegisthus's lineage with yet another violent act.

Alternate Versions

An alternate telling of Aegisthus's sordid biography twists and turns the details into variations of criminality. The rape of Pelopia is described as taking place in two possible locations. She may have been attacked outside Epirus at a stream where she cleansed herself of ritual blood after dancing in a ceremony honoring Athena. Another setting suggests that Thyestes deflowered Pelopia without recognizing her. Because she lived at the court of King Thesprotus, she may have grown up too far from her father to appear familiar and was raped in an anonymous encounter. This version states that Thyestes, in his haste to depart the lurid scene, dropped his sword.

A variant names Aegisthus's cousins, Agamemnon and Menelaus, as captors of Thyestes, whom Aegisthus is said to have confronted in his jail cell. Aeschylus's *Agamemnon* describes a malignant relationship with Thyestes, whom Aegisthus drove from the city that he claimed for himself. Aegisthus sometimes appears dissolute, but innocent, until Clytemnestra lures him with her sexual charms, unused during Agamemnon's absence. In other versions Aegisthus appears as a skilled horseman and smooth despoiler of women who corrupted the blameless Clytemnestra. Also, Aegisthus is pictured as impetuously murdering Agamemnon in his bath at the Argive palace before the banquet began. Pindar's version describes the brave act of Laodameia, who substitutes her own child for Prince Orestes so that Aegisthus will kill the wrong child, thus fooling himself into believing that his royal line is safe. A variation on Aegisthus's death describes Electra, deadly with loathing since the birth of Clytemnestra's illegitimate children, as inflaming her brother against the usurping Aegisthus.

Other variations have Aegisthus's daughter Erigone marrying Orestes and giving birth to Aegisthus's grandson Penthilus, journeying to Athens to serve the goddess Artemis as priestess, or hanging herself after Orestes's acquittal on charges of matricide.

Symbolism Aegisthus, whose name derives from the Greek for goat, which nourished him in childhood, has been pictured in ancient and classical frieze and vase art as falling to Orestes's knife while Clytemnestra, restrained by the nurse and house servants, raises an axe in her lover's defense. Usually he is depicted as a conniving villain and shameless womanizer, although Hugo von Hofmannsthal's libretto set to Richard Strauss's music, *Elektra*, places greater blame on Clytemnestra for seducing Aegisthus. Other writers, such as the tragedian Lucius Seneca, have found Aegisthus's fate worthy, notably in works such as the Roman Varius's *Thyestes*, the Elizabethan playwright Prosper Crébillon's *Atrée and Thyeste*, and Voltaire's *Oreste*. In the twentieth century, Jean Paul Sartre, Paul Claudel, Eugene O'Neill, and T. S. Eliot have continued the tradition of the Oresteia, with Aegisthus playing a major role in the crimes of the house of Atreus.

See Also
Agamemnon.

𝕎 Ancient Sources

Aelian's *Various Narratives;* Aeschylus's *Agamemnon* and *The Suppliants;* Apollodorus's *Epitome;* Aristotle's *Politics;* Cinaethon of Lacedaemon's *Oedipodeia;* Dictys Cretensis's *Trojan War Diary;* Dio Chrysostomus's *Orationes;* Euripides's *Electra* and *Orestes;* Eustathius on Homer's *Iliad* and *Odyssey;* Hesiod's *Catalogue of Women;* Homer's *Odyssey;* Hyginus's *Fables;* Ovid's *Ibis;* Pausanias's *Description of Greece;* Photius's *Library;* Pindar's *Pythian Odes;* Ptolemy Hephaestion on Homer's *Iliad;* Scholiast on Euripides's *Medea;* Seneca's *Agamemnon* and *Thyestes;* Sophocles's *Electra;* Johannes Tzetzes's *On Lycophron.*

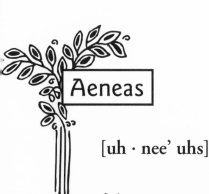

Aeneas

[uh · nee' uhs]

Genealogy and Background

Aeneas, a military success story and a descendant of Tros, father of Troy, was the son of the goddess Aphrodite and Anchises, a member of the Dardanian royal family, who claimed Zeus as their progenitor. At Aeneas's conception, Aphrodite, whom Zeus manipulated into marriage with Anchises to curb her promiscuity, deceived her lover by passing herself off as a Phrygian princess. Their child, born atop Mount Ida southeast of Troy, was reared in the mountains as a shepherd. After Aeneas was brought to Troy at the age of five, his tutor, Alcathus, trained him well and molded him into one of Troy's boldest, most renowned fighting men, the leader of the Dardanians, and second only to Hector.

Because of his mother's pride in him, Aeneas was fated to sire a lineage that would know no end. He married Creusa, eldest daughter of King Priam and Queen Hecuba, and is described as holding a grudge against the king for failing to credit him for defending Troy against the Greeks, although his performance in battle close-ups fail to establish his claims of extraordinary performance. Aeneas fathered Ascanius, also called Iulus, progenitor of the Julian line, including Julius Caesar and his successor, Augustus, Rome's first emperor. From Aeneas's union with Lavinia, his second wife, came Silvius, founder of Alba Longa.

Journey

In Book 5 of Virgil's *Aeneid*, as the Trojan War raged, stout-hearted Aeneas, defended by Poseidon, fought Achilles and suffered a broken hip from a stone hurled by Diomedes, who tried to steal Aeneas's horse. With the protection of his mother, who concealed him in a cloud, Aeneas, attended by Artemis and Leto, recuperated well enough to strike down Crethon, Orsilochus, and other enemy warriors, to besiege the Achaean camp, to assist Hector

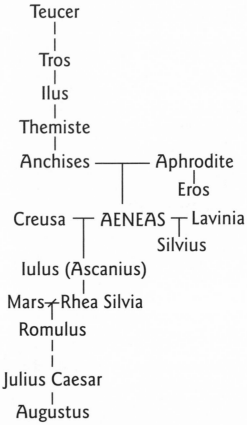

Teucer
|
Tros
|
Ilus
|
Themiste
|
Anchises ——— Aphrodite
|
Eros

Creusa ⊤ AENEAS ⊤ Lavinia
| Silvius
Iulus (Ascanius)
|
Mars⊤Rhea Silvia
|
Romulus
|
Julius Caesar
|
Augustus

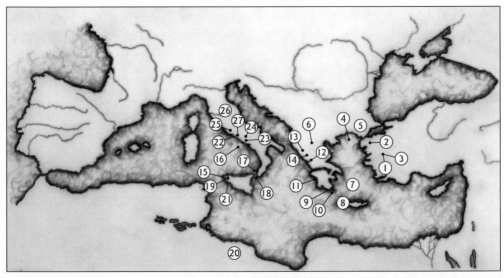

1. Mt. Ida 2. Troy 3. Mt. Ida 4. Samothrace 5. Aeneadae, Thrace 6. Macedonia
7. Delos 8. Pergamum, Crete 9. Boeae 10. Cythera 11. Strophades 12. Actium
13. Buthrotum 14. Dodona 15. Drepanum, Sicily 16. Aeaea 17. Scylla and Charybdis
18. Strait of Messina 19. Mt. Eryx 20. Libya 21. Drepanum 22. Latium
23. Cumae 24. Mt. Vesuvius 25. Tiber River 26. Etruria 27. Latium

against the Greeks, and to face off against Idomeneus. At the high point of the war, Aeneas joined other Trojans in the fight for Patroclus's corpse. In Book 20, during Aeneas's second battle with Achilles, Poseidon rescued him by dimming Achilles's sight and removing Aeneas from the battlefield so that he could fulfill his destiny.

When Hector lay dead, Aeneas replaced him as chief protector of Troy, the kingdom whose downfall the outspoken priest Laocoon predicted. Following the priest's death, Aeneas, eager to avert the vengeance of Athena, helped the Trojans drag the wooden gift horse into the city. That night, Aeneas received a visitation from Hector's weeping, blood-encrusted corpse and heard his command, as recorded in Book 2 of Virgil's *Aeneid:*

> Ah, fly, goddess-born ... and rescue yourself from these
> flames. The foe holds our walls; from her high ridges
> Troy is toppling down.... Troy commends to you her holy
> objects and household gods; take them to accompany your
> fate; seek for them a city, which, after all the seas
> have known your wanderings, you shall at last establish
> in might.

To accomplish this dangerous mission, Aeneas stripped a Greek corpse and decked himself in the enemy's armor. Before he could flee his rooftop, he observed the slaughter of the royal family by the savage Neoptolemus, Achilles's son, and blamed Helen for the destruction of his homeland.

Catching sight of Helen cowering at Hestia's shrine, Aeneas threatened to kill her. Aphrodite turned her son's thoughts from vengeance to the rescue of his family, particularly Iulus. A divine omen in the form of a flaming aura appeared over Iulus's head. Anchises begged for more heavenly guidance, which came in the form of thunder and a shooting star. Aeneas, his family's safety assured by the heavens, gathered a small band, shouldered his aged father, and led his small son by the hand from the noise and confusion of Troy's fiery collapse. In the press of desperate fighting, Aeneas lost sight of Creusa, his wife. He shepherded his father and son to a mountain haven, then returned to locate his wife. Detained by Aphrodite, her spirit appeared on the steps of her ruined home and urged her widowed husband:

> Don't weep for me. At least I shall never be a minion
> in the palaces of the haughty Greeks. And now,
> farewell. Continue to love our son.

(Virgil's Aeneid)

Three times he reached out to embrace her and each time clasped the empty air. In dismay, he abandoned the ruin that was Troy and returned to his followers.

At dawn, Aeneas rejoined the survivors. Bearing holy relics crucial to the survival of the Trojan race—the Penates, or household gods, a statue of Hestia, goddess of the hearth, and the Palladium, the likeness of Pallas Athena-Aeneas, accompanied by his eighty-year-old father and faithful companion, Achates, assembled his followers on Mount Ida, southeast of Troy. He established a temporary realm, but was ousted that summer by Hector's two sons, Oxynius and Scamander, who bore greater claim to the Troad. Thus pushed out of known territory by destiny, Aeneas and his band boarded twenty ships and set sail toward an undisclosed destination.

The route that Aeneas followed led northwest to the island of Samothrace and on to Thrace, now called Bulgaria, where the Trojans established the town of Aeneadae. The ghost of Polydorus, Hector's brother, impelled them to flee to avoid a bloodthirsty race. From Macedonia, west of Thrace, Aeneas moved southeast to Delos, King Anius's island of the Cyclades, east of the Peloponnesus, and heard the oracle's voice urging them to locate their "ancient mother; there the race of Aeneas shall dwell and reduce all other nations to their sway." (Virgil's *Aeneid*) This hopeful but cryptic message, according to Anchises, had to refer to Crete, the home of Teucer, their prehistoric forbear; yet, as they began building the city of Pergamum, they encountered only starvation, disease, and death on the island. With a holy charge from the Penates, Rome's guardian spirits, to seek Hesperia, or Italy, Dardanus's home, Aeneas returned to sea, stopping briefly at the harbors of the island Cythera and Boeae in Laconia on the southeastern tip of the Peloponnesus.

The small fleet was severely buffeted in a storm near the Strophades island cluster in the Ionian waters off western Greece, where the Harpies, vicious clawed bird-women, ripped at their flesh and fouled their food. The lead Harpy, Calaeno, prophesied greater trials on their circuitous route to the new Troy, including such great hunger that the Trojans would devour their tables. The next segment of their odyssey took them in a northwesterly direction up Greece's coastline to Actium, Buthrotum, and Dodona, where Aeneas shared a joyful reunion with Andromache, Hector's widow, and her husband Helenus. The Trojan forces spent the winter reminiscing and recuperating from their flight.

After recapping the final moments of the war, Aeneas pressed Helenus to prophesy the destiny of his small band. Helenus urged him to look for a huge sow with a white brood of thirty piglets lying under an ilex tree on a riverbank, the site of the future Troy. Helenus also pointed out the one-sided gods, particularly Apollo, who would benefit his quest, and Hera, who would spare no pains to thwart it.

With Helenus's words as guide, Aeneas located Drepanum on Sicily's northwest coast. The fleet sailed past Aeaea, Circe's enchanted isle, and the twin terrors, Scylla and Charybdis, the sea monsters that guarded Sicily; the mariners, heeding the warning of one of Odysseus's marooned sailors, also skirted the Cyclops Polyphemus's craggy lair. To Aeneas's dismay, the one tragedy not predicted was the death of Anchises, his beloved father, "solace of my every care … my sire." (Virgil's *Aeneid*) Aeneas buried the old man on Mount Eryx.

The goddess Hera, jealous of Rome's future greatness, intervened, forcing Aeolus, god of the winds, to drive Aeneas's fleet southward to Libya on the North African coast near the city of Carthage. There, Poseidon overruled Hera's fury and brought Aeneas and seven of his ships to safe harbor. In one of Virgil's most cited passages, Aeneas addresses his remaining forces:

> My companions, you and I have long known sorrow and
> even worse sufferings. These too shall pass. Summon
> your courage as you drive out fear. Perhaps some day
> it will please us to recall our toils.

Aeneas and his devoted armor-bearer, Achates, directed by Aphrodite disguised as Diana the hunter, departed from the weary band and explored the territory, which boasted a handsome temple amid a thriving city.

At sight of prosperity, Aeneas's fortune appeared to improve. Rested and royally entertained for the first time in weeks, he enjoyed the company of Dido, the Tyrian queen and widow, who was smitten by Eros's arrow and fell deeply in love with her Trojan visitor. In her eyes, he stood out in a sheen of brilliance, like a deity in demeanor and posture; for his mother had marked him with brilliant locks, the glow of young manhood, and the sparkle of gladsome eyes; just as ivory grows lustrous in the carving, or when silver or Parian marble is crafted with gold.

Dido, dazzled with his divine charms, plied him with celebrations and feasts. Long at the banquet table, she leaned toward Aeneas to catch every word of his trials during the Trojan War. To delay Troy's new foundation, Aphrodite and Hera conspired to further a romance between Dido and Aeneas. During a heavy storm, the pair took shelter from a storm in a cave where fires flash forth above their embrace and nymphs called from the mountaintop. The moment foretold ill fortune and death, for Dido flaunted her love, which she claimed was a marriage to shield her hasty coupling. Driven by passion and the need for a royal mate, Dido offered Aeneas a dignified post as consort and co-ruler.

At the end of their year's dalliance, Zeus was eager to speed his human agent on his way and twice sent Hermes to quell Aeneas's human desires and reignite his commitment to destiny. Extricating himself from Dido's wiles, Aeneas sped across the Mediterranean Sea to the north. He looked back briefly where a curl of smoke marked the funeral pyre of his lover, who stabbed herself in grief at his sudden departure. Suspecting the cause of the fire, Aeneas, by no means deterred from his duty to the gods, hurried back toward Drepanum in Sicily, met with King Acestes, and halted long enough to honor his father with funeral games, where young Iulus brought honor to his father during a cavalry review.

Fomented by Iris, Hera's messenger, a mutiny of Trojan women worn ragged by seven years of voyages cost Aeneas the burning of four ships. For a brief time, Aeneas considered abandoning his quest. Prayers to Zeus brought rain to extinguish the

flames. With advice from Nautes, an aged orator, Aeneas saw the wisdom in regrouping and left behind the most disgruntled and least stout-hearted of his following to found Acesta in western Sicily.

Accompanied by handpicked mariners, Aeneas moved northwest toward Italy's Tyrrhenian coastline. His mother, seeking a cessation of Hera's spite, begged Poseidon to lighten Aeneas's load. Poseidon agreed to make the final leg of the voyage easy on the Trojan band, but he demanded a sacrifice. And so Palinurus, the pilot of Aeneas's lead ship, fell asleep and was swept overboard at the strait of Messenia near the Sirens' rocks, leaving the leader to serve as captain and helmsman.

Undaunted, Aeneas sailed through the Tyrrhenian Sea northwest up the coast of Italy to Latium, near modern-day Naples, to a cliffside cave near Cumae, where he consulted the Sibyl, Deiphobe. Inflamed with the brain-rattling message of Apollo, the prophetess sounded a dire warning:

> The descent to Avernus is easy: the gate of Hades
> stands open night and day; but to retrace one's steps
> and return to the upper air, that is the toil, that the
> difficulty.

> (Virgil's *Aeneid*)

The Sibyl prophesied wars and bloodshed, but Aeneas, the pious defender of Troy's gods, remained true to his quest. Deiphobe sent him in search of a gift for Persephone—a golden bough, which Aeneas, aided by Achates and two doves sent by Aphrodite, located in a grove of ilex.

Farther east near the Avernian crater, where Mount Vesuvius belched sulfurous gases, Deiphobe guided his journey into a rift in the earth leading to the netherworld to gain advice from his father's spirit and to view the coming greatness of Rome, which his progeny would found. The first part of the fearsome journey brought Aeneas past a host of monsters and face to face with Palinurus, who, because his corpse remained unburied, was forced to tread the far side of the Styx. Genuinely sympathetic, Aeneas promised to locate his body and offer it a ritual interment so that the faithful pilot could find peace.

At sight of the golden bough, Charon, Hades's ferryman, fearsome with his shaggy locks and flaming eyes, agreed to ferry Aeneas and his guide into Hades. Among the souls Aeneas glimpsed in the Underworld were those who died in childhood and suicides, including Dido, who refused to notice her former lover and turned instead to the embrace of her husband, Sychaeus. Past Greek heroes of the Trojan War, who cowered at his might, past Tartarus, the region of the damned, and beyond the awesome burning river Phlegethon, Aeneas trod on in search of Anchises.

In the fields of the blessed, Aeneas reunited with his father, who cried out:

> Have you come at last, long expected, and do I behold
> you after such perils past? O my son, how have I
> trembled for you as I have watched your career!

> (Virgil's *Aeneid*)

The two were unable to clasp each other, but took seats in a pleasant grove where they could observe the spirit world. After explaining the process by which souls are cleansed and reborn, Anchises described the future greatness of Rome, naming future leaders Silvius, Romulus, Numa, Tarquin, Brutus, Cato, Scipio, Gracchus, Julius Caesar, and Augustus, and climaxing the prediction with visions of a golden age. In Virgil's words:

> Heaven's star band all. Direct your gaze now here and
> view the Romans, your future offspring! These children
> Iulus will father, a race like no other.

Aeneas, at heart's ease, retraced his steps, passed through the ivory portion of the twin gates of sleep, and prepared his ships for departure to Latium.

Again sailing in a northwesterly direction, Aeneas paused to bury his nurse Caieta and found a city named in her honor. He skirted Circe's isle, and at last sailed into the Tiber River at Latium, where he located a white sow nursing thirty piglets, symbols of Rome's future abundance. He forged an alliance with the noble King Latinus, scion of Saturn and son of Faunus, a woodland deity. During a meal in which the Trojans ate large round cakes, Aeneas realized that a prophecy had been harmlessly fulfilled— they were truly eating their tables.

Far from finished with adversity, Aeneas fought a sturdy band of Rutulians, then, by virtue of the guest code, forged an agreement with his father's friend, King Evander, who placed him in charge of the troops of his son, Pallas. Against the connivance of Hera and Lavinia's mother, Amata, Aeneas, decked in ornate armor made by Hephaestus to Aphrodite's specifications, faced the threat of total war. Latinus, acting on an oracle that predicted Lavinia would marry a foreigner, abandoned his throne. Hera, who was only too glad to thwart Aeneas, set loose Alecto, one of the Erinyes or Furies, from the Underworld and, to declare war, spread wide the entrance to Janus's temple, thus indicating a formal challenge.

In Etruria, the district to the northwest of Latium, Aeneas returned to his forces in time to stop the annihilation of the Trojans by Turnus, a Rutulian hothead and Aeneas's rival for the princess Lavinia. With the backing of Italian leaders, Camilla and Mezentius, and the Volsci, Turnus put up a strong opposition to Aeneas, his ally Pallas, and the Etruscans. Divine intervention salvaged Aeneas's ships from fire by transforming them into Naiads, which swam to safety. Turnus gained ground by killing Pallas; Aeneas countered by slaying both Mezentius and his son, Lausus. After a truce failed, the death of Pallas and an arrow wound to their leader lessened the hopes of Aeneas's forces. Aphrodite, faithful to her son, dropped dictamnus petals in ambrosia, applied the tincture, and caused the arrow point to drop from the wound. With Aeneas restored to vigor, the war was reduced to single combat. Zeus tried to keep the fight fair by forbidding Hera's interference. Man to man, Aeneas at last settled his fight with Turnus and killed him in a duel by plunging his sword into Turnus's chest.

When peace returned to Latium, Aeneas wed Lavinia and adopted her nation and language. Lavinia's people reciprocated by accepting the Trojan Penates as household gods. Thus the ascendance of Rome was assured. Later episodes in Aeneas's life find him safely housed in a palace in Laurentum, where Anna, Dido's sister, was shipwrecked on her way north from Libya. Aeneas received her hospitably and listened to the woeful tale of Dido's suicide and self-immolation. Fearful of Aeneas's new wife, Anna fled, was rescued by a river god, and changed into a nymph. As Anna Perenna or Ann the Eternal, her cult was allied with that of Aeneas.

For four peaceful years, Aeneas remained in power alongside his Latian wife, Lavinia, and son, Ascanius. Poets have revealed few details of the conflict, but a return assault by Rutulians caused Aeneas a fitting end on the battlefield. At his death, Aeneas, lifted in the arms of his mother, Aphrodite, is said to have shrugged off mortality and joined the immortals. Lavinia, who was pregnant with Silvius at the time of Aeneas's death, raised a monument in her husband's honor.

Alternate Versions

Alternate tellings of Aeneas's family connections list Eurydice as his wife and Euryleon, Anius, Romulus, and Remus as his sons. Other name variants include Elissa as an alternate to Dido. In an early version of the myth, Aeneas consults the Trojan Sibyl of Marpessus rather than the more familiar Cumaean Sibyl. Roma, a sketchy mythic figure said to be Telemachus's daughter and Odysseus's granddaughter, is sometimes identified as Aeneas's wife and sometimes as Ascanius's. She appears to be important only as the personification of the city founded on the banks of the Tiber.

Other cities claim a connection with Aeneas's wanderings. One source credits Aeneas with founding Aeneia in Macedonia, another with the establishment of Capua, a prominent Roman city on Italy's west coast. He is said to have founded shrines to Aphrodite in Aeneia, Ambracia, the island of Leucas, Zacynthus on the Peloponnesian coast, and Aphrodisias on the Boeotian coast. Orchomenus in Arcadia is named as an alternate place where Anchises died and was buried. A journey mentioned in later literature brought Aeneas's great-grandson, Brutus, to an island beyond France and established New Troy. He named his kingdom Britain and his people Britons.

| Symbolism | Aeneas, the stoic ideal, resembles numerous mythic figures. Like the Kiowa in Scott Momaday's *The Way to Rainy Mountain,* he |

observed with heartsick regret the death of his nation, the altarless gods, and the end of a noble culture. Like the Greek Odysseus, Herakles, Orpheus, Theseus, Dionysus, and Pirithous, and the Melanesian Malekula, Aeneas suffered the buffeting of unfriendly gods and ventured into hostile territory, including the Underworld, in order to complete a meandering voyage. Like Abraham, the Hebrew patriarch, he received a divine blessing in the form of a covenant that his lineage would never die. Predestined by sacred trusts, Aeneas had little choice in his journeys but to follow whatever god controlled him. His divine mother hovered nearby to offset the enmity of Hera, patron of Carthage, a Phoenician city fated to suffer a ruinous clash with Rome.

Before Virgil turned Aeneas into an epic warrior, the Romans worshipped him as Jupiter Indiges, Rome's founder and the creator of the sisterhood of vestal virgins, whose round temple Aeneas is said to have built. The veneration of Aphrodite, Aeneas's mother, in the form of the Roman Venus resulted in the adoration of Venus Genetrix, the founding mother of the city of Rome. According to Ovid's *Fasti,* the February holiday of Parentalia, which presaged the hope of spring and nature's rejuvenation, evolved from Aeneas's funeral offerings to Anchises. A second Roman spring holiday, which honored Venus Verticordia or the "changer of the heart," recalled that Aeneas's mother had caused the powerful sea god to allow her son to found a new Ilium on the banks of the Tiber.

Other depictions show Aeneas heading Lavinium and as leader of the Latin League, an association of small municipalities. Appropriately, from Virgil he earned the Latin descriptive *pius* for his selfless devotion to the gods, especially to Poseidon and his mother, Aphrodite. His protected passage through Hades is connected with mistletoe, which may have been the true identity of the magical golden bough. Aeneas's lineage is symbolized by *robor,* the oak, the tree most frequently named as host to the parasitic mistletoe. Throughout Rome's history, vestal virgins, in honor of Aeneas, burned only oak on their sacred fires.

As reward for devotion, Aeneas's posthumous son Silvius founded Alba Longa, and his scions, the twins Romulus and Remus, established Rome. Virgil molded the story of the epic beginnings of Rome in order to flatter Augustus's vanity by giving Rome a noble link with Homeric lore. The epic, thus replacing more sordid tales of opportunism and treachery, provided Romans a history dating back to the *Iliad,* a source of pride. The cult worship of Aeneas is represented on a bas-relief on the Altar of Peace, housed in Rome's Terme Museum; other likenesses are found in Etruscan statues from the ancient city of Veii, a few miles north of Rome. Additional shrines can be found in Thrane, Chalcidice, and Elymus in Sicily.

Aeneas's legendary exploits greatly influenced world literature, particularly Dante Alighieri's *The Divine Comedy,* Christopher Marlowe's *Tamburlaine* and *Dido Queen of Carthage,* and six of William Shakespeare's plays: *Antony and Cleopatra, Hamlet, King Henry VI, Midsummer Night's Dream, The Tempest,* and *Titus Andronicus.* Christian writers of the Middle Ages as well as Publius Statius, Torquato Tasso, Johann von Schiller, and Luiz de Camoens refer to Aeneas. Greater emphasis appears in Geoffrey Chaucer's *House of Fame* and *Legend of Good Women,* Ben Jonson's *To William Roe* and *The New Inn,* John Dryden's *The Hind and the Panther,* Elizabeth Barrett Browning's *The Battle of Marathon,* Alexander Pope's *The Rape of the Lock,* Thomas Wyatt's *Jopas' Song,* and John Milton's *Paradise Lost.* In more recent times, Aeneas found his way into the poetry of C. Day Lewis, Walt Whitman, and Jean Giraudoux.

To passing generations, Aeneas represented the dedicated man of god who spurned an earthly love in order to concentrate on a lofty calling. Like earlier heroes, Aeneas, in a milieu of cosmic forces, including dreams, prophecies, the terrors of Hades, and visitations by spirits and gods, became the prototype of the self-disciplined man of action endowed with human strength, wisdom, and a sense of mission. As such, his likeness adorns Macedonian coins and Etruscan scarabs and terra-cotta vases, which date his legend to the sixth century B.C. In Rome, the symbolic connection between Aeneas appears at the base of a statue of Augustus at the Primaporta, where a dolphin and a cupid allude to Venus, mother of both oceangoing Aeneas and Eros, the winged god of love. Musical and artistic tributes include Benjamin Britten's romantic suite, *Dido and Aeneas,* Gian Francesco Malipiero's symphony *Vergilii Aeneis,* a ballet by Henry Purcell, paintings by Giovanni Battista Tiepolo, Joshua Reynolds, and Pierre-Narcisse Guérin's *Aeneas Telling Dido the Disasters of the City of Troy,* and Giovanni Lorenzo Bernini's sculpture, *Flight from Troy.*

❦ See Also

Achilles, Andromache, Diomedes, Leto, Palinurus.

❦ Ancient Sources

Apollodorus's *Epitome;* Arctinus of Miletus's *Sack of Troy;* Catullus's *Poems to Lesbia;* Dionysius of Halicarnassus's *Roman Antiquities;* Ennius's *Annales;* Euripides's *Andromache* and *Hecuba;* Fabius Pictor's *History of Rome;* Hellanicus's *Roman Antiquities* and *Troica;* Homer's *Hymn to Aphrodite* and *Iliad;* Lesches's *Little Iliad;* Livy's *From the Foundations of the City;* Lucretius's *On the Nature of Things;* Lycophron's *Alexandra;* Macrobius's *On Pisander;* Naevius's *The Punic Wars;* Ovid's *Fasti* and *Metamorphoses;* Pausanias's *Description of Greece;* Servius on Virgil's *Aeneid;* Sophocles's lost plays; Stasinus of Cyprus's *Cypria;* Stesichorus's *Iliu Persis;* Timaeus's *History;* Tryphiodorus's *Sack of Troy;* Varro's *Hebdomades;* Virgil's *Aeneid.*

Agamemnon

[ag' uh · mihm' nahn]

Genealogy and Background

A fourth-generation noble—son of Atreus, grandson of Pelops, and great grandson of Tantalus—Agamemnon, whose name means "strongly resolved," was born in Argos to Aerope, whose seduction by her brother-in-law, Thyestes, set off a chain of intrafamilial warfare. Because Atreus was murdered by Aegisthus, Agamemnon and his brother Menelaus were rescued from Thyestes and brought up in Calydon, on the northwestern shore of the Gulf of Corinth, and Sicyon, in the northeast Peloponnesus. As the vengeance code demanded, the brothers later searched out Thyestes at Delphi, but made peace with him.

As an adult, Agamemnon, beloved by Hera and assisted by the Spartan king Tyndareus, returned south to his rightful realm of Argos, ousted Thyestes, and, along with Menelaus, ruled Mycenae and eventually all of Argolis and Sicyon, one of Greece's most ancient and strategic cities. Aeschylus, in his tragedy *Agamemnon,* refers to the royal brothers as "twin-throned, twin-sceptered, in twofold power of kings from God." Thus, by virtue of his power and strategic placement, Agamemnon achieved a significant political gain over all of the Peloponnesus.

The victor of the long-standing family feud, Agamemnon executed Thyestes's heir, Tantalus, the infant of Clytemnestra, by smashing the child's skull against a wall. As claimant of Thyestes's wealth, Agamemnon chose to marry Clytemnestra, the twin of Helen fathered by Zeus, who sired the pair of girls as well as Castor and Pollux following his rape of Leda, the queen of Sparta. Agamemnon, too, fathered a noteworthy pair of twins, Electra (also called Laodice) and Orestes, as well as Chrysothemis, Iphianassa, and the ill-fated Iphigenia. Menelaus, with his brother's influence over Tyndareus, married Helen, whose abduction by Paris led to the Trojan War, the pivotal event of ancient literature. While at Troy, Agamemnon may have fathered a son, Chryses, by Chryseis, who was later reunited with Orestes and Iphigenia on the island of Zminthe.

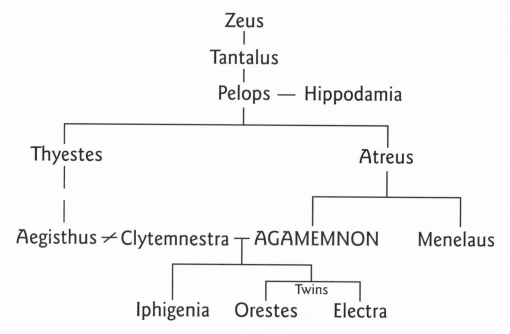

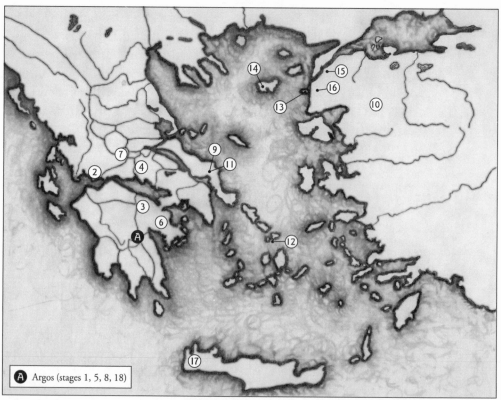

A Argos (stages 1, 5, 8, 18)

1. Argos 2. Calydon 3. Sicyon 4. Delphi 5. Argos 6. Mycenae 7. Aetolia 8. Argos
9. Aulis 10. Mysia 11. Aulis 12. Delos 13. Tenedos 14. Lemnos 15. Hellespont
16. Troy 17. Polyrrhenia 18. Argos

Journey As Homer describes him in the *Iliad,* Agamemnon was brave, but, because of his stubbornness, egotism, and lack of pragmatism and foresight, he fell short of the characteristic strengths of the determined man of action. Bound by oath to Tyndareus, all of Helen's suitors, including Agamemnon's brother Menelaus, vowed that they would serve as her champions. After her abduction, goaded by Menelaus's entreaty, Agamemnon enforced the promise, yet realized the insanity of unbridled patriotism and, according to Euripides's *Helen,* noted, "Some god has sent Greece mad and you [soldiers] with her." Dutifully, he traveled about the neighboring realms, summoning Greece's most promising leaders into a single fighting force dedicated to returning Helen to her lawful husband. Among his personal Argive troop were the seer Calchas, Eurymedon the charioteer, Ptolemaeus, the king's charioteer, Periphetes, and the poet Demodocus.

This prefatory task was not without considerable risk. As Agamemnon enlisted Telephus, he became embroiled in Telephus's grudge against Achilles, who had inflicted a stubborn wound in his foot. In his fury at the affront, Telephus threatened to kill Agamemnon's only male heir, the infant Orestes. Achilles assuaged Telephus's anger by massaging in rust from his spear and healing the wound.

As commander-in-chief of the Achaean fleet, Agamemnon, chosen unanimously at a general session held at Diomedes's palace, led this notable collection of heroes like a feudal lord in a historical quest for vengeance against Troy. Even Menelaus commented in Euripides's *Helen* on his brother's opportunism:

> How suave you were, how friendly to each clown,
> doors open to the world, so affable,
> Ready to talk with all, even when they would not!
> And so you bought your power. But power won,
> my lord has changed. He scarcely could be seen,
> his old friends friends no more.

However, as later squabbles demonstrated, Agamemnon lacked the authority of supreme commander, the spontaneous acclaim of *primus inter pares* (meaning "first among his peers").

Crucial to Agamemnon's combat role was his leave-taking, which required the sacrifice of his eldest daughter, Iphigenia. His armada of a thousand ships, arriving south of their destination in the region of Mysia, fell victim to a storm and were blown back to their home port. After eight years, to relieve boredom, disinterest, starvation, and the collapse of their wooden ships, they made a second foray from Aulis, a coastal village in Boeotia northeast of Athens. An omen appeared in the form of two eagles devouring a pregnant rabbit, which Calchas, the prophet, interpreted as a favorable sign for Agamemnon's hosts. Having insulted the goddess Artemis by claiming that he could out-hunt her, Agamemnon appeased the angry divinity with promise of "first fruits." He then learned that his fleet would remain land-bound in Aulis until the slaughter on the hallowed altar of Princess Iphigenia, the most beautiful "fruit" of the year in which he promised Artemis his best effort.

To secure the transport of his daughter from home, Agamemnon concocted a lie that Iphigenia was to wed Achilles, a splendid example of young manhood and one of the youngest of the Greeks to fight for the return of Helen. Achilles, his name dishonored by this sleazy deception, carped that Agamemnon should have asked permission before using betrothal to Achilles as an excuse for summoning Iphigenia to her death. Agamemnon chose Diomedes and Odysseus, two believable spokesmen, to convey the shabby falsehood to the queen. In Euripides's *Iphigenia in Aulis,* Agamemnon relented and sent a second messenger to overtake the first, but Menelaus stopped Agamemnon from summoning the little princess for slaughter.

Agamemnon sobbed at the sight of his wife, infant son, Orestes, and doomed daughter. Menelaus also wept when he realized that his brother had chosen to sacrifice his own family in order to rescue Menelaus's wife. Agamemnon determined that slaughtering the child was the will of the gods and proceeded with preparations. The little girl, dressed in a saffron yellow burial wrap rather than the customary bridal veil, approached her father. A touching scene ensued in which the king conversed with the girl, who wanted to accompany her father on his long voyage. Cryptically, he replied that she, too, was going on a long journey.

Clytemnestra accompanied Iphigenia to Aulis and refused to be dismissed from her daughter's betrothal to Achilles. A loyal servant betrayed Agamemnon by disclosing to Clytemnestra that the marriage plans were a hoax. Both the queen and princess confronted the king with their knowledge of his heinous plan. Agamemnon, a beleaguered patriarch and warlord pressed by familial ties, was forced to explain that, unless he obeyed the will of the gods, the Greeks might invade Argos and kill the entire royal family.

Blaming warfare for prematurely truncating her childhood, Iphigenia, a model of selflessness and bravery, faced her father's decision to slit her throat with his own hand, but warned prophetically, "I will avenge myself by utterly annihilating my father's house, I will stand and watch with grim satisfaction as it crumbles to nothing before my eyes." (Euripides's *Iphigenia in Aulis*) Sidetracked by Menelaus, the queen did not witness the beheading of her daughter with a ceremonial sword. Too late, Clytemnestra discovered her husband's treachery and her daughter's pitiable demise, which guaranteed fair winds for the royal armada. Enraged beyond control, the queen confronted Agamemnon, who offered a lame fiction that the gods rescued Iphigenia at the last minute and carried her to safety. Thus, the family parted until their bitter reunion at the end of the war.

Along the way to the Troad, a projection of land on Turkey's Asian Coast, Agamemnon's men passed Delos, among the Cyclades southeast of Greece, where they encountered the Oenotropae or "changers into wine," who provided the fleet with amphorae of wine. Agamemnon unwisely decided to take the maidens along on the journey. Only the intercession of their great-grandfather, Dionysus, who changed them into doves, saved them from involvement in the Trojan War.

The fleet moved on in a northeasterly direction to Tenedos, a small island (today called Bozcaada, Turkey), due west of Troy's coastline. The home of Apollo Smintheus, god of mice, was the scene of Agamemnon's first major difference with Achilles, a foreshadowing of a greater imbroglio ahead. Then the Greek host moved farther west to the larger island of Lemnos, where, on the advice of Odysseus, Agamemnon marooned Philoctetes before proceeding to the Troad on the coast of modern-day Turkey and camping along the Hellespont, the strait separating Europe and Asia, where he quickly conquered the lesser of Trojan supporters on the outskirts of the realm. At length, Agamemnon's fleet arrived north of the learning center of Pergamum at the war theater, Alexandria Troas, a propitious site for a city, which survived into Roman times.

Because of the king's petty quarreling and egotism, in the tenth year of the war, Agamemnon, as an oracle predicted, precipitated a rift with Achilles, the kingpin of his fighting force and symbol of Greek might, by seizing Briseis, Achilles's captured war bride. Agamemnon had received Chryseis, also called Astynome, his own prize of honor. Because the girl exceeded Queen Clytemnestra herself in beauty, skill, and brilliance, he refused to relinquish her, even after Chryses, her father, offered substantial ransom. His haughty words in the opening lines of Book 1 of Homer's *Iliad* suggest a disdainful ruler guilty of *hubris*:

> Do not let me find you by our hollow ships, old man, or
> even Apollo will not be able to protect you! I refuse
> to free your daughter. Instead, Chryseis will grow old
> in my house in Argos, far from you and her country.
> There she will weave on the loom and serve me.

At length, Apollo punished the Greeks by sending a deadly plague on the troops. An oracle indicated that Agamemnon had to relinquish the girl to her father if the Greeks were to survive.

In a regal fit of pique, Agamemnon demanded reparation in the form of Briseis. His high-handedness caused Achilles great humiliation before the gathered warriors. Vowing never to fight again, Achilles, supported by Zeus, lay down his arms. During the period that he withdrew to his tent to sulk, the tide of combat swept toward the Trojans, who impelled the commander to fear for himself and his rapidly dwindling forces.

As reported in Book 11 of Homer's *Iliad*, Agamemnon, though not excelling in word or deed, was a man of honor. Called to action by a dream sent from Zeus, Agamemnon led his forces well and earned the epithet "shepherd of his people." In Book 4, after Pandarus broke the truce with a forbidden arrow, Agamemnon expressed both shock and outrage that Menelaus suffered so treacherous a blow. In Books 7 and 8, when the Greeks targeted Hector, Agamemnon refused to allow Menelaus to volunteer for a suicide mission, but did countenance a lottery to decide

who should face the formidable warrior. Another example of Agamemnon's fairness was his agreement to a truce with Priam so that both sides could honor their dead.

After Agamemnon received a serious wound through the flesh under his elbow, he continued to rage among the Trojan attackers in an attempt to compensate for their recalcitrant champion, Achilles. At length, weakened by pain and loss of blood, Agamemnon was spirited by chariot back to his camp, which the Trojans attacked. In Book 9, terrified lest the Greeks lose, Agamemnon wept as he toyed with the idea of returning to Argos. In desperation, he met with his advisers and decided to restore Briseis to Achilles along with other valuables, including seven cities and one of his daughters in marriage if only Achilles would relent and stem the Trojan siege. After Achilles refused, Agamemnon lost sleep and called a late-night council of his advisers to determine strategy.

Achilles, who easily eclipsed Agamemnon's fighting ability, dominated the remainder of the crucial war scenes. By Book 19, when Achilles had rejoined the Achaians, Agamemnon nobly greeted him, blaming Zeus for arousing his anger. In Book 23, Agamemnon resurfaced briefly at the funeral games in honor of Patroclus, where he demonstrated his prowess with the spear. Another episode revealed Agamemnon conspiring with Diomedes and Odysseus to hide a forged message from Priam in the tent of Palamedes. As a result of their conspiracy, Palamedes was stoned to death.

Agamemnon remained active in Greek affairs as the war wound down. Following Achilles's death, it was Agamemnon who interceded between Ajax the Great and Odysseus to settle the matter of an heir to Achilles's armor. In the final days following Troy's downfall, Agamemnon, as a central figure in the formation of the fighting force, demanded Cassandra, a prize Trojan princess, whom he claimed was raped by Ajax. After Ajax's suicide, Agamemnon ordered the body left unhonored, but he acceded to the wisdom of Teucer and allowed a ritual burial.

Against the wishes of Menelaus, who wanted to set sail for Greece as soon as the city gates were breached, Agamemnon, influenced by a visitation of Achilles's spirit, remained long enough to curry favor with Athena. In Euripides's *Hecuba*, Agamemnon took custody of the aged Trojan queen and helped her avenge the murder of her one remaining male child. In the meantime, Cassandra, whom Edith Hamilton's *Mythology* calls "the flower of all the captive women," proved a worthy concubine and bore Agamemnon twin sons, Pelops and Teledamus.

With the blessing of the goddess Athena, the homeward journey of Agamemnon's men, as contrasted with the god-cursed wanderings of Odysseus, was unremarkable. Agamemnon is said to have called at the port of Polyrrhenia in northwest Crete before reaching Argolis. At Tenea near Corinth, the king settled his Trojan captives, who devoted themselves to the worship of Apollo. The final leg brought him in sight of the cheering masses of his own people, who thrilled to his safe return and escorted him over a red carpet.

The significance of Agamemnon's might and authority flamed briefly upon his victory parade in Argos. There Clytemnestra, in league with her lover Aegisthus, had rejected the story that Iphigenia had been rescued and for ten years had cunningly plotted the murder of her deceptive husband and, more recently, his royal war bride, Cassandra, and her twin sons. According to Book 3 of the *Odyssey*, Aegisthus, aware that Agamemnon had posted a singer to serve as a spy on Clytemnestra's activities, had long before kidnapped the spy and abandoned him to die on a desert island.

For a year, the queen and her illicit consort, left to their plotting, kept watchmen posted on mountaintops to light signal fires and warn of the king's return. With traditional ritual, Agamemnon entered his kingdom and immediately thanked the gods for bringing him safely home and set about cleaning the city of symbolic evils. Clytemnestra, wearing the welcoming smile of a loyal wife, called handmaidens to spread royal tapestries in the king's path as he walked the final steps into his palace. Not altogether comfortable with what ancient Greeks termed a fashion too womanly for warriors, the king allowed himself to be led onward, encased in the homage of the conquering lord, a pomp more suited to gods.

Ironically, Cassandra, a seer cursed with a vision that no one believed, described from afar the infamous scenario as it took place. Looking into the middle distance and calling to Apollo, Cassandra experienced vicariously Agamemnon's last moments as he submerged himself into a steaming bath, then floundered in a net thrown by his murderous wife, who hacked him to death with an ax. Agamemnon's subjects listened to Cassandra's ravings, but were unable to decipher her meaning.

After Agamemnon's murder, Clytemnestra slew Cassandra and the two sons fathered by Agamemnon over his very tomb. As a necessary part of the ancient code of vengeance, it fell to Orestes to avenge his father by murdering his mother, a no-win situation, which placed Orestes in the hands of the avenging Furies and Apollo himself. Apollo, impelled by Agamemnon's unrequited spirit, drove Orestes mad, thus fulfilling the cursed fate of Atreus's noble house.

Upon Odysseus's visit to Hades in Book 11 of Homer's *Odyssey*, he met the ashen shade of Agamemnon, who drank a blood offering so that he could address his old comrade. Tearfully, he explained to the astonished Odysseus that Clytemnestra, his "sluttish wife," killed him like a pig being slaughtered for a wedding feast. In her rush to dispatch Cassandra, the queen even failed to perform the ritual closing of the eyes and mouth as Agamemnon's soul struggled free of his body and journeyed on its way to the Underworld.

So aghast was Agamemnon's ghost that he warned Odysseus to expect treachery upon his own reunion with his family. Cynically, the ghost, before asking about Orestes's welfare, confided: "When you bring your ship in to your own dear country, do it secretly, not in the open. There is no trusting in women." (Homer's *Odyssey*) Upon return, Odysseus acknowledged Agamemnon's advice, which circumvented a parallel murder of Penelope's rightful lord.

Alternate Versions Both Hesiod and Aeschylus name Pleisthenes as Agamemnon's father and Cleolla as his mother, with Menelaus still his brother and Anaxibia his sister. Because of Pleisthenes's death at an early age, both Agamemnon and Menelaus were reared by their grandfather, Atreus. Agamemnon's role in the killing of Thyestes is often assigned to Atreus, who is said to have cooked Tantalus and Pleisthenes into a stew and served it to the boys' father. Thyestes's outrage produced the hellish curse on Atreus's lineage, producing Greek literature's most tortured tales of family carnage and blood-lust. In addition to Argos, Agamemnon is said to have ruled Lacedaemon or Sparta; his death scene is sometimes given as Amyclae, where local worshippers honor a tomb that is thought to belong to Cassandra.

Agamemnon's name is attached regularly to Artemis, whose temple at Ephesus he is said to have built to relieve his soldiers' bout with an annoying malady of the hindquarters. One version of Agamemnon's insult to Artemis revealed him in the act of slaughtering a stag in the goddess's sacred grove, for which sin he was commanded to murder his newborn daughter, Iphigenia. The scenario, a foreshadowing of the later sacrifice of his firstborn, proved so repugnant that Agamemnon disobeyed the goddess. The most questionable segment of the Agamemnon story is the death of Iphigenia, which is mitigated in some versions so that she is snatched away at the fatal moment to live among the Taurians in the Crimea and serve as Artemis's votary. In her place, the priest slaughtered a stag. Other tellings describe her as Agamemnon's foster child and the daughter of Helen and Theseus, and therefore less of a loss to Agamemnon or Clytemnestra.

Another variation claims that Clytemnestra was so envenomed at Agamemnon for his savagery that she plotted to kill Orestes and Electra as well. Some versions declare that it was Aegisthus who plotted the carnage. One source claims that Oeax, in retaliation for the Greeks' stoning of Palamedes, convinced Clytemnestra to murder Agamemnon, possibly out of jealousy of his war bride, Cassandra, and her twin babes. These variations describe Agamemnon as assassinated by a band of twenty cutthroats at a feast arranged by Aegisthus, stabbed with a black horn, or impaired by a shirt cunningly sewn so that he could not ward off Clytemnestra's well-honed dagger. Afterward, weighted down by conscience, Clytemnestra sent her easily manipulated Chrysothemis with honeyed gifts to heap on Agamemnon's tomb.

Symbolism Several symbolic events attach to Agamemnon's lore. Most prominent is his scepter, which was forged by Hephaestus and passed to Agamemnon from his grandfather Pelops. The scepter was a holy object venerated in Chaeroneia in Boeotia. In Sophocles's *Electra*, Clytemnestra dreamed that Agamemnon erected his scepter in the soil and that it grew into the shape of a tree and shadowed his realm.

Before sailing from Aulis, Agamemnon witnessed a dragon devouring eight chicks and a mother bird from their nest. Some sources interpret the sacrifice of Iphigenia and the ultimate destruction of Agamemnon's family as symbolic of the preservation of the greater good through loss of personal happiness. The prophet Calchas interpreted the bird and eight biddies as symbolic of the number of years that Troy would remain inviolable to Greek seizure. The dragon served as a direct link to Agamemnon, who bore a blue dragon on his belt and three dragon emblems on his cuirass.

Other emblems of Agamemnon's importance include statues at Amyclae and Olympia and his death mask, which is displayed in Athens' National Archeological Museum. An obscure tale depicts Agamemnon as smitten with lust for Argynnus, a handsome youth who drowned in the Cephissus River in Boeotia. In his honor, Agamemnon raised a temple to Aphrodite Argynnus. Another localized connection declares that Lappa or Lampa, a Cretan town, was founded by Agamemnon and named after Lampos, a Tarrhaean colony. Claims have been made that the Cretan town of Pergamum was also established by Agamemnon.

The Argive king appears on archaic vase paintings as the stifler of the fight between Ajax and Odysseus for Achilles's armor; two scenes—his sacrifice of Iphigenia and his demand for the surrender of Briseis—are recreated on a wall painting at Pompeii. The arrival of Briseis is shown on a similar wall decoration at Tiepolo. Other artistic recreations depict him on the pedestal of the Rhamnusian Nemesis, as part of a Delphic frieze painted by Polygnotus, on a royal monument erected by Menelaus on the Aegyptus River, and on Cypselus's carved cedar chest in the Heraion, the oldest building in the Sacred Grove of Olympia. Agamemnon figured at the center of several cults, one at Sparta in which he supplanted Zeus.

The dismal tale of the Atreides, or ancestors of Atreus, reaches into the arts and astronomy. In the first decade of the twentieth century, a planetoid named Agamemnon was added to the group called the "Trojan Camp." A musical tribute, *Clitennestra,* by Ildebrando Pizzetti, concentrates on the marital climate between Agamemnon and his wronged wife; a similar emphasis exists in Martha Graham's dance *Clytemnestra.* Agamemnon and his family relationships also survive in these works: *Iphigenie's Monologue,* a song by Franz Schubert; *Iphiginie,* an opera by Bernardo Aliprandi; *Iphegénie,* Pierre Corneille's tragedy; Eugene O'Neill's play *Mourning Becomes Electra;* Jean Paul Sartre's *Les Mouches;* Christoph Gluck's operas *Iphigénie en Aulide* and *Iphigénie en Tauride;* Jean Racine's *Iphigénie;* and Johann Goethe's *Iphigenie auf Tauris.*

English and American verse paying tribute to Agamemnon includes Geoffrey Chaucer's *Troilus* and *Criseyde;* Christopher Marlowe's *Jew of Malta;* John Masefield's *Clytemnestra;* William Shakespeare's *King Henry VI* and *Troilus and Cressida;* Elizabeth Barrett Browning's *Aurora Leigh;* Algernon Swinburne's *On the Cliffs;* William Butler Yeats's *Leda and the Swan;* Dylan Thomas's *Greek Play in a Garden;* Walter Conrad Arensberg's *Chryseis;* and T. S. Eliot's *The Family Reunion* and *Sweeney among the Nightingales.*

Perhaps the greatest tribute to Agamemnon's role in the Trojan War is the devotion of the German archeologist Heinrich Schliemann, who taught himself Greek, then in 1870 journeyed to the Troad and defied the scholars of his day in proving that the myth was attached to a real man. According to Irving Stone's historical novel, *The Greek Treasure,* at Hissarlik, Turkey, Schliemann and his Greek wife employed a team of eighty diggers for a year before locating a cache of 9,000 objects that proved the tale of Agamemnon's forces was grounded in history.

Confounded by the discovery of nine Troys, the second of which was destroyed by fire, Schliemann diverted his search from the site to the man and began to scout the eastern Peloponnesus for Mycenae. The identification of Agamemnon's tomb alongside a burial cluster of a woman and two infants, possibly Cassandra and her murdered twin sons, clashes with the gold burial mask, which predates the historic Agamemnon. Still, the mask remains as a relic of Agamemnon's lore.

Schliemann's jubilant telegram to the king of Greece indicated his belief that the burial grounds were authentic. He claimed that they contained the magnificent shafts holding Atreus's and Agamemnon's remains and a lesser barrow honoring Clytemnestra along with gold shirt buttons, intaglios, a silver cowhead with gold inlaid rosettes, bronze daggers, and gold funeral masks. The archeologist's monomania carried him through 1890, when he died praying to "Agamemnon Schliemann, best beloved of sons, greeting!"

❦ See Also

Achilles, Aegisthus, Ajax the Great, Cassandra, Dionysus, Menelaus, Odysseus, Teucer.

❦ Ancient Sources

Aeschylus's *Agamemnon, Eumenides,* and *The Suppliants;* Agias of Troezen's *Returns of Heroes;* Apollodorus's *Epitome;* Athenaeus's *The Learned Banquet;* Dictys Cretensis's *Trojan War Diary;* Euripides's *Electra, Hecuba, Helen, Iphigenia in Aulis, Iphigenia in Tauris, Orestes,* and *Trojan Women;* Eustathius on Homer's *Iliad;* Hesiod's *Histories;* Homer's *Iliad* and *Odyssey;* Horace's *Carmina;* Hyginus's *Fables;* Pausanias's *Description of Greece;* Pindar's *Pythian Odes;* Scholiast on Euripides's *Electra* and *Orestes;* Seneca's *Agamemnon* and *Trojan Women;* Servius on Virgil's *Aeneid;* Sophocles's *Ajax* and *Electra;* Stasinus of Cyprus's *Cypria;* Stesichorus's *Helen* and *Iliu Persis;* Virgil's *Aeneid.*

Ajax the Great

[ay' jaks]

Genealogy and Background More familiar to readers than Ajax the Lesser, the Great Ajax was Telamon's son and grandson of Aeacus, for whom he was later called Aeacid. Ovid depicts Ajax's lineal boasts in Book 13 of the *Metamorphoses:*

> Telamon was my father, who in company with valiant Hercules took the walls of Troy and [sailed] to Colchis. His father was Aeacus, who is passing judgment in that silent [Underworld] where Sisyphus strains to his heavy stone and most high Jupiter acknowledges Aeacus as his son. Thus Ajax is the third remove from Jove.

The nature of the ancient world being unfamiliar with modesty, these words are meant to ennoble Ajax, who had every right to be proud that his great grandfather was the Olympian high god.

His mother, Periboea, a Megaran princess who served as a tribute to Minos of Crete, brought honor to Salamis, the city of peace on an island west of Attica and north of Aegina in the Bay of Eleusis, where Telamon ruled. His kingdom, extending to Ageirussa, Nisaea, and Tripodiscus on the mainland, increased his wealth and influence. Heir to his father's kingdom was Ajax, blessed with looks, strength, size, and character, but not overly endowed with intelligence. Ajax was a devout man, tight-lipped, but good-hearted. A mighty warrior second only to his cousin Achilles in strength, he lacked the Greek leader's gentle nature and artistic training. A half-brother to Ajax and significant figure in his career was Teucer, borne by Hesione during Telamon's journey with Herakles.

Before leaving home, Ajax married Lyside and fathered Philaeus, for whom the Athenian suburb of Philaedae is named. In Asia Minor, Ajax's foreign wife, Tecmessa, is said to have borne him a son, Eurysaces or "broad shield," who was named for his father's body -

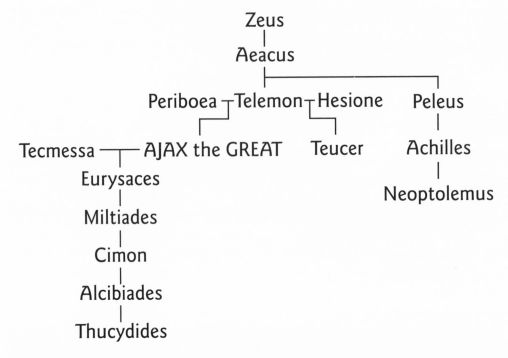

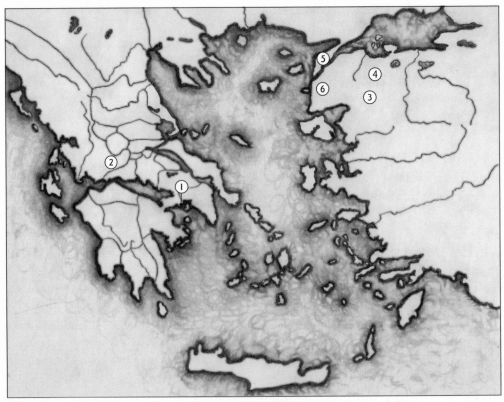

1. Salamis 2. Aetolia 3. Mysia 4. Phrygia 5. Hellespont 6. Troy

protector. The boy passed to the care of Teucer after Ajax's death and succeeded to his father's inheritance upon Teucer's return to Salamis following the war. From Eurysaces came a long line of noble Greeks, including Miltiades, Cimon, Alcibiades, and the historian Thucydides.

Journey Before Helen's abduction, Ajax had been one of her suitors in Aetolia and was thus honor-bound to join Agamemnon's forces to retrieve her from Troy. Before taking leave of his family, Ajax received Telamon's advice to fight with his hands, but to rely on the gods. Ajax, who depended on his keen spear, retorted impiously that cowards relied on celestial intervention. To illustrate his determination to make his own way, he yanked from his shield the symbol of Athena, thus angering the goddess for so foolhardy a demonstration of *hubris*. The insult haunted Ajax to his grave but did not deter his contributions to the war effort. Joining Phoenix and Achilles as fleet commanders, Ajax quickly assumed a position as decisionmaker and led twelve ships from Salamis.

The Achaean force made its way north and east to Troy. At Mysia, south of the target beachhead, Ajax killed Teuthranius, Telephus's brother, as the local forces charged the Greeks. In another foray, Ajax abducted the Princess Tecmessa from Phrygia, where her father, Teleutas, ruled. He also enslaved Glauce, daughter of Cycnus, after her father was strangled by Achilles. In a second prefatory battle, Ajax overcame the Chersonese of Thrace on the north shore of the Hellespont, receiving the child Polydorus, Priam's kinsman, as a hostage to exchange for Helen. After the Trojans refused the trade, Polydorus was stoned to death outside the walls of Troy.

As Agamemnon's left wing commander, Ajax, Greece's tallest and second swiftest warrior after Achilles, guarded one end of the Trojan walls and Achilles the other. Ajax stood behind his eight-layered shield, composed of multiple ox hides topped with bronze, behind which his brother Teucer frequently cowered or darted out to aim shots at the enemy. For this stalwart pose, Homer nicknamed Ajax "Greece's bulwark." In one episode, after Agamemnon was removed from command for slaughtering Artemis's sacred deer, Ajax served as replacement leader.

Still, Ajax was not immune from the unfocused anger of his leader, who threatened to revoke his war prizes after Chryses demanded the removal of his daughter from Agamemnon's possession. Ironically, when Agamemnon sought to appease Achilles for taking Briseis, he sent Ajax among the embassy to Achilles's tent. Ajax had the courage to scold his comrade: "But you, Achilles, will not bend because of one woman, when we have offered you seven of the best women and many other gifts besides." (Homer's *Iliad*) Achilles did not take the bait and retorted that Ajax and Odysseus could return with the message that he intended to stay out of the war until Hector pushed all the way to the Greek fleet.

In Books 7 and 8 of the *Odyssey*, while Nestor oversaw the choice of a warrior, Ajax drew his lot from Agamemnon's helmet and won the right to a duel with Hector in a key battle, which Helen watched from the battlements. In Homer's words, before advancing on the best of the Trojans, Ajax courted the help of his comrades:

> See friends, the lot is mine, and I myself am made happy in
> my heart, since I think I can win over brilliant Hector. Do
> this then; while I put on my armor of fighting, all of you
> by praying to the lord Zeus, son of Cronos, in silence.

As beautifully arrayed as Ares, Greek god of war. Ajax, carrying his seven-ply ox-hide shield, drew near. Hector's spear pierced six of the layers and was stopped by the last leather oval. In retaliation, Ajax waylaid him by hurling a great boulder, which Homer compares to a millstone. It crashed through Hector's shield. Zeus's heralds, reserving the Trojan favorite for the ultimate battle with Achilles, halted Ajax before he completed the kill.

In token of their mutual respect for each other, Hector complimented his enemy and exchanged his silver-studded sword for Ajax's purple war belt. A second encounter with Hector returned the favor, with the Trojan leader stopping short of killing the wounded Ajax. Their third meeting, which followed Ajax's recovery, occurred at the harbor, where Trojans, undeterred by Achilles, pushed their way to Greek ships. Ajax, in the lead, again struck Hector a telling blow, then found himself shoved against his own ship. After Hector split his ash spear, Ajax recognized that the gods did not intend him to kill his old enemy. As Homer describes the god-fearing Ajax in the *Iliad*, he "knew in his blameless heart, and shivered for knowing it, how this was the gods' work, how Zeus high-thundering cut across the intention in all his battle." Thus chastened, Ajax swiftly withdrew.

Shortly afterward, as Greeks struggled over Patroclus's body, the Great Ajax came under Zeus's protective cloud when Hector once more menaced him. With the help of Diomedes, Ajax managed to retrieve the corpse and deposited it reverently in Achilles's tent. At the funeral games in Patroclus's honor, Ajax wrestled the wily Odysseus, who tried to cheat his opponent. Their protracted match ended in a tie because Achilles called a halt to their struggle. After a stray arrow killed Achilles, Ajax extracted the corpse from the roiling fray that broke out over it, while Odysseus held off the Trojans. Ajax then fought to glorious victory over the pursuing Trojans, killing Glaucus.

A varied view of Ajax is his role as foster father to Neoptolemus, Achilles's undisciplined son, in the final year of the fighting after Achilles's death. Other positive roles allotted to Ajax include friend of Teucer (the Attic archer, not his brother Teucer) and of Philoctetes, the bowman fated to help end the war. A more uncompromising role for Ajax came at war's end, when he pressed for Helen's assassination. Odysseus advised otherwise and thus humiliated Ajax.

The most tragic aspect of Ajax's part in the Trojan War involves his demand for the arms of Achilles, the possession of which would have adorned Ajax as worthy successor and second most valuable warrior. Thetis marked Achilles's arms for Odysseus. Ajax, degraded a second time by his jealous comrades' denial of this honor, lost control and ran amok, taking arms against a flock of sheep that he misperceived as Menelaus and Agamemnon, the men who had voted against him. He selected one stout ram, which he identified as Odysseus, and tied it to his tent pole to abuse. Then, appalled at his own madness, he called on his son and half-brother for succor.

To save himself a dishonorable return to Salamis, Ajax chose suicide, despite the pleas of Tecmessa to save her and her son the disgrace. Calchas, prophesying that ill could come to him on this day alone, begged Teucer to protect Ajax from self-destruction. At the shore, Ajax resolved to die, begged the gods for immediate transfer to the Underworld, and impaled himself on the sword that Hector had given him. Both Agamemnon and Menelaus mourned his loss and withheld his body from funeral rites. In deviation from the Greek custom of the funeral pyre, the remains of a suicide could not be honored with funeral games and decorated urn and so were interred by Teucer.

When Odysseus visited Hades, he gave blood for the shades to drink so that he could talk with them. After speaking at length to Agamemnon's spirit, he turned to those of Achilles, Patroclus, and Ajax, "the most impressive-looking of the long-haired Greeks after Achilles." (Homer's *Odyssey*) Ajax still sulked that Odysseus claimed Achilles's armor. Odysseus, a skilled peacemaker, admitted that Greek strength was never the same after the loss of Achilles and Ajax. Ajax, refusing to yield to flattery, stared silently, then stalked away to join his fellow shades.

Alternate Versions

Ajax's mother's name is also given as Eriboea, Eeriboea, Meliboea, or Phereboea. One family linkage has Telamon's sister, Alcimache, married to Oileus, father of Ajax the Lesser, an arrangement that would make the two Ajaxes cousins. On Teucer's return from the Trojan War, Telamon blamed him for not taking better care of his half-brother and banished him to Cyprus.

Ajax's love life is also the subject of conjecture. A woman linked romantically with Ajax is Glauce or Glauca, his slave girl, and mother of Aeantides. Another variation recasts how Ajax died. He chose the Palladium as his allotment of the spoils. Odysseus again intervened and denied him the reward. Boiling with uncontrolled rage, Ajax menaced Odysseus and considered murdering Agamemnon and Menelaus for not supporting his cause. The next day, Ajax's body was found run through by his own weapon. Other tellings have Ajax killed by one of Paris's arrows or buried alive by the Trojans, who believed him invulnerable.

After Ajax's death, one version depicts Menelaus as so angry that he forbade mourners to move his body from the shore so that birds could denude his bones.

Odysseus, out of respect, persuaded Agamemnon to intervene so that Teucer could prepare the body for honorable burial. Another tradition pairs Achilles and Ajax as immortals on the White Island in the Black Sea. In Book 10 of Plato's *Republic*, Ajax appears before the throne of the Fates and is allowed to select a new incarnation. Symbolic of his early life, he chose to become a lion.

Symbolism

As one of the founders of Athens' ten tribes, Ajax's name is linked with the lion and the eagle, *aietos,* for which he was named Aias after Zeus sent the bird overhead as a positive omen at his birth. There is a legend that Herakles saw his father reposed on a lion skin at a banquet. Herakles prayed that Zeus would send Telamon a child with the strength of the lion. Alternate versions depict Ajax as an infant swaddled in a lion skin. When Herakles visited Ajax's parents, he interceded with Zeus to strengthen the child. As with the story of Achilles's dip in the river Styx, Ajax grew to be invulnerable in every part of his body except shoulder, hip, and armpit, which were not protected by the lion skin that swaddled him.

Ajax's death parallels the early myths of Hyacinthus. After his demise, Ajax, who died of despair and disappointment, earned the respect of his peers, who paid annual tribute to him at Salamis at the festival of Aiateia. Other cults sprang up at Megara, the Troad, Athens, and Byzantium. His grave was said to have sprouted purple flowers engraved with AI, an abbreviated form of his Greek name, Aias. Another interpretation of the phenomenon is that the flowers represent a cry of grief, Ai! Ai! A modern interpretation suggests that Ajax was a supernatural figure rather than a human made invulnerable by the gods. A later interpretation, based on Homer's familiarity with the armor of Mycenae, links him with Mycenaean lore as the epic figure armed with a shield.

Ajax's name, ignobly immortalizing a heavy-duty household cleaning product, also graces the arts and sciences. In the early twentieth century, Ajax's name was immortalized among the Trojan planetoids. On the stage, William Shakespeare drew on Ajax's lore in *Antony and Cleopatra, Cymbeline, King Henry VI, King Lear, Titus Andronicus, Troilus and Cressida,* and *The Rape of Lucrece.* In verse, Ajax receives mention in Samuel Butler's *Hudibras,* Ben Jonson's *Epistle to Elizabeth,* Andrew Marvell's *The Unfortunate Lover,* George Crabbe's *The Village,* Matthew Prior's *On Fleet,* and an oft-quoted line from Alexander Pope's *Essay on Criticism,* which contrasts laborious composition with epic struggle: "When Ajax strives some rock's vast weight to throw."

❦ See Also

Achilles, Agamemnon, Teucer.

🌿 Ancient Sources

Apollodorus's *Epitome;* Arcinus of Miletus's *Aethiopis;* Athenaeus's *The Learned Banquet;* Dictys Cretensis's *Trojan War Diary;* Herodotus's *Histories;* Hesiod's *Catalogue of Women;* Homer's *Iliad* and *Odyssey;* Lesches's *Little Iliad;* Lycophron's *Aethiopis;* Ovid's *Metamorphoses;* Pausanias's *Description of Greece;* Pindar's *Isthmian Odes;* Plutarch's *Parallel Lives;* Quintus Smyrnaeus's *Post-Homerica;* Sophocles's *Ajax;* Stephanus Byzantium's *Philaedai;* Johannes Tzetzes's *On Lycophron.*

Ajax the Lesser

[ay' jaks]

Genealogy and Background

The lesser and shorter of classical mythology's two champions of the same name, Ajax was born in Naryx, Locris's coastal capital northwest of Athens, son of one of the Argonauts, Oileus of Opus, "sacker of cities," and of Eriopis, also called Alcimache, or the nymph, Rhene. Additional tales give Ajax an illegitimate brother, Medon, son of Oileus and Alcimache or Rhene. Like his brother, Medon served at Troy as commander of a division of Pythians and later of the Methonians after Philoctetes was wounded and marooned on the island of Lemnos. Medon earned Homer's admiration for smiting Periphetes and other bold Trojans.

Journey

As one of Helen's numerous suitors, Ajax the Lesser was obliged to join the forces that sought her recovery and commanded a fleet of forty ships. A Greek trooper at Troy, Ajax the Lesser fought alongside the Great Ajax. Homer seems to take a liking to Ajax the Lesser, whom he admires in Book 14 of the *Iliad* as

> Ajax the fast-footed son of Oileus [who] caught and
> killed most, since there was none like him in the speed
> of his feet to go after men who ran, once Zeus had
> driven the terror upon them.

Thus, Ajax earned a reputation for baiting and killing escaping Trojan cowards. In one of Homer's graceful epic similes in Book 13 of the *Iliad,* the poet compares the lesser with the greater Ajax.

> [Ajax] the son of Oileus, would not at all now take
> his stand apart from [Ajax the Great], not even a little,

Rhene ⚭ Oileus ⚭ Eriopis

Medon   AJAX the LESSER

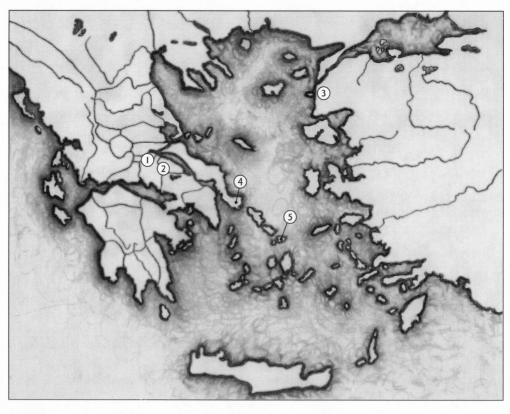

1. Naryx 2. Opus 3. Troy 4. Cape Caphareus 5. Mykonos

but as two wine-colored oxen straining with even force drag the compacted plow through the fallow land, and for both of them at the base of the horns the dense sweat gushes; only the width of the polished yoke keeps a space between them as they toil down the furrow till the share cuts the edge of the plowland; so these took their stand in battle closer to each other.

Armed with a bow and covered in humble linen breastplate, he fought mightily in some of the worst of the fray and drew his lot to determine who would face Hector, Troy's best warrior. A favorite of Homer, Ajax the Lesser appeared in the hand-to-hand struggle in the harbor, and in the tenth year of the war, during the battle over Patroclus's corpse.

The lesser Ajax gained a reputation for savagery, contention, sleazy character, and conceit springing from his skill as a spearsman. Idomeneus reviled him at the games honoring Patroclus: "Ajax, surpassing in abuse, yet stupid, in all else you are worst of the Argives with that stubborn mind of yours." (Homer's *Iliad*) Their set-to might have reached dangerous proportions if Achilles had not stepped in with shaming words and separated them. Ajax, the Greeks' second fastest runner after Achilles, vied against Antilochus and Odysseus in the footraces and lost because Athena tripped Ajax with a pile of cow dung so that her favorite, Odysseus, could win. Ajax whimpered, "That goddess made me slip on my feet, who has always stood over Odysseus like a mother, and taken good care of him." (Homer's *Iliad*) Onlookers, amused by Ajax's unbecoming behavior, laughed at him.

Most crucial to the story of Ajax the Lesser is his sacrilege the night that Troy fell. With fire engulfing the palace and residences, he dashed to the shrine of Athena, stole the Palladium, the goddess's likeness, three cubits high, which formed the center of the city, and ravished Cassandra, a votary and royal daughter of Priam, on holy ground. His comrades, aghast at his audacity and sacrilege, threatened to stone him. To save himself from an ignominious death, he clung to the Palladium and hid behind Athena's altar.

The foolhardy Ajax earned a place in Greek mythology as proof that the gods would not be mocked. Just as the prophet Calchas had warned on the way west from Troy to Greece, Athena retaliated against Ajax's impiety by demanding a bitter homecoming for the Greeks, filled with crashing waters, overturned ships, and corpses choking the shoreline. At Poseidon's bidding, high seas, engulfing much of Agamemnon's armada, threw them against the whirling rocks in southern Euboea at Cape Caphareus. Ajax, a passenger on one of the luckless ships, feared death and took refuge behind the mighty Gyraean rock, then bragged that he survived a divinely inspired storm. At Athena's insistence, Poseidon smashed the rock and filled Ajax's lungs with salt water. His drowned remains floated up on a spot along Euboea's coast later named the Rocks of Ajax. His tomb lies farther to the southeast on the island Mykonos in the Cyclades.

Alternate Versions   One farfetched legend describes the lesser Ajax as victor over a dragon five cubits long, which became so docile that it followed its master like a house pet. A retelling of his sacrilege to the Palladium describes the statue as falling face forward and another as looking skyward in horror. A resetting of the rape scene describes Cassandra as so terror stricken that she clung to the Palladium and dragged it along behind her as Ajax removed her from the temple. The Greeks turned their contempt on Ajax for his villainous act, which jeopardized the entire army. Ajax repented of his sacrilege against the Palladium but not his crime against the priestess. By condemning Odysseus for lying about the rape, Ajax changed the opinion of some, since many recognized Odysseus's disregard for the truth. A version following Homer's *Iliad* accuses the Thracian priestess Theano, wife of Antenor, of betraying Troy and handing over the Palladium to the Greeks. Ajax is not mentioned in this resetting. An alternate version has Agamemnon making up the rape of the Trojan princess as justification for keeping the lovely Cassandra for himself. Another telling of Ajax's death describes Athena avenging herself on the defacer of her temple by piercing him with a bolt of lightning. The family line of Oileus appears to be truncated by the Trojan War, which killed both Ajax and his illegitimate brother Medon before they sired children. If Oileus was indeed a "sacker of cities," as Homer declares, his sons must have made him proud, even though Ajax raped a priestess of Athena and Medon was banished from Phylace for killing his uncle. As is common with professional soldiers, the brothers lives were short, brutal, and cataclysmic, and their lineage ended in ignominy far from Locris.

Symbolism   Ajax the Lesser became patron of Opus. Future armies, loyal to Ajax's military might, left an opening in their battle lines for his invisible presence, which they believed protected them from harm. According to a first century legend, the retribution suffered by Ajax did not relieve his fellow Locrians of his sin. They returned to starvation from ruined fields. After consulting an oracle for relief from their misery, Ajax's comrades learned that, for a thousand years, the clan of Ajax had to dispatch two maidens every year to Troy to atone for the rapist's impiety. When the first pair were delivered, vengeful Trojans killed and cremated them, then sprinkled their remains on the waves. Later pairs, forewarned of what lay ahead, fled immediately from the cruelty of Trojans seeking to murder them like sacrificial sheep. The ones who survived took sanctuary at the altar of Ilium and, like Vestal Virgins, remained in service to Athena until their retirement.

❦ See Also

Achilles, Cassandra.

❦ Ancient Sources

Apollodorus's *Epitome;* Euripides's *Trojan Women;* Homer's *Iliad* and *Odyssey;* Hyginus's *Fables;* Pausanias's *Description of Greece;* Philostratus's *Heroica;* Scholiast on Homer's *Iliad;* Strabo's *Geography;* Virgil's *Aeneid.*

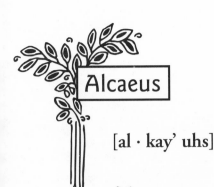

Alcaeus

[al · kay' uhs]

Son of Androgeus, a noted wrestler, and brother of Sthenelus, Alcaeus is an obscure child from an illustrious family. His grandfather, Minos, claimed kinship with Zeus and Europa. Alcaeus's uncles included Deucalion and Glaucus; his aunt was the winsome Ariadne. When Alcaeus became a minor figure in the epic voyage of Herakles, he was living with Minos and Pasiphae, the sordid royal family of Crete, who became his guardians following Androgeus's death. Alcaeus's father had participated in the Panathenaeic festival and won all the events. After Aegeus sent him to face the bull of Marathon, Androgeus was mysteriously killed. Because of the taint that clung to the episode, Minos waged war on the Athenians. Afterward, Androgeus was worshipped at the Androgeonia and games celebrated in his honor at Cerameicus.

Journey When Herakles beached his ship at Paros, King Minos's sons slaughtered four of Herakles's crew. After Herakles overran Paros and demanded reparations, the locals gave him his choice of two men to enslave. Herakles selected the Parian king, Alcaeus, and his brother Sthenelus as hostages to assure safe passage through the Black Sea to the home of the Amazons. Perhaps Herakles took a liking to Alcaeus because Herakles had borne the same name at birth and later named one of his sons Alcaeus.

Journeying eastward through the Hellespont and Bosporus to Mysia, Herakles completed his trip and retrieved Hippolyta's belt, one of the goals of his twelve labors completed for King Eurystheus. On the return voyage, Herakles installed Alcaeus and Sthenelus on the island of Thasos, south of Thrace off the Macedonian shores, where the brothers ruled jointly. Nothing further is recorded about their reign.

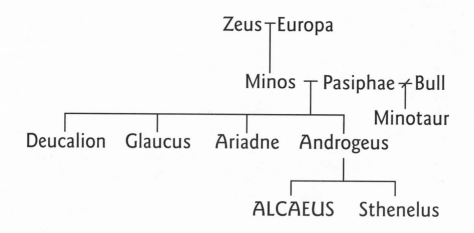

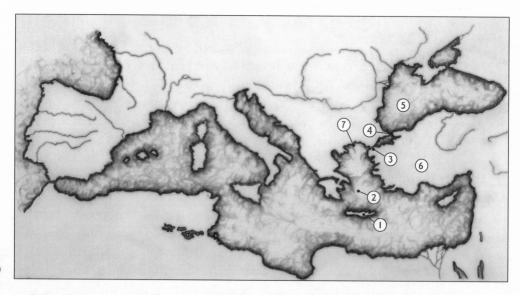

1. Crete   2. Paros   3. Hellespont   4. Bosporus   5. Black Sea   6. Mysia   7. Thasos

Alternate Versions

Diodorus Siculus credits Alcaeus's father's death to an ambush near Oenoe on the road north from Athens to the border separating Attica from Boeotia. The slaying was engineered by Aegeus out of fear of so strong a contendor at the Panathenaeic games. After Minos countered the killing of his son and took charge of his fatherless grandsons, he raised a shrine to Eurygyes the Plowman, the symbolic name for Androgeus, at Phalerum, Athen's harbor. Minos also exacted from the city an annual tribute of seven maids and seven youths to be fed to the Cretan bull, the Minotaur. Pausanias alters this tale by claiming that Asclepius restored Androgeus to life.

Symbolism

Alcaeus's name, meaning "mighty one," indicates his family's hopes for his future, which were brightened considerably after Rhadamanthys ceded him the island of Paros, one of the Cyclades west of Naxos in the Aegean Sea, as a Cretan colony.

See Also

Herakles, Sthenelus.

Ancient Sources

Apollodorus's *Library;* Diodorus Siculus's *Library of History;* Hesiod's *Catalogue of Women;* Justin's *Apology;* Pausanias's *Description of Greece;* Scholiast on Apollonius of Rhodes's *Argonautica;* Strabo's *Historical Sketches.*

Andromache

[an · drah' muh · kee]

Genealogy and Background

Andromache, the daughter of Eetion and Astymone of Imbros, was born in Thebes, a city in Cilicia, south of the Troad and opposite the north shore of the island of Cyprus. One of the most pitied of Trojan women, she was sister to seven brothers, the wife of Hector, and mother of Laodamas and Astyanax or Scamander. According to Homer in the *Iliad,* before Hector's last foray into the war, she clung to his hand and wept,

> You are too brave and will cause your death by attempting too great a victory. Pity your infant son and me, who will soon be widowed and orphaned. The avid Greeks will strike against you in a single rush and you will surely die.

To strengthen her case against Hector's departure, she reminded him that her entire family had been slain by Achilles. She pled that he not abandon her to another loss.

Hector, who recognized his place in the Trojan conflict and knew that his warriors depended on his example, replied, "All this I will bear in mind, my dear, but I would draw down shame on my lineage if I hung back like a coward." (Homer's *Iliad*) With a hug for Astyanax and a brisk command that Andromache return to her spinning and weaving, he went out to face certain death. As worthy daughter-in-law to Queen Hecuba and King Priam of Troy, Andromache found emotional support during her grief over her husband. Helpless on the battlements, she watched as Achilles slew Hector outside the city gates. Ironically, Andromache recognized that the war was fought over a woman of questionable morals whom Hector's brother Paris stole from Argos.

After Hector's death, Andromache cringed at the sight of his killer, Achilles, slayer of her brothers as well, dragging Hector's body about

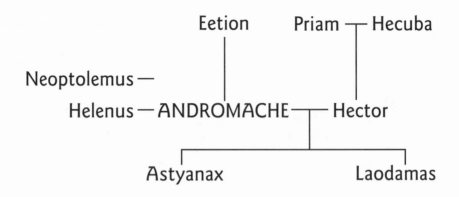

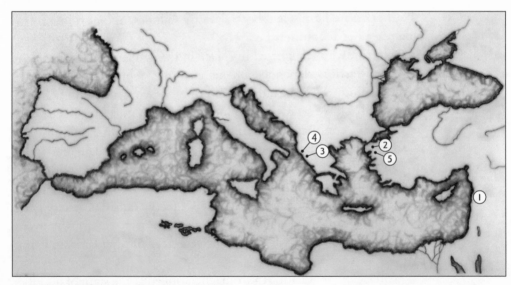

1. Thebes, Cilicia   2. Troy   3. Ephyra   4. Chaonia   5. Pergamum

the city and then abandoning it near Patroclus's pyre. That night the aged Priam intervened and, humbling himself before the Greek Achilles, recovered the remains for the appropriate rites. Andromache and her serving women bathed Hector's body in a warm bath and prepared it for interment. At the ceremony, the loving Andromache stroked Hector's head, which lay in her lap.

When the war ended, the seer Calchas predicted that Astyanax would grow up to avenge his father if left alive. Following lengthy debate by the Greek council concerning the fate of royal Trojan children, Astyanax was tossed over the battlements to his death on the rocks below in sight of his mother. Neoptolemus is credited with his execution; according to Euripedes's *Trojan Women,* Talthybias, Agamemnon's herald, removed the child from Andromache's arms before the execution, and carried the small, crushed form back to his mother after it was recovered. Laodamas's fate is unknown.

Journey | Like other war prizes, Andromache—a royal wife married to a Trojan prince—had no control over her future after Troy fell to the Greeks. Like bartered chattel, she passed to Neoptolemus or Pyrrhus, Achilles's savage son, who built a city on Lake Pambotis in Epirus, in northwestern Greece bordering Macedonia. On the journey from Troy, Andromache went into labor at sea; she and Neoptolemus were cast up at Ephyra on the Acheron river delta in Epirus, where she gave birth to Molossus. She later bore Pielus, Pergamus, and Amphialus, and endured the jealousy of Neoptolemus's younger wife Hermione, Helen's daughter, who took advantage of Neoptolemus's journey to Delphi to torment his Trojan concubine. Rescued by Peleus, Neoptolemus's grandfather, Andromache and her children remained in Epirus after Neoptolmus returned to Phthia.

During his absence, Andromache was again widowed and passed into the hands of the Trojan priest Helenus, Hector's brother, ruler of Chaonia. She bore Cestrinus, her last son, and lived in peace. When Aeneas visited her, he found her well and serene and tending a shrine to Hector. As Virgil writes in Book 3 of the *Aeneid,* she was

> by chance walking in a grove of trees outside Buthrotum,
> placing traditional gifts of food on Hector's remains at a
> green-topped barrow she had made in his honor. She stood
> weeping and calling to his spirit.

At sight of Aeneas, her brother-in-law whom she had not seen since the fall of Troy, she fainted from the rush of memories of the city's final days. Confused as to whether she had died or was still alive, she asked "if the light has failed me, then where is Hector, my husband?" (Virgil's *Aeneid*).

Temporarily traumatized by so great a pain from the past, she realized that she was still alive and narrated to Aeneas how she had fared after marriage to Neoptolemus and then to Helenus. Like a well-bred court lady, she remembered her manners and asked about Aeneas's welfare, particularly about his son Ascanius, whose mother died in Troy the night the Greeks burned the town. At Helenus's death, Andromache's half-Greek son Molossus succeeded him as regent of Chaonia. The aged Andromache traveled to Mysia in Asia Minor and established her son Pergamus in a kingdom later named Pergamum or Pergamon, where she was enshrined.

Alternate Versions

Andromache's father and brothers, all victims of Achilles, were unmutilated. Eetion is said to have impressed Achilles who, out of respect, burned his hostage without stripping away his glittering armor. Nymphs buried Eetion's ashes in a sacred elm grove. The bark and leaves were widely sought as bindings for wounds. Andromache's tragic story has few variations. An alternate version of Astyanax's death credits Odysseus with taking the child from his mother's arms to hurl him from the battlements and thus end the royal line of Priam.

Stories about Andromache's sons are less unified. One version omits Laodamas and claims that Astyanax was Hector's only son. According to Euripedes's *Andromache*, a strange turn of events surrounded Molossus's birth and infancy. Andromache is depicted as abandoning the child, who survived and was reclaimed by Neoptolemus, who recognized his child during a visit to Delphi. Because Thetis wanted the descendants of Aeacus to survive, she commanded Andromache to shelter Molossus. The boy ameliorated some of the past enmity against Neoptolemus and Achilles by succeeding his Trojan stepfather, ruling Epirus, and establishing the Molossian line.

Symbolism

In literature and art, Andromache is pictured as a tall, stately wife who bears well her multiple sorrows. A symbol of the effects of war on women and children, Andromache with her son clasped in her arms epitomizes the disenfranchisement and powerlessness of females and small children in the ancient world, where the valor of warriors was ranked above family. The artist Polygnotus drew her with Astyanax in the treasury at Delphi. Jacques-Louis David's *Andromache Mourning Hector* depicts Andromache grieving for her fallen warrior-husband. Poets refer to her as a pawn of war, as depicted in Geoffrey Chaucer's *Nun's Priest's Tale*, John Skelton's *Philip Sparrow*, William Shakespeare's *Troilus and Cressida*, Jean Racine's *Andromaque*, Dante Gabriel Rossetti's *Cassandra*, Charles-Pierre Baudelaire's *The Swan*, and Elizabeth Barrett Browning's *The Battle of Marathon*. A musical setting of Euripides's *Andromache* is the tragic scenario of Samuel Barber's *Andromache's Farewell* for soprano and orchestra in which the heroine tells Astyanax that he must soon die.

🌿 See Also

Achilles, Aeneas.

🌿 Ancient Sources

Apollodorus's *Epitome;* Dictys Cretensis's *Trojan War Diary;* Euripides's *Andromache, Hecuba,* and *Trojan Women;* Homer's *Iliad;* Hyginus's *Fables;* Lesches's *Little Iliad;* Ovid's *Metamorphoses;* Pausanias's *Description of Greece;* Pindar's *Nemean Odes;* Quintus Smyrnaeus's *Post-Homerica;* Seneca's *Trojan Women;* Servius on Virgil's *Aeneid;* Tryphiodorus' *Sack of Troy;* Johannes Tzetzes's *On Lycophron;* Virgil's *Aeneid.*

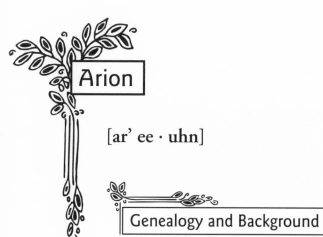

Arion

[ar' ee · uhn]

Genealogy and Background

A well-known legendary singer born in approximately A.D. 700 in Methymna, a fishing village on the north shore of the island of Lesbos near the eastern end of the Mediterranean, Arion was the son of Poseidon and Oncaea, a sea nymph, and the student of Alcman, the Spartan love poet. Arion earned fame in Italy for the creation of the metrical dithyramb in honor of Dionysus and for arranging choruses in a circle around the sacred altar to chant a processional hymn. Upon settling in Greece, Arion was hired by his master Periander, tyrant of Corinth, to organize religious music.

Journey

Arion received his master's permission to compete in a music contest and to pay his way on a lengthy voyage by singing original dithyrambs and playing the lyre. Traveling from Tarentum in southern Italy back to Corinth, on the isthmus connecting mainland Greece to the Peloponnesus, the young singer saw a vision of Apollo, patron of musicians, warning him that his life was in danger. Fearful that the crew planned to harm him and steal his purse, which his successful tour had filled, Arion requested that the captain turn back, then in vain offered a bribe in exchange for his life. When the doomed singer realized that he would find no pity among conniving freebooters, he begged to sing a final lay.

Dressed in formal minstrel garb, Arion perched on the prow and strummed a sweet verse to Apollo, which touched the hearts of a passing school of dolphins. As they swam close to the gunwales, Arion leaped on the back of the closest dolphin and was borne to the shores of Taenarum in Laconia on the southernmost tip of Greece. Once more in Corinth, he told his adventures to Periander, who brought the charmed dolphin to his palace and accorded it a pension and, at its death, a royal funeral.

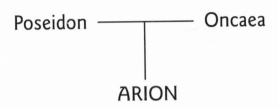

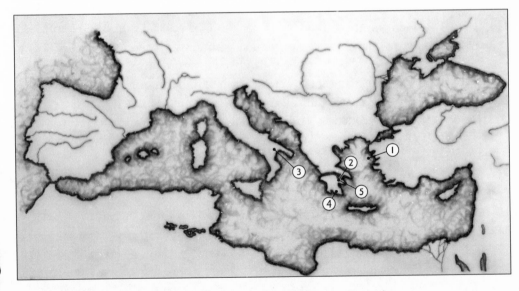

1. Methymnia 2. Corinth 3. Tarentum 4. Taenarum 5. Corinth

The authorities questioned the ship's captain the next time his boat was in port. He lied that Arion had not survived the voyage. Periander, who made the crew swear to their version of the story on the dolphin's monument, produced Arion and had the captain and his crew skewered or crucified on the spot.

Alternate Versions

Another telling of the legend describes how Periander doubted Arion's outlandish rescue. When the captain returned to port and explained that Arion had remained behind in Sicily, the singer's sudden appearance in formal robes stunned the captain to silence.

Symbolism

The story of Arion, which resembles rescues of Enalus and Phineis and early myths of Dionysus, reflects a popular New Year's ceremony during which a child rode on the back of a trained dolphin, symbolic of Apollo. Apollo himself immortalized Arion in a constellation shaped like a *cythara* and a school of dolphins. The story of rescue by sea creatures charmed by song reflects resurrection, a theme echoed in Christian lore by Symeon Metaphrastes's story of Lucian of Antioch, a martyred saint thrown overboard in A.D. 312 and carried by dolphins as though laid out on a catafalque.

The residents of Taenarum honored a bronze likeness of Arion astride his dolphin; the painter Exekias commemorated the myth in the form of a ship guarded on each side by paintings of dolphins. The myth remained in vogue during Rome's height and found artistic expression in statues, painted vases, frescoes, coins, charms, and mosaic floors and pool bottoms in Pompeii, Herculaneum, Paestum, and Agrigento. Poets have incorporated the myth into verse, as in Edmund Spenser's *Amoretti* and *Faerie Queene*, William Shakespeare's *Twelfth Night*, Michael Drayton's *The Barons' Wars*, Edward Young's *Ocean* and *Sea Piece*, John Milton's *Lycidas*, William Wordsworth's *The Power of Sound*, John Keats's *Endymion*, Percy Shelley's *The Witch of Atlas*, and Robert Browning's *Fifine at the Fair*.

See Also

Dionysus.

Ancient Sources

Aelian's *On the Nature of Animals*; Arion's *Hymn to Poseidon*; Aulus Gellius's *Attic Nights*; Herodotus's *Histories*; Hyginus's *Fables* and *Poetic Astronomy*; Ovid's *Fasti*; Pausanias's *Description of Greece*; Scholiast on Pindar's *Olympian Odes*; Suidas.

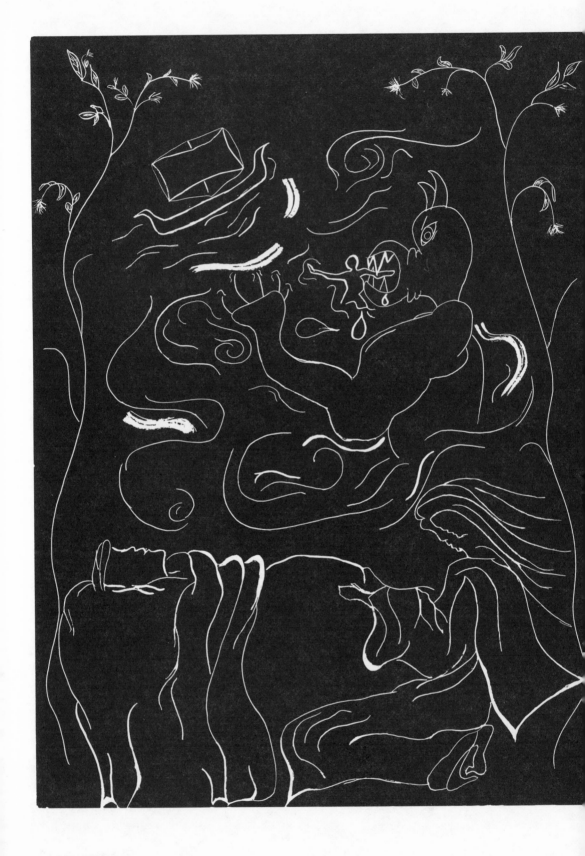

Auge

[ow' gay]

Genealogy and Background The story of Auge's maidenhood is a grim reminder of the place of women in ancient society, especially that reserved for royal daughters. The princess Auge was the daughter of Neaera, Pereus's daughter, and Neaera's uncle, King Aleus, founder of Tegea in the southeast of the Peloponnesus and importer of Athenian worship to Arcadia. Auge and her brothers—Cepheus the Argonaut, Lycurgus, grandfather of Atalanta, and Aphidamas—were grandchildren of Apheidas. Auge was the mother of the hero Telephus and grandmother of Tarchon and Tyrrhenus, founders of Etruria and the cities of Tarquinia, Mantua, and Cortona. Auge's granddaughter, Telephus's daughter, Roma, is said to have married Aeneas and contributed her name to the new city of Rome, thus linking Auge's story with the history of Italy.

As was common with royalty, Auge's name is alternately given as Alea, the feminine form of her father's name. One version of Auge's wretched teen years has Aleus consulting with the Delphic oracle, who related the message that Auge's son would one day kill her mother's brothers. To prevent the murders, Auge's father pledged her to chastity as a votress of Athena and vowed to slay her if she broke her promise.

On one of his wanderings, either to oppose King Augeias or on his way back from Sparta, Herakles stopped at the Tegean palace. As a good host, Aleus plied the hero with wine and entertained him at Athena's temple. Herakles, under the influence of alcohol, seduced Auge near a holy fountain, although her lack of struggle suggests that she gave herself willingly, perhaps out of boredom with her celibate role as priestess. She was able to conceal her pregnancy and the birth of a son, Telephus, whom she hid in Athena's temple, thereby profaning holy ground.

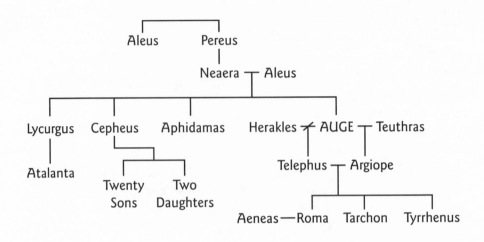

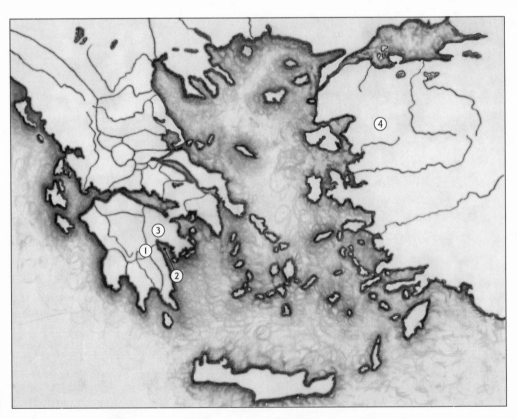

1. Tegea   2. Argolid Bay   3. Nauplia   4. Mysia

Journey The king, faced with decreasing agricultural yield, traveled north to Delphi to consult the oracle and learned that Auge's impious act had angered the goddess. To alleviate his people's sufferings, Aleus publicly humiliated his daughter in the town plaza. He exposed the infant boy on Mount Parthenius, on the border of Argolis and Arcadia, and remanded Auge to Nauplius, who had a choice of selling her into slavery or drowning her.

Removed from Arcadia, Auge traveled aboard Nauplius's vessel to Nauplia, a coastal town on the Argolid Bay. At length, he chose the greedy way out and traded Auge to Carian pirates, who resold her to Teuthras, king of Mysia, a powerful realm southeast of Troy in Asia Minor. King Teuthras cared for the pair and raised Telephus to manhood, then pledged the princess Argiope to him in marriage. Later, Telephus visited the Delphic oracle and learned that he should return to Mysia to discover his real parentage. Because of his likeness to Herakles, Telephus accepted the story that his mother had once been the famous warrior's mate.

Alternate Versions A variety of retellings suggest the instability of Auge's myth as it grew on two continents.

Auge herself is said to have exposed her son on Mount Parthenius to hide her guilty secret.

A violent version suggests that Nauplius, given free rein over his property, manhandled the pregnant girl and forced her to kneel. She supposedly gave birth on the ground or possibly hid in nearby bushes to bear her son in privacy.

Another setting has her giving birth to the child on Mount Parthenius, where a deer suckled the child until King Corythus's herdsmen discovered the boy and named him Telephus after the Greek for *suckle* and *doe.*

A tender version of Auge's misfortunes describes how Aleus confined her and her son to a locked chest and how Athena, forgiving and protective of a former priestess in spite of the girl's desecration of a temple, directed its drift to Asia Minor, where King Teuthras discovered it where the Caicus River flows into the sea. Entranced with the lovely priestess, the king married her and accepted Telephus as his son.

A more romantic telling links Auge to Danae by describing her immurement in a chest, which was set afloat to the whims of the sea nymphs and gods.

A completely different myth has Auge living at Laomedon's court in Troy, where Herakles coupled with her when he came to Troy to capture Laomedon's horses. This version places Telephus in the Trojan cycle by having him marry Laodice, Hiera, or Astyoche, one of Troy's princesses.

Hyginus's account links Auge's exposure of her son with that of Atalanta's abandonment of Parthenopaeus. Both boys were discovered by local shepherds and reared on Mount Parthenius. The boys grew up like brothers. After Telephus fulfilled his destiny by killing his uncles, he is said to have fallen mute. Like the Hebrew Aaron speaking for Moses, Parthenopaeus became his foster brother's spokesperson.

As a grown man, Telephus, accompanied by Parthenopaeus, consulted Pythia, the priestess of Apollo, who urged him to locate his mother. At Mysia, Telephus reunited with Auge and allied himself by marriage with King Teuthras, Auge's foster father (or by some accounts her husband) after helping the king defeat the usurper Idas, a mighty Argonaut. In one version, Teuthras wed Auge to her son, whom, like Oedipus's mother, Jocasta, she failed to recognize because of their long years of separation.

Two versions of this story provided alternate endings. In the most popular, Auge, still loyal to Herakles and spurning union with a mortal, held a sword at the ready to murder Telephus upon his arrival to the nuptial chamber when a serpent menaced her, thus sparing the couple the crime of incest. In the ensuing uproar, Telephus tried to kill Auge. Her cries to Herakles revealed her identity as Telephus's mother, whom he returned to her home in Arcadia. The lesser known version has Herakles returning to prevent the consummation of Telephus's marriage to his mother.

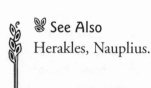

Symbolism

At Tegea, Aleus raised a shrine and sacred couch to Athena Alea, who served as local corn goddess. The current holy shrine of Eileithyia, the goddess of childbirth, still contains a statue of Auge on her knees, a suggestion that the girl paid heavily for her violation of holy vows of chastity. Auge is said to have been buried at Pergamum near the Caicus River in Mysia, even though she spent her old age in Arcadia. To accommodate the discrepancy, Pergamum's natives created a mythic immigration led by Telephus from Arcadia to Asia Minor. To give authority to the story, the Mysians venerate the heroic son of Herakles, as do residents of Mount Parthenius in Greece.

Artistic and literary evidence of the Auge myth is scattered. She appears on an altar carving in Pergamum, in a temple painting in Tegea, and as a New Year goddess or fertility symbol on local coins. The painter Polygnotus included Auge among the Lesche of Delphi, a dramatic pair of murals depicting the fall of Troy and the terrors of damnation.

The traumatized behavior of Telephus, the confused and abandoned son of Herakles, gave rise to the expression *the silence of Telephus* because of his refusal or inability to speak after murdering his uncles. Telephus's wife, Hiera, is said to have been immortalized in the Turkish town of Hieropolis, destroyed twice in A.D. 17 and A.D. 60 by earthquakes, then rebuilt. Both Hadrian and Caracalla, sybaritic Roman emperors, cultivated the ancient site for its thermal baths.

❧ See Also

Herakles, Nauplius.

🌿 Ancient Sources

Alcidamas's *Odysseus;* Alexis's *Plays;* Amphis's *Government by Women;* Apollodorus's *Epitome;* Apollonius of Rhodes's *Argonautica;* Aristotle's *Poetics;* Callimachus's *Hymn to Delos;* Dictys Cretensis's *Trojan War Diary;* Diodorus Siculus's *Library of History;* Euripides's *Auge* and *Telephus;* Hecataeus's *Mythologic History;* Hesiod's *Oxyrhynchus Papyrus;* Hyginus's *Fables;* Pausanias's *Description of Greece;* Sophocles's *Aleadai* and *Mysians.*

Bellerophon

[behl' luhr · uh · fahn]

Genealogy and Background

According to Homer in Book 6 of the *Iliad*, "Bellerophon the blameless," a chaste, heroic demigod originally named Hipponous, was the spirited, muscular, handsome grandson of Sisyphus and son of Glaucus and Eurymede. Born in "horse-pasturing Ephyre," the village that developed into Corinth on the northeastern edge of the Peloponnesus, Bellerophon grew up north of his birthplace in Potniae, a city in Boeotia on the road from Thebes south to Plataea. Bellerophon's father was deranged and reportedly kept his mares from mating and (to spite Aphrodite) fed them human flesh to increase their competitiveness in races. The goddess retaliated by upsetting Glaucus's four beauties, which hurled him to his death beneath competitors' wheels. Another setting describes the horses as rending Glaucus with their teeth.

Like his doomed father, Bellerophon suffered tragedy after he accidentally killed his brother Bellerus during a forest hunt. At the time of his trial and banishment, Bellerophon was wooing Aethra, daughter of King Pittheus of Troezen in Argolis. Defeated in his first suit, Bellerophon is said to have journeyed on a pilgrimage to Lycia in southwest Asia Minor and earned the right to marry Philonoe, with whom he produced a daughter, Laodameia, and two sons, Isandros and Hippolochus. Isandros died young in battle against Ares, the Greek god of war. Glaucus, Bellerophon's grandson by Hippolochus, made a name for himself as Lycian commander during the Trojan War, from which he did not return alive. Laodameia, who was later killed by Artemis while weaving, bore an equally famous warrior, Sarpedon, the son of Zeus, whom the Greek Patroclus killed. Bellerophon also fathered Hydissus by Asteria.

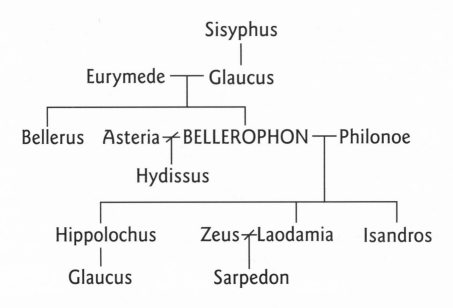

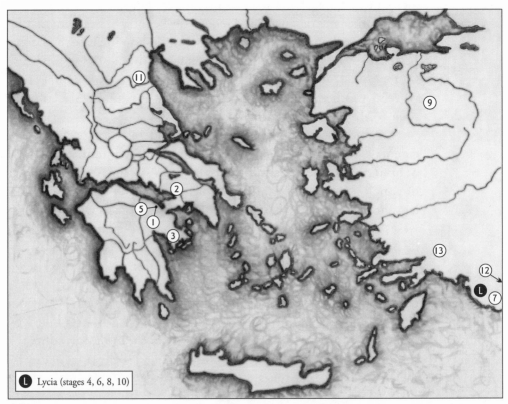

L Lycia (stages 4, 6, 8, 10)

1. Corinth 2. Potniae 3. Tiryns 4. Lycia 5. Corinth 6. Lycia 7. Solymnes, Cilicia
8. Lycia 9. Amazons 10. Lycia 11. Mt. Olympus 12. to Aleius, Cilicia 13. Caria

According to one evaluation, the name Bellerophon translates as "dart bearing" or "slayer of Bellerus," thus labeling him forever with the treachery of fratricide. For this atrocity, Bellerophon suffered exile. Remanded southeast of Argos to the court of Proetus at the ancient city of Tiryns on the Gulf of Argolis, Bellerophon achieved ritual purification. His peace of mind came to an end, however, after Proetus's haughty, conceited Lycian queen, Stheneboea, made lewd advances to her guest. When Bellerophon refused her, she salved hurt pride by lying to Proetus. In Homer's *Iliad*, the wily queen simpered, "Would you be killed, oh Proetus? Then murder Bellerophontes who tried to lie with me in love, though I was unwilling."

To end the contretemps, Proetus, impeded by ancient courtesy codes, dispatched his unwanted guest southeast across the Aegean Sea to Stheneboea's father, King Iobates of Lycia, near the River Xanthus in Asia Minor, where for nine days Iobates fed his guest by sacrificing nine oxen. Unwittingly, Bellerophon carried a sealed tablet containing coded instructions that Iobates assassinate the bearer for foully dishonoring Queen Stheneboea. Before facing execution, Bellerophon accepted a challenge, one that had ended the lives of all who had previously attempted it. He had to kill the Chimaera, a monstrous oriental beast offspring of Echidna and Typhon, akin to Cerberus, Orthus, and the Hydra. The Chimaera, which was formed of a fire-breathing triad of lions' heads tipped with pitch-filled nostrils, goat's trunk, dragon's hind parts, and snake's tail, had burned up the country's pastures and herds. It had already borne two more monsters, the Nemean lion and the flesh-hungry sphinx, and was threatening the very existence of Lycia.

The task terrified Bellerophon, who had fallen in love with Princess Philonoe and feared that he would never see her again. Because Athena, the horse deity, pitied Bellerophon for the false charge, she led him back to Greece to her Corinthian temple, showed him Pegasus, the gallant, white-flanked winged horse that sprang from blood spurting from Medusa's neck onto sea foam. The goddess advised him on bridling and mounting so spirited a beast, which she had already tamed with her magic bridle. Bellerophon crept up on the incredible steed at the Pirenean spring in Corinth's citadel and, fully outfitted in bronze armor, leaped onto his back. Reputedly armed with a deadly lead spear point that the Chimaera's fiery breath would melt, Bellerophon hoped to strangle or poison its vital organs. He rode Pegasus across the Mediterranean Sea to the volcanic valley of Lycia, flew in a great arc, and surprised the monster, which he shot in the mouth, thus turning it into a ravenous phantasm at the entrance to Hades.

Iobates was so pleased with the hero's courage that he assigned him a second quest: to defeat the fierce Solymnes, warlike coastal neighbors who threatened the security of Lycia. He accomplished the mission by flying out of bow range and crushing the Solymnian warriors with boulders. Bellerophon undertook a third quest to the north to defeat the Amazons, female archers, ax-wielders, and fierce man-killers. On the road back to Lycia, Bellerophon had to ward off a band of armed attackers whom Iobates sent to murder him. According to Homer's *Iliad*, "Then when the king knew him for the powerful stock of the god, he detained him there, and offered him the hand of his daughter."

Exonerated at last of Stheneboea's false charges and cheered by grateful Lycians, Bellerophon married Princess Philonoe, accepted half the kingdom as a worthy reward, including arable wheat fields and an olive orchard, fathered three royal children, and later inherited the Lycian crown. Before settling down, he returned to Proetus's court to clear his name. The queen, caught in an obvious lie, mounted Pegasus and spurred him upwards. Unable to remain in the saddle, Stheneboea toppled off and drowned in the Mediterranean Sea.

Happier times came to Bellerophon, such as a twenty-day visit to Oineus at Pleuron, west of Calydon, the outstanding city of Aetolia on the southern coast of the Greek mainland, where he received a guest token of a red war belt. But the latter portion of the hero's life was filled with mental or emotional aberrations. For an unspecified reason, he abandoned his family and wandered about the plain of Aleius, mentally unbalanced and incapable of normal contact with other human beings. Bellerophon's fatal journey took him up Olympus toward the throne of Zeus. For this impiety, Zeus sent a stinging fly to nettle the soft spot beneath Pegasus's tail, thus goading the horse into bucking Bellerophon headlong down a precipice. On the Plain of Aleius in Cilicia, a part of southern Turkey, he landed in a thorn bush, which tore out his eyes. Still, his death at the hands of the almighty did not deter honor, which came from both Lycians and Corinthians.

Alternate Versions

Bellerophon or Bellerophontes, sometimes called the son of Poseidon, god of the sea, and a mortal mother, Eurynome, is often assigned other brothers, including Deliades, Peiren, and Alcimenes. Likewise, Proetus's wife is in one major source called Anteia. Stheneboea, alternately listed as the daughter of Aphidas, King of Arcadia, is depicted as committing suicide rather than face her wronged accuser, who had married her sister Philonoe. In Euripides's lost play *Bellerophon,* the hero flings the conniving queen from Pegasus's back to her death. Bellerophon's wife is sometimes named Anticleia, other times Cassandra; his daughter is alternately named Deidameia, who is sometimes listed as a second daughter.

Other variations depict Pegasus as returning to earth periodically to drink from the Hippocrene, a spring in Troezen on the eastern promontory of the Peloponnesus, which appeared miraculously at the point where Pegasus first alighted on earth, striking Delphi with his hooves and creating the Castalian spring between the rocky slopes of the Phaeriades.

Alternate episodes in Bellerophon's exploits list a follow-up to the defeat of the Solymi. On the plain of Xanthus, he is said to have bested the pirate Cheimarrhus (a name suggestive of *Chimaera*) and his band of Carian cutthroats, who flaunted their prowess in a ship adorned fore and aft by lion and serpent. An alternate explanation of Bellerophon's defeat of the waylaying band of Lycians on his return route is that Poseidon, in answer to his favorite's prayer, sent flood waters to engulf the plain of Xanthus much as Yahweh washed away Pharaoh's army, who pursued Moses and the fleeing Children of Israel. For Bellerophon's bravery, the Lycian women offered their favors, which he modestly declined.

Homer's *Iliad* offers an account of Bellerophon's exile. He lists the spite of Proetus, who "devised evil things against him, and drove him out of his own domain, since he was far greater." The seer Polyidus of Corinth gave Bellerophon the useful tip of spending a night in Athena's sanctuary, where a vision of the goddess awarded him a golden bridle and instructed him to sacrifice to Poseidon. At the completion of ritual worship, the winged horse appeared to aid Bellerophon on his quest.

Bellerophon's punishment for climbing to the court of the gods is alternately given as blindness or severe physical handicap. He is said to have become a vagabond who wandered the Aleian territory speaking nonsensically and died in Caria, an Argive colony south of Lycia. Pegasus, the immortal steed that enjoyed a more pleasing fate than his master, received quarter in Zeus's Olympian stable and forever afterward bore the sacred lightning bolt.

| Symbolism | The story of Bellerophon the blameless probably sprang from eastern sources and parallels a similar story about Ireland's hero, Cuchulain. Akin to Phaethon, Talos, Daedalus and Icarus, and John Milton's Lucifer, who tempted fate by imitating the gods, at first Bellerophon avoided the tragedy associated with these characters before succumbing to greed and overreaching his status enough to call down Zeus's wrath. Bellerophon's conflict with Stheneboea, the outgrowth of folklore, parallels the experiences of Hippolytus, who was enticed by his stepmother Phaedra; of Acastus, who was lured by Hippolyta; and of Joseph at Potiphar's court, where a lustful wife offered herself to the Hebrew prophet, then, stung by his refusal, labeled him a rapist. Cursed like Cain and the wandering Jew (a legendary figure who was denied death and condemned to wander forever), Bellerophon is depicted as a pariah, spurned by fellow beings as odious to the gods and therefore dangerous.

In another biblical similarity from the canon of the Hebrew King David, Bellerophon, like Bathsheba's husband Uriah, carried his death warrant in the form of a letter to another authority. From this diabolical experience, the phrase *Bellerophontic letters* came to mean a damning message carried by the victim. Other monster-slayers, notably Perseus, Herakles, and Saint George, as well as knights and even rodeo stars and cowboys, develop the mythic pattern of Bellerophon by conquering a terrifying challenger—the Chimaera.

Much analysis equates Bellerophon's fate with that of the misogynist and narcissist. Relying upon Athena, he defied a she-dragon, whom he bested in the style of Beowulf over Grendel or Perseus over Medusa, but the heady ring of victory deluded the young strutter. Bellerophon's downfall evolved from an ill-advised testosterone surge—an attempt to compete with the father, represented by Iobates.

Having attained the status of hero, Bellerophon was honored in a sacred grove of Craneion on the outskirts of Corinth, where locals adapted the myth to accommodate post-Homeric lore. The defeat of the Chimaera was sculpted in bas-relief on a throne in Amyclae, an ancient Laconian town on the east shore of the River Eurotas south of Sparta. The hero's likeness appears on Boeotian vase paintings, a glass plaque at Dendra near Mycenae, Tarquinian frescoes near Rome, and Etruscan bronzes in Arezzo and Florence, Italy. Corinthians adopted Bellerophon as a favorite son, who figured heavily in local lore as well as on coins, which permeated both the city and its colonial markets. As depiction of the three segments of the year, the lion as spring, the goat as summer, and the snake as winter, the tripartite Chimaera appears on Hittite architecture at Carchemish on the Syrian border. The monster's name is preserved in Mount Chimaera, a Lycian volcano near Phaselis, where, like the ancient Lycians, local people dread the fire-breathing exhalations that threaten their lives and land.

An alternate interpretation of Bellerophon's fate describes the tale as a sun myth similar to that of Phaethon. Named *Bellero* for "power of darkness or evil" and *phon* from the Sanskrit for "killer," the character attained symbolic significance when enticed by Anteia or "dawn" and pitted against the Chimaera, a symbol of drought or belching volcanic gas, outmatched by Pegasus, a thunderhead or moon goddess sprung from sea mist. Bellerophon's earthly reward was Philonoe, whose name means "twilight." As a balance to the character's ambition, Zeus struck him with a lightning bolt and cast the blinded demigod from Olympus's zenith into darkness as punishment for overreaching human limitations. The heavenly constellation Andromeda commemorates Pegasus in its four brightest components, which make up the square of Pegasus.

Bellerophon's flights on Pegasus's back, representations of arrogance, set others against him because they envied his freedom from earthly restrictions. His punishment, like that of Herakles and Orestes and, to a lesser degree, Icarus, brought on *ate*, a passionate episode of insanity, which gave free rein to consuming emotion. The result, *nemesis*, led to Bellerophon's fall from Pegasus, permanent injury of limb and sight, exile, and self-destruction.

Pegasus is not alone among flying mythological beings. Other examples of winged beings include Amon-Re, the Egyptian sun deity who mounted a heavenly cow and appeared as a sun disc flanked by wings; Hermes, Zeus's wing-hatted, wing-sandaled messenger; Eros, the cherubic love god; Harpies, Griffins, and Nemesis, the winged Greek swordswoman who exacted punishment for deadly sins; the sphinx, a flying female monster; the Mesopotamian flying bull; Roc the dragon, and the Phoenix from the *Arabian Nights*. Later evolutions, particularly angels; Peter Pan; Aladdin's flying carpet; William Shakespeare's Puck, Oberon, Titania, and the fairies of *Midsummer Night's Dream*, were more kindly disposed, more likely to bestow benevolence or grace.

Bellerophon's legend usually bears the marks of physical perfection and *arete* or excellence and the resultant *hubris*—vaunting pride as demonstrated by unbridled ambition or godlike pretensions—as demonstrated in the seventh book of John Milton's *Paradise Lost*, Andrew Marvell's *To That Renowned Man*, poet Edward Young's *Night Thoughts*, verse by Johann von Schiller, C. Day Lewis's *Hero and Saint* and *Pegasus*, John Dryden's *Aureng-Zebe*, William Wordsworth's *Sonnet from the Dark Chambers*, Henry Wadsworth Longfellow's poem "Pegasus in Pound," William Shakespeare's *King Henry IV*, and George Meredith's *Bellerophon*.

See Also
Daedalus and Icarus, Phaethon.

Ancient Sources
Antoninus Liberalis's *Metamorphoses;* Apollodorus's *Epitome;* Euripides's *Bellerophon* and *Stheneboea;* Eustathius on Homer's *Iliad* and *Odyssey;* Hesiod's *Theogony;* Homer's *Iliad;* Horace's *Carmina;* Hyginus's *Fables;* Ovid's *Metamorphoses;* Pausanias's *Description of Greece;* Pindar's *Isthmian Odes* and *Olympian Odes;* Plutarch's *On the Virtues of Women;* Scholiast on Homer's *Iliad;* Stephanus Byzantium's *Hydissos;* Strabo's *Geography;* Johannes Tzetzes's *On Lycophron;* Virgil's *Aeneid.*

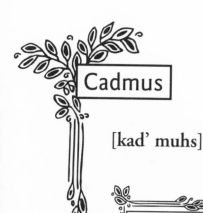

Cadmus

[kad' muhs]

Genealogy and Background   The legendary founder of Thebes, Cadmus, grandson of Poseidon and Libya and son of King Agenor of Sidon or Tyre, and Telephassa, had two sisters, Electra, and the shepherdess, Europa. Zeus abducted Europa by changing himself into a white bull and infiltrating her flock. Cadmus's uncle, Belus, was Egypt's king and founder of a parallel lineage of Mediterranean kings. At the command of Agenor, Belus's twin brother, Cadmus, and his brothers—Phoenix, Cilix, Phineus, and Thasus—had to retrieve Europa or live forever in exile. Later, Europa made Cadmus the uncle of her notable children—Minos, the king of Crete, Sarpedon, the king of Lycia, and Rhadamanthys, a judge of the Underworld.

Cadmus wed Harmonia, child of Aphrodite and Ares. Their children included sons Actaeon and Polydorus and four daughters, Autonoe, Ino or Leucothea, Agave, and Semele, whose son Dionysus was fathered by Zeus. Of the six children, the daughters created the most ignominy for the Cadmian line. Polydorus brought the most notoriety to his father's lineage by siring Labdacus, father of Laius, grandfather of Oedipus, and great-grandfather of Antigone, Ismene, Eteocles, and Polynices.

Much suffering afflicted Cadmus's offspring, including the terrifying dismemberment of Actaeon by hunting hounds and the destruction of Semele by Zeus's thunderbolt. Ino was driven insane for daring to shelter Dionysus from divine wrath. She leaped to her death in the sea. After Dionysus's deification, Cadmus joined his rejoicing entourage, which savaged Pentheus for concealing himself in a pine tree to spy on worshippers. *The Bacchantes,* a defective version of one of Euripides's tragedies, depicts the killing as the work of Agave, Pentheus's mother, who, in the fury of Dionysic fanaticism, ripped Pentheus's arms from their sockets while Ino, his aunt, rent his flesh. Cadmus, moved by the sight of the rabid Agave carrying her son's head, gently gathered his grandson's remains and abandoned his hopelessly deranged

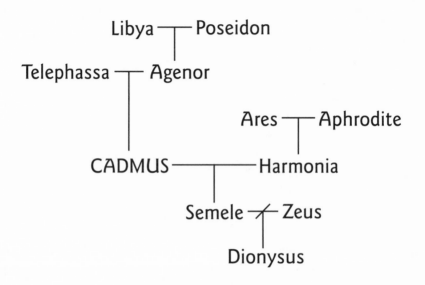

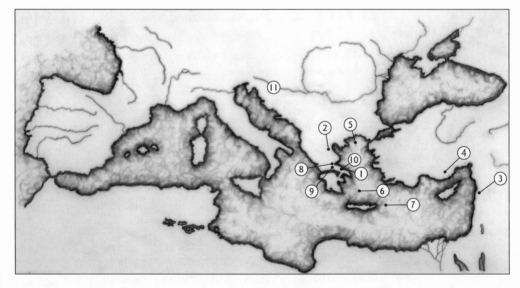

1. Thebes   2. Mt. Olympus   3. Phoenicia   4. Cilicia   5. Thasos Island   6. Thera
7. Lindos   8. Boeotia   9. Delphi   10. Thebes   11. Buthoe

daughter as he led the Maenads through the countryside. Because there was no royal family member left to rule Thebes, Cadmus returned to the throne.

Cadmus is also credited with immuring Semele and her babe in a chest and setting it adrift. The ark is said to have floated ashore at Brasiae in Laconia. Semele did not survive, but the infant Dionysus was rescued by Poseidon and became a god. Near the end of their lives, Cadmus and Harmonia abdicated in favor of their grandson, Pentheus. In Illyria, Cadmus fathered a third son, Illyrius, who succeeded his father on the throne of Buthoe.

Journey On the fruitless quest to locate Europa, Cadmus, accompanied by his mother, tracked the bull that had abducted his sister. A side venture joined Cadmus and Zeus against Typhon or Typhoeus, a man-monster born of Hera and covered with one hundred scaly heads. Girdled by serpents, Typhon could fly and shoot flames from his 200 eyes. So bold was Typhon that he attacked Olympus, removed Zeus's sinews, and hid them in the lair of his snaky sister, Delphyne.

Cadmus intervened, calmed Typhon with chords from his lyre, and convinced Delphyne that he had to have the sinews to restring his lyre. Cadmus then returned the sinews to Zeus, who was paralyzed without them. A chase across the Mediterranean world ended with Zeus obliterating Typhon by hurling Mount Etna into the monster's body.

On the way to recover Europa, Cadmus set sail and left his brothers to establish colonies throughout the Mediterranean, namely Phoenicia and Cilicia on the eastern Mediterranean and the gold-rich isle of Thasos, south of Thrace. At Calliste or Thera, Cadmus established Membliarus, a cousin, as head of a new colony. At Lindus, a harbor town on the island of Rhodes, Cadmus dedicated a bronze cauldron to Poseidon to commemorate the sufferings of the voyage and established a brotherhood of attendants to maintain the shrine. From Lindus the search party continued to Boeotia and raised a shrine to Poseidon. While living among the Edonians in Thrace, Telephassa died suddenly. Her death marked a turning point in Cadmus's roving.

Still searching for his missing sister, but growing less certain that his mission could be completed, Cadmus traveled overland to Delphi to consult Pythia and was directed to establish a city where a cow lay at rest. Journeying south from Delphi, Cadmus bought a cow from Pelagon that was marked with two lunar-shaped spots, one on each flank. The animal wandered from Phocis to Mycalessus, an ancient town in southern Boeotia named for the lowing of Cadmus's cow. On the Asopus River, the cow finally lay down. Cadmus, realizing the importance of the spot, kissed the ground and established a shrine to Athena Onga and built his city, Cadmeia, alongside a spring. The city was later named Thebes.

Needing fresh water in order to complete the ritual sacrifice of the cow, Cadmus dispatched a contingent of men to the Castalian Spring. When they failed to return, he followed and discovered that a sacred dragon or serpent had devoured the men. To assure ownership and safe passage on his land, Cadmus cast a boulder and slew the beast, which was sacred to Ares, the god of war. Athena materialized and ordered Cadmus to collect the dragon's teeth. At the goddess's direction, he seeded the soil with half of them. Armed men sprang up and menaced him. To protect himself from overwhelming odds, he threw a stone into the roily mob. The warriors began attacking each other and killed off all but five mystical sown men or Sparti. These men— Chthonius, Echion, Hyperenor, Pelorus, and Oudaeus or Udaeus—halted the slaughter and became the lords of Thebes.

To appease Ares, Cadmus served a penance of eight years, thus expiating his crime. At the completion of his penalty, Athena proclaimed him king of Thebes, which he adorned with a citadel on the highest point of land. Zeus blessed Cadmus's accession by initiating him into the cult of Iasion. Ares's reward was the divine Harmonia and a nuptial ceremony blessed by the gods themselves, who watched a mortal wedding for the first time. To reciprocate their courtesy, Cadmus seated them on golden thrones.

The wedding, graced with the melodies of Apollo and the nine muses, yielded a splendid array of wedding gifts. From Hermes came a lyre, from Aphrodite, a jeweled gold necklace wrought by Hephaestus that made its wearer beautiful, from Athena, flutes and a gold peplos woven by the Charities to enhance the dignity of the wearer, and from Demeter, the goddess of agriculture, barley seeds and a rich harvest, guaranteed by her coupling with Iasion in a thrice-plowed plot. Cadmus presented his bride with a bright-colored robe; Electra initiated Harmonia into the cult of the Great Goddess.

An oracle foretold that Cadmus and his queen would ride in a chariot pulled by cows and would master distant cities. In fulfillment of the prophecy, in their old age, Cadmus and Harmonia fled the scene of their children's and grandchildren's wretched demise. Reestablished in Illyria on Greece's far northwest coast after Agave murdered her husband, King Lycotherses, Cadmus ruled the Illyrians. When the Encheleans, an uncivilized Illyrian tribe, offended the gods by desecrating Apollo's shrines, Ares changed Cadmus and his wife into inky snakes or blue-spotted dragons, and placed them in the Elysian Fields. The Illyrians honored them with a state funeral at Buthoe, Cadmus's Illyrian capital.

Alternate Versions   Cadmus's mother is sometimes given as Argiope and his father as Phoenix or Ogygus. A variant lists Antiope, his Egyptian cousin, as his mother. Another variance in Cadmus's lore describes Harmonia as a gift of Athena when Cadmus journeyed to Samothrace, an island in the northern Aegean Sea off the coast of Thrace. An alternate end for Cadmus and Harmonia pictures Zeus changing them into lions, which are featured at the Mycenaean Lion Gate.

Symbolism The story of Cadmus, whose name means "eastern," is a blend of Greek and eastern mythology and contains strong Phoenician elements, which in some respects confuse the events and meaning. Cadmus's father is called Chnas in Phoenician and Canaan in *Genesis.* The spread of Cadmus's lore from Egypt connects it with Ugandan mythology and indicates that Cadmus and his brothers probably migrated north and west around 2000 B.C., possibly after displacement by invaders. Thus the story of Cadmus is the mythic explanation of Phoenician colonization of Greece.

According to one analyst, the early segment of Cadmus's life connects with sun myths. Europa, whose name means "light spread abroad," was lured from her east Mediterranean birthplace by Zeus. Cadmus, a symbol of light, traversed many miles and slew a dragon, a symbol of darkness or barbarity, in order to recapture Europa. By extension, Cadmus, who, like Herakles and Prometheus, was forced into years of expiation for slaying darkness, demonstrates a pre-Christian martyrdom, thus emulating a bringer of light and savior of humankind.

The Spartan nation took the name Cadmeians in honor of their founder and enshrined their hero at Sparta, where they still note the wedding site where the gods applauded the festivities from golden chairs of honor, with the muses and Apollo providing the entertainment. Illyrians also claimed Cadmus as a patriarch, primarily to legitimize their connection with Greece and to establish the Illyrian role in the Olympic Games. In Macedonia, Mount Pangaeum is linked with Cadmus's mining activities and the invention of metal casting, which the Thasians later took over; Tanagra, a Boeotian city on the Asopus River, claims a direct connection to Cadmus's immigration.

In Laconia, Cadmus was exalted as the legendary carrier of the thirteen-consonant Pelasgian or Phoenician alphabet to Greece, which he brought from either Egypt or Asia Minor. As creator of the Greek alphabet, he is said to have reordered the letters, but he deliberately preserved *aleph* or alpha in first place because it means ox, the chief product of Boeotia. With some excitement, Herodotus remarked on these letters in his *History:* "I myself saw Cadmeian characters engraved on some tripods in the temple of Apollo Ismenias in Boeotian Thebes, most of them shaped like Ionian letters."

Cadmus was immortalized in the naming of the Cadmeia, the Theban acropolis where the Seven against Thebes launched their fruitless revolt. The expression *sowing dragon's teeth* indicates any attempt to provoke war. The wholesale loss of life resulted in a doleful military term, Cadmeian victory, similar to the Roman Pyrrhic victory, in which the battle is won at such a high price that it is not worth the cost in human life.

Science also links discoveries to Cadmeian lore. The element cadmium earns its name from cadmia, an ore mined near Thebes. In 1964, archaeologists located decorated Mesopotamian cylinder seals at the Cadmeion, the mythic king's royal residence, which dates to 1400 B.C. The presence of these objects casts doubt on the truth of Cadmus's myth, which belongs centuries before that era.

Cadmus and Harmonia's divine connections were symbolized by their metamorphosis into snakes, symbols of blessing and godly protection, which are featured on pottery created in Paestum in the fourth century and currently housed in the Louvre. The shape of the serpent's bite marked future offspring, as demonstrated in Antigone's myth, and continued into Roman times as sacred emblems. Like other heroes from the classical era and from later periods in other cultures such as Jason, Saint George, Beowulf, Siegfried, Herakles, and Perseus, Cadmus was a noted dragon slayer and savior of humankind.

The version that credits Cadmus with setting Semele and Dionysus adrift is very similar to the story of Acrisius immuring his daughter Danae and his grandson Perseus in a wooden chest and sending them out to sea.

Herodotus credits Cadmus with passing on Dionysian worship to Melampus and ultimately to all of Greece. For this reason, and for his connection with writing and metalwork, Cadmus is depicted on numerous ancient vases and urns. His marriage and ill-fated children served as the impetus of Jean-Baptiste Lully's 1673 opera *Cadmus et Hermione.* Cadmus's adventures found favor with numerous British poets, as evidenced in Geoffrey Chaucer's *Knight's Tale,* Samuel Daniel's *Civil Wars,* Edmund Spenser's *Faerie Queene,* William Shakespeare's *Midsummer Night's Dream,* Michael Drayton's *Polyolbion* and *The Owl,* Robert Herrick's *Women Useless,* William Diaper's *Dryades,* Lord Byron's *The Isles of Greece,* Alfred Lord Tennyson's *Tiresias,* and Algernon Swinburne's *Tiresias,* Robert Bridges's *Prometheus the Firegiver,* and Louis MacNeice's *The Island.*

🌿 See Also

Adrastus.

🌿 Ancient Sources

Apollodorus's *Epitome;* Apollonius of Rhodes's *Argonautica; Coins of Gortyna* (anonymous); Diodorus Siculus's *Historical Library;* Euripides's *Bacchants* and *Phoenician Women;* Herodotus's *Histories;* Hesiod's *Theogony;* Homer's *Odyssey;* Hyginus's *Fables;* Isidore of Seville's *Origins;* Juba's *Roman Questions;* Moschus's *Idylls;* Nonnus's

Dionysiaca; Ovid's *Fasti* and *Metamorphoses;* Pausanias's *Description of Greece;* Pherecydes's *Heptamochos;* Philostratus's *Heroica;* Pindar's *Pythian Odes;* Pliny the Elder's *Natural History;* Plutarch's *Symposiacs;* Ptolemy Hephaestion on Homer's *Iliad;* Scholiast on Euripides's *Phoenician Women;* Scholiast on Homer's *Iliad;* Servius on Virgil's *Aeneid;* Theocritus's *Idylls;* Theophrastus's *History of Plants.*

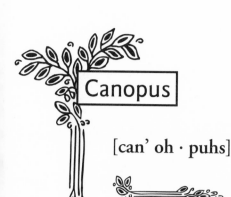

Canopus

[can' oh · puhs]

Genealogy and Background

The seafarer Canopus, like a cadre of rootless voyagers and wandering adventurers in ancient lore, left very little historical fact and no genealogy. Perhaps, like the soldier of fortune or the stereotypical escapee to the French Foreign Legion, he chose his destiny in an effort to distance himself from an unsatisfactory or sordid past. He may have joined Menelaus's Spartan fleet out of wanderlust, greed, boredom, or an ambition to develop his piloting skills on the way to the Trojan War. If the last surmise is correct, he chose wisely by signing on for the most noted undertaking in Greek naval history.

The only tie between Canopus and a woman is a dim legend of his unrequited love for Theonoe, a clairvoyant, granddaughter of Poseidon and daughter of King Proteus, and either the Thracian princess Torone or the Egyptian Psamathe. It is likely that Canopus's death from snakebite occurred while he was still a youth and may have been the reason for the foreshortened relationship with Theonoe.

Journey

Canopus was the pilot for Menelaus on his voyage from Greece to locate Helen in Egypt and return her to Sparta's throne. Canopus is said to have sailed south from the Troad and threaded his way south past the islands of Tenedos, Limnos, and Lesbos, through the Dodecanese cluster off the west coast of Asia Minor, and past Crete and Rhodes to the mouth of the Nile River. There Menelaus reclaimed Helen from Egypt where, according to one legend, Hera, goddess of matrimony, in order to show her disapproval of the adulterous union, transformed Helen into a *ka*, or phantasm. The duped Paris returned to Troy with the ghost woman while the real Helen spent the war years in safety under the protection of King Proetus and the spirit double took her place as Paris's lover at Troy.

As often happens on these early voyages, Menelaus's fleet was becalmed. During this hiatus, Canopus fell in love with the prophetess Theonoe. Having survived the Trojan War, it is ironic that he was bitten by an adder and buried in a shrine on a delta isle, many miles from home. In his honor, Menelaus and Helen gave the name Canope to both the western Nile tributary and the island where Canopus died. The site is also renowned for Lord Nelson's successful battle against Napoleon's fleet in 1801.

Alternate Versions

Canopus's name is alternately given as Canobus. A variant of his lore turns the love story of Canopus and Theonoe into a one-sided affair, with Canopus spurning the girl, possibly out of respect to the gods she served or perhaps out of devotion to the landless, wifeless state of the professional sailor. He is said to have piloted Osiris, god of the Egyptian underworld. According to one source, he starved to death on the island of Pharos while awaiting the return of Menelaus to his crew. Another variation of this same tale give the pilot's name as Pharos, a privateer who offered to spirit Helen away from Troy, reunite her with Menelaus, and speed them home to Sparta. The plot was foiled by a storm, which wrecked the ship near Egypt. Pharos was cast ashore and bitten by a poisonous snake. In his honor, Helen and Menelaus named an island in the mouth of the Nile after Pharos. The version that names the sting of an adder as cause of death is unlikely, since the venom of this snake is rarely fatal to human victims. If Canopus did die from snakebite, it was more likely to have been the sting of an asp or Egyptian cobra, an indigenous hooded serpent reputed to have killed Cleopatra.

Symbolism

Canopus appears to represent a series of ill-fated pilots in Greek and Egyptian lore. Like Palinurus, Aeneas's ill-fated steersman, Canopus remained faithful to his captain and came to an unforeseen bad end. Not

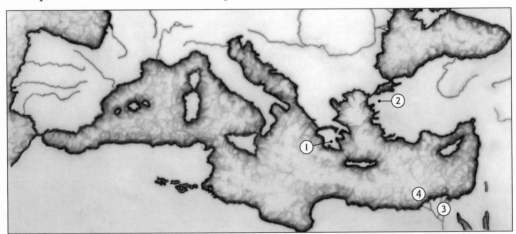

1. Sparta   2. Troy   3. Nile River Delta   4. Canope

all cognate place names refer to him, as is the case with Lake Canope near Pleuron, and Calydon in Aetolia, which bear no direct connection with the steersman. However, it is certain that, in his honor, Egyptians named a canal and one of the Nile river tributaries the Canope, which was honored as the lying-in spot where Ino gave birth to Epaphus, one of Egypt's most energetic kings. Fleet commanders from Greece and other trader nations called at the port of Canope from 664–525 B.C. Two hundred years later, as Alexandria grew into a center of finance and a military superpower, the site served as home port for the Egyptian fleet. Along the road to Canope, wealthy Egyptians built vacation villas. A splendid temple to Serapis, the corn god who dwelt in the Underworld, served droves of sufferers who sought healing from the golden bull, housed inside.

Canopus's legend influenced the naming of the canopic jars, a set of four oval ritual containers dedicated to Horus, the sky god, and guarded by Isis, who took the shape of a kite. After evisceration of a corpse and the beginning of the embalming process, each limestone or basalt jar was used to store a single wrapped internal organ of the dead, including the lungs, stomach, liver, and intestines, or, in some cases, liver, intestines, kidneys, and stomach. The canopic jars, which were placed in an ornate canopic chest, were inscribed with invocations to Hapi the ape, Duamutef the jackal, Qebsennuef the falcon, and Imsety, a human male. The more elaborate jars were stoppered with carved likenesses of each god.

Rome, too, was touched by the myth of Canopus. At Tivoli, outside Rome in A.D. 126, the mournful Roman emperor Hadrian named an oblong chamber of his villa the Canopus, a *nymphaeum* where he honored the ashes of his beloved Antinous, who committed suicide at Canope, Egypt. The pool leading up to the structure of the apse end suggests the layout of the Egyptian city. Hadrian's Canopus is said to swirl the viewer in a grand display of chiaroscuro, the interplay of light with dark.

Also mentioned as Jason's helmsman, Canopus may have steered the *Argo,* which is honored in the stars with its own constellation, of which the yellowish-white star Canopus shines brightest. Low in the southern sky in what is now known as the constellation of Carina, the star Canopus is named the second brightest heavenly body after Sirius, the Dog Star. In ancient times the Canopus star was worshipped, possibly in connection with the healing properties of the Serapic temple. Alfred Lord Tennyson honored Canopus with brief mention in *A Dream of Fair Women.*

❦ See Also

Helen, Jason and Medea, Menelaus, Palinurus, Paris.

❦ Ancient Sources

Aristophanes's *Thesmophoriazusae;* Euripides's *Helen;* Homer's *Odyssey;* Plato's *Cratylus;* Strabo's *Geography.*

Cassandra

[kuh · san' druh]

Genealogy and Background

The clairvoyant daughter of King Priam and Queen Hecuba of Troy, Cassandra, the twin of the prophet Helenus, received her prophetic gift from licks on the ear by the snakes that guarded Apollo's shrine or from a love relationship with the god himself, who blessed her with the powers of prophecy on the night that she spent at his altar. When she rejected the god's embrace, Apollo spat on her tongue to curse her prognostications so that no mortal would believe her.

An early example of her peculiar position as the unbelieved seer was her identification of Paris as her long lost brother, whom she observed at the games of Troy. Citizens insisted she was mistaken because he was exposed on a mountain and most certainly died in infancy. At length, King Priam and Queen Hecuba concurred that the young man had to be Paris. Against the dire wailings of Cassandra, they welcomed him home.

Cassandra viewed the events leading to the Trojan War with deeper understanding than her peers: she knew that Paris would be Troy's firebrand and that the arrival of the Spartan Helen on Trojan soil spelled doom. Likewise, she supported Laocoon, the priest who rejected the Trojan Horse from the city gates because it contained a Greek assault party. Convinced his daughter knew too much, Priam locked her in the citadel and left a guard to record her babblings. During the war, Cassandra lost three suitors, Coroebus, whom Diomedes or Neoptolemus killed; Eurypylus, killed by Neoptolemus; and Othryoneus, slain by Idomeneus.

Journey

The day before Troy's collapse, after jubilant Trojans dragged the gift horse into their walls, Cassandra warned the citizens in vain that the wooden structure was filled with Greek

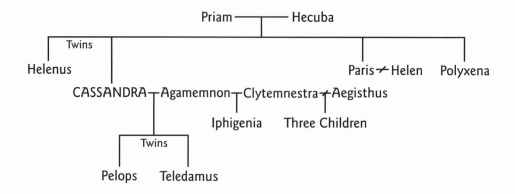

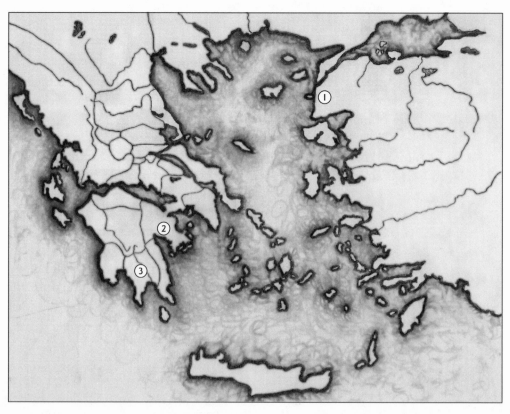

1. Troy   2. Mycenae   3. Amyclae

soldiers. As recorded in Book 2 of Virgil's *Aeneid,* she "cried out the coming doom, but the Trojans, at Apollo's command, rejected her warning." When the war came to its inevitable fiery end, the virginal, pious Cassandra crept to Athena's temple and cowered behind the statue that stood in place of the Palladium, a treasured likeness of Athena, which Diomedes stole. On sacred ground, Ajax the Lesser assaulted and captured Cassandra. Her hands tied behind her and her hair streaming, she was dragged before his compatriots, who made no effort to assist the prophetess. For this sacrilege of Athena's sanctuary, the Greeks later suffered catastrophic events on their victorious journey homeward, and Athena ensured the death of Ajax the Lesser at the end of the voyage. Before their departure, Cassandra, called "the flower of all captive women" in Edith Hamilton's *Mythology,* was allotted to Agamemnon, who fell in love with her.

Cassandra sailed with Agamemnon to Mycenae and bore him twins, Pelops and Teledamus. Outside his palace, where she prayed to Apollo, Cassandra foretold her own death and that of her infants at the hands of Agamemnon's jealous wife Clytemnestra and her lover Aegisthus, who had just slain Agamemnon. According to Odysseus in Homer's *Odyssey,* the spirit of Agamemnon was tormented by his Trojan bride's shrieks that penetrated the Underworld as she died. According to Pindar, she was buried near a shrine dedicated to her outside of Amyclae on the Eurotas River south of Sparta. Another sanctuary at Leuctra in Laconia contains a likeness of Cassandra and a temple.

Alternate Versions

Homer's *Iliad* makes no mention of Cassandra's unusual prophetic gifts and concentrates on her beauty, which surpassed that of the other Trojan princesses. A separate tradition claims that Cassandra, who was alternately named Alexandra, received her gift of prophecy as an infant, when she crawled about the temple of Apollo and was licked on the ear by one of his sacred serpents. The tongue of the sacred snake purified her and made her worthy of serving the god of prophecy.

Cassandra is often cast in the role of fanatic or lunatic. According to Lycophron's *Alexandra,* her hysterical ravings caused King Priam such grief and humiliation that he had her shut away from public view. She may have been unfairly allotted to Agamemnon, who is accused of fabricating the story of the rape by Ajax the Lesser to make her seem less desirable as a war trophy. Another variant reports that Agamemnon, to curry favor with Cassandra, attempted to stop the slaughter of her younger sister, Polyxena, who was sacrificed by the Greeks over Achilles's barrow.

The time span that follows the parceling out of Trojan women suggests that the Greeks spent a few months at the Troad before leaving for home. A justification for this logic is the birth of Cassandra's twins, who were probably conceived in Troy and were born on board Agamemnon's ship before it reached Mycenae or Amyclae, where some sources say Cassandra and her babes were slaughtered and buried. During a nineteenth-century dig, the German archaeologist Heinrich Schliemann disputed the Amyclaean tomb site after he excavated some circle graves at Mycenae. He located a tomb containing the skeletons of a woman and two babies, which he declared to be Cassandra and her twins.

Symbolism

Cassandra, who figures in numerous artistic works, forever symbolizes the cry of the unheeded prophet. Her name suggests the frenzied "jeremiad," evolved from the name of the Hebrew prophet Jeremiah whose alarms were discounted and ignored. The term *Cassandra* attached to Winston Churchill in the 1930s, when he warned British and world leaders that Hitler's rise presaged a conflict greater than World War I.

In art, Cassandra is often depicted at the direst moment of her life, when Ajax the Lesser violated her virginity and her petitions to Athena. In Athens, she was included in a mural showing her clutching the Palladium and warding off the advances of Ajax. At Delphi, Polygnotus depicted her in a frieze in a similar pose of distress.

Cassandra also is characterized in verse and dramas, notably these: Geoffrey Chaucer's *Troilus and Criseyde* and *Book of the Duchess;* William Shakespeare's *Troilus and Cressida;* Edward Young's *Night Thoughts;* Lord Byron's *English Bards and Scots Reviewers;* Elizabeth Barrett Browning's *Wine of Cyprus;* Dante Gabriel Rossetti's *Cassandra;* Alfred Lord Tennyson's *Oenone;* George Meredith's *Cassandra;* Algernon Swinburne's *Athens* and *On the Cliffs;* John Masefield's *Cassandra;* and C. Day Lewis's *Transitional Poem.*

❦ See Also

Agamemnon, Ajax the Lesser, Diomedes.

❦ Ancient Sources

Aeschylus's *Agamemnon* and *Eumenides;* Anticlides's *Nostoi;* Apollodorus's *Epitome;* Arctinus of Miletus's *Sack of Troy;* Dictys Cretensis's *Trojan War Diary;* Euripides's *Andromache, Electra, Iphigenia in Aulis, Orestes,* and *Trojan Women;* Eustathius on Homer's *Iliad;* Homer's *Iliad* and *Odyssey;* Hyginus's *Fables;* Lesches's *Little Iliad;* Lycophron's *Alexandra;* Ovid's *Art of Love;* Pausanias's *Description of Greece;* Pindar's *Pythian Odes;* Scholiast on Homer's *Iliad* and *Odyssey;* Seneca's *Agamemnon;* Servius on Virgil's *Aeneid;* Sophocles's *Electra;* Stasinus of Cyprus's *Cypria;* Stesichorus's *Oresteia;* Triclinius on Sophocles's *Electra;* Johannes Tzetzes's *Hypothesis of Lycophron's Alexandra* and *On Lycophron;* Virgil's *Aeneid.*

Daedalus and Icarus

[dehd' uh · luhs] and [ih' kuh · ruhs]

Genealogy and Background

One of Greek mythology's most poignant and widely read stories is the tale of Daedalus, which dates to 1450 B.C., and is always linked to the fate of his son, Icarus, the boy who flew too high and sank into the sea that bore his name. Daedalus, an Athenian born to the house of Cecrops, a king of Athens, earned fame as a cunning architect, engineer, sculptor, and inventor. Daedalus, whose name means "cunning" or "artful," came from impressive stock. His father is listed as Eupalamus, or "skillhand," son of Metion. Most often, Metion himself is named as Daedalus's father, his mother as Alcippe, daughter of Ares, Eupalamus as his brother, Metiadusa as his sister, and the famed warrior Erechtheus as his grandfather. Thus, Daedalus sometimes bears the patronymic Metionides.

In her early youth, Daedalus's mother, Alcippe, Metion's distant cousin, was connected with a bitter court case, the first to be tried at Athens' famed Areopagus hill. After Halirrhothius raped the girl, Ares avenged his daughter by killing her attacker. Poseidon, father of the rapist, brought Ares to the Acropolis before a divine tribunal. The court found in Ares's favor. The hill came to be known as the Areopagus or "Ares's Hill."

Although a privileged member of the royal household, Daedalus was the prototypical self-made man who came to notoriety through his technical skills. Similarly, his brother Sicyon, through determination and resourcefulness, founded the city of Sicyon on the Peloponnesus. In manhood, Daedalus found work in Athens. There, Talos (also called Calos or "partridge"), his nephew by his sister Polycaste or Perdix, served as apprentice and is said to have rivaled the master by inventing the handsaw, which he modeled on a serpent's jaw or fish's backbone, as well as the chisel, compass, and potter's wheel. Daedalus's envy grew so great that he murdered Talos by hurling him to his death from the roof of Athena's temple atop the Acropolis. Daedalus was apprehended while burying the boy's corpse; Perdix, too saddened to live

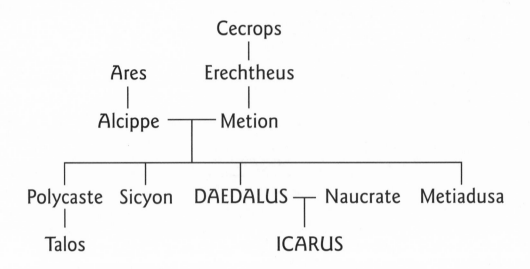

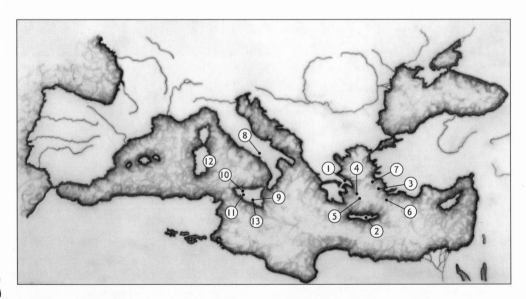

1. Athens 2. Knossos 3. Samos 4. Delos 5. Paros 6. Calymne 7. Icaria 8. Cumae
9. Camicos 10. Mt. Eryx 11. Selinus 12. Sardinia 13. Camicos

with her grief, hanged herself. Curiously, Daedalus, who lied to investigators by claiming that Talos slipped, bridled at the public outcry that followed his vicious, cowardly deed.

Journey For his crime, the Areopagus, a select jury of Attic aristocrats, exiled the inventor. Armed with Talos's saw, Daedalus journeyed to the court of King Minos on Crete, the island southeast of Greece, where he pleased the renowned priest and king so thoroughly that he was immediately named staff inventor. Daedalus married a palace slave, Naucrate, and produced a son, Icarus.

As part of his job, Daedalus designed an elaborate dance floor at Knossos patterned after the Egyptian labyrinth in a white marbled relief maze, which Homer describes in his *Odyssey* as picturing "youths and seductive maidens [joining] hands in the dance … and a divine bard [setting] the time to the sound of the lyre." Locals flattered Daedalus's ego and easily converted him into a self-important dandy. Minos's daughters, Ariadne and Phaedra, haunted his workshop and observed the intricacy of his toils. For them, he contrived dancing dolls that could bob, curtsy, and wink; for the queen, he created a folding parasol to ward off the midsummer sun.

While employed as royal smithy, Daedalus learned the secret lusts of the queen, the notorious Pasiphae, condemned by Aphrodite to crave sexual union with beasts. Because Pasiphae longed to mate with a magnificent white bull, which Poseidon sent from the sea, she used her influence with the exiled engineer to satisfy her bizarre lust. At the direction of the wanton queen, who had the power to kill, torment, or deport Daedalus, he took pity on her desire and designed a wooden cow to accommodate her perversity. By climbing into the model, Pasiphae exposed herself to the great bull, consummating the act she had long desired. For the pleasure of coupling with the snorting beast, she rewarded Daedalus with gold.

After the birth of "Minos's bull" or the Minotaur, the monstrous bull-headed human who was also called Asterius, Daedalus assisted the king in hushing up the shameful episode and its vicious offspring. According to Watts's translation of Ovid's *Metamorphoses:*

> The palace blazed with trophies; but within
> was scandal dark and hideous fruit of sin,
> the household shame, full-grown and foul to see,
> the illicit half-and-half monstrosity.

Daedalus worked for years on the design and construction of the Labyrinth, a subterranean maze shaped like a double axe, edged in thorny hedgerows and designed to confine the grotesquely gluttonous Minotaur:

A multiplex of courts and cloisters blind
Where misdirections led, in mazes long,
The cheated eye circuitously wrong.

(Ovid's *Metamorphoses*)

The Minotaur fed annually on seven youths and seven maidens, a yearly tribute that King Minos exacted on Athens for the death of his son, Androgeus, who died while trying to subdue the Cretan bull. This ritual sacrifice was stopped by Theseus, who killed the Minotaur by following a plan devised by Daedalus and passed along to Theseus's lover, Princess Ariadne. His idea was to mark a trail through the dark Labyrinth with string by tying it to the lintel, then following it to the bull, completing the kill, and rewinding the string safely back to daylight. For this, Daedalus and Icarus suffered imprisonment in the Labyrinth so that the secret would remain forever immured.

Suffering homesickness, Daedalus grew desperate. Pasiphae felt some responsibility for his plight and tried in vain to gain his exoneration. To free himself and his teenage son, Daedalus outwitted Minos, who guarded both land and sea, by escaping on homemade wings, which carried the duo west toward Cumae on the Tyrrhenian coast of Italy. As Ovid pictures this beloved myth, the child Icarus dawdled by his father's workbench, puffing at feathers and dipping his fingers into gluepots while the inventor, drawing an elaborate analogy from nature, meticulously laid out feathers resembling a gull's wing—in ascending order, small to large, "the way that panpipes rise in gradual sequence."

Daedalus lovingly explained their undertaking; Icarus had to listen carefully, for they risked their lives in taking to the skies. As Rolfe Humphries translates the father's advice:

I want you, Icarus, to fly the middle course:
Don't go too low, or water will weigh the wings down;
don't go too high, or the sun's fire will burn them.
Keep to the middle way. And one more thing,
no fancy steering by star or constellation,
follow my lead!

(Ovid's *Metamorphoses*)

With that said, Daedalus busied himself adjusting the wings to fit their shoulders. He must have hidden serious concerns, for silent tears wet his cheeks and his hands shook.

They launched forth, Daedalus leading the way as though guiding a fledgling from the nest.

With hand signals, Daedalus pointed the way. Fishermen watched in amazement, as did shepherds and farmers, who assumed that the winged beings were gods. Possibly to conceal their plan to fly to Italy, the pair soared in a wide circle north and east over the Cyclades—the islands of Samos, Delos, and Paros—and past Calymne in the Sporades (scattered) chain. Icarus, thrilled with the power of flight, thought boyishly, "This is wonderful!"

The fliers separated, Icarus winging higher in the thrill of freedom from the earth. The closer he came to the sun, the weaker grew the hold of wax on feathers. At length, Icarus flapped bare arms, quickly losing altitude as he dropped toward the Aegean Sea near Samos, off the shores of Asia Minor. As Humphries describes the desperate situation:

> *Father!* he called, and *Father!*
> Until the blue sea hushed him, the dark water
> men call the Icarian now. And Daedalus
> father no more, called "Icarus, where are you!"
> Below, empty wings floated on the waves.

(Ovid's Metamorphoses)

Daedalus, quick to blame himself for his heady scheme, cursed his skill. The twitter of a partridge abraded the wounds, reminding Daedalus that his pride brought about his son's death. After burying Icarus west of Samos on the island of Icaria, named in his child's honor, Daedalus placed two columns on the Amber Islands, one inscribed "Icarus," the other, "Daedalus." For the portals to Cumae's temple facing the Bay of Naples, he sculpted a frieze depicting the ill-fated flight from Crete. According to Book 6 of Virgil's *Aeneid,* he dedicated his wings to Apollo, the creator's god, in whose honor he built a gold-crowned temple.

Daedalus migrated to Camicos on the southern shore of Sicily. He earned his keep at the court of King Cocalus by designing noble buildings and public works, especially the dam on the River Alabon, a fort at Agrigento, a plaza and gold filigreed grille dedicated to Aphrodite on Mount Eryx, and a steam-bath at Selinus, which channeled the vapors of natural hot springs into public chambers. Meanwhile, Minos scoured the Mediterranean for Daedalus's whereabouts. To locate so clever a man, Minos devised a test: he offered a reward to the person who could thread a spiral seashell. Cocalus's engineer easily passed the test by tying the thread to an ant's leg and allowing the insect to traverse the circuitous path. Cocalus presented Minos the shell, thus indicating that Daedalus dwelt in Sicily.

Because of Cocalus's admiration for his maligned guest, he fought off Minos's warriors and killed Minos himself. Daedalus remained at Cocalus's court, wandered briefly in Sardinia, but never returned to Athens.

Alternate Versions

A minor variation to the well-known story of Daedalus and Icarus pictures Icarus as the son of Iphinoe, Merope, or Phrasimede. An alternate tale of Daedalus's murder of Talos describes how the boy had begun an invocation to Athena. The goddess intervened in the murder, changing Talos into a partridge.

A more inventive version of Minos's death claims that Cocalus lured Minos to a banquet. As Minos soaked in a tub to prepare for public presentation, Cocalus's daughters, performing a ritual guest ablution, either scalded or suffocated Minos in steam, thus ending the Cretan king's torment of Daedalus.

An alternate setting describes Icarus as searching for his father after their mutual banishment for Daedalus's murder of Talos. Far from his home in Athens, the luckless boy drowned in a shipwreck off Samos. His remains washed ashore on Icaria, where Herakles performed funeral rituals. Another version depicts Daedalus and his son sailing on a merchant ship secretly supplied by Pasiphae; an even more creative tale has them rowing away from their Cretan prison in sailboats, for which Daedalus had invented masts, yardarms, and sails. Because Icarus was unfamiliar with the art of sailing, he capsized his vessel. An alternative to this ending is the story that Icarus, already in sight of Icaria, jumped from his boat and drowned.

Although Icarus lived a short life, he is credited with the invention of carpentry and woodwork. Usually, mythographers list this accomplishment beside Daedalus's name, alongside the invention of the ax, auger, plumb bob, wedge, level, drafting compass, and glue. Other tidbits associated with Daedalus's name include the creation of puppetlike statues with moveable limbs and eyelids, particularly the giant Talos, which guarded Crete until Medea removed the nail in its calf and caused the robot to bleed to death.

Engineering works that have been attributed to Daedalus extended throughout the Mediterranean, from Athens to Sicily and Sardinia and as far south as Ptah's temple in Memphis, Egypt. He created a wooden likeness of Aphrodite at Delos as a gift to Ariadne. While on Crete, he is credited with honoring Artemis Britomartis with a temple. At Knossos he is said to have dedicated a temple to Athena and a second at Athens, where a folding chair demonstrated his cunning devices. In Sardinia, Daedalus supposedly constructed the Daedaleia, a series of cone-shaped towers dating to the Bronze Age.

That Daedalus built everything to which local tradition links him is unlikely; even if he had commanded the world's largest engineering corps, such a feat would have been impossible. Perhaps the creations of other inventors gained legendary stature by forced attachment with a builder of Daedalus's reputation, as did the artist Eucheir's kinship, which ennobled his invention of painting. Whatever the source of such engineering wonders, Daedalus apparently earned a noteworthy enough reputation to have a district of Attic Cecropis named after him.

Symbolism

Scholars question whether Daedalus the risk-taker grew into a cult-hero or whether craftsmen were amalgamated into the single legendary figure of Daedalus the technician. One suggested reason for the popularity of his myth is that it embodied Minoan culture, which spread throughout the Mediterranean world.

In Daedalus's honor, fifth century B.C. inventors referred proudly to themselves as Daedalids, some even claiming kinship with the famed artificer. A festival of the Daedaleia was observed around Attica. Daedalus's name evolved into *daedal,* or *daedalian,* English adjectives meaning "intricate."

Not everyone had a great liking for the Daedalus myth. Bullfinch failed to mention it at all in his work. Edith Hamilton disdained Ovid's sentimental appraisal of the designer as one of the great mythic adventurers. Like Prometheus, his name was equated with creativity and, tragically, over-confidence or *hubris.* Similarly, the Daedalus and Icarus story as imparted by Ovid reflects the Roman philosophy contained in the unearthly yearnings of Phaethon to drive the sun's chariot. Like the doomed driver, Icarus and his grief-bowed father learned the Greek golden mean that "one goes safest on the middle," balancing emotion with control and acting responsibly, regardless of the godlike buoyance of power.

From Daedalus's two-legged sculptures sprang the convention of living statues, like those that appear in the myth of Pygmalion and Galatea and continue in the Renaissance with William Shakespeare's *Winter's Tale,* in modern times with Karel Capek's *R.U.R.,* where he peopled his mythic island with robots, and George Lucas did the same in his movie, *Star Wars.* James Joyce names the hero of *Portrait of the Artist as a Young Man* Stephen Dedalus for the ambitious young Dubliner yearning to fly the confines of his native city; Joyce's novel concludes with an invocation to the "old father, old artificer," whose unfettered risk-taking inspires the hero to test his own wings.

Artists, jewelers, technicians, writers, and astronomers have drawn on the story of Daedalus and Icarus for centuries. Walter Baade named a planetoid for Icarus because of its precarious lurch toward the sun. Roman floors and walls depict the tale in mosaics, bas-relief, and frescoes; vases, too, reveal views of the first men to fly like gods. Painter Sir Anthony Van Dyck depicts Daedalus as he fits the wings onto his son's shoulders; Peter Brueghel the Elder's representation, *The Fall of Icarus,* captures the fearful moment as the boy tumbles to his death. Peter-Paul Rubens and Auguste Rodin also re-created the myth. Rich with images of Apollo's blessings, grim, forbidding evils, soaring ambition, and youthful folly, the myth is often interpreted metaphorically in terms of the intellect in conflict with a rebellious spirit, as represented by Icarus's ineffectual fluttering of wings which, pierced by Helios's heated rays, lost their feathers. As symbols of technology, the wings represent frustrated ambition and functional insufficiency.

The story of Daedalus and Icarus holds a prominent place in later literature. Perhaps William Shakespeare pays the most touching tribute to the hopeless situation of father, Daedalus, and his doomed son. In *King Henry VI,* Part III, Act V, the playwright recalls the plight of the central figure with these words:

> I, Daedalus; my poor boy, Icarus;
> thy father, Minos, that denied our course;
> the sun that seared the wings of my sweet boy,
> thy brother Edward; and thyself, the sea
> whose envious gulf did swallow up his life.

The myth also forms the nucleus of Lauro de Bosis's antifascist tragedy *Icaro,* and historical fiction, notably V. Cronin's *The Golden Honeycomb* and Mary Renault's *Bull from the Sea.* Poets, too, incorporate the myth of Daedalus/Dedalus, as demonstrated by Geoffrey Chaucer's *Book of the Duchess* and *House of Fame,* Christopher Marlowe's *Dido Queen of Carthage,* William Cowper's *Anti-Thelyphthora,* Winthrop Praed's *The County Ball,* Ralph Waldo Emerson's *Sea Shore,* and Algernon Swinburne's *Ballad against the Enemies of France.*

Other creative minds have turned to the Daedalus myth for inspiration. Modern painter and sculptor Michael Ayrton's *The Maze Maker* reflects on Daedalus as logician and problem solver. Geneticist and popular science writer J. B. S. Haldane's *Daedalus or Science and the Future* provoked the famed reply from the philospher and mathematician Bertrand Russell, *Icarus or the Future of Science.* Other writers, including Philippi Destuches, Johann Goethe, Nanina Alba, and André Gide, allude to the touching story of the boy who flew too high and the father who rued the day that he taught his son to fly.

❦ See Also

Theseus.

🦋 Ancient Sources

Apollodorus's *Epitome;* Cicero's *On the Nature of the Gods;* Diodorus Siculus's *Library of History;* Euripides's *Electra* and *Hecuba;* Horace's *Carmina* and *Odes;* Ovid's *Metamorphoses;* Pausanias's *Description of Greece;* Pherecydes's *Heptamochos;* Pindar's *Olympian Odes;* Plato's *Meno;* Pliny the Elder's *Natural History;* Plutarch's *Parallel Lives;* Scholiast on Sophocles's *Oedipus at Colonus;* Johannes Tzetzes's *Chiliades;* Virgil's *Aeneid.*

Danaides

[duh · nay' uh · deez]

Genealogy and Background

The Danaides, or Danae, included fifty daughters born to various mothers (Melia, Atlantia, Crino, Elephantis, Europa, Herse, Memphis, Phoebe, Pieria and, Polyxo), were sired by King Danaus of Libya on Africa's northern coast. When the girls reached marriageable age, they eluded their uncle Aegyptus, who pledged them to his fifty sons so he could kill the girls and usurp their father's realm, as Danaus learned from an oracle. To save his girls, Danaus, like Noah, built the Mediterranean's first two-prowed vessel to accommodate them.

Journey

Praying to Zeus to drown the pursuers so the girls could retain their maidenhood, the family rowed northeast to the ancient town of Lindos on the island of Rhodes off the coast of Asia Minor and, from there, northwest toward their Argive ancestors at Apobathmi near Lerna in Argos.

The Danaides, bearing the olive branch woven with white wool, signaled to King Pelasgus their wish for sanctuary and threatened suicide by hanging themselves by tying their sashes to fifty statues of goddesses if he betrayed them. Intent on avoiding multiple sacrilege, the king complied and allowed them to remain in Argos. At length, the girls earned the hospitality of all of Argos and taught the local women the mysteries of the Egyptian Demeter.

One of Danaus's daughters was Amymone, who enjoyed the outdoors and who was handy with a bow. One day, wearied of boar hunting, she lay down to sleep. She accidentally wounded a Satyr, who attempted to ravish her. Poseidon drove the Satyr away and raped the girl himself. In payment for her favors, Poseidon struck the ground with his trident and made sweet water flow from three openings onto the parched land. The son born to Amymone was Nauplius, who gained fame as Jason's helmsman on the *Argo*.

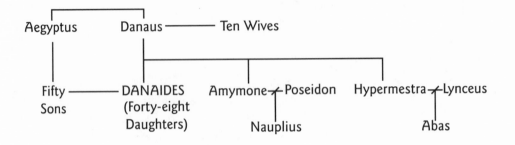

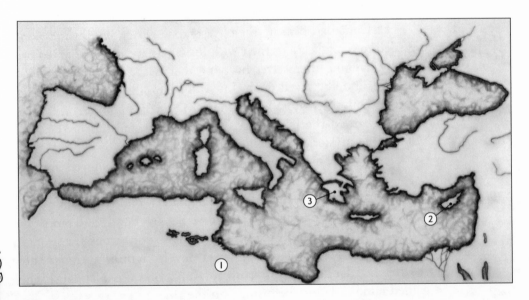

1. Libya   2. Lindos   3. Lerna

Danaus's family reconciled with their uncle Aegyptus. His fifty sons, tempted by Danaus's improvements to his new kingdom, again pledged their love to the girls in hopes of aggrandizing themselves in Argos. Danaus, who was not persuaded of their sincerity, mated the pairs by drawing names from his helmet and organized a multiple wedding. The cousins were paired in this order:

Actaea	Periphas	Glauce	Alces
Adiante	Daiphron	Glaucippe	Potamon
Adite	Menalces	Gorge	Hippothous
Agave	Lycus	Gorgophone	Proteus
Amymone	Enceladus	Hippomedusa	Alcmenor
Anaxibia	Archelaus	Hippodameia	Diocorystes
Anthelia	Cisseus	Hippodameia (2)	Istrus
Asteria	Chaetus	Hippodice	Idas
Automate	Busiris	Hyperippe	Hyppocorystes
Autonoe	Eurylochus	Hypermestra	Lynceus
Bryce	Chthonius	Iphimedusa	Euchenor
Callidice	Pandion	Mnestra	Aegius
Celaeno	Hyperbius	Nelo	Menemachus
Chrysippe	Chrysippus	Ocypete	Lampus
Cleite	Cleitus	Oeme	Arbelus
Cleodore	Lixus	Phartis	Eurydamas
Cleopatra	Agenor	Pirene	Agaptolemus
Cleopatra (2)	Hermus	Podarce	Oeneus
Dioxippe	Aegyptus	Pylarge	Idmon
Dorium	Cercetes	Rhode	Hippolytus
Electra	Peristhenes	Rhodia	Chalcodon
Erato	Bromius	Scaea	Daiphron
Euippe	Argius	Sthenele	Sthenelus
Euippe (2)	Imbrus	Stygne	Polyctor
Eurydice	Dryas	Theano	Phantes

Danaus armed each bride with a dirk and made them pledge to kill their treacherous cousins that same night.

As their father commanded, the forty-nine brides dispatched, then beheaded their grooms. Overcome by the loss, their father Aegyptus, collapsed at Aroe and was honored at a temple or Serapis at Patrae. On Artemis's advice, only Hypermestra or Hypermnestra, the eldest, let her mate, Lynceus, remain alive because he had respected her virginity. She helped him escape to Lyceia and signaled with a bonfire when he could safely return. Hypermestra stood trial in Argos and was acquitted for disobeying her father.

To rid themselves of blood guilt, the forty-nine brides honored their grooms with funerals and interred their heads in the Lernean swamp. At Zeus's request, Hermes absolved the Danaides of murder. Because men shied away from the notorious daughters of Danaus, the king was forced to offer decorated shields and his daughters as prizes in a footrace called the Hymenaean Contest. The girls lined up at the finish line and left with the Egyptian runners as they reached the goal. The resulting offspring were named Danaians and populated the area with loyal citizens.

Alternate Versions

According to one account, Lynceus later slew the forty-nine Danaides and their conniving father and seized the kingdom of Libya. He was succeeded by Hypermestra's son, Abas, founder of the city of Abae in Phocis. The girls reassembled in the Underworld and, among Tantalus, Sispyphus, and Ixion, were condemned by the judges of the dead to the impossible task of carrying water in sieves to fill a leaking or bottomless water urn.

Symbolism

The myth of the fifty Danae indicates the long history of the olive branch as a symbol of peace, which messengers carried wrapped in white wool to assure their safe passage. The olive branch was replicated in Roman lore as a prop in the hand of Pax, goddess of peace. In a seventeenth-century engraving, the olive flourishes under the motto *Planta dei, pax est,* meaning that peace is god's plant. Christians adapted the plant plus a white dove as symbols of peace and love in catacomb paintings.

The maidens are also connected with the white flag, a sign of surrender. Ironically, the daughters of Danaus also represent retribution in the Underworld, where they work perpetually at a meaningless, infernal task, an existential symbol of life's futility. The adjective *danaidean* reflects the endless back and forth of the doomed maidens, forever carrying water in sieves to fill a bottomless vat. The plight of the Danaides is mentioned in Geoffrey Chaucer's *Legend of Good Women,* Edmund Spenser's *Faerie Queene,* Samuel Daniel's *Complaint of Rosamond,* John Milton's *Paradise Regained,* and Alfred Lord Tennyson's *The Princess.*

❧ See Also

Jason and Medea, Nauplius.

❧ Ancient Sources

Aeschylus's *Amymone* and *Danaides;* Apollodorus's *Epitome;* Apollonius of Rhodes's *Argonautica; Danais* (anonymous); Diodorus Siculus's *Library of History;* Eustathius on Homer's *Iliad;* Herodotus's *Histories;* Hesychius's *Hippeion;* Horace's *Carmina;* Hyginus's *Fables;* Lucian's *Dialogues of Sailors;* Ovid's *Amores, Heroides,* and *Metamorphoses;* Pausanias's *Description of Greece;* Pindar's *Pythian Odes;* Plato's *Axiochus;* Plutarch's *On the Malice of Herodotus;* Scholiast on Euripides's *Hecuba;* Scholiast on Pindar's *Pythian Odes;* Servius on Virgil's *Aeneid;* Tibullus's *Elegies.*

Dardanus

[dahr · day' nuhs]

Genealogy and Background

Dardanus was one of mythology's most noted pioneers. The son of Zeus and Electra, he and his brother Iasion were born in Arcadia and settled on Samothrace, an island in the northern Aegean Sea off the coast of Thrace. Dardanus fathered Idaeus and Deimas by his first wife, Chryseis, Athena's daughter. His father-in-law, the prophet Chryseis, entrusted Dardanus with Arcadia's sacred objects, particularly the Palladium, the wooden likeness of Athena said to have fallen from the sky. Chryseis also set Dardanus in charge of the cult mysteries of Cybele in Phrygia. The city of Dardania, named for its founder, was later changed to Ilium, after Dardanus's son Ilus built Troy to the northwest of Dardania. The city was ideally situated on the triangular land mass, the Troad, that maintained a valuable overlook of east-to-west grain shipments through the Hellespont and overland journeys through Mysia. Tros's wife Callirrhoe bore Scamander, Cleopatra, Ilus, and Assaracus. Tros's last son, Ganymedes, was so handsome that the gods claimed him as their cupbearer. Dardanus's second grandson, Laomedon, was a mortal and father of Priam, who was king of Troy at the time of the Trojan War and father of Hector, Troy's champion. The royal line ends with Hector and Andromache's son, Astyanax, whom the Greeks tossed from the battlements to jagged rocks below to halt the succession of Trojan kings.

Journey

After a flood swept Iasion away, Dardanus inflated a one-man skin raft, weighted it with four stones, and paddled east to Teucer's realm on the Troad near Mount Ida. Dardanus, by then a widower, made a favorable impression on the king, married his daughter Batieia (or Arisbe), and ruled jointly in Dardania, the forerunner of Troy, on Mount Ida, where he introduced the worship of Cybele, the Anatolian earth mother. Dardanus's second family

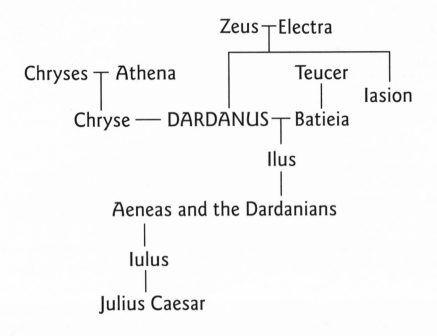

```
                              Zeus ┬ Electra
                                   │
        Chryses ┬ Athena        ┌──┴──────────────┐
                │            Teucer                │
        Chryse ── DARDANUS ┬ Batieia           Iasion
                           │
                          Ilus
                           │
            Aeneas and the Dardanians
                           │
                         Iulus
                           │
                     Julius Caesar
```

1. Arcadia 2. Samothrace 3. Mt. Ida 4. Dardania 5. Troy

included Ilus, Erichthonius, Idaea, and Zacynthus. By his sister-in-law, Neso, Dardanus fathered the first Sibyl, who introduced Sibylline prophecy to the Troad.

Dardanus is responsible for erecting the Trojan citadel, from which he ruled the Troad. He consulted an oracle and learned that he could keep his realm intact if he guarded his wife's dowry and the Palladium at the shrine of Athena. On his voyage from Troy after the Trojan War, Aeneas, leader of the remains of the Dardanians, sought to reestablish the ancestry of Dardanus, whom he viewed in the Underworld.

Alternate Versions An alternate account of the Palladium has Zeus presenting it to Dardanus at the time of Troy's founding. In a curiously larcenous retelling for so honored a hero, Dardanus is said to have stolen the Palladium and carried it back to Troy. A lesser tale reports that Boreas, god of the wind, was changed into a stallion, mated with the horses in Dardanus's stables, and created twelve mounts of unsurpassed swiftness which, like the Palladium, guarded Troy.

Several versions of Dardanus's myth confuse his history:

- Dardanus's brother Iasion is also called the son of Corythus, King of Tusca and Electra's husband, rather than the son of Zeus. Like the Dioscuri, the brothers would have shared a doppelganger relationship—a mother and one mortal and one immortal father.
- One telling gives Dardanus and Iasion a sister, Harmonia, who is the source of an extensive branch of Greek mythology. An alternate mating for Iasion makes Cybele Iasion's wife and Dardanus's sister-in-law.
- Dardanus and his brother are said to have been born in Italy and migrated to Samothrace or born in Samothrace and migrated to Crete or Italy to establish an altar for the Palladium. Other variations claim that they separated amicably after the Deucalian Flood to seek their fortunes, Iasion in Samothrace and Dardanus in Phrygia.
- More violent versions claim that Zeus skewered Iasion with a thunderbolt for coupling with Demeter or that Iasion was eaten by his horses. More murderous is the myth that Dardanus, like Cain, slew his brother before leaving home to wander the world.
- Dardanus, Chryse, and their son, Ideaus are said to have traveled back to Samothrace from Troy to establish Cybele's cult. Because of Dardanus's influence, the island was called Dardania.
- Alternate accounts of the Palladium have Athena tossing it out of Olympus because it was touched by Electra, a rape victim of Zeus and therefore unworthy to handle holy objects. A different version has Zeus presenting it to Dardanus at the time of Troy's founding to guard the city. However it

arrived, the Palladium was a token of protection from Athena, goddess of war.

Dardanus is connected historically with a belligerent Illyrian nation. Sprung from nomadic roots, they coalesced under a strong leader in 284 B.C. As enemies of Rome, the Dardani faced both Sulla and Appius Claudius Pulcher in the first century B.C. The continued unrest of the area caused the Romans to draft the Dardani into their occupation troops, whom Marcus Aurelius legitimized as soldiers of the empire in the second century A.D.

| Symbolism |

In Virgil's *Aeneid*, Aeneas recalls Cassandra's prophecy that he should settle in a land to the west. At the decree of Augustus, Rome's first emperor, Virgil has Aeneas honor Dardanus, his ancestor and fellow colonist, in a passage that ties Rome's rather tawdry, insubstantial beginnings with the dignity and glory of Homer's Troy, originally called Dardania:

> There is a lush, promising land the Greeks called Hesperia,
> which is blessed with valiant children ... This nation of Italy
> was the birthplace of King Dardanus and Iasius. Such an
> auspicious land should be our starting place.

According to Roman tradition, Dardanus answered a call to battle that reflected divine intervention: after losing his helmet on the field, he returned for it, renewed the fray, and won a significant victory. In honor of Dardanus's victory, a town was founded and named Corythus, for the Greek *corys* or helmet.

A second factor in the hero's fame was the decree of the gods that Dardanus should keep watch over his wife's dowry, the Palladium, a wooden statue depicting Athena, which her father gave his son-in-law at the time of the betrothal. The coastal vantage point of Dardania was renamed Hellespont and later returned to the honor of Dardanus after being renamed the Dardanelles, a major city at the crossroads of Asia and Europe.

In Roman history, the passage of the Palladium from the burning city of Troy to Alba Longa resulted in a promise of longevity for Rome. Aeneas, the rescuer of the statue, placed it in the care of the Vestal Virgins, attendants of the *focus* or hearth of Rome. The statue figures in numerous occasions when Rome was endangered. One variation of this talisman reports that Aeneas's statue was a copy of the original, which Diomedes delivered personally to Aeneas. It is likely that many regions revered copies of the likeness of Athena in an attempt to propitiate the goddess of wisdom and war.

Geoffrey Chaucer referred to Aeneas's Trojan ancestor in *Troilus and Criseyde.*

🌿 See Also

Aeneas.

🌿 Ancient Sources

Apollodorus's *Epitome;* Conon's *Narrations;* Diodorus Siculus's *Library of History;* Dionysius of Halicarnassus's *Roman Antiquities;* Eustathius on Homer's *Iliad;* Hesiod's *Theogony;* Homer's *Iliad;* Lycophron's *Alexandra;* Servius on Virgil's *Aeneid;* Stephanus Byzantium's *Arisbe;* Strabo's *Geography;* Johannes Tzetzes's *On Lycophron;* Virgil's *Aeneid.*

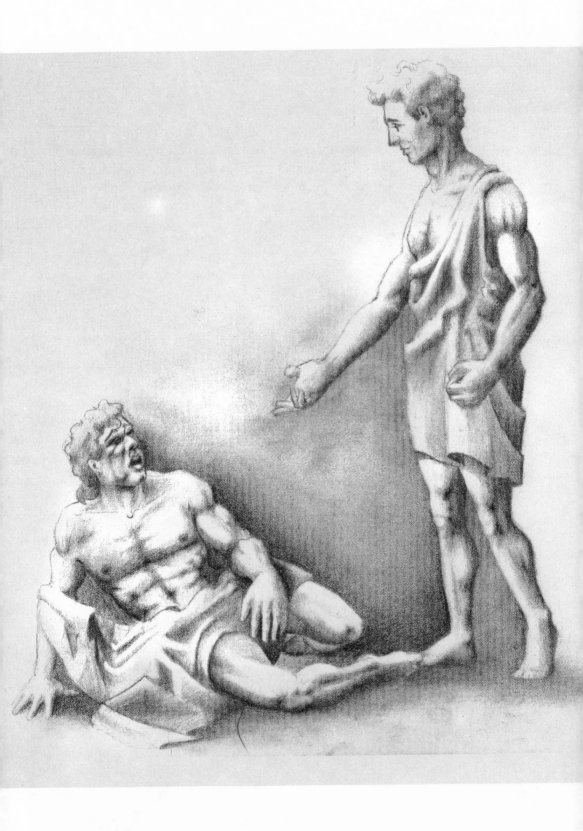

Diomedes

[di · oh · mee' deez]

Genealogy and Background The hard-fighting Aetolian, Diomedes, son of Deipyle and Tydeus and husband of Aegialea, his mother's sister, traveled widely in his lifetime from his home in central Greece to Italy's southeastern shore. He earned a reputation as a professional soldier by vindicating his father on the march of the Seven against Thebes, an aggression encouraged by Athena. Still in his youth, Diomedes helped restore Oeneus, his grandfather, to his throne in Calydon.

Journey As a suitor of Helen who still ached with longing at the sound of her name, Diomedes served as one of Agamemnon's lieutenants and headed a fleet of eighty ships to the Troad. He accompanied Odysseus on the trip to Scyros to enlist Achilles. At Aulis, it was Diomedes who cast a vote for the butchering of Agamemnon's daughter Iphigenia to secure winds for the journey east to the Troad, where he also urged the framing (probably carried out at Odysseus instigation) of Palamedes as a Trojan spy; he was stoned to death by the Greeks for treachery.

Often paired with Odysseus, Diomedes fought Trojans with unusual elan. His deeds form a regular, but disconnected echo throughout the war:

- On the battlefield, he set an example of reason by exchanging armor with his Trojan kinsman, Glaucus.
- After Penthesilea's death at the hands of Achilles, he repudiated Achilles's desecration of her corpse by hurling it into the Scamander River.
- In the thick of battle, Diomedes, the main character of Book 5 of Homer's *Iliad,* attacked Aphrodite and Ares.

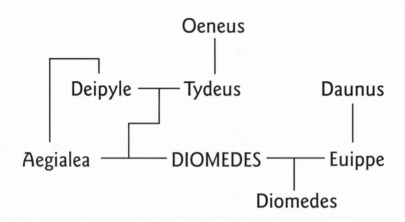

Oeneus

Deipyle —— Tydeus   Daunus

Aegialea ———— DIOMEDES —— Euippe

Diomedes

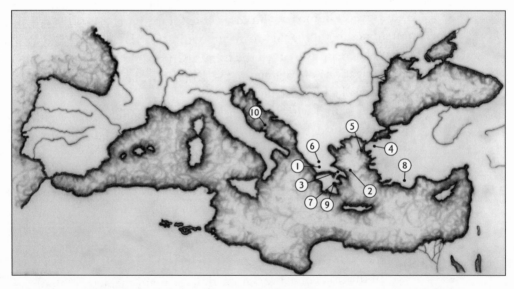

1. Calydon 2. Scyros 3. Aulis 4. Troy 5. Tenedos 6. Aetolia 7. Argos 8. Lycia
9. Argos 10. Isle of Diomedes

- He hurled a boulder and smashed Aeneas's hip, killed Pandarus, Dolon, and Rhesus, and rescued Nestor.
- He cast lots with the other Greek warriors vying for a private duel with Hector.
- He joined Odysseus in launching a foray against Troy during Achilles's absence. To achieve this last exploit, Diomedes had Odysseus beat him bloody so that he could clothe himself in beggar's rags and pose as an abused servant.
- Diomedes helped recover Patroclus's body and carried it back to Achilles's tent.
- A less familiar story connects Diomedes with Briseis, Calchas's lovely daughter, whom he loved so spiritedly that he repeatedly engaged Troilus, her Trojan suitor, in the crush of battle.
- In council, Diomedes stood his ground among the best and promised that all could return home, but he intended to see the war to its conclusion.

Other accomplishments attach to Diomedes's name:

- He assisted Odysseus in sailing to Lemnos to persuade Philoctetes to help end the war by bringing his bow and arrows to Troy.
- He sailed with the deputation bound for Scyros to bring Achilles's twelve-year-old son, Neoptolemus, to Troy.
- He also figures in the theft of the Palladium, which he and Odysseus stole by climbing through the Trojan water system and forcing Theano, Athena's priestess, to surrender it. On the way back to the camp, Diomedes is said to have carried the statue. Because Odysseus wanted all the glory, he raised his sword against his accomplice. The moon glinted off the metal and warned Diomedes to duck.
- On the night that Troy fell, Diomedes joined the attack party in the belly of the hollow horse.

Compared to Agamemnon, Menelaus, and Odysseus, with whom he parted at the island of Tenedos off the Troad, Diomedes enjoyed an uneventful journey west from Troy to Aetolia. However, his good fortune ended on the way to Argos. His ship foundered off Lycia on the east coast of the Mediterranean Sea. Callirrhoe, daughter of Lycus, helped him elude capture. Diomedes was forced to continue his westward voyage, leaving Callirrhoe to mourn his departure. She hanged herself. On his arrival at Argos, south of his home, Diomedes learned that Aegialea, who had committed adultery with Cometes, planned to kill him because of his role in the stoning of Palamedes.

To save himself an ignoble death, Diomedes hid at Hera's shrine before departing to seek his grandfather's help. He was either defeated or disheartened and migrated west to Daunus's kingdom in southern Italy. He ingratiated himself by fighting Daunus's war against the Messapians and was rewarded with marriage to Princess Euippe, who bore a son and named him Diomedes. His relationship with Daunus was fraught with battles and his intention to aid Turnus in the fight against Trojan Aeneas was foiled by Aphrodite, who still bore a grudge against the human warrior who had attacked her in battle.

Alternate Versions Many Italian cities, including Agyripa and Brundisium, claim Diomedes as their founder. Two myths describe his death: in the first, Daunus bests him at last and deposits his remains on an eastern Italian island in a cluster called the Diomeds or Tremiti, on the Apulian shore off Cape Garganus; in a second version of his death, he vanishes, leaving behind a flock of shorebirds.

Symbolism The memory of Diomedes remains alive in a local cult in Venetia, in Apulia, and at Luceria, where Athena's worshippers venerate him and his bright armor. A temple to Athena stands on the Messenian shores in Sicily to watch over the windswept strait that separates the island from Italy's southern tip. In art, Diomedes, named for "divine cunning," appears in murals in warrior's stance or as thief of the Palladium as well as a conniving sinner in Dante Alighieri's *Inferno*. He also figures in Geoffrey Chaucer's *Troilus and Criseyde*, William Shakespeare's *Troilus and Cressida* and *King Henry VI*, and Samuel Butler's *Hudibras*. He is portrayed as a hero in Jean-Auguste-Dominique Ingres's painting *Venus Wounded by Diomedes*.

See Also

Achilles, Agamemnon, Menelaus, Odysseus.

Ancient Sources

Aeschylus's *Philoctetes*; Antoninus Liberalis's *Metamorphoses*; Apollodorus's *Epitome*; Conon's *Narrations* and *Cypria*; Dictys Cretensis's *Trojan War Diary*; Euripides's *Oineus* and *Rhesus*; Hesychius's *Lexicon*; Homer's *Iliad* and *Odyssey*; Hyginus's *Fables*; Lesches's *Little Iliad*; Ovid's *Metamorphoses*; Pausanias's *Description of Greece*; Philostratus's

Heroica and *Imagines;* Pliny's *Natural History;* Plutarch's *Greek Questions;* Quintus Smyrnaeus's *Post-Homerica;* Scholiast on Euripides's *Orestes;* Scholiast on Pindar's *Nemean Odes;* Servius on Virgil's *Aeneid;* Sophocles's *Philoctetes;* Stasinus of Cyprus's *Cypria;* Strabo's *Historical Sketches;* Johannes Tzetzes's *On Lycophron;* Virgil's *Aeneid.*

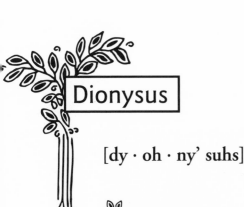

Dionysus

[dy · oh · ny' suhs]

Genealogy and Background

The jovial, horned wine god, Dionysus, whom the Greeks treasured and the Romans revered as Bacchus or Liber Pater, was the foster child of Silenos. Also called Nysus, the "lame god," Dionysus, was born to Olympian Zeus and the Theban princess, Semele, in Dracanum in Icaria, an island west of Samos in the southern Aegean. His birth brought immediate death to his mother, who, in her sixth month of pregnancy, was beguiled by Hera, disguised as an aged crone, and enticed to view the mighty Zeus. The flash of lightning that burst from him instantly incinerated her. The god secured the immortal fetus in a slit in his thigh.

When the child was developed, he was born a second time. Hera attacked him through her intermediaries, the Titans, who dismembered the boy and stewed him in a great pot. From his blood grew a pomegranate tree. Rhea, his grandmother, gathered up his remains, reformed him, and passed him into the care of Persephone, who located worthy foster parents to raise him in a land where Hera would be least likely to look—North Africa.

Nurtured at the court of Athamas and Ino, Semele's sister, at the cave of Macris and by her sister nymphs on Mount Nysa in Libya, Dionysus grew fat on milk and honey or mead. As his father directed, to protect him from the constant vigilance of Hera, who punished Zeus's paramours and baseborn children, Dionysus, like Achilles after him, wore only female garments and cultivated feminine gestures. The complicated ruse failed to conceal from Hera the product of yet another of Zeus's adulteries. After she repaid the royal couple with lethal insanity, Zeus changed the boy into a goat named Eriphus, "the kid," as another form of disguise.

By the time he reached adulthood, Dionysus was ripe for his great role in human history: the evolution of wine making from table grapes. As a fertility god, Dionysus grew appealingly handsome, with fair skin, sanguine cheeks, and soft, serpentine ringlets. Although he

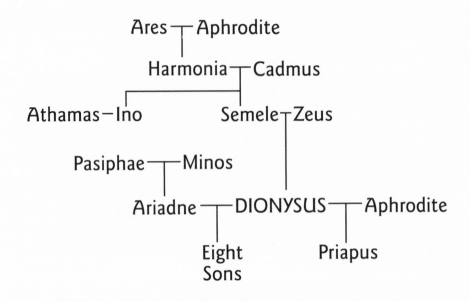

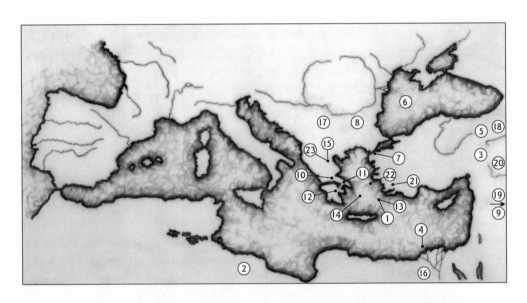

1. Icaria 2. Libya 3. Syria 4. Pharos 5. Phrygia 6. Black Sea 7. Hellespont
8. Thrace 9. to India 10. Delphi 11. Thebes 12. Argos 13. Icaria 14. Naxos
15. Mt. Olympus 16. Egypt 17. Macedonia 18. Euphrates River 19. Ganges River
20. Tigris River 21. Ephesus 22. Samos 23. Mt. Olympus

never developed skill with a sword or a macho demeanor, his enthusiastic temperament and accuracy with bull-roarer and thyrsus—the draped fennel stalk or pine scepter that came to symbolize Dionysus, the phallus, and the sexual excesses of his worshippers—suited the persona of an orgiastic wine god. He wed Ariadne, the Cretan princess who was jilted by Theseus. Their children included eight sons: Latromis, Thoas, Phanus, Oenopion, Peparethus, Euanthes, Tauropolus, and Staphylus. Dionysus and Aphrodite are named as parents of Priapus, the fertility god endowed with a grotesquely swollen phallus. Dionysus also sired Dejaneira by Althaea, Phlias by Araethyrea, Ceisus by Araethyrea, Carmanor by Alexirrhoe, Medus by Alphesiboea, Telete by Nicaea, the river goddess, and Narcaeus or Arcaeus, a faithful worshipper, by Physcoa.

Journey Following his discovery of the power of the vine, Dionysus, one of mythology's wide-ranging characters, fell victim to Hera, who set him blathering about Syria and Pharos, an island north of the Egyptian delta. By supporting the Libyan Amazons, he helped defeat the Titans and restore Ammon to the throne. He traveled to Phrygia, east of Troy, took refuge in Cybele's cult, and surrounded himself with exulting Satyrs, Bassarids, and Bacchantes. Completely rehabilitated from his mental breakdown, he and his entourage, copulating and reveling into the night, emerged from the Black Sea area near the Hellespont. The *Homeric Hymn* describes him as

> the son of glorious Semele, how he appeared on a
> jutting headland by the shore of the fruitless sea,
> seeming like stripling in the first flush of manhood:
> his rich, dark hair was waving about him, and on his
> strong shoulders he wore a purple robe.

As the youth crossed into Thrace, King Lycurgus arrested his followers and drove him into the sea. Zeus avenged his son by causing Lycurgus to slice at his own leg and his son Dryas's limbs as though he were pruning a vine.

Armed with mystical powers, Dionysus retraced his steps into Asia and, with his hosts, journeyed to India and overcame the inhabitants, who danced free of their inhibitions and merged with the god. So joyous was his train that its members—Satyrs, the flute-playing Pan, the god of pastures, votaries, Maenads shaking tambourines, Sileni, Bacchantes, disheveled Lydian women banging cymbals, and his son, Priapus, the god of carnality—preceded his chariot, woven with ivy and grape vines and pulled by a matched pair of panthers. The vanguard led Dionysus back to Europe to Boeotia, where he honored Semele, and on to Delphi, where Apollo allowed his cult to fling themselves at Dionysus in unbridled adoration.

Dionysus's most profitable foray was to Thebes. He marched northwest from Mount Cithaeron, lured ecstatic women into his service, and enchanted local citizens to march along into the wild. Among them were the prophet Teiresias and Dionysus's grandfather, Cadmus, both decked in ritual costume. Shocked by troops of Bacchantes draped in serpents, which they fed on breast milk, and beset by complaining husbands and fathers, King Pentheus halted the mad entourage. To prove his divinity and justify the celebration, Dionysus summoned wine, milk, honey, and water from bare rock. Pentheus rejected these miracles as evidence of Dionysus's powers and cast him into prison, preparing to have him decapitated. Dionysus retaliated by bursting his shackles and calling down Zeus's lightning to set fire to the royal halls.

The wild entourage, draped in linen hoods, fawn skins, and snoods, moved on its way toward the River Asopus and Mount Cithaeron, carrying off infants and holding live coals in their hands on the way. As King Pentheus perched in the top of a pine to glimpse the frenzied females at their titillating rites, Dionysus set them on him. Led by the king's mother, Agave, they ripped the tree from its roots, tore Pentheus apart, and strewed his fragmented body about the meadow. The bedazzled queen mother speared her son's head on a thyrsus.

In Argos, Dionysus struck madness into the three daughters of Proetus, who remained cold to his worship. The trio, known as the Proetides, ran crazily about the Peloponnesus until Iphinoe collapsed and died and the remaining pair, Lysippe and Iphianassa, drank purifying herbs sprinkled on spring water. To punish the Argive women's impiety, Dionysus forced them to kill and eat their infants. A parallel incident at Orchomenus in Arcadia involved Minyas's daughters, Arsippe, Leucippe, and Alcithoe, who declined to join the god's Maenads. In the changing form of lion, panther, and bull, he menaced them into a frenzy. The women sacrificed Hippasus, Leucippe's son, ate his flesh, and metamorphosed into birds or bats.

Dionysus's juggernaut frolicked on toward a band of Tyrrhenian pirates, who ferried them southwest from Icaria toward the island of Naxos. Once the group boarded the vessel, the pirates attempted to overpower them, sexually abuse them, and force them into slavery in an Asian port. According to the *Homeric Hymn,* the one dissenter, the pilot Acoetes, cried:

> Madmen! what god is this whom you have taken and bound,
> strong that he is? Not even the well-built ship can
> carry him. Surely this is either Zeus or Apollo who has
> the silver bow, or Poseidon, for he looks not like mortal men but
> like the gods who dwell on Olympus.

 As the helmsman prophesied, Dionysus performed one of his most exotic miracles—he caused the oars to become snakes and the masts to twist into a network of vines. A lion roved the deck and devoured the pirate leader. Other beasts created a Noah's ark out of the pirate boat. Amid the playing of unseen flutes and the draping of ivy, the pirates—except for the pilot—lost their senses and leaped into the sea, where they were changed into benevolent dolphins and later became constellations as warnings to pirates still on earth.

When Dionysus's worship was widely accepted along the eastern Mediterranean, he withdrew to Mount Olympus in northeastern Greece to sit in the chair vacated by Hestia and join Ganymede in pouring nectar into the gods' cups. Euripides, like John the Baptist presaging Christ, marked the event with his *Bacchantes,* in which an invocation asks:

> Who is abroad, who is abroad? Who is within? Let him withdraw, let each man keep his lips hallowed in silence; for I am about to sing to Dionysus the hymns that were ever customary. Blessed is he who, having the good fortune to know the secret mysteries of the gods, consecrates his life and hath his soul filled with the spirit.

Introduced to Corinth and Sicyon between 625 B.C. and 585 B.C., the new god took his place on the completed Parthenon in 432 B.C.

Since both Hephaestus and Dionysus had reason to hate Hera, they teamed up early in Dionysus's residency among the divine. Among his earliest acts as a deity was the deifiction of his foster parents as Palaemon and Leucothea. Having learned the way into Hades, Dionysus dived into a hellmouth at Lerna on the Bay of Argos to visit Semele in the Underworld. There he turned her into her old self, escorted her north to Mount Olympus, and renamed her Thyone. In exchange for his mother, the god traded Hades the myrtle vine, which became part of the ritual decoration of Bacchantes.

Warlike as well as majestic, Dionysus led forces into Egypt. While wandering the desert, he made a ram appear to mark the spot of a spring. To commemorate the life-giving water that bubbled forth, he cast the ram into the stars as the constellation Aries. In the Olympian war on the Titans, Hephaestus accompanied Dionysus, who, with one blow of the thyrsus, slew the giant Eurytus. Pursued by the monster Typhoeus, Dionysus disguised himself as a goat and hid in Egypt until Zeus could rescue him.

Dionysus's itinerary carried him north into Macedonia and east over the River Euphrates and the far Ganges as well. As he approached the Euphrates, he met an adamant king of Damascus, whom he skinned. In triumph, Dionysus lay down a natural bridge woven of vines and ivy and crossed the Tigris River, named for the tiger on which he rode. While visiting Midas in Phrygia, it was Dionysus who told the doomed king how to rid himself of the golden touch.

The journey back to Olympus put Dionysus in the way of the Libyan Amazons, whom he dispersed to Artemis's temple at Ephesus on the Lydian coast. By sea, he caught up with the rear guard of his entourage, fleeing west to the island of Samos off the Lydian shore. The result of their all-out battle was a blood-soaked field later named Panhaema or "full-bloodied." Pausanias remarks that Dionysus lost some of

his Indian elephants at Phloeum, where they rotted in the sun and left huge skeletons as a landmark.

On his way home to Olympus, Dionysus saw Ariadne, whom Theseus had cast aside on the island of Naxos in the southern Aegean. He consoled her and placed a crown on her head so that she and her *corona borealis,* or bride's tiara, a gold chaplet set with red rosettes, could rise into the heavens as a constellation. Dionysus was destroyed by Titans, but Athena, like Isis, reclaimed his vital organs and fed them to Zeus, the father who gave him life.

Alternate Versions

Among the places claiming Dionysus's birth are Naxos, Icarus, Mount Nysa in India, Thrace, and Libya. Dionysus's parents are also listed as Zeus and Persephone, and Ammon and Amaltheia. From the former union, Dionysus was born under the name Diounsis or Zagreus. Amaltheia is said to have been led by Hermes to safety on the island of Nysa in India (or Thrace or Africa) to keep her out of sight of Ammon's wife, Rhea. While thus hidden and nurtured by either Ino, Euboea, or a dozen other names suggested as his foster mother, Dionysus was free to study vine cultivation. Under Silenos's tutelage, he learned to chew ivy as a mild intoxicant and bestower of immortality, which inspired him to form a company of worshippers and return in triumph to Europe.

Pausanias restructured this land-based idyll with a marine version, in which Cadmus ejected Semele and her infant from Thebes, locked them in a chest, and cast them in the Mediterranean Sea. Washed ashore at Brasiae or Prasiae in Laconia on Greece's southern tip, Semele did not survive the voyage, but Dionysus was rescued by his aunt, Ino, and sheltered in a cave by the sea. Nursed by the Dodonidae or Hyades, Dionysus later showed his gratitude in his characteristic fashion—by enshrining them as stars in the heavens.

Aristophanes's comic retelling of Dionysus's visit to the Underworld has him stopping by Herakles's house on his way to the entrance to Hades. Accompanied by his servant Xanthias, Dionysus caused him to appear before the three judges of the Underworld as Herakles, the thief of Hades's dog, three-headed Cerberus. When a sideline competition arose between Aeschylus and Euripides as to who deserved the place of honor beside Hades's throne, the god of the Underworld chose Dionysus to judge the disagreement. He at first could not decide which deserved selection. Hoisting a scale, he eventually selected Aeschylus, who returned to earth with the gift of peace.

Symbolism

The god of blood, wine, sap, and semen, Dionysus—whom Ovid called the "twice-born" and others named "child of the two doors," "son of Lethe," Lenaeus or "wine-presser," Bromios or "thunderer," Dendrites meaning "tree-man," and Lyaeus or "liberator"—reflects numerous orgiastic cults nurtured along the east end of the Mediterranean rather than in the less-sybaritic Greek theology.

Following the route of the grape from the southern Black Sea to Palestine, Libya, Crete, and India, Dionysus found a grateful populace for his gift of fermented juice. His deification, which influenced the philosophy of Friedrich Nietzsche, involved processions through the wild in honor of the earth's regenerative powers, as symbolized by the pruning of the vine, which stirs to life each spring with vigorous new growth. Thus evolved the adjectives *dionysian* and *bacchanalian,* epitomizing the most decadent forms of indulgence.

Depicted in art either decked with ivy and crowned with vines or naked, Dionysus is borne aloft on the shoulder of Silenos or Pan. Sacred to the god were grapes, ivy, laurel, asphodel, figs, yew, and fir trees and numerous animals, particularly the lynx, panther, tiger, ass, dolphin, and magpie, whose loose chatter mimicked the babbling of Bacchantes. The processional figure of Dionysus is often pictured in a chariot pulled by tigers or other ravenous beasts, whose yoking symbolizes tenuous control over deadly powers that threaten to break free. Unlike more sedate deities, Dionysus provoked his followers to extremes of ribaldry, drunkenness, and sexuality, and rewarded them with visions of goats and bulls. The power of these festivals caused the death of Orpheus, who interrupted a gathering in Thrace and was torn to bits by raging celebrants. Dionysus punished the indiscriminate Bacchantes by turning them into oaks.

A resurrected god linked with Osiris (from whom he may have originated), and compared to Christ, Dionysus symbolized a paradoxical divergence of youth and depravity, as well as law, healing, prophecy, and the spread of peace and civilization. Around 700 B.C., he served as the impetus to theater, which offered the Greeks a cathartic form of worship and a sanctioned emotional release. Venerated in the four annual festivals, his rituals coincided with the December festival of the Vintage or Rural Dionysia, the February festival of the Winepress or Lenaea, a March festival of Tasting or Anthesteria, and the most spirited festival, the City Dionysia, held in April.

In worship of Dionysus, inebriates dressed in goat skins and danced with leather phalluses tied to their waists as an encouragement to sexual potency and fecundity. Their capers presaged the arrival of the god, who rode on a gilded float strung with vines, reminiscent of Dionysus's arrival from the shore. Hymns to carnality and fertility preceded prayers for a full harvest, healthy children, and governmental stability. Celebrants bought almond and honey cakes, chestnuts, chickpeas, broadbeans, and flat bread and sipped wine.

After orgiastic debauchery, worshippers settled down to serious concerns by watching the early chorus, composed of fifty male dancers, process into a circle or orchestra, reminiscent of early threshing floors. Their songs warned celebrants that harvest must be preceded by pruning, just as future generations follow the deceased who came before them. These melancholy ceremonies, similar to Lenten festivals and the Christian Maundy Thursday, balanced the more joyous celebrations, which compare to the Caribbean Carnaval, Brazilian Carnival, or New Orleans' Mardi Gras.

Over time, Dionysian dithyrambs or hymns acquired an antiphonal arrangement, with the leader addressing recitatives to the chorus and awaiting their chanted response. By 534 B.C., Thespis had evolved these antiphonies into staged actions, with characters playing the roles of noteworthy characters in mythology. From this neophyte dramatic form came the first plays of Aeschylus in 499 B.C. and the glory of Greece's golden age, which influenced theater throughout the Western world.

Pericles and the Athenians built a theater to Dionysus in 435 B.C., which grew into a megastage with seating for 17,000 people. From this model, adorned with statues of playwrights Aeschylus and Menander, architects around the Mediterranean created theaters in dug-out hillsides to enhance acoustics. The front row traditionally belonged to dignitaries and Dionysus's priests. Actors attained such importance that guild membership exempted them from military service.

The Romans, too, found much use for Dionysus's example. Virgil recast the story of Dionysus in Book 7 of Virgil's *Aeneid,* in which Amata, the Latin queen, led the women of Latium in a Dionysian orgy. In Virgil's *Georgics,* the poet encouraged husbandry by

> giving Bacchus due honor in ancestral hymns, and bearing
> cakes and platters, and led by the horn, the victim goat
> shall stand by the altar, and the fat flesh roast on
> spits of hazelwood.

This rich bounty, Virgil stressed, supplants the warlike urge to kill and waste, the antithesis of Dionysus's worship.

An attempt to halt the bacchanalia by official decree in 186 B.C. is recorded in Livy's *History.* By the time Rome's empire was thoroughly established, Dionysiac cults drifted about Italy, despite the Roman Senate's efforts to search out hidden cells and quell them. The excesses of Dionysian fanaticism, offset by the more sedate worship of Demeter or Ceres, the goddess of grain, suited the confluence of imperial debauchery, which by then had weakened Rome through the decadent and immoral excesses of the imperial family and their sycophants.

Tibullus concurred with Virgil by pairing Ceres and Dionysus, whom Virgil referred to as Bacchus, in Book 2 of his *Elegies,* which urges rest at the rural festival. As the plowman stops his furrow and the spinster guides no more yarn through the spindle, all come to Bacchus's altar to worship:

> Ah, wretched they upon whom our god bears mightily; and
> happy is he on whom Love in his graciousness breathes
> gently. Come to our festal cheer, holy lord ... Let each
> one call him for the herd aloud, but in a whisper for
> himself.

Thus refined in the Roman version, Dionysus epitomizes the reason for human thanksgiving. Worshippers, spreading their noontide meal on the grass, bear little

resemblance to the more abandoned worship of Greece, when Dionysus identified strongly with wine and less with nourishment.

The bearded Dionysus, usually designated with his Roman name, is common in artistic works, either robed or naked with upraised bowl or drinking horn and either grape basket or winnowing fan in his other arm and clustered about by sybaritic Satyrs and ecstatic women. Among the most notable depictions are a sixth century B.C. cup painted by the Athenian Exekias with Dionysus on the pirates' ship with mast sprouting vines and waters surrounded by seven dolphins, a fourth century B.C. statue by Scopas, a subdued mosaic in Antioch, Turkey, the Elgin Marbles in the British Museum, a second century B.C. mosaic of the god astride a panther, and clouded by mystical secrecy in Pompeii, Italy, on the Villa dei Mistri's frieze. In later times, Dionysus's myth continued to influence artistry, as with Christian sarcophagi near Arles, France, representing the resurrected god, the silver dish of Mildenhall from the fourth century A.D., Titian's painting, *Bacchus and Ariadne,* which features the god in his chariot pulled by panthers, Tintoretto's *Marriage of Bacchus and Ariadne,* Correggio's, Nicholas Poussin's, and Diego Velazquez's versions of *Bacchus,* Piero di Cosimo's *The Discovery of Honey* and *The Discovery of Wine,* Pablo Picasso's *Bacchanal,* a cover for *Punch* magazine, and two magnificent statues: Auguste Rodin's *Bacchante* and Michelangelo's earliest work, *Bacchus,* which he decked in the traditional style and carved with wild eyes and abandoned gesture. References were made to Dionysus in the following literary works: Geoffrey Chaucer's *Parliament of Fowls;* John Skelton's *Garland of Laurel;* Edmund Spenser's *Epithalamium, The Shepherd's Calendar, Tears of the Muses,* and *Faerie Queene;* Michael Drayton's *Elinor Cobham to Duke Humphrey;* Giles Fletcher's *Christ's Victory on Earth;* Phineas Fletcher's *Purple Island;* Abraham Cowley's *Elegy on Anacreon;* William Diaper's *Dryades;* George Crabbe's *The Borough;* Christopher Marlowe's *Jew of Malta* and *Hero and Leander;* William Shakespeare's *Love's Labours Lost* and *Midsummer Night's Dream;* Ben Jonson's *And Must I Sing* and *Dedication of the King's New Cellar;* Edward Young's *Night Thoughts;* Thomas Carew's *To My Friend G. N.;* William Shenstone's *The Judgment of Hercules;* Robert Herrick's *The Vine* and *Hymn to Bacchus;* Jonathan Swift's *Vanbrugh's House;* Thomas Hood's *Progress of Art;* John Milton's *Comus, Paradise Lost,* and *L'Allegro;* Alexander Pope's *Ode for Musick;* William Cowper's *On the Death of Mrs. Throckmorton's Bullfinch* and *Truth;* Lord Byron's *Don Juan;* Percy Shelley's *Adonais, Lines Written During the Castlereagh Administration, Ode to Liberty,* and *Prometheus Unbound;* John Keats's *Otho the Great, Sleep and Poetry, Lamia, Endymion,* and *Ode to a Nightingale;* William Wordsworth's *Ecclesiastical Sonnets* and *River Duddon;* William Blake's *The Mental Traveller;* Winthrop Praed's *Modern Nectar;* Robert Browning's *Apollo and the Fates* and *Balaustion's Adventure;* Elizabeth Barrett Browning's *The Dead Pan* and *Wine of Cyprus;* Alfred Lord Tennyson's *Pierced Through with Knotted Thorns, Semele,* and *The Coach of Death;* Alfred Noyes's *The Burning Boughs;* Matthew Arnold's *Bacchanalia* and *The Strayed Reveller;* Ralph Waldo Emerson's *Bacchus;* Algernon Swinburne's *Atalanta in Calydon;* William Butler Yeats's *Two Songs from a Play;* Hillaire Belloc's *In*

Praise of Wine; D. H. Lawrence's *Medlars and Sorbapples, They Say the Sea Is Loveless, Late at Night,* and *Middle of the World;* Walter F. Otto's *Dionysus: Myth and Cult;* Robert Graves's *The Ambrosia of Dionysus;* Ellen Hooper's *To Ralph Waldo Emerson;* and Wallace Gould's *Drunken Heracles.*

❦ See Also

Arion, Herakles, Orpheus, Theseus.

❦ Ancient Sources

Aelian's *Varia Historia;* Aeschylus's *Edonians* and *Orphic Hymns;* Alcaeus's *Hymn to Dionysus;* Antoninus Liberalis's *Metamorphoses;* Apollodorus's *Epitome* and *Library;* Apollonius of Rhodes's *Argonautica;* Arian's *Indica;* Aristophanes's *Frogs;* Aristotle's *Poetics;* Athenaeus's *The Learned Banquet;* Bacchylides's *Dithyrambs;* Catullus's *Poems to Lesbia;* Cicero's *On the Nature of Gods;* Clement of Alexandria's *Address to the Greeks;* Conon's *Narrations;* Diodorus Siculus's *Orphic Hymn;* Eratosthenes's *Star Placements;* Euripides's *Bacchants* and *Oineus;* Eustathius on Homer's *Iliad;* Hesiod's *Theogony;* Hesychius's *Antheia, Bassarai,* and *Lenai;* Homer's *Hymn to Dionysus, Iliad,* and *Odyssey;* Horace's *Carmina,* Hyginus's *Fables* and *Poetic Astronomy;* Livy's *From the Foundations of the City;* Lycophron's *Alexandra;* Megasthenes's *Indica;* Nonnus's *Dionysiaca;* Onomacritus's *Orphica;* Ovid's *Fasti* and *Metamorphoses;* Pausanias's *Description of Greece;* Philostratus's *Life of Apollonius of Tyana;* Pindar's *Pythian Odes;* Plato's *Phaedo;* Plutarch's *De E apud Delphos, Greek Questions, On Rivers,* and *Table Talk;* Scholiast on Apollonius of Rhodes's *Argonautica;* Scholiast on Persius's *Saturae;* Scholiast on Pindar's *Olympian Odes;* Scholiast on Theocritus's *Idylls;* Servius on Virgil's *Eclogues;* Sophocles's *Oedipus Rex;* Stephanus Byzantium's *Brisa;* Strabo's *Historical Sketches;* Theocritus's *Idylls;* Theon on Aratus's *Phenomena;* Theophilus's *Poems;* Thucydides's *History;* Tibullus's *Elegies;* Virgil's *Aeneid, Eclogues,* and *Georgics.*

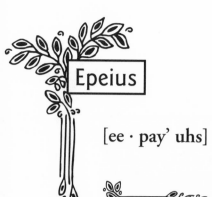

Epeius

[ee · pay' uhs]

Genealogy and Background

Epeius, son of Panopeus or Phanoteus from Parnassus and of Asteria or Asterdoeia, sprang from an illustrious family and carried a name meaning "successor." His sister Aegle, who may have been one of the maidens chosen to be fed to the Minotaur, deserves fame for luring Theseus away from Ariadne on the island of Naxos. In contrast to Epeius's sister's notoriety, because Panopeus reneged on his promise to Athena not to steal after the Amphytrion defeated the Taphians, Epeius bore the brunt of his father's foolishness. Afterward Epeius, an effeminate boy, was dogged by the undeserved epithets of coward and sissy.

After leading thirty Phocian ships from the Cyclades to the Trojan War, Epeius served in a minor post as water carrier for Agamemnon and Menelaus. Athena took pity on his lowly station and placed in his mind the kernel of a plan to build the Trojan Horse, a feat that earned Epeius everlasting honor as a craftsman. The grandson of Phocus and Asteria, Epeius had an uncle Crisus, a twin and mortal enemy of Panopeus. Epeius was the cousin of Strophades and second cousin of Pylades, Orestes's companion during the wretched era of blood-letting that marked the murder of Orestes's parents, Agamemnon and Clytemnestra.

Journey

Epeius, who was a sculptor and artist by trade, earned no honors for battlefield heroics, but was better known among his peers as a racer and a boxer. In Book 23 of Homer's *Iliad*, during the funeral games honoring Patroclus, Epeius addressed other contenders for a hard-working mule:

> Let the man come up that will carry off the two-handled goblet. I say no other of the Achaians will beat me at boxing and lead off the jenny. I claim I am the champion.

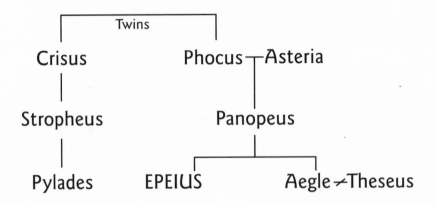

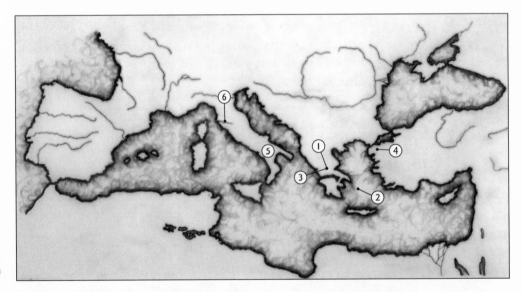

1. Mt. Parnassus 2. Naxos 3. Mt. Parnassus 4. Troy 5. Southern Italy 6. Pisa

Admitting that he fared poorly in combat, Epeius reminded his comrades that no man possesses all skills. As the fight began, Epeius raised his fists and snarled at Euryalus, his adversary:

> Let those who care for him wait nearby in a huddle about him to carry him out after my fists have beaten him under. I will smash his skin apart and break his bones on each other.

Epeius proved his proud, disdainful words by grounding Euryalus with severe injuries to his cheek, producing dizziness, weak legs, and blood from the mouth. As Homer describes the scene, "the great-hearted Epeius" reaches out and catches Euryalus in his arms and returns him to his feet. But the words came back to unseat Epeius in the sixth event, the tossing match. Achilles, master of ceremonies for the events, provides a valuable lump of pig iron as both projectile and prize, hurling it in a fashion more similar to the graceful twirl accompanying the Olympic discus throw than the awkward heft accompanying the tossing of the Scottish caber. Against Epeius stand Polypoites, Leonteus, and Ajax the Great, ranked Greece's strongest warriors. First to compete, Epeius steps to the mark, whirls and throws. According to Homer, his aim was so poor that the Greeks laughed at him.

As emphasized in Book 8 of Homer's *Odyssey*, Epeius's carpentry skills outweighed his athleticism. While constructing the horse that would end the ten-year war, Epeius called on Athena to supervise the job, which Homer describes as "an ambuscade, manned by the warriors who then sacked the town." Epeius used fir planking to make the hollow image, cut a trap door in the side, and, according to Homer's *Odyssey*, dedicated the horse with this inscription: "In thankful anticipation of a safe return to their homes, the Greeks dedicate this offering to the Goddess." So certain was Epeius that Odysseus's ruse would work that he volunteered for the assault party. As depicted in Virgil's *Aeneid*, on the night that the Greek forces entered Troy, Epeius—coward or not—was one of the handpicked squad hiding in the belly of the wooden horse.

Rightfully, Epeius, the most knowledgeable about the device, took the last seat by the trap door and manipulated the complicated lock. The ingenious breach of Trojan walls succeeded after Priam proclaimed it a gift to Athena and had a crew pull it to the ramparts on rollers and wedge it through the main gate, a feat that required four tries. The priest Laocoon declared it dangerous: to his dismay, twin serpents from the sea wrapped him and his sons in their coils and throttled him. Suspecting no harm, Trojan women decked the wooden image with flowers and sprinkled petals in its path. The most fearful of the Greeks inside, Epeius earned his reputation for cowardice by quaking and crying in terror of being found out. According to Virgil's retelling in Book 2 of the *Aeneid*, at the signal from Antenor, Epeius joined the others in shinnying down the rope and burning and ravaging the doomed city. In later years,

Odysseus, belittled Epeius's role by claiming the lion's share of credit for the horse, which swiftly concluded a ten-year war.

At the end of the war, Epeius set out for home, but lost his way. He arrived in southern Italy, where he enshrined his carpentry tools in Athena's temple to honor her assistance in planning and constructing the Trojan horse. He is credited with migrating up the western coast of Italy and founding Pisa on the Arno River.

Alternate Versions

A minor side episode in Epeius's lore describes his creating a statue of Hermes, messenger of the gods. When the river Scamander rose up to quell Achilles, floodwaters carried away the statue. It turned up at Ainos, where it caught in fishing nets. The locals disliked the image and tried to hack it into kindling. Except for a meager slice on one shoulder, the statue remained unharmed. The fishers, intent on completing the destruction of the statue, tossed it into a fire, but the wood refused to burn. Exasperated by the unusually tough image, they threw it back into the ocean. When the statue again washed up in Ainos, the finders realized that the image was a message from Hermes. They installed the statue in a beachside shrine.

Symbolism

In art, Epeius is immortalized as a water-bearer on Apollo's temple walls at Carthaea on the island of Ceos. In epic literature, he epitomizes the hard lot of men who excel at fine arts but do poorly in the manly or athletic arts, as demonstrated by the lot of Paris, whom Homer degraded as a skilled dancer and stylized perfumed womanizer, but who was, ironically, the bowman who killed Achilles. The myth also weighs the dilemma of Ajax the Great, who like Epeius, had body and mind out of balance, with brawn outdistancing brain.

Epeius's stylized horse—which theorists have linked with siege machinery covered with horse hides—has remained a constant in mythic imagery and has permeated mosaic, painting, frieze art, opera, dance, verse, movies, book illustrations, and advertising. In literature, Epeius appears in John Masefield's *The Horse* and Christopher Marlowe's *Dido, Queen of Carthage*. Giovanni Battista Tiepolo's eighteenth-century canvas pictures Epeius leading his workers in the final sculpting of the Trojan Horse, which is still anchored with scaffolding. A comic version appears in *Monty Python and the Holy Grail*, a British spoof that turns the wooden horse into an ungainly rabbit that, having been taken inside the fortress walls, is catapulted back over the ramparts to land on the beseiging force.

🌿 See Also
Odysseus.

🌿 Ancient Sources
Apollodorus's *Epitome;* Athenaeus's *The Learned Banquet;* Callimachus's *Iambi;* Cicero's *Tuscan Debates;* Dictys Cretensis's *Trojan War Diary;* Euripides's *Trojan Women;* Eustathius on Homer's *Iliad;* Hesychius's *Epeius;* Homer's *Iliad* and *Odyssey;* Hyginus's *Fables;* Pausanias's *Description of Greece;* Plato's *Ion;* Scholiast on Theocritus's *Idylls;* Stesichorus's *Iliu Persis;* Johannes Tzetzes's *On Lycophron.*

Helen

[heh' lihn]

Genealogy and Background

One of two sets of twins born of Zeus's rape of Leda, Helen was an immortal endowed with tantalizingly fair skin, dancing tresses, and superhuman features. Like her twin brothers Castor and Pollux, Helen shared a single periwinkle blue egg with Clytemnestra. Paternity, as often occurred in mythology, was shared with Leda's husband, King Tyndareus of Aetolia. After Theseus abducted the pubescent Helen to Aphidna outside Athens, she may have borne Iphigenia and given her to Clytemnestra to raise.

As Helen grew to adolescence, her surpassing loveliness and wealth were fabled about the Mediterranean, luring Agapenor, Ajax the Great, Ajax the Lesser, Amphimachus, Antilochus, Ascalaphus, Diomedes, Elephenor, Enarephorus, Epistrophus, Eumelus, Eurypylus, Ialmenus, Idomeneus, Leitus, Leonteus, Meges, Menelaus, Menestheus, Odysseus, Patroclus, Peneleus, Phemius, Philoctetes, Podaleirius, Podarces, Polypoetes, Polyxenus, Protesilaus, Schedius, Sthenelus, Teucer, and Thalpius. Because these youths clamored for the glamorous Princess Helen, the king feared that he would initiate a civil war if he chose one over the others. On Odysseus's advice, Tyndareus forced the suitors to mount a ritually dismembered horse and swear to protect Helen. Of her own accord, Helen placed a symbolic wreath on the Laconian Menelaus, her choice, who immediately succeeded Tyndareus and crowned Helen his queen. She resided in the palace in Sparta with Menelaus. As wife to the Laconian king, Helen bore a daughter, Hermione, and three sons: Maraphius, Aethiolas, and Pleisthenes.

Journey

No journey compares with the voyage that carried Helen from Greece to Troy and back again. At the time that Paris, Troy's reclaimed prince, visited Sparta, Menelaus was called to attend the funeral games of his maternal grandfather, Catreus, king

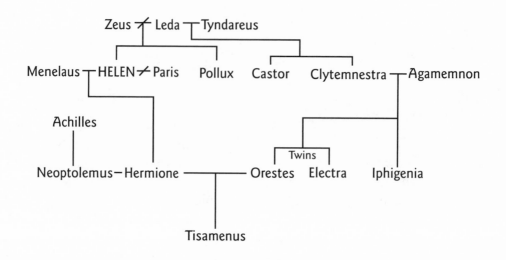

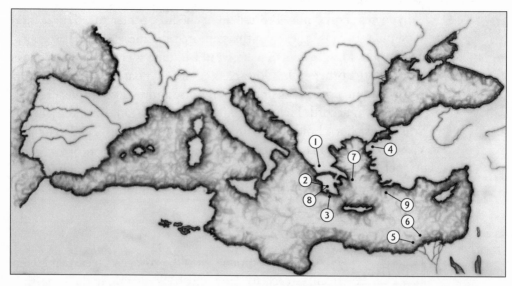

1. Aetolia 2. Sparta 3. Cranae 4. Troy 5. Canope 6. Pharos 7. Helena 8. Sparta
9. Rhodes

of Crete, leaving Helen to entertain their guest. The question of Helen's complicity in the notorious abduction from Sparta remains moot. Whatever the circumstance—adultery, violated guest code, or Olympian conspiracy—she became Paris's reward for selecting Aphrodite the most beautiful of the goddesses in an Olympian beauty contest and he lured Helen away from Sparta to Troy.

Upon the couple's departure to the eastern Mediterranean kingdom of Troy, Helen, sometimes described as self-absorbed and larcenous, looted Sparta's treasury and took along her pick of slaves. According to Pausanias, the couple consummated their union on Cranae, a tiny island in the Laconian Gulf; Lycophron accorded this honor to Salamis, an island off the western shore of Attica.

Driven by a storm east to Sidon on Phoenicia's coast and later southwest to the mouth of the Nile in Egypt and to Cyprus, the pair felt the wrath of Hera, goddess of matrimony, who disapproved of their union. Helen and Paris finally arrived in Troy, where great-hearted Hecuba and Priam accepted them among their huge family of fifty sons, fifty daughters, and scores of sons-in-law, daughters-in-law, and grandchildren.

Helen bore three sons with Paris—Bunomus, Aganus, and Idaeus—and a daughter, who stirred her parents to controversy. Helen wanted to call the infant Helena; Paris chose Alexandra, a version of his other name, Alexander. The couple decided to throw the dice to settle the question. Helen won the toss and named the girl after herself.

Many ambassadors sought Helen's return, but the Trojans, enamored of their prince's wife, rejected Odysseus, Acamas, Diomedes, and even Menelaus, her wronged husband. In keeping with the pledge they swore Tyndareus, Helen's former suitors formed the world's most famous body of crusaders bound for the Troad to bring Helen home.

When war brought suffering to the Trojan nation, their love changed to hatred toward Helen, who became the scapegoat. Although Homer in Book 3 of the *Iliad* describes her standing on the battlements and identifying for Priam the Greek leaders who once sued for her hand, Helen still bore a double label: a dangerous turncoat whom neither side could trust with a terrible likeness to divine beauty, deadly enough to cause Troy's destruction. During the war, after Paris was killed by an arrow wound, Helen was forced to wed his brother Deiphobus, who beat out the envious Helenus and Idomeneus.

Helen's conduct at Troy was exemplary in most respects. She endeared herself to Priam and was surrounded with luxury and a staff of serving women. As Homer describes her in Book 24 of the *Iliad*, she took her place among the mourning women who honored Hector and, because of his courtesy, genuinely regretted his loss:

> In this time I have never heard a harsh saying from you, nor an insult. Now, but when another, one of my lord's brothers or sisters, a fair-robed wife of some brother, would say a harsh word to me in the

> palace ... then you would speak and put them off and restrain them by your own gentleness of heart and your gentle words.

Helen, somewhat melodramatic at this moment, concluded that she mourned both Hector and her ill fortune on the Troad, where "all other[s] shrank when they saw me."

A minor legend notes that Achilles saw her standing on the lofty towers and fell so completely in love that he risked punishment for treachery in exchange for a single tryst. A parallel to this tale tells how Odysseus obscured his identity in beggar's rags and entered Troy's front gate. Helen recognized him, but did not sound the alarm. On a second foray by Odysseus, Helen aided him in stealing Troy's treasured icon, the Palladium. She also agreed to signal the Greek fleet, which appeared to sail away, but merely hid behind the island of Tenedos. Standing on the highest point, she lighted a torch to set in motion the fiery capture of the city. During the fall of Troy in a disastrous fire and night assault, Helen's Trojan sons died when a palace roof caved in; Hecuba murdered the baby Helen to rid the world of another dangerous beauty.

Virgil added his bit to Helen's lore by describing Aeneas's encounter with her as he departed the city. As flames devoured the city walls and the fierce Neoptolemus, Achilles's son, strode through the wreckage killing any Trojan within reach of his sword, Helen cowered alongside Vesta's altar, unsure whether safety lay with the conquerors or the conquered. Aeneas spied her there and raised his hand in anger against her for all she had caused his homeland. Aphrodite, his mother, stopped his hand and reminded him: "Son, why do you thirst for vengeance? ... Blame not Helen or Paris for Troy's destruction." (Virgil's *Aeneid*) As Aphrodite rationalized the cataclysm, the gods alone shouldered blame for Troy's toppling.

To prove her loyalty to her Spartan husband, Helen hid Deiphobus's weapons. With Helen's assistance, Menelaus killed her Trojan mate, then attempted to impale her on his sword to repay her earlier treachery. However, one glimpse of her loveliness as she cowered behind the statue of Aphrodite restored Helen to his heart. In Euripides's *Trojan Women*, Helen had a ready excuse for adultery: she claimed Aphrodite misguided her and vowed to her stern husband that she frequently tried to escape to the Greek side by dropping ropes over the battlements.

Hecuba, grown bitter with multiple losses, retorted that Helen was an opportunist who did whatever suited her whim. Hecuba alleged that she tried to help Helen leave Paris, but Helen could not depart so luxurious a role as Trojan princess. As Helen and Menelaus glimpsed each other for the first time since her departure for Troy, Hecuba grew angry and ordered him to slay Helen to stop her lying mouth and maim the divinely alluring face. Menelaus, mesmerized anew by her grace, was transfixed. The Greeks, less eager to acclaim the woman who had kept them in the field for a decade, raised stones and menaced her, but, like Menelaus, could not bring themselves to mar her divine beauty.

Like Aeneas and Odysseus, Helen did not enjoy an easy voyage home. Menelaus vowed to reserve judgment on her until he reached Sparta. For seven or eight years, Menelaus and Helen, possibly facing death on her reunion with the Spartans, sailed the eastern Mediterranean. At length, their ship, piloted by the faithful Canopus, was beached in Egypt. Canopus died of the sting of an adder; Helen and her husband lovingly interred him on the isle of Canope north of the Egyptian delta.

King Thon received the royal couple with solemnity, then in secret tried to rape Helen. The queen, Polydamna, recognized the king's lechery and hid Helen on the island of Pharos. To protect her from Egyptian asps, Polydamna provided a medical chest stocked with antivenin. Menelaus killed Thon and recovered his wife once more. After a brief journey to the northwest, he landed at Helena, a thin rocky islet off the southeastern shore of Attica and escorted her overland to Sparta where Helen returned to her former role of Spartan queen and bore Menelaus a fourth son, Nicostratus.

Homer again turns to Helen in Book 4 of the *Odyssey*. As Odysseus journeyed toward home, his son, Telemachus, eager for news, arrived at Menelaus's sumptuous palace on the day of a double royal wedding for Menelaus's son, Nicostratus, and daughter, Hermione. Helen, whose entourage seated her alongside a golden distaff and a wheeled silver basket, shone like Artemis and graciously extended welcome to Odysseus's handsome son, who looked like his father. She referred to herself as "shameless" because Odysseus and the other warriors who sought her at Troy wasted their manhood "upon reckless warfare."

As melancholy overwhelmed the gathering, Helen, herself moved to tears, made a potion of heartsease to brighten the court's mood. Homer pointed out that such skill in medicines was appropriate to a daughter of Zeus who had known Polydamna of Egypt, where mood-altering herbs were common. Helen's soothing words included a recounting of Odysseus's bold appearance in Troy at a time when her allegiance had reverted to Greece, where she longed to return. To account for her departure from Menelaus, Helen blamed "the madness that Aphrodite bestowed." This night of re-tellings prompted Menelaus to describe how Helen, accompanied by Deiphobus, walked three times around the Trojan Horse and called to the men in the voices of their wives until Athena pulled her away. The ambiguity of this memory does not indicate whether Helen was taunting the men for Deiphobus's benefit or summoning the Greeks in order to assist them.

In Book 15 of the *Odyssey*, Helen concluded Telemachus's visit in grand style. Menelaus gave him a two-handled drinking cup, but Helen added the romantic touch of a robe woven by her own hands, which she asked him to save for his wedding day. As Telemachus prepared for the long and dangerous journey home, Helen assumed the role of prophet and predicted correctly that he would reunite with his father and cleanse Pylos of the suitors who warred for the hand of his mother, Penelope.

The conclusion of Helen's life brought more controversy and strife. After Menelaus's death, the Spartans chose not to crown Nicostratus king and Helen was forced off the throne of Sparta by Menelaus's squabbling illegitimate sons. Following Hermione's

brief marriage to Neoptolemus, Achilles's son who died ignobly in a brawl in Delphi, she wed her cousin, Orestes, whom the Spartans chose to replace Menelaus on the throne. Their son, Tisamenus, Helen's grandson, continued the family rule in Sparta. Ostensibly safe far to the east on the island of Rhodes, Helen was hanged by servants disguised as the Erinyes or fell under the knife of Polyxo, a widow who blamed Helen for instigating the Trojan War and causing the death of Tlepolemus, Polyxo's husband. At her death, Helen was buried alongside Menelaus at Therapne outside Sparta and wandered the fields of the blessed with her husband.

Helen's spirit was said to have joined with those of her brothers, the Dioscuri, to protect Sparta from treachery, to have transformed ugly infant girls into beauties, and to have blinded the poet Stesichorus for his unflattering verses. Lucian, in *Dialogue of the Dead,* penned a poignant reminder of earthly fragility with his conversation between Hermes and the cynic, Menippus, who wanted to see examples of beauty that were preserved in the Underworld. Hermes held up Helen's skull. Menippus sneered his rhetorical question, "Was it for this then that the thousand ships were launched from all of Greece and so many Greeks and non-Greeks fell and so many cities were destroyed?" Hermes, like a patient teacher, replied that flowers must be enjoyed while they bloom.

Alternate Versions

Many non-Homeric variations of Helen's story exist. She is sometimes said to have been born to Oceanus, Aphrodite, or Nemesis, who eluded Zeus by changing into a goose, but was circumvented when the god metamorphosed into a swan. In this version, Nemesis abandoned an egg near a Spartan grove, where shepherds or Hermes carried it to Queen Leda. The swan egg or eggs are alternately described as producing Helen paired with Clytemnestra, Helen paired with Pollux, or Helen and her brothers from one egg and Clytemnestra born normally. Another possibility is that Helen and Pollux, the children of Zeus and Leda, hatched from one egg while the children of Leda and Tyndareus, their mortal step-siblings, Clytemnestra and Castor, hatched from the matching egg.

Theseus and his friend, Pirithous, are said to have seduced Helen in girlhood as she performed rites before Artemis Orthia. The pair cast dice for Helen; Theseus won and abducted her from Tyndareus's watchful eye. Taken first to Athens, then placed outside the city at Aphidna in the care of Aethra, Theseus's mother, Helen remained until her pugnacious brothers, Castor and Pollux, recovered her, but not before she bore Theseus's daughter, Iphigenia.

The Trojan episode is even more blurred with varied details. Some say that Tyndareus himself gave Helen to Paris. An alternate to Helen's abduction to Troy appears in Herodotus's *History,* Stesichorus's *Palinode,* and Euripides's *Helen,* far-fetched fantasies that describe how she traveled to Egypt with Paris and took refuge at Aphrodite's shrine. Before the prince returned to Troy, the spiteful Hera transformed Helen into a *ka* or phantasm, which he conducted on board his ship as though it were his treasured paramour. The real Helen stayed under the protection of King Proteus, whose offer of marriage she spurned until she had proof of Menelaus's fate.

By the time the war ended, Proteus had died and left Theoclymenus as his heir. Helen was rescued either by Menelaus or by her brothers, the Dioscuri. In the former scenario, depicted in Euripides's version, Helen cursed her fair face and contemplated suicide. Captive Greek women echoed her words. To end her decade of limbo, Helen sought out Theonoe, Proteus's daughter, who could divine the future possibilities of a reunion with Menelaus.

Meanwhile, Menelaus, forced south by strong winds, washed up on Egypt's shores, much like Odysseus before Nausicaa, and sought help at a temple. He learned that Helen lived nearby. Reunited by the unlikeliest of circumstances, the couple mourned bitterly that a decade of war was waged over a phantasm. They plotted to outwit Theoclymenus. First, Menelaus brought false tidings of his own death in battle. Helen, ostensibly a widow, agreed to marry the Egyptian king if he would arrange for ritual offshore offerings. When the boat pulled out of sight, she drowned Theoclymenus's menials and sped with Menelaus to Sparta. The myth concluded with an appearance of the Dioscuri, who deterred Theoclymenus from murdering their duplicitous sister and prophesied that Helen would once again reign in Sparta before attaining divinity in the Isles of the Blessed.

An even more far-fetched variation is the tale of Pharos, a privateer who offered to spirit Helen away from Troy, reunite her with Menelaus, and speed them home to Sparta. The plot was foiled by a storm, which wrecked the ship near Egypt. Pharos was cast ashore and bitten by a poisonous snake. In his honor, Helen and Menelaus named an island in the mouth of the Nile after Pharos.

The ill-fated voyage continued toward Greece. In Euripides's *Orestes,* Helen and Menelaus beached their ship at Argos at a memorable time—the day that Orestes avenged Agamemnon's death by the ritual murder of his mother Clytemnestra and her lover Aegisthus. Helen, too vain to perform the ritual self-mutilation and tonsure of the next of kin, snipped only tips of her hair to honor her twin and dispatched Hermione to perform the sacrificial offering of wine at the tomb.

Orestes was tempted to add his aunt Helen to his list of vengeful murders because he blamed her for the family's sufferings. Zeus, content with the status quo, sent Apollo to intervene. Thus, just as Orestes raised his sword, Helen was spirited away and welcomed among the immortals at the throne of Zeus alongside Hera and Hebe. As an adjunct to her brothers, the Dioscuri, she was sent as a guide to mariners. Numerous shrines honor her deification and that of Menelaus, whom she had arranged to be compensated for his life of struggle.

Alternate death scenes picture Helen suffering Iphigenia's fate—as a sacrifice alongside Menelaus in a Taurian ritual. Another version describes how Thetis murdered her by calling down a storm to requite the death of Achilles. As Helen Dendritis, or Helen of the olive groves, she, like Ariadne the weaver, is said to have died by hanging and is commemorated by charms bearing her likeness, which are suspended from fruit and olive boughs.

Symbolism

Like Guinevere of Camelot and King David's concubine, Bathsheba, Helen of Troy travels a narrow literary path between victim and unprincipled temptress. Acclaimed more for loveliness than guile or lechery, Helen was an anomaly, the heavenly child born from an eggshell, which Pausanias claims fell from the moon, an eventuality that would account for her name, which means "moon." The significance of Helen's unequaled parentage is preserved in the constellation Cycnus, "the swan."

The Spartans preserved the egg in a chest, ironically shielding the unhatched woman doomed to sever east from west in a disastrous war between Greece and Troy. So extraordinary was her fabled loveliness that old men were willing to fight for her, although the playwrights Aeschylus and Euripides immediately blamed Helen for the Trojan War. With similar vituperation, Iphigenia held Helen responsible for impeding her marriage to Achilles, and the Cyclops accused her of lusting for variety in her sexual conquests.

Possibly a goddess herself from prehistoric times, Helen is associated in early Rhodes lore with nature, the medicinal herb *Inula helenium*, and plane trees, from which she was said to have been hanged. Unlike heroes who died in the style by which they lived, residents of Himera and Crotona believed that Helen journeyed with Achilles, her abductor, to Leuce, a white isle in the Black Sea, a deathless demise suggestive of King Arthur's tenure on Avalon. Wed in a ceremony attended by the Olympians, she remained untouched by further pain and bore Achilles a winged son, Euphorion. A spa on the Saronic gulf at Cenchreae honors her with the Baths of Helen.

Helen figures either as a character or a symbol of womanly allure in many literary works, notably: Dante Alighieri's *Inferno;* Pierre de Ronsard's *Sonnets pour Hélène;* Sir Philip Sidney's *Astrophel and Stella;* Edmund Spenser's *Faerie Queene* and *Shepherd's Calendar;* Henry Surrey's *When Raging Love;* William Shakespeare's *Troilus and Cressida, As You Like It, Henry VI* (Part III), *Midsummer Night's Dream, Sonnet 53,* and *The Taming of the Shrew;* Christopher Marlowe's *Dr. Faustus* and *Tamburlaine;* Ben Jonson's *Epistle to Elizabeth;* Sir John Denham's *Friendship and Single Life;* John Dryden's *Aureng-Zebe;* John Milton's *Comus;* Alexander Pope's *To Belinda;* Thomas Gray's *Agrippina;* Robert Herrick's *His Age;* Johann Goethe's *Faust, Iphigenie,* and *Helena;* Lord Byron's *Siege of Corinth* and *Don Juan;* Elizabeth Barrett Browning's *Battle of Marathon* and *The Fourfold Aspect;* Robert Browning's *Fifine at the Fair, With Charles Avison,* and *The Ring and the Book;* Dante Gabriel Rossetti's *Troy Town;* Matthew Arnold's *Palladium* and *On Translating Homer;* Edgar Allan Poe's *To Helen;* George Seferis's *Helen;* William Butler Yeats's *Leda and the Swan, Long-Legged Fly, When Helen Lived, Prayer for My Daughter, Double Vision of Michael Robartes, A Man Young and*

Old, No Second Troy, Three Marching Songs, Rose of the World, Lullaby, and *Parnell's Funeral;* Algernon Swinburne's *Atalanta in Calydon;* Rupert Brooke's *It's Not Going to Happen Again;* D. H. Lawrence's *Body of God;* John Masefield's *A King's Daughter, Tale of Nireus,* and *Clytemnestra;* C. Day Lewis's *Transitional Poem;* Robert Graves's *New Legends* and *Judgment of Paris;* Eda Lou Walton's *Leda, the Lost;* Lizette Woodworth's *A Puritan Lady;* Walter de la Mare's *Ages Ago;* Jean Giraudoux's *The Trojan War Shall Not Take Place;* and Hilda Doolittle's *Helen in Egypt.*

Art and music, like literature, depict Helen on vase paintings, drinking cups, frescoes, bas-reliefs, coins, pedestals, such as the presentation of Helen to Nemesis carved by Agoracritus at Rhamnus outside Athens, and opera, particularly Richard Strauss and Hugo von Hofmannsthal's *Die Aegyptische Helena,* Camille Saint-Saens's *Hélène,* and Christoph Gluck's *Paride ed Elena.* Usually, Helen is identified by her basket, called a *helene,* in which she tended sacred objects pertinent to orgiastic cult worship. A panel carved in a basilica near Rome's Porta Maggiore depicts Helen with the Palladium, Troy's sacred icon, which she defiled. In contrast to such carnal and sacrilegious symbolism, Fra Angelico painted her as young and maidenly in his *Rape of Helen,* which hangs in London's National Gallery, whereas Jacques-Louis David gave her a more mature grace.

❦ See Also

Achilles, Aeneas, Agamemnon, Canopus, Cassandra, Menelaus, Odysseus, Paris, Pirithous, Theseus.

❦ Ancient Sources

Aelian's *Varia Historia;* Aeschylus's *Agamemnon;* Agias of Troezen's *Returns of Heroes;* Antoninus Liberalis's *Metamorphoses;* Apollodorus's *Epitome;* Arctinus of Miletus's *Aethiopis* and *Sack of Troy;* Athenaeus's *The Learned Banquet;* Callimachus's *Epithalamion for Helen* and *Hymn to Artemis;* Colluthus's *Rape of Helen;* Conon's *Narrations;* Cratinos's *Dionysalexandros* and *Nemesis;* Dares of Phrygia's *Trojan War;* Dictys Cretensis's *Trojan War Diary;* Eratosthenes's *Star Placements;* Eugammon's *Telegony;* Euripides's *Andromache, Electra, Helen, Iphigenia in Aulis, Orestes, Philoctetes, Rhesus,* and *Trojan Women;* Eustathius on Homer's *Iliad;* First Vatican Mythographer; Gorgias's *Encomium of Helen;* Herodotus's *History* and *Persian Wars;* Hesiod's *Catalogue of Women;* Homer's *Iliad* and *Odyssey;* Horace's *Ars Poetica;* Hyginus's *Fables* and *Poetic Astronomy;* Isocrates's *Encomium of Helen;* Lactantius's on Statius's *Thebaid;* Lesches's *Little Iliad;* Lucian's *Dialogue of the Gods* and *Dialogue of the Dead;* Lycophron's *Alexandra;* Ovid's *Fasti, Heroides, Ibis,* and *Metamorphoses;* Parthenius's *Love Stories;* Pausanias's *Description of Greece;* Philostratus's *Heroica* and *Life of Apollonius of Tyana;* Photius's *Library;* Pindar's *Nemean Odes;* Plato's *Phaedrus;* Plutarch's *Symposiacs;* Proclus's *Chrestomathy;* Ptolemy Hephaestion on Homer's *Iliad;* Quintus Smyrnaeus's

Post-Homerica; Sappho's *Fragments;* Scholiast on Euripides's *Andromache;* Scholiast on Euripides's *Iphigenia in Aulis;* Seneca's *Moral Essays;* Servius on Virgil's *Aeneid;* Sophocles's *Philoctetes;* Stasinus of Cyprus's *Cypria;* Stephanus Byzantium's *Arisbe;* Stesichorus's *Recantation;* Suidas's *Herophila;* Theocritus's *Idylls;* Tryphiodorus's *Sack of Troy;* Johannes Tzetzes's *On Lycophron;* Virgil's *Aeneid.*

Herakles

[hehr' uh · klees]

Genealogy and Background

Called Herakles by the Greeks and Hercules by the Romans, the handsome, muscular, six-foot son of Zeus by the beautiful Alcmene, claimed a notable family tree that developed into the Heraclid dynasty, a significant link between myth and history.

His mother was Perseus's granddaughter and wife of Amphitryon, her first cousin and also Perseus's grandchild, who involved himself in a military expedition to the Taphian Islands. As Amphitryon was returning to his family in Mycenae, Zeus, who, according to Hesiod in *Shield of Herakles*, "wanted to produce a son who would one day be a powerful protector for gods and men alike," changed himself into Amphitryon's likeness and won Alcmene's love by describing how he avenged the wrongful death of her brothers. The pleasure Zeus took in Alcmene's body inspired him to stretch the night over three days.

The next morning, the real husband returned to find himself cuckolded by a surprised wife, a woman of inviolable reputation who believed that she shared her bed the night before with the famous war hero. In the Roman playwright Plautus's ribald version, *Amphitryon,* the Theban general grew angry enough to threaten divorce. In the Greek mythic version, Teiresias, the blind seer and sage of the ancient world, settled Amphitryon's unjust accusations against a wife who, by remaining true to the face and form she supposed to be her husband, carried out fidelity at least in intent. The problem of Zeus's infidelities also roused Hera to anger at his boast that the son Alcmene carried would one day be a mighty ruler over Argos. Having taken a vow to oppose forever Zeus's superchild, Hera tricked Zeus by sending Eileithyia, goddess of childbirth, to hold back Alcmene's contractions so as to confer the divine promise on Sthenelus's son, Eurystheus, who controlled Mycenae and Tiryns.

Meanwhile, Alcmene, her labor delayed, lay in danger of dying until her serving woman, Galinthias, burst out in shouts that Alcmene had given birth. Eileithyia, who had been holding legs and fingers

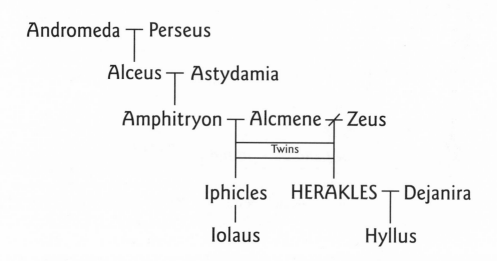

Andromeda ⊤ Perseus

Alceus ⊤ Astydamia

Amphitryon ⊤ Alcmene ⟋ Zeus

Twins

Iphicles   HERAKLES ⊤ Dejanira

Iolaus   Hyllus

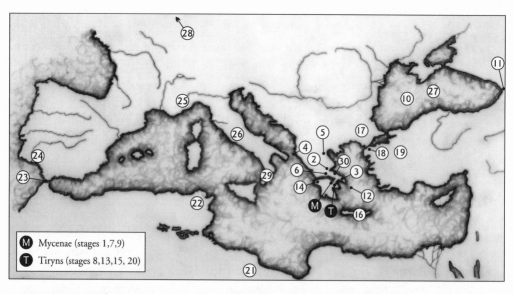

M   Mycenae (stages 1,7,9)
T   Tiryns (stages 8,13,15, 20)

1. Mycenae   2. Thespiae   3. Athens   4. Drepane, Phaeacia   5. Thessaly   6. Delphi
7. Mycenae   8. Tiryns   9. Mycenae   10. Black Sea   11. Colchis   12. Tenos   13. Tiryns
14. Elis   15. Tiryns   16. Crete   17. Thrace   18. Hellespont   19. Mysia   20. Tiryns
21. Libya   22. Numidia   23. Strait of Gibraltar   24. Eurytheia   25. Liguria
26. Tiber River   27. Black Sea   28. to England   29. Rhegiem   30. Euboea

crossed, leaped up, thus freeing Alcmene of the charm. (Eileithyia was so angry at being deceived that she turned Galinthias into a weasel.) Immediately, Alcmene bore twins, Iphicles and Herakles. She called the latter Palaemon, "the wrestler," or Alcaeus, a name suggesting "Alce" or "strength."

The threat of Hera's vengeance caused Alcmene to suckle Iphicles while rejecting Herakles, who was left to die near Thebes on the Plain of Herakles. The goddess Athena rescued the infant, carried him to Mount Olympus, and presented him to the sleeping Hera to nurse. Unknowingly, she nuzzled him to her nipple, which he bit. The milk that spurted from her breast dotted the sky, forming the Milky Way and anointed the infant, thereby assuring his immortality. The unwanted child eventually found a home with his family. Alcmene, at Athena's urging, took the boy back to raise with Iphicles.

Amphitryon confronted the problem of two sons and questionable paternity by trying to guess which son he had fathered. When the boys were eight months old, an event established unquestionably which child bore immortal blood. The children were sleeping under a lambskin in their shield-cradle when Hera sent twin blue serpents baring poisonous fangs to kill the babies. Iphicles cried out in fear while Herakles took charge and squeezed the snakes in his baby fists.

At that moment, Amphitryon, hearing the shrieks of the nurse, grabbed a sword and dashed to the nursery. He immediately recognized the touch of the god in Herakles. A brief consultation with Teiresias, the noted blind seer, settled the child's future. As Pindar's *Nemean Odes* cites the episode:

> Herakles himself, in peace for all time without end,
> will win rest as the choice reward for his great
> labors, and in the palaces of the Blessed he will
> take Hebe to be his youthful bride. Feasting at his
> wedding beside Zeus, Cronus's son, he will praise
> the holy customs of the gods.

Hence, the boy, no longer a pariah, acquired a patronym, Alcides, based on his grandfather, Alcaeus, a Theban hero whose name means "valiant" and whose reputation as a lion killer foreshadows his illustrious grandson.

Rumor of the infant Herakles's immense powers spread. Amphitryon educated him in handling the chariot; Autolycus demonstrated wrestling holds; Harpalycus trained him in boxing; Eurytus taught archery, at which Herakles excelled all men ever born. Others added their expertise: Castor taught fencing, Rhadamanthys lectured on wisdom and virtue, and Linus taught literature and music, although Herakles did not take to the lyre as had Linus's father, Orpheus. A difficult child, Herakles often raged out of control. In retaliation against his teacher for chastising him, Herakles struck the abusive Linus over the head with the lyre and killed him. The incident foreshadowed later bouts with an unmanageable temper and the fateful onset of madness, which plagued his adult life.

Altogether, Herakles demonstrated his sizeable sexual appetites and stamina by fathering around eighty sons. The following list of his offspring leads to a suspicion that either Herakles populated much of the Greek world or that his exploits made trumped-up family trees a popular pursuit:

- Deicoon, Creontiades, Therimachus, Mecistophonus, Glenus, Clymenus, Polydorus, Aristodemus, Anicetus, Patroclus, Toxoclitus, Menebrontes, and Chersibius.
- Antilochus, son of Meda, a Dryopian princess.
- Echephron and Promachus, twin sons of Psophis of Sicania.
- Triplets by the monster Scylla.
- Ctesippus, son of the Thessalian princess Astydameia, King Amyntor's daughter.
- Palaemon, nicknamed "the wrestler," child of Antaeus's widow, called Autonoe or Iphinoe.
- A second Hyllus, born to the nymph Melite, daughter of a river god.
- Gelonus, Agathyrsus, and Scythes, leader of the Scythians, all of whom were borne by the snake-queen who ruled the shores north of the Black Sea.
- Lamius, Maleus, Tyrrhenus, and Agelaus, all royal princes sired during his service to Queen Omphale of Lydia.
- Cleodaeus, the by-blow of Malis, a serving woman at Omphale's court.
- Bargasus, child of Barge, also a resident of Omphale's court.
- Bolbe, son of the nymph Olynthus.
- Thestalus, son of Epicaste, King Augeas's daughter.
- Latinus, the son of the Italian Faula or Fauna, figures significantly in Virgil's *Aeneid*, although paternity is often ascribed to either Faunus, Odysseus, or Telemachus.
- An Indian dynasty fathered through Pandaea, mother of the royal line, during Herakles's sojourn in India.
- Aechmagoras, son of Phialo or Phillo, who secreted her unwanted boy on a cave on Mount Ostracina, where a jay imitated the child's cry and summoned Herakles to the abandoned baby.
- Telephus, who became a significant figure in the Trojan Cycle, sired during Herakles's final exploits in Tegea after he seduced Auge, the sister of Cepheus, who hid her son in a temple.
- Thessalus, father of two heroes at Troy, sired after Herakles killed Eurypylus, the Meropian king, and wed his daughter.
- Pallas, for whom the Palatine Hill may have been named, the offspring of Herakles and Dyna, Evander's daughter.
- Tlepolemus, son of Astyoche, Phylas's daughter, sired after Herakles married Dejanira, thus leading to her jealousy and the fateful application of poisoned Centaur's blood to Herakles's tunic.
- Alexiares and Anicetus, born to Hebe after Herakles's deification.

- Herakles's daughter, Eucleia, was born to Myrto in Boeotia, and at Locris, she was deified as a virgin goddess.
- Another possible daughter was Manto, a seer for whom Mantua, Italy, was named.
- Hyllus, Ctesippus, Glenus, Hodites, and Macaria, four sons and one daughter of his last wife, Dejanira. Of the five, Hyllus, head of the Heraclids, was the most important. Macaria committed suicide in response to an oracle, which promised victory to Athens only after the sacrifice of one of Herakles's children. She was immortalized by the Macarian Spring at Marathon.
- The Thespiades, fifty sons from one visit to Thespius's home, where Herakles, then only eighteen years of age, lay on successive nights with the host's fifty daughters or their serving women. The offspring and their mothers were given as follows:

Mother	Son	Mother	Son
Aeschreis	Leucones	Hippocrate	Hippozygus
Aglaia	Antiades	Iphis	Celeustanor
Anthippe	Hippodromus	Laothoe	Antiphus
Antiope	Alopius	Lyse	Eumedes
Argele	Cleolaus	Lysidice	Teles
Asopis	Mentor	Lysippe	Erasippus
Calametis	Astybies	Marse	Bucolus
Certhe	Iobes	Meline	Laomedon
Chryseis	Onesippus	Menippis	Entelides
Clytippe	Eurycapys	Nice	Nicedromus
Elachia	Buleus	Nicippe	Antimachus
Eone	Amestrius	Olympusa	Halocrates
Epilais	Astyanax	Oreia	Laomenes
Erato	Dynastes	Panope	Thresippas
Euboea	Olympus	Patro	Archemachus
Eubote	Eurypylus	Phyleis	Tigasus
Eurybia	Polylaus	Praxithea	Nephus
Euryce or Euryte	Teleutagoras	Procris	Hippeus and Antileon
		Pyrippe	Patroclus
Eurypyle	Archedicus	Stratonice	Atromus
Eurytele	Leucippus	Terpsicrate	Euryopes
Exole	Erythras	Tiphyse	Lyncaeus
Heliconis	Phalias	Xanthis	Homolippus
Hesychia	Oestrobles	an unnamed daughter	Creon
Hippo	Capylus		

The sum of Herakles's ancestors bore out the dynasty's reputation for greatness and courage.

Journey At this point in Herakles's maturation, he was becoming a family problem—an overactive temper in a phenomenally strong teenager. After the
courts found Herakles not guilty for the death of Linus by reason of self-defense,
Amphitryon rid himself of his unruly ward by dispatching him to Thespiae to tend
Thespius's herds and ward off dangerous predators. Thespius, grateful for the favor,
took an interest in Herakles's hunting skills and kept the young man at his table for
fifty nights. Each evening at bedtime, the king assigned one of his fifty daughters to
share Herakles's bed, possibly to assure his lineage worthy grandsons. Only one girl,
Anthea, refused the guest's embrace and was remanded to temple duty as a virgin
votary. Procris's twins rounded out the births of the forty-nine women to an even
fifty grandchildren. An oracle advised Thespius to keep seven of the babies with their
mothers and dispatch three to Thebes. Iolaus took charge of the remaining forty male
infants and set up a nursery for them in Sardinia, where they established a colony.
Only two returned to Thebes. Thus Thebes and Sardinia added to the expansive dynasties springing from the mighty Herakles.

Outside Mount Cithaeron south of Thebes, Herakles fashioned a crude club from
an olive tree, then picked off a foraging lion that had been depleting the royal flocks.
He decked himself in the animal's pelt, shaping the jaws about his head as a helmet.
On the path from Mount Cithaeron, Herakles encountered messengers journeying
to Thebes to exact the yearly tribute to the city of Orchomenus in the central Peloponnesus. He overpowered the men and hacked off their noses and ears, which he hung
about their necks on cords. Spurning Orchomenus, he called a halt to the annual
tribute. King Erginus led his Minyan military toward Thebes, which had long been
disarmed.

Herakles, a resourceful warrior, called his peers to battle and outfitted them with
ancient armor that returning war heroes had suspended from temple walls. The youth
army, spoiling for a good fight, cut off the Minyans in a narrow gap and ended their
advance. Herakles exacted penalty on the Minyans by raiding Orchomenus in the
dark and setting fire to the king's hall. Erginus died in the fire and Herakles, his
conqueror, set the city's tribute at twice the amount that Thebes had been paying
Orchomenus. In commemoration of the successful battle, Herakles commissioned
two stelae to honor Athena Zoster, the incarnation of the goddess in full battle dress.

His reputation established, Herakles accepted a fitting reward—marriage to princess Megara, King Creon's daughter. Herakles fathered numerous children with
Megara, alternately identified as Deicoon, Creontiades, Therimachus, Mecistophonus, Glenus, Clymenus, Polydorus, Aristodemus, Anicetus, Patroclus, Toxoclitus,
Menebrontes, and Chersibius.

After Creon's death, Lycus, usurper of Thebes, threatened to kill Megara and her
children, who stood to inherit their grandfather's throne. Herakles overcame Lycus
and rescued his family and Thebes. Hera's bitter enmity caused her to dispatch
Lyssa, the daemon of madness, who caused Herakles to have a sudden fit of insanity. In a maniacal state, Herakles killed his wife, children, and the two children

of his nephew, Iolaus. Some say he shot them; others say that he hurled them into the altar flames. Athena's quick toss of a stone knocked him senseless and prevented more carnage.

To shed the awful guilt of parricide, Herakles first shut himself in a darkened room and contemplated suicide. As Seneca, the Roman tragedian, depicts in the melodrama *The Mad Hercules,* the crazed Herakles repined:

> I haste to purge the earth of such as I. Now long enough has there been hovering before my eyes that monstrous shape of sin—so impious, savage, merciless, and wild. Thus come, my hand, attempt this mighty task, far greater than the last.

To escape the torment of his crime, the Roman Hercules joined Theseus in Athens and sought a place where he could properly atone.

When Herakles once more gained self-confidence, he sought recompense through voluntary exile to Drepane, a Phaeacian isle of the west coast of Epirus later named Corfu, where Nausithous and Macris exonerated him through purification rites. During this recovery period, Herakles journeyed to Anticyra in Thessaly to partake of the hellebore, an herbal cure for insanity, and south to Delphi to ask Apollo's advice, which was delivered through the words of the votary Pythia. Her instructions to seek King Eurystheus in Mycenae and over a period of twelve years perform a series of labors led Herakles on one of mythology's greatest adventures. At the successful completion of this trial period, Pythia changed his name from Palaemon to Herakles (Hera's Glory), because Hera granted him perpetual fame.

Recalling the trickery that caused Eurystheus to be born first, Herakles did not put himself into servitude to his usurper cousin Eurystheus without serious contemplation. Abased before his old rival, Herakles willingly accepted a series of assignments, each more demanding than the last because he felt genuine remorse for killing his family. The resulting exploits, which reached the far corners of the Mediterranean coast and filled Greek literature, notably Book 9 of Ovid's *Metamorphoses,* were favorite adventure stories known to every generation born in the ancient world.

The first half of Herakles's tasks kept him close to Tiryns, an ancient city in the Peloponnesus. Eurystheus initiated the quests by demanding that Herakles kill the Nemean lion, a freakish beast born of Orthus and Echidna and possibly nurtured by a moon goddess. Herakles—armed with a homemade club, Apollo's bow and arrows, Hermes's sword, horses from Poseidon, a robe from Athena, and armor and a bronze club crafted by Hephaestus—traveled from Mycenae to Cleonae and took shelter with Molorchus, a poor laborer who was so impressed with his oversized visitor that he begged to offer a sacrifice to him. Herakles instructed him to wait for one month. If he did not return to Cleonae in that time, Molorchus might consider him a hero.

Scouting his prey in the Argolid region between Argos and Corinth at Mount Tretos, Herakles cornered the lion in a cave, where he easily made the first shot. His arrow failed to penetrate the thick hide, so Herakles abandoned arrows and club, barricaded the beast in its lair, and menaced it bare-handed. The ensuing battle cost him a finger. When the animal lay dead, Herakles recycled the pelt, which was impermeable to stone, bronze, or iron, into a rather stylish and individualistic armor. He used its sharp claws to skin the carcass, then draped the pelt over his shoulder and head, arranging the jaw to encircle his head like a helmet. By return route, he reached Molorchus's hut on the last day of the month and bade the laborer offer sacrifice to Zeus, the savior. Molorchus honored the defeat of the Nemean lion by launching the Nemean games at the city of Molorchia.

Setting out to Tiryns, Herakles found the cowardly Eurystheus quavering in a huge bronze storage container buried in the soil. The tremulous king asked that Herakles leave evidence of the kill at the gate. To avoid further contact with the strongman, the king promised to dispatch future assignments through Copreus, the royal messenger. In addition, Eurystheus refused the hide of the Nemean lion, so Herakles kept the natural armor, his trademark.

A more difficult job was the second labor, subduing the Hydra, a multiheaded beast, fathered by Typhon and akin to the Nemean lion through their mother, Echidna. Suckled by Hera, the Hydra and its companion, a monstrous crab, lurked under a plane tree alongside the Amymone spring at Lerna on the marshy Argive plain. Herakles forced it out of its hiding place with flaming arrows. The Hydra menaced him with its nine mouths, one of which he grasped in his fist. The beast attached itself to his ankle and the crab to his other foot as he methodically decapitated the Hydra head by head. As each head came off, two more sprang up on the oozing neck. Moreover, the central head was insuperable.

To end this losing battle, Herakles summoned his nephew, the charioteer, Iolaus, to cauterize each wound and so prevent more heads from appearing. At length, Herakles capped the work by ripping away the final head and secreting it under a rock alongside the road to Elaeus. To reward himself for his ingenuity, he soaked his arrows in the Hydra's poisonous gall and stored the deadly weapons for later use. These arrows had a noteworthy history, including a role in the Trojan War.

On the return journey, Herakles complimented Iolaus for his courageous intervention. At Mycenae, however, Eurystheus used Iolaus's help as reason to nullify the second labor because Herakles had not completed it singlehandedly.

The third chore demanded a different approach: Herakles had to capture Artemis's sacred stag, the gold-horned, bronze-hoofed Ceryneian deer, which wore a collar inscribed with the name of Taygete, one of the Pleiades. For twelve months, the wily hunter stalked Oenoe, the region in Argolis where the deer lived, and crossed the Artemisian mountain. He outwitted the stag near the Ladon River in Arcadia by sneaking up on its resting place and tossing a net over its body.

The trip back to the king required Herakles to walk southeast through the forest with the stag across his shoulder. Along the way he encountered Apollo and Artemis, who chastised the hunter for waylaying one of her sacred beasts. Herakles explained that he had no choice but to obey Eurystheus, who had devised the task. Artemis acceded to his explanation and allowed him to carry the stag to Tiryns.

Eurystheus, eager to keep Herakles occupied, sent him on a trip, this time to bag the Erymanthian boar, which threatened the people near Psophis. Herakles halted beyond Mount Pholoe to consult with Pholus, the wisest, most just Centaur and son of Silenos. Pholus welcomed the famous hero by pouring a fragrant wine, a divine vintage given him by Dionysus. The fragrant beverage drove the other Centaurs into fits and caused them to hurl boulders, torches, uprooted trees, and axes.

Taken aback by the unexpected assault, Pholus hid from his fellow Centaurs while Herakles scattered them in all directions, killing Ancius and Agirus, then wounding Chiron so badly that he prayed to be granted mortality so he could die. Herakles tried to save the old Centaur by applying healing herbs to the wound. At length, Chiron died; the gods established him in heaven as Sagittarius. While helping to bury his fallen comrades, Pholus realized his visitor's importance and grew curious about his lethal arrows. While turning one over in his hand, the Centaur dropped it, nicked his foot, and died. Herakles returned to his labor. The hunt ended with Herakles miring the Erymanthian boar in a snow bank, then chaining it to his shoulder. He transported it to Eurystheus, who remained hidden in the subterranean bronze jar.

At the completion of this labor, Herakles, sidetracked by Jason's search for worthy seamen, chose to journey on the *Argo* to Colchis on the southeastern shore of the Black Sea. He was welcomed by all and voted captain, but he wisely passed that honor to Jason.

After the Argonauts accidentally slew King Theiodamas, Herakles adopted Hylas as his companion. Following the snap of his oar, Herakles scoured the Mysian forest for a pine suitable for a new oar. Hylas, who separated from his companion to fill a bucket with water, met a peculiar fate at the spring, where admiring nymphs drew him into the pool. As Herakles roamed the woods in search of his squire, the *Argo* sped on its way, leaving him behind. Later on the Cycladean isle of Tenos in the Aegean Sea, north of Delos, Herakles located the Borean brothers, Zetes and Calais, who had urged the crew to abandon him. He slew them, and buried them under two stelae that were said to fluctuate with the wind, just as the sailors bowed to the opinion of Zetes and Calais.

On Herakles's return to Tiryns for the fifth assignment, Eurystheus berated him for deviating from the prescribed course, which was meant to expiate Herakles's sin of murdering his family. To remind the strongman that he was still in charge, Eurystheus devised a disgusting task: mucking out the stables of King Augeas of Elis, the area's richest herdsman. The task required immediate attention to prevent disease from spreading throughout the Peloponnesus, so Herakles meekly agreed to go west to Elis on the Alpheus River in Arcadia and survey the heaped manure that clogged Augeas's land.

Shrewdly exacting a commitment for one-tenth of the king's herd, Herakles sealed the arrangement with the signature of Prince Phyleus, who sided with the visitor. Then, seemingly without effort, Herakles knocked out the upper wall of the barn and dug a trench so that the Alpheius and Peneus rivers (probably the current Menius River) would do his work for him. The water pressure quickly scoured the barn clean of cattle and sheep dung.

On return to Augeas, Herakles was not surprised that the king reneged on his promise of one-tenth of his cattle in exchange for unclogging the barn. Lepreus, a somewhat dim-witted ally, suggested that Augeas chain Herakles, but Lepreus's mother Astydameia persuaded Lepreus to unlock the chains. Herakles demonstrated his willingness to forget the incident by inviting Lepreus to a friendly duel. The two hurled the discus and tried to out-drink and out-eat each other. Herakles was twice the victor, in hurling and drinking; Lepreus won the ox-eating contest. The resulting ill will led to a fight in which Herakles smashed Lepreus to the ground with his club.

Prince Phyleus, too, urged the king to pay his debts as agreed, but the king retaliated by booting his own son from the kingdom. Herakles departed along with the prince north to Olenus in Achaea and enjoyed hospitality at the palace of Dexamenus. As a gesture of thanks, Herakles rid Princess Mnesimache of the unwelcome suit of Eurytion, a lustful Centaur.

From Achaea, Herakles returned to Elis to collect his pay. Augeas refused, on the grounds that Herakles was really working for Eurystheus. Herakles then made a quick trek to Tiryns to complete his obligations. The renewed hostilities with Eurystheus continued doublefold as the king once more discounted the labor because Herakles had bargained with Augeas. Thus Herakles gained nothing from this labor.

Dispatched again to Arcadia for the sixth labor, Herakles undertook the expulsion of the Stymphalian birds, which cluttered the lake of Stymphalus, devoured crops, and soiled the surroundings with their droppings and feathers while raising a ferocious clatter. With the help of Athena, Herakles dispersed the birds by making more noise than they did. He clacked a set of brass rattles or clappers, which Hephaestus had crafted, and frightened the birds into the air. Once the birds were aloft, the sure-shotted Herakles slew great numbers and drove off the rest, which made their way east to the Isles of Ares in the Black Sea. Later representations of this myth depict the birds as local women whom Herakles ejected for their failure to extend hospitality to strangers.

By this time, Eurystheus was frustrated that Herakles completed his tasks so easily. To make the work more demanding, the vengeful king sent him farther from Tiryns for the seventh labor, to Crete to capture the Cretan bull, the notorious mate of Queen Pasiphae and sire of the Minotaur. Herakles had no difficulty persuading King Minos to rid the island of the beast, which had brought ill repute to his kingdom. The expedition went smoothly. After Eurystheus recognized the snorting bull, he agreed that Herakles should free it. The bull disappeared, resurfacing near Marathon and terrifying locals. Androgeus lost his life in an attempt to subdue the bull; it took the work of Theseus to end the beast's life on the altars of Athens.

Still eager to rid himself of Herakles, Eurystheus conceived a greater assignment for the eighth labor: rounding up Diomedes's four flesh-eating mares, named Deinus, Lampon, Podargus, and Xanthus. Because of his fear of strangers, Diomedes had bred the animals to devour all newcomers. Note that this Diomedes is unrelated to the Diomedes of Trojan War fame.

Along the way north and east to Thrace, Herakles visited King Admetus's home, where the royal family simulated pleasant welcome by concealing the recent death of their queen, Alcestis. Herakles, caught in a contretemps not of his making, relieved Admetus of the burden of feigned hospitality by intercepting Thanatos, the personification of death, and returning the queen from the Underworld to life.

At sea on the final leg of his voyage to the Bistones' land near Cape Bulustra, Thrace, Herakles arrived at the corrals of the king, Diomedes, bested the stable boys, and rounded up the herd, which their owner kept tied to their bronze feeding shed by iron tethers. Local uproar over the theft led Herakles to fight for himself while his companion Abderus guarded the horses. By the time Herakles drove off his attackers and killed Diomedes, he discovered that Abderus had been nearly devoured by the ravenous mares. Herakles, grieved that the appealing young man died so ignobly, buried his remains and founded the city of Abdera adjacent to his tomb. As an appropriate end to Diomedes's cruelty, Herakles fed the king's remains to the mares just as the king had often fed them on the flesh of his enemies.

The return to Eurystheus in Mycenae repeated earlier completions of difficult tasks. The king acknowledged that the mares were indeed the horses of Diomedes and bid their deliverer to free them. The horses wandered northwest toward Mount Olympus and were themselves overcome and devoured by wild animals.

Eurystheus showed a bit more practicality with his ninth labor: he commissioned Herakles to reward his daughter, Admete, with Hippolyta's belt, a symbol of sovereignty that the princess coveted. Like Jason had done in the voyage to fetch the Golden Fleece, Herakles sought the most reliable of sailors, including Telamon and Theseus, to travel through the Hellespont to Themiscyra near the Thermodon River on the south coast of the Black Sea. Along the way, the crew were forced to battle the inhabitants of Paros, an island ruled by King Minos's sons. Two of Herakles's men died in the fray and were replaced with Alcaeus and Sthenelus, Parian hostages.

Herakles's ship cruised northeast up the coast of Asia Minor toward Mysia, where Lycus, king of the Mariandyni, welcomed the mariners. The crew joined the Mariandyni in a brief uprising against the Bebryces, their local enemies. The war ended in Lycus's favor, with Mygdon, the Bebryces's king, slain by Herakles and a sizeable portion of land annexed, which Lycus named Heracleia in honor of his famous guest.

At Themiscyra, Herakles encountered Hippolyta, the Amazon ruler, who came on board to size up Herakles, by now famous across the entire Mediterranean. She was so impressed with his handsome figure, boldness, and pleasant personality that she voluntarily handed over the belt, which Ares had given her as an emblem of his warlike power. The queen also prepared to offer herself to Herakles, possibly in hopes of producing a child who might combine the strength of two audacious parents.

Hera, who disapproved of both the potential mating and of a task that required so little daring, decked herself out as an Amazon and incited the other female warriors to attack Herakles, whom she claimed was about to kidnap their queen. Herakles, confused by the subversive action, instinctively warded off the attackers. In the first wave, he killed Aella, the swiftest Amazon, then slew Philippis, Prothoe, Eriboea, Celaeno, Eurybia, Phoebe, Deianeira, Asteria, Marpe, Tecmessa, and Alcippe, before knocking Hippolyta from her mount. She refused to beg for mercy, so Herakles crushed her skull with his club.

The victory voyage brought the Greek company near Troy, where Herakles answered Laomedon's plea for assistance. In punishment for cheating Aeacus, Apollo, and Poseidon, Laomedon had been forced to chain his daughter Hesione to a crag overlooking the sea as an offering to a dire sea monster. Herakles agreed to rescue the maiden if King Laomedon promised him both the princess and a pair of mares given to Laomedon by Zeus.

The king, eager to rescue Hesione from a grisly end, agreed to Herakles's offer. To assist the Greek he-man, the Trojans and Athena built a redoubt behind which Herakles could retire during his furious battle with the monster. When his daughter was restored to safety, Laomedon did as others had done and refused to keep his promise to Herakles. The Greeks set sail without their reward. Herakles, too shorthanded to wreak vengeance, vowed to come back and settle with the treacherous Trojan king.

A series of unrelated incidents marked the remainder of the return voyage: at Ainos, Herakles's crew enjoyed the hospitality of King Poltys; by accident, Herakles shot Sarpedon, the king's brother. At Torone on Sithonia, Herakles wrestled and killed Proteus's sons, Polygonus and Telegonus.

The voyage ended with the deposit of the Amazon queen's belt into Eurystheus's hands. Rather than enrich himself, Herakles dedicated the other loot. To Queen Omphale, he gave Hippolyta's battle-ax. Before Apollo at Delphi, he laid lavish garments on the altar.

For the tenth labor, Eurystheus, still creative in his demands for Herakles to work off penance for killing his wife and children, sent the strongman after the oversized red cattle of King Geryon of the island of Eurytheia, a monster with three bodies joined into one. Traveling southwest to Libya on Africa's coast and due west through Numidia and over the Atlas Mountains, Herakles killed a number of wild animals before arriving at the Strait of Gibraltar, which he marked with the Pillars of Herakles, one on the continent of Africa and one to the north in Europe. Today called the Rock of Gibraltar or Calpe and Abyla near Ceuta, Morocco, these monuments attest to Herakles's far-flung exploits.

Herakles, fretting at the intensity of the sun, took aim at Helios himself. The sun god, somewhat taken aback by so self-confident a warrior, rewarded his audacity with the loan of a golden chalice shaped like a lotus and large enough to be used as a boat. Herakles boarded the cup and sailed it up Spain's west coast to the island of Eurytheia, now named Cadiz, where he faced the three-bodied king as well as his herdsman Eurytion and Orthus or Orthrus, a double-headed watchdog.

The first battle for Geryon's cattle took place on Mount Abas and pitted Herakles against Orthus. Herakles beat Orthus with his weapon and set out to deliver the same medicine to Eurytion, clearing the way for the capture of the cattle. Menoetes, Hades's herdsman, warned Geryon that both Eurytion and Orthus were dead and that Herakles was about to seize the cattle. Geryon charged the invader, then fell dead as Herakles pierced his triplicate body with a well-placed poisoned arrow.

Herakles, who liked tidy conclusions, returned the golden cup-boat to Helios. Having beached his own craft at Tartessus, Herakles, like Hannibal crossing the Alps with his elephants, decided to drive the cattle back to Eurystheus's court on the overland route through Europe, leading him from Abderia to Marseilles to Liguria in northern Italy. Rustlers led by Dercynus and Alebion tried to steal the herd. For the first time, Herakles came near death from the fierce Ligurian force that charged him. Zeus intervened and deposited a load of stones with which Herakles could arm himself. The hail of projectiles drove the pursuers away and marked the territory around Marseilles with an inordinate number of boulders.

Turning south, Herakles set off for Italy. While Herakles slept near the Tiber River, Cacus, a notorious giant, snatched some of the cattle by the tail and yanked them into his cave. Herakles, confused by the lack of tracks, listened for lowing and located the stolen animals in Cacus's cave. With one swift motion, Herakles snatched the barrier from the cave entrance and throttled Cacus. For ridding the Italian coast of so despicable a brigand, natives proclaimed Herakles their hero.

An unexplained detour took Herakles north of the Black Sea into what is now Russia. While he rested in the forest, his horses wandered off. When Herakles became aware of their disappearance, he scoured the neighborhood and discovered a cavern inhabited by a monster queen that was half woman and half serpent. To persuade the monarch to release his stolen horses, Herakles remained long enough to sire three sons—Scythes, Gelonus, and Agathyrsus. Years later, only Scythes had the strength of his father, as demonstrated by his skill with Herakles's bow. In his honor, the Scythians took his name and proclaimed him their king.

On Herakles roved, toward Rhegium on the southernmost tip of Italy where the finest specimen of Geryon's cattle eluded its herdsman and swam east to Sicily. Herakles, faced with a rough crossing at the Strymon River, created a ford with stones, thus damming the river and forming a cataract. He petitioned the god Hephaestus to guard the rest of his herd and scouted the island nation as far as Mount Eryx, where the king hid the magnificent bull among his own herds. Herakles agreed to a duel of strength and won back the bull by killing the king in a wrestling match.

The return trip to Tiryns is sometimes set over a rambling route through the British Isles. At length, Herakles returned to Eurystheus and handed over the fabled cattle. The king selected the best of the lot to sacrifice to Hera.

In Herakles's eighth year of service to Eurystheus, the eleventh and next-to-last labor took the famed strongman to the earth's edge, where grew the golden apples of the Hesperides, nymphs who tended the orchard. Possessed by Hera and guarded by Ladon, a one hundred-headed serpent, the glittering fruit was hidden from human thieves. In order to retrieve the apples, Herakles had to locate the grove. Nymphs living on the Eridanus River dispatched Herakles to Nereus, the wily sea god who could change himself into any shape he chose. Herakles wrestled Nereus through multiple metamorphoses as a fire, lion, snake, and waterfall before forcing him to point the way to the earth's end, which authors alternately name as Oceanus, southern Libya, or the land of the north wind.

Along a meandering path on his way to retrieve the apples (which suggests the geographic naivete of the composers of his myth), Herakles had the following adventures:

- In the Caucasus Mountains, he shot the eagle that had daily fed off Prometheus's liver and restored Prometheus to normalcy and eventual immortality.
- In Arabia, Herakles slew Emathion, Tithonus's son.
- At King Busiris's city in Egypt, Herakles discovered a bizarre ritual requiring annual sacrifice of a visiting stranger. Pretending to accept his fate as the next victim, Herakles followed in procession to the sacred altar, then burst his chains and slew Busiris and Prince Amphidamas.
- To the west, Herakles embroiled himself in a wrestling match with Antaeus, son of Gaia or "earth." When Herakles realized that Antaeus regained his strength from even the slightest contact with earth, he held the wily wrestler in the air and squeezed out his breath.

Farther west, Herakles reached the end of the earth—the point where the titan Atlas supported the sky on his shoulders. In exchange for Atlas's help in retrieving the golden apples, Herakles boosted the earth onto his own back while Atlas sought the orchard. Atlas returned with the apples, and like many before him, he proved false to his promise and refused to shoulder the earth's weight again. Herakles agreed to a compromise plan by which Atlas would carry the apples to Eurystheus. At the last moment, Herakles asked Atlas to support the heavens for a short while so that Herakles could shift his back into a more comfortable position. Atlas realized too late he had been fooled; Herakles grabbed up the golden fruit and hastily departed east.

The golden apples were so dangerous a treasure that Eurystheus lacked the courage to keep them. He passed them back to Herakles, who dedicated them at Athena's shrine. The goddess, so as to avoid squabbles with Hera, returned them to the Hesperides.

The twelfth and last labor was the most fearful of Herakles's tasks: to kidnap Cerberus, the three-headed, serpent-tailed dog that guarded the entrance to the Underworld. A relative to the Nemean lion, the nine-headed Hydra, and Orthus (the watchdog over Geryon's cattle), Cerberus posed a deadly challenge to Herakles. If he failed this mission, he might never return to earth. He prepared himself for the assault by being adopted by Pylias, a helpful Athenian, so that he could claim Athenian citizenship, enter the Eleusian mysteries, and exonerate himself of the Centaurs' deaths. At length, Eumolpus, Orpheus's son, accepted Herakles into the holy orders of Demeter and Dionysus, divinities of bread and wine, so that Herakles could be forgiven.

From Taenarum on Greece's southern tip, Hermes, pathfinder of the gods, joined Athena in directing Herakles's way down the murky path to Hades's kingdom. Herakles glowered so fiercely at Charon that the ferryman rowed him over the Styx River without comment. On the far shore, the ghosts of Medusa and the warrior Meleager hovered menacingly, but Herakles was not cowed. He stopped to hear Meleager's pitiable fate and promised, upon return to the upper air, to marry his sister, Dejanira, who no longer had a male family member to protect her.

Then Herakles pushed on into the murk. Along the route, he performed some acts of mercy:

- At the seat of forgetting, he loosened Theseus, a living mortal who was being punished for trying to abduct Persephone. Herakles also tried to free Pirithous, but an earth tremor warned him that he dared too much.
- He loosened a stone with which Demeter had immured Ascalaphus for revealing to Hades that Persephone had eaten a pomegranate seed, thus sealing her fated marriage to the god of the Underworld.
- He slaughtered a cow so that shades could sip the blood and taste a momentary rejuvenation. Menoetes, Hades's herdsman, threatened Herakles, who hugged him in a rib lock and crushed his bones. Persephone stepped in to prevent Herakles from doing Menoetes more damage.

At last, Herakles arrived at the throne of the god himself. Upon hearing Herakles's demand for Cerberus, Hades nodded, then added a single proviso: the act had to be carried out with bare hands. Herakles accepted the challenge and snatched the fearful dog by its snake-covered neck and, avoiding the stinger in its tail, forced it into the upper world by a side entrance at Troezen and went directly to Tiryns. Eurystheus, more cowardly than usual, begged Herakles to take the dog back to Hades. Once more, Herakles headed for the Underworld, this time to dispose of its guard dog. Herakles's labors were over.

A long time in claiming his promised immortality, Herakles continued to face the living hell of Hera's spite toward her wayward husband's offspring. Herakles grew lonely and sought a wife to replace his unfortunate alliance with Megara. In Oechalia, in Messenia in the southwesternmost province of Greece, Herakles challenged King Eurytus to an archery match so that he could claim Princess Iole as his bride. Although Herakles won, Eurytus refused to allow Herakles his daughter, fearing that Iole and her children would suffer the same fate as that of Megara and her children.

Herakles departed in anger and took along some of the king's herds. Eurytus ordered his son, Iphitus, to follow Herakles and retrieve the horses. Iphitus, who sided with Herakles, joined him and halted at Tiryns, where Herakles grabbed up the unsuspecting Iphitus and tossed him from the battlements. One explanation of this undeserved mayhem was a second visitation from Hera, who caused a temporary fit of insanity.

Herakles, struck down with disease in retribution, sought cleansing from Neleus at Pylus. Neleus, however, took Eurytus's side and withheld medical attention. At

Amyclae in Laconia, a few miles south of Sparta, Deiphobus interceded and healed Herakles, but the disease recurred. Herakles, like most dwellers of the ancient world, put his trust in the Pythian oracle, Xenocleia, who refused to give him an explanation of his sudden insanity. He spitefully snatched her tripod and menaced all of Delphi. Threatening to establish his own oracle, Herakles called down the anger of Apollo. The resulting wrestling match caused Zeus to settle the unseemly uproar with a bolt of lightning. Xenocleia, who was convinced that Herakles was too dangerous to refuse, extracted a terrible promise: that Herakles would return to normal by allowing himself to be enslaved for three years. He also had to pay a blood price to Iphitus's survivors.

Herakles had little choice but to comply and journeyed east to the far end of the Mediterranean. As the slave of Omphale, the Lydian queen, he served the royal household in women's dress as spinner of yarn and singer while the queen wore his trademark lion pelt and occasionally swatted him with her slipper if he pricked his finger or snarled the wool. During one evening's charades, Omphale and Herakles spent the night in a distant grotto. Pan, who lusted for Omphale, made a grab at the shadowed figure dressed in wig and laced girdle. To his surprise, a masculine foot protruded from the coverings and booted him to the door.

After winning the queen's affections, Herakles passed into a more fitting service as strongman and bodyguard by performing numerous tasks:

- At Omphale's command he journeyed to Oechalia in Euboea on the east coast of Greece to capture the Cercopes, a pair of rascally gnomes who stole from Herakles while he slept.
- Farther east at Aulis he killed both Syleus and his daughter Xenodice with a hoe for waylaying strangers and forcing them to do farm work.
- He defeated Itoni, an enemy city, and rid the Sagaris River of a monstrous snake.

At length, Herakles earned manumission and fathered Maleus, Tyrrhenus, Agelaus, and Lamius, all of whom led illustrious lives. Once more free of disease, he returned to Greece. Along the way, he came upon the corpse of Icarus and interred the body on an island later named Icaria.

Unhampered by heavenly constraint, Herakles set out to settle scores with all who had wronged him. He outfitted eighteen ships, each equipped with fifty oars, and sailed northeast to punish Laomedon, Troy's king, for reneging on the reward for rescuing Princess Hesione. With Telamon as his crew chief, Herakles arrived at his destination, beached his ships, and launched an attack. Telamon forced a way into the city gates, deeply humiliating Herakles. Quick-wittedly, Telamon set up an altar honoring Herakles, thereby avoiding another insult to Herakles's list of wrongs to avenge.

The war against Troy, a miniature version of the later Trojan War, won Herakles the devotion of Podarces, Laomedon's unfaithful son, and the hand of Princess Hesione. Laden with treasure and herding the mares that the king had originally offered,

Herakles forced Hesione to select a survivor to claim the city and to ransom that person with some of her personal goods. Hesione selected Podarces and offered her scarf as a symbolic payment. Podarces, renamed Priam, remained as Troy's sovereign.

Out of gratitude to his noble lieutenant and lover, Herakles offered Hesione to Telamon. In further repayment for Telamon's assistance, Herakles prayed that Telamon would sire a great son. Zeus sent an eagle to drop a feather, emblem of the might and blessing accorded Ajax, son of Telamon and Eeriboea. So mightily did this benediction inflame Hera that she persuaded Hypnos to give Zeus a sleeping potion, then, without his interference, Hera summoned winds to beach Herakles's fleet on Cos, an island in the Aegean Sea opposite the Gulf of Halicarnassus. The act was the breaking point with Zeus, who suspended Hera by her hands from Mount Olympus and weighed her feet with anvils.

The Greeks overcame the inhabitants of Cos. Herakles bested the king, Eurypylus, but sustained a wound and hid in a hut, where he put on women's garments to escape detection. Zeus rescued his favorite son and enlisted him to fight off the Giants. At Phlegra, Herakles joined the divine ranks and helped Apollo blind Epialtes, one shooting out the right eye and the other shooting out the left. As the Giants descended on the seductive Aphrodite, Herakles leaped from his hiding place in a cave and smashed their heads together. Bare-handed, Herakles subdued Alcyoneus, then departed the carnage to return to civilian life.

The second faithless monarch to encounter Herakles's vengeance was Augeas, Elis's king. Herakles gathered men in Arcadia and, mounted on Arion, the flying moon-horse, sprang forth in good faith that he would exact a worthy toll. An unforeseen illness weakened Herakles; his men were overwhelmed. Herakles sought refuge in Tiryns, but Eurystheus ousted him. Herakles, weakened and exiled, had little choice but to settle in Pheneus, a small town in Arcadia, until he could recuperate.

Once more hearty, Herakles waited until Augeas's allies approached the Isthmian games and destroyed them. Without their help, Augeas faced a second and much bloodier invasion. In this attack, Augeas died. Herakles replaced him with his son, Phyleus, who had remained Herakles's staunch ally. Thus restored to confidence, Herakles honored his great-grandfather Pelops with an Olympian shrine and established the Olympic Games near the Alpheius River in Arcadia.

A third unfinished matter lay in Pylus, where Neleus had rejected Herakles after he sought purification from the death of Iphitus and had also tried to steal some of Geryon's herd. Herakles exacted a terrible penalty by killing Neleus and eleven royal princes, and wounding both Ares and Hera, who fought on Neleus's side. Only Nestor, Agamemnon's great sage and adviser, survived. Herakles left Nestor to rule Pylus, but made it clear that one day Herakles's own sons would assume control of the kingdom.

From Neleus's realm, Herakles marched on Hippocoon, Neleus's spartan ally. During this bloody engagement, Herakles's brother Iphicles died in the field. The war also claimed Hippocoon and his twenty sons. Herakles himself received a wound on his hand; Tyndareus helped him regain his health by leading him to Asclepius, priest at Demeter's shrine in Eleusis, west of Athens. Because this battle marked the first episode in Herakles's life that Hera did not oppose, he concluded the event by raising a shrine to her at Sparta. Since no other sacrificial animal was available, he was forced to offer a goat, thus earning for Hera the name of Aegophagos or "goat-eater." To make certain that Athena would not be jealous, Herakles also built an altar to her.

Herakles departed the Peloponnesus and settled in Calydon, considered the greatest town of Aetolia. He wrestled Achelous, a river god, for the maiden Dejanira (or Dejaneira or Deianeira), the daughter of King Oeneus, for whom the spirit of Meleager had sought a provider. This love match, interrupted by a war in which Herakles guided the Calydonians against Ephyra, a Thesprotian city to the northwest, resulted in another uprooting. Herakles, while being served by a wine steward, grew annoyed and smacked the child Eunomus, a house slave who knelt to wash the hero's feet, and instantly killed him. Although the boy's father, Architeles, held no grudge, for this deed Herakles paid the blood price of yet another exile, which he served in Trachis in southern Thessaly in the company of Dejanira.

One of the most poignant episodes of Herakles's eventful life occurred at the Evenus River in Aetolia. The ferryman, Nessus the Centaur, offered to bear Dejanira across the river on his back while Herakles forded at a distance. As the party set out, Dejanira screamed in rage as Nessus, aroused by her perfume, attempted to rape her when he reached the opposite shore. Herakles impaled the deceitful Centaur with a single arrow through the heart.

Lying on the shore in the last moments of his life, Nessus earned his revenge by deceiving Dejanira. He yanked the arrow from his body and, as Sophocles reports his words, said:

> If you mix the seed which I have spilt on the ground with blood from my wound, add olive oil, and secretly anoint Herakles's shirt with the mixture, you will never again have cause to complain of his unfaithfulness.

(Sophocles's *Trachinian Women*)

Dejanira, who knew well her glamorous husband's penchant for female conquests, collected Nessus's blood and semen, which were tainted with the poison of the Hydra, which Herakles had long ago soaked into his arrows.

Beyond Mount Parnassus near Mount Oeta, the couple pressed on toward Trachis, where Dejanira gave birth to Hyllus, Herakles's most famous son, and four other children. The marriage did not satisfy the lusty Herakles. Just as Nessus had predicted, as Dejanira aged and busied herself with domestic matters, including caring for her husband's sixty-five sons by other women, he was drawn to repeated adulteries and greater roving. Sophocles, who pitied Dejanira, named her the "bird lorn of its mate."

Herakles continued to push himself to the extremes of human strength. He fought the Dryopes and Lapiths, dueled with Cycnus, and his battle with Ares brought a second lightning bolt as a warning from Zeus. Herakles made one last drive for vengeance by leading a great force against Oechalia, where Eurytus failed to keep his promise of granting Herakles the hand of Iole. The war went well. At length Iole became Herakles's newest concubine.

At her husband's request Dejanira sent a fresh robe for her husband to wear at the altar he raised to Zeus at Cape Cenaeum in Euboea. She commented with great insight:

> So now the two of us lie under the one sheet awaiting his embrace.
> This is the gift my brave and faithful Herakles sends home to his dear
> wife to compensate for his long absense ... to live in the same house
> with [Iole], to share the same marriage, that is something else. What
> woman could stand that?

> (Sophocles's *Trachinian Women*)

The fearful wife, hearing about Iole's beauty, had smeared the garment with Nessus's body fluids. She handed it to Lichas, who hurried away to serve his master. As he drove out of sight, Dejanira caught sight of a drop of the poisonous liquid, which burned through wool. Too late to stop Lichas, she envisioned how her husband would die and vowed to kill herself for her foolish belief in the wicked Nessus's dying words.

At the altar, Herakles had already begun the rites involving sacrifice of a dozen unspotted bulls and the mixing of frankincense in the holy chalice to spill over the flame. On first touch to his naked skin, he recognized well the poison by which he had killed so many enemies. As Ovid describes in Book 9 of the *Metamorphoses*:

> Then as he tried to strip the shirt away,
> his flesh came with it. Horror to his sight,
> it scarred his bones and clung or stripped them bare;
> like white hot rods thrust into icy water;
> his blood steamed with the heat of Hydra's venom,
> its flames burned inward to his vital parts ...
> and all his limbs turned black with hidden fires.

Blaming Lichas for his torment, Herakles ripped off the offending robe, but could not halt the flow of the Hydra's blood into his skin. Fated to die at the hand of no living man, he struggled in vain against the slow-acting agony, which ate into his bones.

Mottled like a burn victim, Herakles tore off his own flesh, and deranged with agony, snatched up his valet Lichas, twirled him three times overhead, and hurled him into the ocean, where the boy was immortalized in the naming of the Lichades Islands. Slowly succumbing to the poison that seeped into his veins, Herakles was borne on a litter and across the sea to Trachis by boat and returned to Dejanira, only to learn that she, in recompense, had slain herself on her husband's sword and had fallen full-length atop their bed. Along with his faithful son, Hyllus, Herakles forced himself to the summit of Mount Oeta near the town of Callium outside Aetolia in Thessaly, and awaited the heaping of live oak and olive branches to fuel the funeral pyre.

In a dramatic scene, Herakles laid himself out and, while awaiting the torch, gave parting commands to Hyllus, which Sophocles reports thus in *Trachinian Women:*

> Swear by the head of Zeus that you will convey me to the highest
> peak of this mountain, and there burn me, without lamentation,
> on a pyre of oak branches and trunks of the male wild olive.
> Likewise swear to marry Iole as soon as you come of age.

The boy, in awe of his father and the prophecy that bound Herakles to a terrible death, nodded in assent.

The time approached for Herakles's death. Hyllus was terrified of the task, so Poeas, a nearby shepherd, agreed to have his son, Philoctetes, light the fire. Grateful to be put out of pain, Herakles handed his euthanizer the bow and quiver that would play an integral role in the conclusion of the Trojan War. Just as Nessus predicted, Dejanira's application of the virulent Centaur's blood did indeed stop Herakles from loving any more women.

The fire burned away the mortal remains of Herakles, releasing the divine spirit in a wondrous cloud and a peal of thunder. As the pyre cooled, Herakles's followers discovered no earthly remains and deduced that their leader had achieved apotheosis, a final purification into godhood. As Ovid notes in his *Metamorphoses:*

> Hercules stepped free of mortal being,
> and took on greater stature with his honors,
> and with an air of gravity and power,
> grew tall, magnificent as any god.

His friend Menoetius raised a shrine to Herakles at Opus, an ancient Locrian settlement on the Opuntian Gulf, and began the tradition of honoring the demigod with the sacrifice of lambs, a bull, rams, or a boar, symbolic of the Erymanthian boar.

Other idiosyncrasies were attached to Herakles's deification. His worship was linked with Galinthias, the trickster who assisted at Herakles's birth and who was punished by being changed into a weasel, which afterward slunk about the unlighted corners of Herakles's temples and became the familiar of the witch Hecate. Herakles remained so grateful to her that he built her a shrine and inaugurated a festival to Galinthias or Historis, as she is called by Pausanias. Alcmene, still loyal to her wondrous son, shepherded his sons to Trachis, far from the spite of Eurystheus, thus preserving the Heracleid dynasty for greater exploits. Like Herakles, Alcmene lived a long and eventful life, then entered the realms of the blessed and was worshipped at Thebes as Herakles's mother and the grandam of the Heraclids, leaders of the Doric invasion.

At rest from human toils and seated among the Olympian deities, Herakles, who came to resemble his divine father, became the adopted son of his long-time enemy, the goddess Hera, who acted out a ritual birth by pretending to go into labor and extract a newborn from beneath her skirts. She offered Herakles her daughter Hebe, the goddess of youth, who bore him two sons, Alexiares and Anicetus. As one of the Olympians, Herakles took his rightful place among the gods and served as guardian of the Olympian gates.

Herakles made earthly appearances by restoring Iolaus to youthful vigor and defending him in battle and by advising Philoctetes to take up Herakles's bow and kill Paris, thus bringing the Trojan War to an end. Herakles and Hebe continued to be worshipped, often in tandem, for centuries in Athens and its environs. Hera, the relentless Olympian fishwife who had dogged Herakles's entire career, changed into a doting mother-in-law, attentive to her daughter's amazing mate.

As destroyer of monsters and earth's defender, Herakles, mythology's most popular hero, was widely venerated, especially in the far south of Greece, where cults followed his simple lifestyle and emulated his courage; among the Sabines, who regarded Herakles as a healer, fire-bringer, and abominator of human sacrifice; with the Romans, who associated him with the lyre and the muses; and on Crete, the island he rid of ravenous beasts. He earned a lengthy list of appended names, such as Index, "the denouncer of thieves;" Melampyges, or "covered in black hair;" Monoecus, "the solitary god;" Ogmius, "the eloquent one;" Charops, "the bubbly one;" Ophioctonus, "killer of snakes;" Buphagus, "the bull-eater;" Alexicacus, "averter of evil;" and Promachus, "the champion."

As demonstrated in verse, prose, and drama, the Romans, who introduced Herakles worship at Tivoli as a protection of traders, preferred swearing in Latin *"me hercule"* than by the Olympian gods, a custom originated by Nestor, Herakles's loyal friend. Herakles's name, meaning "Hera's glory," prophesied the acceptance that he eventually won through an extreme number of physical tests. More than any other ancient hero, Herakles is associated with selfless devotion to duty. Against the deceitful Eurystheus, who extended the required ten labors into twelve, Herakles raised no outcry, even in the face of a journey to the nether regions to fetch Cerberus.

The hero's name figures in a variety of places about the Mediterranean, including:

- Marathon, a small town near Athens, which claims to be the first worship center raised to Herakles.
- Methana, a cape off Troezen, where a statue of Herakles adorns the marketplace.
- Abia, Messenia, where Hyllus's nurse raised a temple to Herakles.
- The island of Chryse, where Philoctetes tended the hero's shrine.
- Cladeus, a river in Olympia where Herakles stepped off a sacred grove and surrounded it with a wall.

- Herakles, a town outside the kingdom of Monaco.
- Melampygos, a hot spring and Heraclean altar near Thermopylae, south of Thessaly.
- The Herakles temple at Gadeira in Cadiz, Spain.
- Heraclea, a common name used by a town near Miletus, a city in Caria; a Macedonian city; a city in Bithynia on the Black Sea; a city on the Chersonesus; a Median city, Heraclea Tarentum, now called Policoro, Italy; and Heraclea Trachinia, a Spartan settlement near Thermopylae.
- Temples in Thespiae near the base of Mount Helicon in Boeotia in Thisbe, a small town in Boeotia described by Pausanias as the setting of an annual festival in Herakles's honor.
- The Heracleion at Thymoetadae outside Athens, a temple overlooking the Strait of Salamis.
- The well of Cyane in Syracuse, Sicily, where, according to Apollodorus, the annual sacrifice of a bull in the well marked the eating of an entire bull by Herakles Buphagus.
- The Heraclean baths of Aedepsus in Euboea.
- Six altars raised by Herakles to the Olympian games, a shrine to Zeus Soter, and a temple to Herakles, excavated in 1912 at Cleonae, a city between Corinth and Argos.
- The healing Heraclean stones in Hyettus, Boeotia.
- The Heraclean shrine at Acharnae north of Athens.
- An altar to Herakles in Hymettus, outside Athens.
- The temple of Heracleion, which names the modern town of Iraclio near Athens; a temple near Athens shared by the four towns of Xypete, Peiraeus, Phalerum, and Thymoetadae; a temple on Thasos, an island in the Aegean Sea off Macedonia where Herodotus visited and commented on the deification of Herakles; and another facing the forum in a Roman settlement excavated at Corinth in 1896.
- Temples to Herakles in Halimus, a coastal city in Attica; at Phera in Thessaly, the home of Admetus, whose wife the hero returned from the dead.
- A shrine at Proschium in Aetolis, where the hero accidentally killed Cyathus, his wine steward.
- Temples that featured an annual tribute ceremony at Siphae on the Gulf of Corinth, on the island of Aegina, and in Sparta near the place Herakles avenged the death of Oeonus.
- A crude sanctuary on a rock ledge and a larger shrine on the island of Delos.
- In Cretan ceremonies at Heracleion, an eponymous city, which honored a local version of the hero as a magician.
- Herculaneum, the famous west coastal Italian city often paired with its neighbor, Pompeii, with which it was immured in ash and lava following the eruption of Mount Vesuvius.

- A depiction of Herakles and Iolaus slaying the Hydra on the metopes of the Delphian temple.
- A sanctuary to Herakles in Dodona in Epirus.
- A fort named Teichos in Dyme near Elis, where Herakles trounced the Eleans, fell in love with Sostratus, and later returned to bury the youth.
- A sanctuary and gymnasium sacred to Herakles at Diomeia in Attica.
- An oracle at Bura in Achaea, where the petitioner receives as answer after tossing four dice.
- Heraclea Pontica on the south coast of the Black Sea.
- The site of Herakles's death pyre, a hexagonal relic discovered in 1919 in southern Thessaly alongside a Doric temple and a small memorial, possibly a gift from Philoctetes, who received Herakles's bow and arrows.

Much of Herakles's lore relates to actual places and pragmatic circumstance. Literal explanation suggests that the duel with the Hydra epitomized the Argolid battle to turn swampland into arable soil. Likewise, Herakles's victory over the Minyans, which he achieved by plugging underground tunnels and flooding their land, probably commemorated an actual neglect of underground limestone channels as the control of the Minyans declined.

The spread of the Herakles myth across Europe placed the name in a variety of unusual places. Oddly, the house of Burgundy linked its ancestry with an alliance of the Greek hero and Alise, a Spanish princess. So widely was his influence felt that early critics deduced that his canon, like that of Robin Hood, Rob Roy, El Cid, and Daniel Boone, was an amalgam of heroic episodes assembled under the aegis of a single warrior. Herakles lived on in human names, especially Heraclitus, the fifth century B.C. philosopher, the middle name of Cyrano de Bergerac, and the humorous detective, Hercule Poirot, master unraveler of Agatha Christie mysteries. In English, the adjective *herculean* denotes anything marked by unusual power, intensity, or challenge. In botany, a small prickly shrub of the rue family bears the name Hercules's Club.

Alternate Versions

The convoluted myth of Herakles, which encompassed the known Mediterranean world as well as Hades, the home of the Amazons, and other terrain not found on maps, contains many side versions and alterations. Among them are the following:

Zeus placed Herakles on Hera's breast while she slept. The milk that leaked from the baby's mouth formed the Milky Way.

Amphitryon put snakes in his sons' bed to determine which son was mortal and which son was fathered by Zeus.

Megara did not die, according to one setting. Herakles feared that their union was destroyed by his murder of the children and passed her into the care of his nephew, Iolaus. Megara's five children are sometimes augmented to include Therimachus,

Chersibius, Areas, Ophites, Deicoon, Aristodemus, Deion, Democoon, Toxoclitus, Oneites, Menebrontes, Mecistophonus, Creontiades, Oxeus, Antimachus, Clymenus, Glenus, Polydorus, and Anicetus.

Thespius sent all fifty of his daughters to enjoy one orgiastic evening with Herakles. Retellings of the twelve labors often reorder them.

The search for the Cyrneian stag is sometimes set across the Ister River in Hyperborean territory or among the Isles of the Blessed.

In one version of the voyage with Jason and the Argonauts, Herakles cut short his search for the Golden Fleece after the talking beam demanded that the *Argo* was not built to accommodate so large a sailor. In this version Herakles departed from the Argonauts at Aphetae on the Gulf of Pagasae, east of Thessaly.

The Stymphalian birds are sometimes described as metal-encased eaters of human flesh capable of impaling enemies with sharpened feathers.

The Cretan bull is identified with the beast that kidnapped Europa.

At Malea in Arcadia, Herakles accidentally shot Chiron with an arrow poisoned with the Hydra's blood. Quick application of first aid failed to stop the pain, but Chiron, an immortal, was unable to die. Prometheus relieved him of his grief so that Chiron could journey to the netherworld. Hera honored him by naming a constellation the Centaur, although some sources say that the star cluster immortalized Pholus, the other Centaur killed by Herakles's arrows.

A variation on the story of Cacus and the stolen cattle has Cacus's sister, Caca, informing Herakles of her brother's theft. In gratitude, Herakles assured her an everlasting honor, a flame to adorn her altar.

The Amazonian revolt was led by Antiope, Hippolyta's sister, who loved Theseus and returned to Greece with him aboard Herakles's ship. A similar variation depicts Hippolyta as surviving the battle, marrying Theseus, and bearing Hippolytus.

In one conclusion to the retrieval of Hippolyta's belt she survives the battle and exchanges the belt for Melanippe, an Amazon whom the Greeks held for ransom.

The bull that escaped from Herakles in Sicily is sometimes described as a large segment of the total herd, some of which did not survive the rigors of the return trip.

Alternate descriptions of the Pillars of Herakles depict them as warnings to sea monsters or as a set of barriers that Herakles separated to create an access to the unknown sea beyond the Mediterranean.

The recovery of the golden apples is sometimes credited to Prometheus, who was grateful to be relieved from eternal bondage. Other versions depict Herakles as completing the job without Atlas's help by slaying the watch-dragon or lulling it to sleep, just as Medea quelled the dragon that guarded the Golden Fleece.

Herakles dug a spring with his toe in the Libyan desert, where the Argonauts, on their return journey, halted for a drink that saved them from dying of dehydration.

Herakles persuaded Hades to free Theseus from punishment in the Underworld.

One setting of Herakles's adventures in the Underworld shows him wounding Hades, forcing the god of the Underworld to seek medical treatment from Paeeon, the Olympian doctor. An alternate arrival point for his return from the Underworld is Hermione, a town in the southern Argolid.

An alternate version of the killing of Syleus and his daughter Xenodice states that Xenodice killed herself after Herakles deserted her. He returned and attempted to immolate himself on her funeral pyre. An altar to Herakles was erected atop her grave.

The nymph Melite was named as the mother of Hyllus.

After the battle against Hippocoon, Herakles raised an altar to Athena, whom he called *Axiopoenos*, "the avenger," for her assistance.

Another version of Herakles's wedding day describes how he arrived at Olenus in Achaia to marry Dejanira (alternately named Hippolyta or Mnesimache), King Olenus's daughter, and found Eurytion, the Centaur, rivaling his suit. Herakles slew the Centaur.

Herakles killed Amyntor, king of Ormenium in Thessaly, for obstructing his journey and for refusing him the princess Astydameia.

After the Centaur's attempted rape of Herakles's bride, Dejanira collected Nessus's semen to use as a love potion.

The inflated warnings of Lichas, Herakles's servant, caused Dejanira to kill her husband.

Numerous variations on who lit Herakles's funeral pyre name Zeus, Hyllus, Morsimus, Poeas, and Philoctetes.

A legend arising from the violent separation of mountains in Tempe, Thessaly, credits Herakles with splitting the mound by hand, much as Paul Bunyan is said to have created topographical changes in the United States.

Symbolism

Sometimes referred to as Alcides or son of Alcmene, Herakles completed a long career of struggle and conquest, which symbolizes the human war against death, a personified terror that Herakles once met face to face and overcame, much as Beowulf, in the epic of the same name, defeated Grendel and the fire dragon; Gareth the squire faced off against death disguised as a knight in Tennyson's *Idylls of the King*. Herakles's rejection and banishment from home, which parallels similar episodes in the lives of Rama, Merlin, and Arthur, demonstrates how completely his success belongs to him alone, although, like Robin Hood and his companions, Aeneas and Achates, Gilgamesh and Enkidu, David and Jonathan, and Arthur and Lancelot, Herakles usually was accompanied by a sidekick, often his nephew, Iolaus.

The relentless search for the golden apples guarded by the Hesperides symbolizes a standard theme, striving for the unattainable, as demonstrated by a host of literary models: Jason's search for the Golden Fleece, the Arthurian knights' longing for the Holy Grail, Hugh Conway's pilgrimage back to Shangri-La in James Hilton's *Lost Horizon*, and the pilgrimage to the unreachable nirvana of Arthur Clarke's *2001* and the sequel, *2010.* Also, Herakles, like Jason, suffered the treachery of a woman, although Dejanira brought about his death out of innocence rather than spite. Like Arthur, Herakles was ferried by boat to his final resting place, and in the style of Moses, Elijah, and Christ, was taken up into heaven and made immortal.

As an object of satire, Herakles's humiliating enslavement in womanly garb delineates how thoroughly service to Queen Omphale unmanned him. Euripides also takes a degrading tack by depicting Herakles as a drunken debaucher during the visit to Admetes's palace. These episodes balance the unselfish dash into the Underworld to snatch Alcestis from the arms of Thanatos as well as the many altruistic moments when Herakles assisted a host to defeat a military enemy, a common motif in his lore. Such isolated episodes, particularly the last minute inclusion of Herakles among the Argonauts for a brief segment of the voyage, and the fiery death that freed him from mortal constraints, demonstrate how loose, dissociated segments of the myth were interpolated into the original tale of Herakles and his twelve labors.

In immortality, Herakles continued to influence earthly events and to represent victory over adversity. Homer honored Herakles in Book 4 of the *Odyssey* by depicting him as one of the heroes Odysseus visited in the Underworld. Armed with his trusty bow, Herakles continued as in life, equipped for action and daunting to behold, even to the limp ghosts who populated the Underworld. The soft side of the great Greek poured out in tearful exclamation at the sight of Odysseus, to whom he cried:

> I see that you, too, endure wretched burdens like
> those I bore in the days of old when I walked the
> earth. Although Zeus is my father, it was my fate
> to serve a man far inferior to me and to perform
> the difficult labors he devised.

Sophocles used Herakles as the *deus ex machina* to end the play *Philoctetes* with an edict from Zeus that Philoctetes must fulfill his role as one of the actors in the concluding episode of Troy's fall.

Euripides used the dire tale of Herakles's fateful marriage to Dejanira as commentary on Phaedra's doomed love.

Aristophanes included Herakles in the delegation of Olympians who established peace in *The Birds.* In *The Frogs,* Herakles's house in Athens is the setting of the comedy.

In Livy's Roman lore, during the rule of Ancus Martius, one of Rome's first kings, Herakles visited his Italian temple and played dice with the groundskeeper. The game, which the god won, netted him a banquet and the sexual favors of Acca Larentia, the Roman deity who became foster mother to Romulus and Remus.

Numerous symbols evolved from events in Herakles's life, for example:

- Hera turned the Nemean lion and Cancer, the crab, into constellations. Herakles himself is found in the constellation of the Kneeler, which depicts

his fight with the Ligurians or his battle with Ladon, the serpent that guarded the apples of the Hesperides. A third constellation, Ophiuchus, "the serpent-holder," honors Herakles's killing of the snake that ravaged the river Sagaris. Likewise, his nurse, the nymph Amalthea, evolved into the star Capella or "nanny goat," the horns of which flowed with ambrosia and nectar. The twelve labors together formed a kind of zodiac.

- The Mysians continued the symbolic hunt for Hylas with a ritual calling of his name.
- While wrestling the water god Achelous, spirit of Greece's most famous river, Herakles severed his horn, which he presented to the Hesperides. They filled it with harvest fruits. In later years, the horn, a parallel of the horns of Amalthea, was known as the cornucopia or horn of plenty, which the Roman goddess Bona Copia (or Bona Dea or Fauna) received as an emblem of bounty. Because the goddess declined to let Herakles drink from her sacred spring, he forbade all women entrance to his shrine. Another explanation of his men-only worship was the exclusion of men from the annual festival of the Bona Dea or Good Goddess, over which Julius Caesar's wife is said to have officiated.
- The Roman Recaranus or Garanus, an alternate version of Herakles, was worshipped at the Ara Maxima or Greatest Altar, where suppliants offered a tithe equal to one-tenth of their worth.
- Herakles, who decked himself in poplar leaves bleached white by his sweating forehead, introduced the silver or white poplar from the Underworld to lower Greece, where its bark became the only fuel used to kindle the flames on Zeus's altar.
- Death from the garment soaked in Nessus's blood gave rise to the phrase *a shirt of Nessus,* denoting a fatal gift.
- Herakles established the most noble dynasties of the ancient world, including Latinus of Italy and Alexander of Macedonia.

Events in Herakles's life also figure in art, music, and literature. Graphic and three-dimensional depictions of Herakles center on miraculous strength, such as poses from babyhood with serpents clutched in his two fists or scenes from adulthood marked by the lion's pelt, which traditionally covered his head and one shoulder, and the club, which won him an impressive list of victories. Vase paintings, coins, amphorae, Samian dinnerware, and mosaics are among the varied recreations of the Greek hero's life, including these:

- A bronze mirror dating from the Etruscan age, now located in the Boston Museum of Fine Art.
- Damaged Roman statuary dating to the second century A.D. at Side, Turkey.

- A silver cup, now located in Copenhagen's National Museum, featuring a frieze in high relief detailing Herakles's relationship with Philoctetes.
- One of the stone heads of gods that look out from Mount Nemrut in Turkey.
- A crater or wine bowl housed in the Corinthian museums.
- A painting by Lysippus.
- A temple in Lindus, Rhodes, featuring Parrhasius's paintings of Herakles and an unusual worship service calling for harsh, abusive liturgy.
- A sixth-century B.C. vase by Exekias.
- A silver platter in the Bibliotheque Nationale of Paris depicting the final gasp of the Nemean lion after Herakles abandons bow, club, and scabbard.
- A statue by Myron that was found on the island of Samos.
- A statue by Scopas and temple within a sacred compound in Sicyon near the Corinthian gulf.
- A wooden statue by Daedalus in Arcadia.
- A stone statue in the city square of Bythium near the Laconian gulf.
- Giovanni Bologna's seventeenth-century sculpture of Herakles clubbing a writhing Centaur.
- A group of statues honoring Herakles's theft of Apollo's deer adorning a temple at Veii, Italy, and a temple at Ostia at the mouth of the Tiber River.
- A fifth-century B.C. sculpture of Herakles flexing his bow.

Overwhelmingly, artistic representations refer to the twelve labors, which are pictured on the metopes of Zeus's temple at Olympia as well as a perfect Ionian vase featuring a comic view of Eurystheus cowering in his vase from the Erymanthian boar, now housed in the Louvre, metopes located in the Palermo National Museum showing Herakles readying himself for the final blow against Hippolyta, and a depiction of Iolaus and Herakles fighting a monster on a vase now shown in the British Museum. The Munich Museum of Antiquities owns a magnificent cup shaped in the sixth century B.C. by Cachrylion and painted by Euphronius with a montage of scenes from the twelve labors. Herakles figures mark the pediment of Aphaia's temple at Aegina and decorate Pompeiian wall paintings. A sculpture made by Glycon in the first century B.C. and housed in the Naples National Museum moves to the end of the hero's hardships to depict a peaceful moment with Herakles propped against his club. One of the best preserved likenesses is the figure of Herakles with a cushion on his shoulder to pad the weight of the world, which Atlas gladly leaves with him.

As sculpted and painted by Michelangelo, Reni, Andrea Briosco, Charles Gleyre, Peter-Paul Rubens, Charles Le Moyne, and other European artists, Herakles in Christian hagiology superimposes the larger-than-life hero over saints. Such art treasures as the Colleoni Chapel at Bergamo, Roman catacombs, and Florence's Campanile honor pagan scenes of the twelve labors alongside biblical stories. In the Renaissance, Nicola Pisano drew Herakles in the Pisa Cathedral. Later works by Agostino Carracci,

Nicolas Poussin, and Paolo Veronese stress Herakles choosing between a life of luxury and a life of commitment to ideals.

Literary tributes, which are heavily laced with Herakles/Hercules references, date from early times in their admiration for the strongman. Book 5 of the *Iliad* describes the deities whom the presumptuous Herakles smote, including Hera and Hades. Homer fumes, "Brute, heavy-handed, who thought nothing of the bad he was doing, who with his archery hurt the gods that dwell on Olympus!" Later writers, on the other hand, glossed over the emphasis of violence and tended to dignify, even deify Herakles, whose life of dedication, forbearance, and earned immortality parallels aspects of Stoic, Cynic, and Christian philosophy. Because the Roman Hercules achieved popularity for his stance against evil and tyranny, the Stoic writers idealized him as a model of superhuman strength, boldness, daring, and altruism; Petrarch stressed Hercules's choice of a life of duty and struggle, a concept he extracted from Cicero's *On Duties.*

Depictions from Ovid and Boethius influenced the Middle Ages, particularly Geoffrey Chaucer's *Monk's Tale,* which compares the Greek hero with Adam, Samson, and Alexander. French poet Pierre de Ronsard featured the hero as "Hercule Chrétien" in his *Hymns.* Additional citations are legion: Geoffrey Chaucer's *House of Fame* and *Parliament of Fowls;* Edmund Spenser's *Faerie Queene, Hymn in Honour of Love, Tears of the Muses* and *Ruins of Time;* John Skelton's *Philip Sparrow;* Samuel Butler's *Hudibras;* George Chapman's *Shadow of Night;* William Shakespeare's *All's Well That Ends Well, Coriolanus, Merchant of Venice, King Henry VI* (Part I), *Love's Labour's Lost, Cymbeline, Midsummer Night's Dream,* and *Much Ado about Nothing;* Christopher Marlowe's *Dido Queen of Carthage* and *Hero and Leander;* Ben Jonson's *And Must I Sing?;* John Milton's *Sonnet 23;* Andrew Marvell's *Letter to Dr. Ingelo;* Sir Philip Sidney's *Espilus and Therion;* Michael Drayton's *Fourth Eclogue, Aureng-Zebe,* and *To My Honoured Friend;* William Wordsworth's *Laodamia;* Robert Southey's *Roderick;* Lord Byron's *The Island* and *On the Death of Mr. Fox;* Robert Browning's *Aristophanes' Apology, Sordello, Balaustion's Adventure, The Ring and the Book,* and *Prince Hohenstiel-Schwangau;* Robert Owen's *Antaeus;* George Meredith's *The Labourer;* Wallace Gould's *Drunken Herakles;* George Santayana's *Odes;* Algernon Swinburne's *Atalanta in Calydon;* Robert Graves's *To Ogmian Hercules;* C. Day Lewis's *Hero and Saint;* and Agatha Christie's *Labors of Hercules.*

Musical settings of the Herakles myth occur in a variety of European vehicles ranging from the anonymous opera *Hercules at the Crossroads* to a Bach cantata to Camille Saint-Saens's piano piece, *Caprice sur les Airs de Ballet de Alceste,* and symphony, *La Jeunesse d'Hercule.* Georg Friedrich Handel wrote two oratorios, *Choice of Hercules* and *Hercules.* A particularly poignant segment of the Herakles canon is the Alcestis myth, a favorite of Robert Browning, which is featured in operas by Christoph Gluck and Jean-Baptiste Lully, and plays by Johann Gottfried von Herder, T. S. Eliot, and Vittorio Alfieri. The American Thornton Wilder wrote *Alcestiade,* which was developed into an opera.

❧ See Also

Ajax the Great, Alcaeus, Jason and Medea, Nestor, Orpheus, Sthenelus, Theseus.

❧ Ancient Sources

Aelian's *On the Nature of Animals* and *Varia Historia;* Agias of Troezen's *Returns of Heroes;* Antoninus Liberalis's *Metamorphoses;* Apollodorus's *Epitome* and *Library;* Apollonius of Rhodes's *Argonautica;* Arian's *Indica;* Athenaeus's *The Learned Banquet;* Bacchylides's *Choral Lyric XVIII;* Callimachus's *Hymn to Artemis* and *Hymn to Delos;* Cicero's *On Duties* and *On the Nature of the Gods;* Conon's *Narrations;* Demodocus's *History of Herakles;* Diodorus Siculus's *Library of History;* Dionysius of Halicarnassus's *Roman Antiquities;* Diotimus's *Heraclea;* Eratosthenes's *Star Placements;* Euripides's *Alcestis, Children of Herakles, Hippolytus, Ion*, and *The Mad Herakles;* Eusebius's *Preparation for the Gospel;* Eustathius on Homer's *Iliad* and *Odyssey;* First Vatican Mythographer; Hellanicus's *Roman Antiquities;* Herodotus's *Histories;* Hesiod's *Catalogue of Women, Shield of Herakles,* and *Theogony;* Homer's *Iliad, Kerkopes,* and *Odyssey;* Horace's *Odes;* Hyginus's *Fables* and *Poetic Astronomy;* Lactantius on Statius's *Thebaid;* Livy's *From the Foundations of the City;* Lucian's *Dialogue of the Dead* and *Dialogue of the Gods;* Lycophron's *Alexandra;* Lysimachus; Macrobius's *Saturnalia;* Mnaseas's *Travels;* Ovid's *Fasti, Heroides,* and *Metamorphoses;* Pausanias's *Description of Greece;* Pherecydes's *Heptamochos;* Philochorus's *Atthis;* Philostratus's *Imagines* and *Life of Apollonius of Tyana;* Photius's *Library;* Pindar's *Isthmian Odes, Nemean Odes, Olympian Odes,* and *Pythian Odes;* Pisander's *Exploits of Herakles;* Plautus's *Amphitryon;* Pliny the Elder's *Natural History;* Plutarch's *Aristides, On Love, On Rivers, On the Face Appearing in the Orb of the Moon, Parallel Lives, Roman Questions,* and *Theseus;* Pollux's *Onomasticon;* Polyaenus's *Stratagems;* Praxilla's drinking songs; Ptolemy Hephaestion's *On Homer;* Scholiast on Apollonius of Rhodes's *Argonautica;* Scholiast on Aristophanes's *Frogs;* Scholiast on Euripides's *Alcestis;* Scholiast on Pindar's *Nemean Odes* and *Olympian Odes;* Seneca's *The Mad Hercules;* Servius on Virgil's *Aeneid* and *Georgics;* Simonides of Ceos's *Verse;* Sophocles's *Trachinian Women* and *Philoctetes;* Stephanus Byzantium's *Bargasa, Psophis, Olynthus,* and *Zoster;* Strabo's *Historical Sketches;* Suidas's *Melite;* Theocritus's *Idylls;* Thucydides's *History;* Johannes Tzetzes's *On Lycophron;* Valerius Flaccus's *Argonautica;* Varro's *On the Latin Language;* Virgil's *Georgics;* Xenophon's *Hellenica* and *Memoirs of Socrates;* Zenobius's *Proverbs.*

Jason and Medea

[jay' suhn] and [muh · dee' uh]

Genealogy and Background

Most readers of mythology can name one voyager along with his ship—Jason and the *Argo*. The mild-mannered son of Aeson and Alcimede, Jason (originally named Diomedes) was born in the seaport of Iolcus in Thessaly, the fertile plain lying in northern Greece south of Mount Pelion. His grandparents were Clymene and Phylacus, a Thessalian hero. After Aeson's brother, Pelias, snatched the throne, Jason's parents reported him stillborn or dead in infancy and smuggled him out of the court and east to a coastal peninsula. Aeson and Alcimede, grieved to part with their infant, passed the time until Jason could mature and reclaim power.

Tutored in medical lore on Mount Pelion by Chiron, the learned Centaur who taught Asclepius and Achilles, Jason, whose name means "the healer," prepared himself well, and in adulthood returned home. A tall, long-haired youth, he presented so good an account of himself that his uncle Pelias wanted him out of the way and dispatched him to Colchis, a distant land beyond the Black Sea that bordered the Caspian Sea. Jason's assignment was to fetch the Golden Fleece. On the outbound voyage, Jason spent time on the island of Lemnos, west of Troy on the Turkish coast, and sired sons Euneus and Nebrophonus by Queen Hypsipyle.

Clothed in the hide of a tiger and clasping a lance in each hand, Jason, dashing and ruggedly handsome at age twenty-one, returned home unannounced on Poseidon's feast day. Having lost a sandal in a river bed, Jason wore no shoe on his left foot. On the day that Jason forded the Anaurian stream, Hera, disguised as an old woman, insisted on being borne across on his shoulder. In performing the deed, Jason lost his shoe, but was in too great a hurry to attend the festival to search the mud for it. He also failed to question the old lady and learn her true identity.

Hera apparently had good reason to choose Jason to wreak vengeance on the impious Pelias. Because Pelias had repeatedly avoided

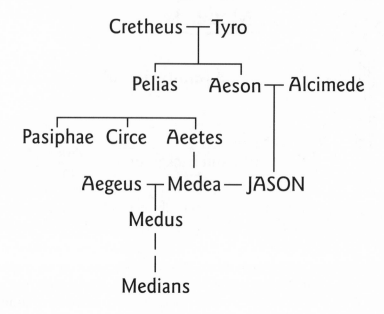

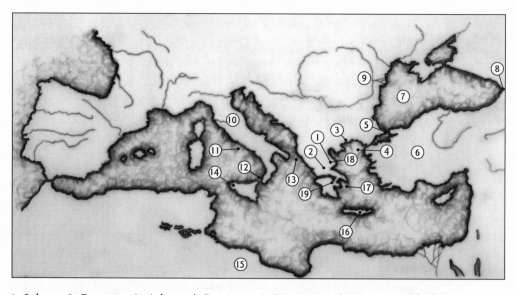

1. Iolcus 2. Pagasae 3. Athos 4. Lemnos 5. Bosporus 6. Mysia 7. Black Sea
8. Colchis 9. Danube River 10. Po River 11. Aeaea 12. Strait of Messina
13. Corcyra 14. Drepane 15. Libya 16. Crete 17. Aegina 18. Iolcus
19. Corinth

her worship, Hera decided to punish him by placing a curse on him to be enacted by a shoeless man. More to her purpose, Hera chose Jason to ally with Medea, a known enchantress with enough occult powers to enact Hera's retaliation. Also, Medea's father had once ruled Corinth, so her interest in the Greek mainland was both romantic and political.

The surprise arrival just as Pelias was performing a sacrifice placed the king in a tenuous position: he had to observe the rules of hospitality, especially during Poseidon's feast day. Pelias was shaken by Jason's one-shoed appearance, which was described by an oracle who warned Pelias to avoid such a man. For five days, Jason, bolstered by his uncles, Amythaon and Pheres, and his cousins, Admetus and Melampus, remained an untroubling guest, then requested an audience with Pelias on the sixth day to claim rule of Iolcus, either for himself or his father.

Pelias, according to Apollonius's *Argonautica,* devised a heinous plot: he pretended to puzzle over a visitation by Phrixus's ghost, which urged the aged king to honor Phrixus's spirit by returning the Golden Fleece from Colchis to Iolcus. To rid himself of Jason and the threat to his rule, Pelias "made ready to his hurt a grievous task of seamanship, that so he might lose his return in the deep or haply among strange folk."(Apollonius's *Argonautica)* Thus, Pelias agreed to abdicate if Jason would accept a fool's quest: to retrieve the fleece of the magical flying ram that had provided Phrixus an escape from his father Anthamas, thus ridding Pelias of the bourne of Phrixus's ghost. Along the way, Jason had to snatch the pelt from an unsleeping dragon owned by Aeetes, king of Colchis. Pelias was so set on destroying Jason that he allowed his own son Acastus to join the crew of a ship Pelias assumed would never return.

Journey For the quest, Jason consulted an oracle and studied the advice of Phrixus's son, Argus. At Pagasae in Magnesia, Athena assisted Jason, Argus, and Glaucus with the building of the *Argo,* the world's first longboat, which Jason named for Argus. The goddess even taught Jason how to use a ruler to measure planking. A devout man, he cropped a bough from Zeus's sacred talking oak at Dodona and installed it aboard as a prow. Because the wood was blessed with the gift of prophecy, it served as a sacred talisman and spoke to the crew in dire moments.

To sail the forty-oared ship, Jason recruited approximately fifty notable sailors, whom the locals termed Minyan chiefs. In Pindar's words in *Nemean Odes:*

> Hera kindled all-persuading sweet desire in the sons of
> gods for the ship *Argo,* so that none should be left behind
> to nurse a life without danger at his mother's side, but
> rather that he should find even against death the fairest
> antidote in his own courage along with the others of his age.

The men, many of whom participated in the Calydonian boar hunt and fathered heroes of the Trojan War, voted Herakles their leader, but he conceded the post to the originator of the expedition.

Jason wisely chose Orpheus as coxswain; Hermes's son, Aethalides, as herald; and the Boeotian prophet, Tiphys, scanner of wind, sun, and stars, as pilot. Four seers—Mopsus, Amphiaraus, Idmon, and Apollonius—accompanied a crew composed of mortals and demigods, the military might of Greece. Most famous of the crew were Idas, Lynceus, Herakles, Theseus, and the semidivine twins, Castor and Pollux. Minor members included Actor; Admetus; Amphidamas; Amphion; Ancaeus; Areius; Ascalaphys; Asclepius; Asterius; Augeas; Autolycus; Butes; Caeneus; Calais; Canthus; Cepheus; Clymenus; Clytius; Coronus; Deucalion; Echion; Erginus; Eribotes; Euphemus; Euryalus; Eurydamas; Eurytion; Eurytus; Hippalcimus; Hyllus, who was Herakles's son; Ialmenus; Iolaus; Iphicles; Iphiclus; Iphis; Iphitus; Laertes; Laocoon; Leitus; Leodocus; Melampus; Meleager; Menoetius; Mopsus; Nauplius; Nestor; Oileus; Palaemonius; Peleus; Peneleus; Periclymenus; Phalerus; Phanus; Philammon; Phlias; Pirithous; Poeas; Polyphemus; Staphylus; Talaus; Telamon; Thersanor; Tydeus; and Zetes. The only warrior Jason declined was Atalanta, who, as the one female among fifty males, might cause squabbling among the sailors.

So magnificent was the flashing armor of Jason's band that throngs gathered around them asking the intent of Pelias, mustering so many heroes. So fierce was the collected might that people feared for Aeetes's palace and predicted that the king would hand over the Golden Fleece without daring to anger so formidable an army. The Argonauts, they believed, were invincible.

When Idmon proclaimed the omens propitious, the Argonauts slaughtered two oxen and prayed to Apollo for a safe departure. The oracle indicated that Jason's sailors would all return, except for Idmon, Apollo's son, who would die in Asia. So Jason, in the embrace of his grieving mother who had clutched him briefly at birth and then during the days of the festival after he declared himself to Pelias, loosed her arms and signaled for his men to launch the ship. In a final farewell gesture, he kissed the hand of the priestess, Iphias, who made no reply, imparted no blessing. The *Argo*, an admirable craft, "scooped out a space as wide as the ship's girth encompassed, and about the prow into the deep they dug out all that she would take to run in, when they hauled her down." (Apollonious's *Argonautica*) Over smooth rollers, the keel slid into Pagasae harbor as Tiphys called out encouragement to the crew.

Seated two to a bench, the rowers dipped dry oars into the brine. In Onomacritus's version, Hera puffed out their sails and the *Argo*, as though endowed with its own spirit, shot forward. As the ship glided smoothly out to sea toward the coastal town of Tisa, Chiron came down to the shore to wave farewell, as did Peleus's wife, holding up the young Achilles to catch a glimpse of Peleus, his departing father.

As Apollonius narrates, the Argonauts pursued a sensible route from the mainland of the Pelasgi, up the shore past the Pelian Cliffs in Magnesia, to the Sepian headland and the island of Sciathos in the Aegean Sea, and on to Peiresia. At length, they arrived at the cairn of Dolops, where they paused at evening, offered sacrifice, and rested for two days. Moving rapidly, they continued past Meliboea and Homole, beyond the mouth of the Amyrus River in view of mounts Ossa and Olympus. By nightfall they were as far east of Greece as Pallene and Canastra. By morning, they had reached the Thracian crest of Athos on what is now the European side of Turkey.

The craft made its way southeast to Myrine on Sintian Lemnos, Queen Hypsipyle's rugged matriarchal stronghold. There a year past, the women had slain their faithless men, leaving only the queen's father, Thaos, alive, whom she set adrift in a small boat. The militant female band, clad in full armor, rushed down to Myrine's shore, fearful of attack. Jason dispatched Aethalides, his messenger, with Hermes's staff, to beg quarter for the Argonauts. At sundown, Hypsipyle, the white-haired regent, on the advice of her nurse, Polyxo, realized that a civilization cannot long endure without procreation. Grudgingly, Hypsipyle welcomed the crew.

Jason, resplendent in a purple and red mantle woven by a goddess and worked in intricate patterns featuring the Cyclopes, Cytherea, chariot racing, Phoebus Apollo in boyhood, and Phrixus on the flying ram, carried a spear given him by Atalanta. After hearing Hypsipyle's recent difficulties, he expressed his concerns for the quest for the Golden Fleece. When his audience ended, he posted Herakles and his associates to guard the *Argo* so that the rest of the crew could visit Hypsipyle's palace and enjoy the all-female populace, who danced a welcome to the Argonauts.

After lengthy delay on Lemnos, Herakles grew testy, and hammering on each lintel with a stout stick, he reminded the sailors that the fleece would not be handed over by godly generosity—they still had to make the effort to obtain it. Hypsipyle, enamored of her new lover, desired that Jason remain and give her sons to repopulate the island with males. Jason, however, rededicated himself to his voyage and requested that, if the queen bore him a son, she should send the child to Iolcus so that his parents might raise a male child in his place.

On advice from Orpheus, from Lemnos the *Argo* sped by night to Electra's island to learn her secrets to help them sail safely over the cold northeast waters. Their course, which avoided the hostile Laomedon of Troy, took them straight through the Propontis, which the Romans called the Sea of Marmara, toward the mouth of the Black Sea with Thrace to port and the island Imbros to starboard. By nightfall, they reached Chersonese, a seaport city on the northern shore of the Black Sea; the next morning, they pressed on, keeping Rhoeteum to port and Mount Ida to starboard. From Dardania, they sailed straight to Abydos, avoided Percote and the shores of Abarnis as they headed northeast from the Hellespont. Among fearsome six-handed monsters, they made landfall at Cyzicus's kingdom in Propontis, the northern shore of Troy, where Jason, mindful of his dependence on the divine, set up an anchor stone to Athena at the Artacian fountain.

The king, a youthful monarch recently wed to Cleite, invited the Argonauts to a sumptuous entertainment and offered them stores to refill the ship's larders. The next morning, Cyzicus escorted Jason to the top of Mount Didymus to determine his position. Below, an attack by giants failed to daunt Herakles, who was again left on watch. From shore patrol he shot the savage brigands with his bow and killed each and every one. Jason set forth again, sailing rapidly the entire day from Cyzicus's kingdom.

That same night, while awaiting the end of a storm, the sailors were driven back over the same course. The native Dolionians feared that the unknown vessel was filled with pirates and opened fire. Cyzicus joined the fray and was killed by Jason. Cleite, overcome with grief, hanged herself. When daylight revealed the grievous error, the sailors spent three days mourning their former host and hostess, performed traditional Greek funeral rites, marched three times about the bier, and honored the king with games. Their responsibilities complete, they prepared to cast off but remained twelve days on shore as wild winds whipped the Black Sea to an angry froth. In the night, Mopsus, who stood guard duty, heard the call of a kingfisher and roused Jason to dedicate the image of Cybele at Mount Didymus to guarantee a fortuitous departure.

Jason rejoiced that he could continue under a propitious wind. The *Argo,* following the Macrian cliffs to starboard and keeping Thrace to port, entered the Bosporus and made its approach to the city of Adresteia on the shore of Mysia, the northernmost portion of the Turkish coast, where the crew cut an old stump and carved out a likeness of Rhea, queen of the earth, which Argus polished. With Orpheus in the lead, they danced in full armor to drum and tambourine, beating swords on shields. Inhabitants showered them with hospitality. So effective was their rhythmic ritual that wild beasts joined in the frolic and a marvelous spring gushed forth. The event climaxed with a feast to Rhea. By dawn, the liturgy complete, the Argonauts rowed on.

The sailors developed a healthy competition, refusing to give up their pull on the oars lest they lose respect. Mightiest of all was Herakles, who rowed so lustily that he jostled the ship's timbers. At the Rhyndacus River and the Aegeon Mound, not far east of Phrygia, Jason collapsed with fatigue and Herakles rowed so stoutly that he broke his oar. The Argonauts moved inland near the Arganthonian mountain at the Cios River.

The Mysians rejoiced to welcome Jason, whom they had spotted on his approach from the west. In record time, they kindled a fire, presented dry straw for beds, and offered fresh mutton and mead for refreshment. At dark, Jason toasted Apollo, the god of embarkation. Herakles, bereft of an oar, went into the woods to find pine suitable for whittling a new one. The crew lost Hylas, whom Dryope and her nymphs lured into the depths of a spring as he sought a fresh pitcher of water, and at dawn, Jason abandoned Herakles, who strode the countryside demanding a search for the winsome Hylas.

The sailors, except for Zetes and Calais, were loyal to their stout oarsman and demanded that Jason return for Herakles, accusing their captain of bearing ill will for losing the rowing contest. Jason declined and pressed for speed. Polyphemus deliberately did not rejoin the crew and remained in Mysia, where he founded the city of Cios midway along the southern shore of the Propontis. The captain urged the pilot to return until the sea god Glaucus sprang up and claimed that the two maroonings were Zeus's will. Jason, a man of god, obeyed and set his sights eastward toward Colchis.

From Mysia the craft sailed east a whole day and was becalmed at Amycus's kingdom of the Bebryces in Bithynia on the southeastern shore of the Black Sea in modern Baykoz, where the eccentric king hurled into the waves any stranger who refused to don leather gloves and meet him in the boxing ring. With a stunning smash, Pollux killed the ruler, who had taken unfair advantage by wearing a metal-studded glove; the crew raided the king's stores and forced an uneasy truce with locals. Orpheus ended the night with soothing hymns to Zeus.

A day later, having navigated more of the swirling Bosporus, the *Argo* reached Salmydessa on the European side in Thrace and encountered blind Phineus, the clairvoyant, who was beset by Aellopus and Ocypete, two foul-smelling, feathered, brass Harpies, female bird demons whose name means "snatchers." This vigilant duo made revolting droppings about the table and snatched away Phineus's food before he could guide it to his mouth. Jason requested advice about his mission, which Phineus pledged as soon as the Harpies stopped plaguing his life. The sons of Boreas, blessed with the gift of flight, warded off the loathsome bird-women and would have killed them, but Iris, the messenger of Hera, warned that they belonged to Zeus and should not be harmed. The befuddled pair of birds flapped in consternation and called back to Phineus with discordant cries.

In gratitude for a respite from the Harpies, Phineus, who recognized the Argonauts from a propitious oracle, warned that at a place where two seas flow together the *Argo* should steer clear of the Symplegades or Cyanean Rocks, possibly errant ice floes, which rushed together in a violent clash. Phineus explained how to test the rocks with a dove. He concluded that the *Argo* should proceed to the Rhebas River and sail directly to the land of the Mariandyni, who lived across from the Thynian isle. He enumerated other landmarks, including the entrance to the Underworld, the plain of Doias, and three cities dominated by Amazons. Beyond lay the Caucasus Mountains and Colchis, which is today one of the southernmost tips of Russia.

So dire was Phineus's counsel that the doughty Argonauts were silent with apprehension. Jason exhorted him for his frightening prophecies and asked,

> How am I to act, how shall I come again over so wide a path of sea,
> in ignorance myself and with a crew alike ignorant, for Colchis lies
> at the uttermost end of Pontus and the earth?

> (Apollonius's *Argonautica*)

Phineus found an uplifting response: "My child, as soon as you have escaped through the Black Rocks, be of good cheer, for a god will guide you on a different route." (Apollonius's *Argonautica*) On Phineus's advice, Jason pledged to follow Athena.

Wafted on summer breezes, Jason's *Argo,* under Athena's guiding hand, moved out of sheltered waters onto the deep sea. Into a sinuous passage steeply walled by cliffs, the crew rowed into treacherous waters. On Tiphys's advice, Euphemus, acting on Phineus's prophecy, released a dove to test the safety of the straits. In Apollonius's words from his *Argonautica*:

> At once the two rocks met again with a clash; and the foam leapt up in a seething mass like a cloud, and grimly roared the sea, and all around the great firmament bellowed. And the hollow caves echoed beneath the rugged rocks as the sea went surging in, and high on the cliffs was the white spray vomited as the billows dashed up them. Then did the current spin the ship round.

The dove slipped by except for its tail feathers. Tiphys urged the sailors to row their hardest. They stalled in the very heart of the gushing strait until Athena stretched out her left hand and gave them a push. So rapid was their passage that Jason lost only the tip of the *Argo's* stern after he scuttled through. Jason soothed his brave oarsmen with a promise, "I vow there will be no other horror in store such as this, if we surely go our way, following the counsel of Phineus." (Apollonius's *Argonautica*)

In Book 12 of the *Odyssey,* Homer lauded Jason's mettle in facing this most difficult point of the journey:

> Sole this voyage hath made, of the ships which fare on the ocean, *Argo* ever renowned, as she sailed from the land of Aeetes. Aye and the *Argo* too on the huge rocks surely had driven save for the guidance of Hera, who showed such favor to Jason.

And the rocks, doomed to immobility after Jason broke the spell, never again threatened a voyager.

The *Argo* toiled on, reaching the Thynian isle, where the crew beached their craft and marveled at the appearance of Apollo, the divine son of Leto. Fearful that they gazed into the eyes of a god, they abased themselves until he had flown away. Orpheus advised Jason, "Be gracious, O be gracious in thy appearing, prince!" (Apollonius's *Argonautica*) Orpheus instructed the crew to name the shrine Harmonia, a sanctuary to Apollo, and to sacrifice the rich thigh meat of a goat and sing "Hail, all hail!" to the god. They also planned to return by the same route and to repeat the rite.

At last in the area east of Turkey, on the third day out, the Argonauts located Cape Acherusia at Acheron's mouth and the cave of Hades, which belched an icy blast from the nether reaches of the Underworld. The ship approached the Mariandyni, ruled by Lycus, a hospitable monarch and enemy of the Bebryces. So thrilled was he with his visitors that he dispatched his son as a member of the crew. During the last hour of their sojourn, Idmon, Aeolus's son, was gored by a wild pig and bled to death in his companions' arms and thus fulfilled the prophecy that he would not return home. Lycus joined Jason in appropriate rites to honor Idmon and heaped his barrow as was fitting to a noble crewman.

Temporarily prevented from departure, the *Argo* remained in Mariandyni territory. A second casualty, Tiphys the pilot, contracted an unspecified fatal illness while Idmon's funeral was being conducted and fell dead. So grieved were the crew that they cast themselves down on the beach and considered giving up the quest for the Golden Fleece. Ancaeus, Nauplius, Euphemus, and Erginus, Poseidon's white-haired son, volunteered to replace the pilot. Jason wisely chose Ancaeus, a worthy helmsman.

Again on the deep sea twelve days later, Jason halted at the tomb of Sthenelus, Actor's son, and conversed with the spirit, which Persephone sent up from Hades. Mopsus advised that Jason appease Sthenelus's spirit by pouring libations. So moved was Orpheus by the event that he dedicated the spot to his instrument, the lyre. From that point on, the strand was called Lyra.

Once more at sea, they passed streams and headlands and other landmarks and heard the hair-raising shrieks of Prometheus, whom Zeus had chained to the Caucasus Mountains to be pecked by an eagle. After a brief pause on Assyrian shores, they passed the Thermodon River and the Amazonian mountains, where Autolycus, one of Herakles's replacements, led a foray against the giant female warriors, and made for Tibareni territory, the Holy Mountain, and Ares's isle, where vicious birds attacked the oarsmen. Moving inland, the reconnaissance party raised a clatter by beating swords on breastplates and shields and routed thousands of birds.

The weather threatened with dark skies and sharp winds. Jason, faithful to Phineus's prophecy, recognized the divine touch in events and rescued four castaways on Ares's isle. Two were kinsmen, Argus and Melus, Chalciope's sons and Aeetes's grandsons, who were marooned on the unnamed island. The *Argo,* its crew restocked, moved closer to the goal: Aea, the realm of Aeetes. After thinking over where the *Argo* was headed, Argus demurred from entering so hostile a court as Aea because the king, Aeetes, was rumored to be a savage killer of all outsiders. Argus also warned Jason that the snaky monster that guarded the fleece never slept. Jason's men, listening to these dreadful words, grew pale. Only the bold words of Pelias reminded the men that they were an august body of warriors fit to face Aeetes.

With Argus and Melus as guides, the *Argo* approached the river Thermodon, avoided the Caucasus Mountains where Prometheus struggled against the chains that held him firm as bait for a ravenous eagle, and reached the muddy Phasis River at the extreme eastern border of the great Black Sea. Near the garden where the fleece lay guarded, King Aeetes warded off all strangers. Jason, maintaining his rule of fairness, opened a free discussion and encouraged his crew to make known their reservations regarding the fearful task:

> For all alike share this quest, and all alike can speak; and he who silently withholds his purpose and counsel, let him know that 'tis he and he alone who robbeth this expedition of its return.

> (Apollonius's *Argonautica*)

Taking the most difficult assignment, Jason, armed with Hermes's staff, prepared to enter Aeetes's halls with only four men guarding him. He announced that he intended to use reason rather than force, thus avoiding ill will.

At this point, Jason, having sacrificed to the earth gods, entered the gorgeous inner court of the palace of Colchis, seaport capital of Aea, the Greek word for "land." He encountered Medea, votary of Hecate, and her sister Chalciope, who rejoiced that Jason had returned her sons. The outcry brought king, queen, and servants, who especially welcomed Argus, the court favorite. Argus introduced Jason to Aeetes and told his life's story and the need to complete the difficult venture so far from Greece.

With little fanfare, Argus, the king's grandson, spoke for Jason and requested the fleece in exchange for a fair price. Aeetes, literally "man of the land (Aea)," angered by his grandson's potential threat to the throne, acceded, but extracted Jason's promise to complete two seemingly impossible tests: to yoke a pair of bronze-hoofed, fire-breathing bulls, and to sow a plowed field with dragon's teeth. Secretly, Aeetes expected Jason to fail and plotted to burn him and his Argonauts within the body of the *Argo*.

Jason was at first stymied by the enormity of the task. He might have despaired had not the princess Medea, a noted enchantress and follower of Hecate, been drawn to him. Their mutual attraction was much more than coincidence, for Hera and Athena had inveigled Aphrodite into hatching a love plot. Unseen, Eros, whom Aphrodite had bribed with a golden bauble, flew among the throng and loosed an arrow at Medea. The goddess of love knew what would tempt a woman of Medea's background and provided Jason with the inyx bird to offer her as a love token.

Battling the powers of love, Medea hesitated to rebel against her father in support of the Greek stranger. She suffered troubling dreams. In Ovid's *Metamorphoses* she remonstrated with herself:

> In vain, Medea, do you fight. Some god or other is opposing you; I wonder if this is not what is called love, or at least something like this. For why do the mandates of my father seem too harsh?

Aeetes attempted to immure her until the Argonauts left, but Medea struggled free. To prepare herself for suicide, she inventoried her medicine chest and wept over the collections of nostrums and potions. Then, under Hera's guidance, Medea opted to embrace both life and love. She prostrated herself on Hecate's dire woodland altar, acknowledging, "I see what I am about to do, nor shall ignorance of the truth be my undoing, but love itself." (Ovid's *Metamorphoses*) Ready to accept Jason as lover and thus to challenge her father, she mounted her chariot and drove back to the palace.

In defiance of Aeetes, Medea urged the local peasants to organize song and dance to welcome the Argonauts. Hera obliged Medea by making Jason much handsomer than before. In the background, a crow uttered a warning to Mopsus, Jason's seer, who withdrew, leaving Jason at the temple with Medea. At first sight of him, Medea grew pale, then flushed and felt faint. Jason, as straightforward as when he addressed his sailors, begged her help in retrieving the Golden Fleece.

Argus formally introduced Medea to Jason, opening the way to their friendship and eventual involvement. As part of her spell, Medea offered Jason enchanted balsam or crocus nectar to rub on his body and armaments to make him invulnerable to fire or weapon. She predicted that the teeth, taken from the mouth of Ares's dragon, would germinate into armed warriors whom he could subdue by tossing a stone into their midst, thereby causing them to fight themselves. She pledged to assist Jason if he would accept her as wife and transport her to Greece.

Jason believed Medea and, as a pledge of honor, promised to treasure her as a lawful bride. That night, Jason made certain of his success by robing himself in black and entering a distant part of the forest to worship Hecate. Visions of the snake-wrapped goddess flanked by hellhounds terrified him, yet he maintained control of his fears as he slowly returned to the *Argo* without a backward glance.

The next morning, Jason anointed his shield and weapon with the drug that Medea provided. He followed her advice and, to the Minyans' amazement, completed both tasks assigned by Aeetes. First he strode up to the bulls and petted them like lapdogs before yoking them to the leader pole. He plowed until sunset. Then, while pricking the beasts with his spear to incite them to pull harder, he reached into a bronze helmet and cast out handfuls of dragon's teeth on Ares's field. When armed men sprang up in the furrow, Jason hurled a stone in their midst and caused the soldiers to combat each other. By sunset, the furrows ran heavy with blood and no more soldiers emerged from the ground.

The Greeks were thrilled at Jason's victory and ran to embrace him. Aeetes, furious that Medea had helped Jason elude the treacherous tasks, set out to murder the Argonauts and destroy the *Argo*. Again, Medea intervened by collecting her potions and fleeing the palace. At the ship she implored:

> Save me, friends, me most miserable, yes, and yourselves as well from Aeetes. For all is discovered by now, and no remedy remains. Let us hurry aboard the ship, before Aeetes mounts his swift horses. And I will give you the golden fleece. . . .

(Apollonius's *Argonautica*)

At once they cast off and sped upstream to the garden and the old oak where the Golden Fleece was suspended.

Medea showed Jason how to employ an incantation, juniper branches, and drops of a potent herb to calm the vigilant thousand-coiled dragon with the three-forked tongue and barbed fangs. As the dragon's eyes sagged shut, Jason clambered up the coils and whisked away the treasured Golden Fleece. To assure a safe departure, Medea, aided by Hera, led the Argonauts out of Aea by a secret route. To safeguard their leaving, she instructed Jason to waylay her half-brother, Apsyrtus, on a deserted island and to take him hostage.

Jason crept up behind Apsyrtus and struck him down, then hacked free his limbs. To ward off the angry spirit, Jason licked blood from the ground and spit it back on the dust. At dawn, as the couple fled, Aeetes set out after them. At the mouth of the Ister River, Medea stopped her father's party by sprinkling parts of her brother's dismembered body in the ship's wake, shocking both the Colchians and the Argonauts with her murderous *sangfroid.* Aeetes, overcome with grief at the loss of two beloved children, halted to collect his son's remains, all the while calling to Medea. The Argonauts demanded that Jason set ashore so villainous a woman, but Jason, benighted by love, insisted that the crew think of her as their rescuer rather than as the killer of her own brother.

On the sea once more, the *Argo* sailed toward the Danube to a link with the Adriatic Sea. A storm, stirred up by Zeus, punished the fleeing Argonauts for the death of Prince Apsyrtus. Blown off course, the talking beam of the *Argo* spoke to Jason and urged him and his consort to expiate their blood crime by sailing up the Po and halting at the isle of Medea's aunt Circe for purification. Over a meandering route, the *Argo* made its way to Aeaea, the same enchanted island Odysseus visited on his journey. Jason achieved atonement for the murder, but Circe spoke only to Medea, whom she chastised and warned that retribution would ultimately catch up with her.

At Hera's command, Thetis the sea nymph led the *Argo* past the three sirens, where Orpheus charmed all of the sailors except Butes with his poesy so that they would not succumb to the sirens and their rocky lair. Butes plunged into the Mediterranean and swam toward the enticing female voices. Only Aphrodite's intervention saved him from death. He remained behind and founded Lilybaeum, Sicily.

With Hera's help, the *Argo,* traversing the treacherous Strait of Messina, avoided death at Scylla and Charybdis, the evil whirlpool and its companion monster, a ravenous man-slayer described as surrounded by snarling dogs, baying at the sea. From there the ship passed the Wandering Isles and took shelter at Corcyra or Corfu, Alcinous's island realm in the Ionian Sea opposite Epirus's shore.

On the island of Drepane under Phaeacian jurisdiction, as a Colchian contingent relentlessly pursued Jason and Medea, Alcinous proposed turning the princess over to her father's soldiers, but only if she could still claim virginity. Queen Arete divulged the plot so that Medea would have time to seduce Jason in the Macrian cave. Jason married Medea and enjoyed a night of wedded bliss in a grotto decked with blossoms and carpeted with the Golden Fleece. Orpheus provided the wedding music.

Once more the Argonauts set out. A sudden storm impelled the *Argo* south to the Libyan shore in northern Africa, where they nearly perished from thirst. Herakles saved them by stopping on his way to fetch the golden apples of the Hesperides and digging out a spring. The crew hoisted the *Argo* to their backs and completed portage by way of rollers across the sandy desert to Lake Tritonis. Triton, the spirit of the waters, appeared and explained where the crew could reconnnect with a channel to the Mediterranean. On the way, they lost Canthus to a shepherd's sling and stone, and Mopsus, the augur, who was bitten on the shin by a poisonous snake.

Traveling northeast round the straits of Malea to Crete, the Argonauts fought the giant Talus, a metallic robot stoked red hot. Hephaestus had fitted out the monster with insuperable strength and a single weakness, a nail at the calf of his leg, which stopped a vital vein that fed his body from top to bottom with life-giving ichor. Talus's daily task was to patrol Crete three times and to embrace and singe any who breached the shores. Medea, standing alone on the deck and wrapped in a dark robe, entranced the glowing brass man with hellish spells and caused him to rave and rip out the nail, causing his body fluid to pour out. Talus weakened and toppled from a cliff into the Mediterranean.

The crew, safe from menace, slept on the shore. The next day, they raised an altar to Minoan Athena and pushed their craft again into the foamy waves. A mysterious blackness engulfed the skies. Jason pleaded with the god Apollo to restore the light. A thin ray appeared and guided the *Argo* to Aegina in the gulf south of Athens. The crew dropped anchor alongside an islet the men named Anaphe or the Isle of Discovery. They gratefully worshipped Apollo with the only liquid they had—fresh water rather than the usual ceremonial wine.

Within four months, Jason completed his mission and returned home to Iolcus in Thessaly as his father Aeson lay near death from old age. Jason begged his wife to intercede and extend his father's life. Ovid's telling depicts the sorceress striding barefoot from the palace, robes flowing behind, her hair loose and unadorned like that of a maiden. According to Ovid's *Metamorphoses,* in the dark of night, "three nights before the horns of the moon would meet and make the round orb," she raised her arms to dark powers of night, earth, and Hecate. A spectral chariot appeared and bore her to Tempe where, for nine days and nights, she plucked herbs and dug roots from Mount Ossa with a bronze pruning hook.

Ignoring Jason, Medea remained in her god-inspired trance and slaughtered a black ram. In the resulting blood she plunged sticks and burned them over Aeson to purify him. She slit the old man's throat and gave him a hellish brew to drink, restoring him to black-haired youth. Although already forty years of age, Aeson frolicked like a youngster. Even Dionysus was impressed by Medea's command of the black arts, and applied her concoction to his attendants.

Jason handed over the fleece and settled again in his boyhood home. Medea, who was not content in a domestic role, worked her occult skills against Pelias, Jason's maleficent uncle. She convinced his daughters to hack his limbs apart and boil them in a magic soup to restore Pelias to vigorous youth. To prove that she was capable of such a stunt, she tried the ploy on an old ram, which sprang from the pot as a frisky lamb.

The stratagem produced the effect that Medea had plotted: the daughters killed their father without the sorceress having to soil her hands with his blood. To escape retribution, Medea boarded her chariot and flew a wide itinerary—over Pelion, Othrys, the Aeolian isles, Dionysus's home on Mount Ida, and over the city of Eurypylus. On she flew over the island of Rhodes, the Telchines, Carthaea on the isle of Cea, Lake Hyrie, Tempe, Pleuron, Cyllene, and back to Corinth. Through the decision of the council, Acastus, Pelias's son, forced Jason to flee Iolcus and the *Argo*, which he had set up as a shrine to Poseidon, in pursuit of his black-hearted bride.

For ten years, the pair lived in Corinth, one of Greece's major cities on the isthmus that connects mainland Greece and the Peloponnesus. During this decade, Medea rid the realm of the usurper Corinth, whom she poisoned and replaced with Creon, who served as interim ruler. Jason was well received and took part in the Calydonian boar hunt, but succeeded only in slaying a hunting dog. Medea, who had a legitimate claim to the throne, failed to find welcome among people who considered her a priestess of the occult from a barbarian eastern nation. Trouble arose after Creon began to arrange Medea's ouster so that Jason could marry the princess Creusa and sire children with a legal claim to the Corinthian dynasty. Learning from her children's nanny that Jason wanted to abandon her, Medea worked black magic by pleading for a day to bid farewell to her husband. Creon feared Medea's reputation for treacherous machinations, yet agreed to a stay of exile for a full day. During this period, she pondered poison, stabbing, and fire, before creating a deadly, ornamented wedding dress and headband for the bride.

In Euripides's version of the end of a marriage, Jason confronted Medea and applauded her exile, which would rid him of a dangerous, shrewish wife. Medea riposted with a list of her past accomplishments on his behalf:

> I made you victor. I held the light that saved you. Father and home—I left them for a strange country. I overthrew your foes, contrived for Pelias the worst of deaths. Now you forsake me.... Oh, I have had in you a loyal husband, to be admired of men. An exile now, O God, O God. No one to help. I am alone.
>
> (Euripides's *Medea*)

Jason, who was inflamed with greed for a royal bride who would guarantee succession to a rich throne, put his trust in Aphrodite and replied high-handedly,

> You women have such strange ideas; you think all is well so long as
> your married life runs smooth. But if some mischance occurs to ruffle
> your love—all that was good and lovely before, you reckon as enemies now.
>
> (Euripedes's *Medea*)

Medea stood bereft of refuge in her native land. With no one to take her side, she
branded him a villain and cursed him and his offspring.

Aegeus, a guest at the nuptials, was attracted to Medea and offered her refuge in
Athens if she promised to bear him an heir to his throne. When the two had welded
a compact, Medea returned her attentions to Jason, whom she intended to skewer
with wizardry before fleeing Corinth. As she made her plans, she ominously intoned
an incantation to death.

Medea sent her children with Creusa's bridal raiment—a dress and chaplet of gold,
which would crown the future queen of Corinth. When Creusa dressed for the wedding, she was engulfed in a circle of flame and burned to death, even after she dived
into a fountain to extinguish the unearthly conflagration. Creon dashed to his daughter's rescue and was also immolated as he clasped the ashen corpse.

To complete her dire plot, while her children cried for mercy, Medea, who did
not want her offspring to be abused by strangers, slew them with a sword at the shrine
of Hera as a perverse offering to the goddess of marriage. Jason hastened to retaliate.
The sorceress then, with the help of Helios, boarded a magic vehicle, possibly Helios's
sun chariot, pulled by flying dragons and, like the earth-goddess of the *Ramayana,*
flew away, leaving Corinth to the rule of Sisyphus.

Jason shouted out insults to the departing villainess, comparing her to a she-lion
and Scylla. In Seneca's version Medea crowed:

> Now, now have I regained my regal state, my sire, my brother!... And
> by the magic of this hour I am a maid once more. O heavenly powers,
> appeased at length! O festal hour! O nuptial day! Oh, no! Accom-
> plished is the guilt, but not the recompense.
>
> (Seneca's *Medea*)

Deranged with power, she also prophesied that Jason would wander the earth without
succor and come to an ignoble end crushed beneath the tattered remains of the *Argo*.
The grieving father gathered up his children's corpses according to an oracle's instructions and buried them in Hera's temple. The children were made immortal.

 Free of encumbrances, Medea flew east to Athens, safely out of Jason's reach, and
sought the aid of Herakles, who was sunk in psychosis and unable to assist her in
reestablishing herself in a hospitable kingdom. So Medea relieved his melancholic
rages. Then she came under the protection of King Aegeus, who had agreed to shelter

her if she promised to end his childless state. Her security remained intact until Theseus appeared and proved to Aegeus that he was Aegeus's son with stronger claim to the throne than Medea's boy, Medus, her son fathered by Aegeus. Medea's plot to poison Theseus with a cup of aconite caused Aegeus to suspect her motives and knock the cup from his son's hand, then, on the advice of the goddess Artemis, to exile his witchy consort as punishment for treachery.

Medea took Medus, returned over the Black Sea toward Colchis, and stopped along the way at Absoros to honor Apsyrtus's grave. At the request of the locals, Medea rid the city of a plague of snakes, which she immured in Apsyrtus's tomb. Aeetes's successor, King Peres, who had usurped Aeetes's throne and feared interlopers, imprisoned Medus. Medea posed as a votary of Artemis and forced the release of her son, whom she directed to kill Peres. Medus did her bidding with the sword she provided, grew militarily strong after ridding the land of the usurper, and forged eastward to subdue a territory that Medus named Media to honor his mother. Medea passed from life into the Elysian Fields, where she became the mate of Achilles.

Jason lived to old age and died while napping under the rotten hulk of the *Argo*, which collapsed and crushed him. Thessalus, his son, returned from Corinth to Iolcus to seize the scepter from Acastus and revive the royal line.

Alternate Versions

A number of alternates suggests the lack of geographical knowledge in ancient times and the complexity of Jason's lore, which must have undergone much retelling by a variety of authors and many interpolations of episodes out of time order. Within the scope of the myth, these facts are listed:

- Jason's mother is sometimes listed as Amphinome, Arne, Scarphe, Periclymene, Polymela, Rhoeo, Polypheme, Perimede, or Polymede, daughter of Autolycus.
- Pelias knew that Jason had been spirited away at birth, but allowed him to grow up as a country bumpkin, whom he did not fear.
- Pelias tricked Jason by asking him to devise a hypothetical penalty for a traitor. Jason replied that he would send the traitor to retrieve the Golden Fleece. Pelias chose this voyage as a test of Jason. An alternate version of this plot has Hera dreaming up the quest as a means of placing Medea in Iolcus to murder Pelias, whom Hera despised.
- The river in which Jason lost his shoe is sometimes given as the Euenus, Evanus, or Enipeus.
- According to Simonides, the Golden Fleece was actually purple and was used as a cloak for Zeus when he rose into the clouds.

- The quest for the Golden Fleece was an actual search for gold, which prospectors sifted from the Rion River and dried on fleeces. In this historical version of the tale, dating to the thirteenth century B.C., Herakles headed the seekers and founded numerous Jasonica, or healing centers.
- Atalanta was chosen to join the *Argo* and its all-male crew.
- Tyro, Jason's grandmother, reasoned with Pelias and caused him to imprison Aeson rather than kill him.
- Nebrophonus, Jason's son by Hypsipyle, is alternately named Thoas or Deipylus.
- The Argonauts deliberately abandoned Herakles because a beam spoke to them and complained that he was too heavy.
- Phineus, the blind king, was being deceived by his wife, who complained to him that birds were stealing his food when actually it was servants acting on her orders to starve him to death.
- Apsyrtus rather than his father was pursuing Medea at the time of his death. Jason killed him near the Danube River and erected a temple to Artemis, the huntress.
- Jason remained in Colchis four years before stealing the Golden Fleece.
- King Aeetes had Medea execute all strangers in Colchis.
- In Ovid's version, Jason thought up the stone ploy as a means of quelling the soldiers who sprang from the dragon's teeth.
- The Golden Fleece was hidden in a cave and a fire-breathing dragon guarded the door.
- Medea drove the robot Talus insane with a potion. An alternate setting describes him as dying from arrows shot by the Argonauts into a vulnerable point in his ankle.
- Jason returned home via a northern route through Oceanus, which brought him back to familiar waters. An alternate version of his route took him home via the Danube River, which connected with the Rhine River and the North Sea, east past England and down Europe's western shores to Gibraltar. A minor possibility is the existence of a mysterious passageway known only to the gods, who guided Jason safely back to Iolcus.
- Jason did not marry Medea until their arrival in Iolcus.
- Pelias heard a rumor that the *Argo* and all its crew were lost at sea. Rid of Jason at last, he secured his throne by poisoning Aeson and murdering Aeson's son, Promachus, by dashing his head open. The boy's mother confronted the king for his treachery and threw herself upon a sword in the palace courtyard. At this point, Pelias believed himself safe from evil destiny.
- Pelias killed outright or drove to suicide all of Jason's family—his younger brother, Promachus, his mother, who hanged herself or knifed herself in the heart to escape murder by Pelias's henchmen, and his father, who was forced to gulp down poisoned bull's blood—and so deserved the crafty scheme by which Medea repaid his cruelty.

- Before her death, Jason's mother placed a curse on Pelias that he would die an excruciating death.
- Rather than launch his fifty weary Argonauts in a military assault against Pelias, Jason allowed Medea to murder him by a deceitful ruse. She made herself old and wrinkled and approached Iolcus with a statue of Artemis under her arm and claimed to know the goddess's secret of eternal youth. Then she restored her own beauty, convincing Pelias that she could also restore him to youth. He submitted to her treatment, allowing his gullible daughters, the Peleides, to hack him to death and boil the chunks in a great cauldron. The women, horror-stricken at their unintentional patricide, realized too late that they were unable to duplicate Medea's magic. The removal of Pelias allowed Jason's men to reclaim Iolcus.
- Pelias watched Medea transform an old ram into a lamb by boiling it in herbed sauce. He willingly allowed her to do the same to him.
- Jason voluntarily abdicated in Acastus's favor and resettled at Corinth, where Medea pursued her claim to the throne.
- Jason left Medea because she concealed their children in Hera's temple in the hopes that the goddess would grant them immortality.
- Medea slew only some of her children, leaving Pheres and Thessalus, who founded the nation of Thessaly.
- Creon wanted Jason to abandon Medea and marry his daughter Glauce, also known as Creusa. Medea killed her and Creon by setting the palace ablaze during the night.
- Medea's children were murdered by stone-throwing Corinthians angry with her for presenting Creon's daughter with the deadly wedding outfit.
- Medea killed Jason at the same time that she slew her children.
- Medea tricked Aegeus into believing that he was no longer sterile by giving birth to Medus, who was actually fathered by an unnamed man.
- Medus was sired by an Asian monarch after Medea fled Athens.
- After his children's deaths, Jason grew despondent and killed himself. Another setting describes his attempt to hang himself on the *Argo's* rotting beam, which broke free and crushed him.

Symbolism   The episodic quest of Jason and his Argonauts, which Moses Hadas in the introduction to Apollonius's *Argonautica* claims was Greece's first "major work of pure *belles-lettres*," was probably the first extensive maritime voyage undertaken by a Greek captain and a rare example of Mycenaean monarchs uniting for a common cause: the establishment of the amber trade with Black Sea nations, as symbolized by the Golden Fleece. The myth, set around 1300 B.C. and prefiguring the Trojan War, was recorded by Apollonius, became common knowledge to children of the ancient world, and graced the heraldic shield of the city of Paris. As historian

Will Durant in *Life of Greece* characterizes Jason's lore, it, like the tales of Perseus, Herakles, Minos, and Theseus, was "true in essence, imaginative in detail." The ship, named "the swift," the place, Aeaea, later called Colchis, meaning "the land," King Aeetes, "landsman," and even Euneus, Jason's son, named "good shipman," all suggest a lyrical setting of what might have been a real voyage screened through poetic fancy.

Numerous parallels spring from a comparison of Jason lore with later mythology. Like the Trojan Horse, Jason's ship bears Greece's most illustrious heroes on a voyage that encompassed the known world, although the geographical details strain the credulity of later generations who owned better maps. The story transcends place and bears biblical overtones, particularly the serpentine dragon that guards the fleece, a motif suggesting the seduction of Adam and Eve into sin. Some analysts suggest that the story may be a corruption of lore surrounding Noah and the ark; others ally the myth with the wanderings of Sinbad the Sailor and even Ferdinand and Isabella's commissioning of Columbus, the visionary Italian gold-seeker bound for Eldorado.

The delineating factors that separate Apollonian poetry from Homer's epics are blatant: Apollonius created a nonconfrontational organization man as hero and also satirized the gods by depicting their foibles. Against the backdrop of petty deities, the poet who worked out Jason's lore injected a revolutionary element—romantic love rather than piety as the prime emotion. To characterize the difference between Jason and Medea, the poet cast them as blond and brunette. The chemistry that welded Jason and Medea's infatuation into real romance produced a touchingly tragic conclusion, the age-old story of the faithful wife scorned and tossed aside by the ambitious husband eager for a younger and/or richer and more prestigious mate.

A twist that transformed the story into classic best-seller was the basis for their union—passion on Medea's side and gratitude on Jason's—and the fact that Medea loved Jason to the death, much like Cleopatra loved Antony and Heloise loved Abelard. Jason's tragic flaw, the obligatory *hubris* that held his feet to earth, was his willingness to dabble in occult arts for the sake of his quest. His value system, shoved out of kilter by his eagerness to succeed, caused his downfall. Drugged with *ate* or madness for the Princess Medea, he risked all and paid the price of greater sins, including the murder of his children.

Medea, whose name means "the cunning woman," is alternately called Aeetis after her father's name or Aeaea from the land Aeetes ruled. No ordinary *hausfrau*, Medea, a binary or dual-natured character sometimes identified as the true offspring of the witch Hecate, was a complex, assertive, passionate female willing to give all for a lasting love, but who refused to be jilted and worked her occult skills to gain vengeance. A liberated woman in the sense that she could subdue passion where business logic was required, she worked toward whatever brought her the greatest emotional or political profit.

Critic Moses Hadas points out a telling shift in Homeric style. Apollonius's *Argonautica,* written some eight centuries after the *Iliad* and *Odyssey,* contains a new form of *ecphrasis,* the traditional descriptive catalog. Apollonius lists warriors by birth and importance in typical heroic style and sprinkles his text with Homeric simile and occasional recaps of the action, but he chooses to omit the convention of the epic shield, symbol of male strength. The rich detail instead analyzes a womanly image—the richness of Hypsipyle's robe. Another stylistic touch is Apollonius's decision to spread the Jason myth over a meandering route, pulling in minor variations from obscure points in the Mediterranean, connecting the illustrious Argonauts with Italy, North Africa, and the rejuvenated populace of Lemnos, and creating a farfetched plot equal to later collected lore, such as the extravagances in the Arabian *One Thousand and One Nights,* Ovid's fanciful *Metamorphoses,* Miguel de Cervantes's flamboyant *Don Quixote,* and Giovanni Boccaccio's picaresque *Decameron.*

Symbolically, Jason, a prefiguration of Agamemnon, bears the persona of the captain rather than a superman or military titan on a par with Achilles, Ajax the Great, or Odysseus. Alternately named Aesonides for his father, Pheraeus for his native land of Pherae, and Pagasae for the town from which the *Argo* set sail, Jason earned the name "healer" for quelling a drought and plague caused by Phrixus's exodus aboard the flying ram. As an educated, ethical man, and a worthy estimator of quality in others, Jason represented civilization accepting the challenge of barbarity.

In reality, the eastward voyage placed Jason's band near a very real prize—a gold-producing shore where prospectors used sheepskins as sieves to capture particles of gold that washed out of rich freshwater lodes. Accompanied by local salts who shared his yen for unknown waters and a handsome purse to show for their adventure, Jason most certainly would have stayed close to the shoreline. Because their quarters were cramped, Jason and his rowers would have been obliged to make frequent stops for fresh water, food, and rest and encountered hostile natives.

For some unknown reason, the *Argo* was forced to return by a different route, one so tedious and fearful that his homecoming transcends geography to ply the waters of fancy. If he used up the finer weather of spring and late summer on the eastward leg, the westward segment, if routed along Russia's southern border, brought him into ice-choked waters, where the clashing rocks might have threatened his small craft as surely as did the ice floe that pierced the oceanliner *Titanic.* The difficult portage that forced his mariners to roll their craft over logs may have taken place near the Crimea in the Sea of Azov, where Jason braved a land mass in order to reconnect with the sea. This prehistoric *tour de force,* successfully breaching the ancient world's *Pontus Axeinus* or "unfriendly sea," led to a new name for the Black Sea—the *Pontus Euxeinus,* the "welcoming sea."

Jason's story, a parable of ambivalence in its blend of passionate love and abominable crimes, remained a favorite throughout ancient times. Like Aeneas, Odysseus, and earlier heroes, Jason valued and tended his relations with the gods and kept Hera's favor always in good stead. Like Theseus, he faced a fearsome bull, but no part of the story indicates that Jason intended to overcome the beast by either strength or craft.

Overall, despite his reliance on magic, Jason risked all for ambition and, except for the murder of his children, remained victorious. The example of his bare right foot illustrates the style of Plataean soldiers who fought with an unshod right foot to improve their grip on slippery turf and who kept on the left shoe to cushion a kick at an opponent. His ship was the greatest of its day, a tribute to the captain's vision. One scene from his lore concisely captures the theme of victory: Pollux, the mythic boxer, bested the king of the Bebryces by trouncing the brute strength of a crusher with the deft, practiced jabs of a scientific pugilist. The boxing crown represented Greece's supremacy over the Dark Age still prevalent in the far reaches of the Mediterranean, which Jason dared to probe in a quest for *arete* or excellence.

Other examples of Jason's humanity include his willingness to confer with prophet and sailor, to delegate responsibility based on individual skills, and to hear out any contributor's advice. Unburdened by the prideful anger that destroyed Achilles, the madness that plagued Herakles, and the bullheadedness that killed Ajax the Great, he formulated his plans as the moment arose, doing what was pragmatically feasible and conciliating rather than drawing arms at the first impediment to his quest. For most situations, he delegated authority to his officers, notably Mopsus, Idmon, and Orpheus. Jason, supported by the piety of Orpheus and Mopsus, observed the courtesies necessary to appease the gods, particularly Apollo, Hera, and Athena, the three who most influenced the success of voyagers and adventurers.

Unlike other Greek heroes, Jason did not receive a full measure of honor. When his own ship betrayed him, he died an ignoble death, received no lavish funeral, and left no sons to inherit his kingdom. On the other hand, the gods did not forsake him. To commemorate Jason's expedition, Poseidon flung the *Argo* into the heavens to join the stars. The four small constellations that comprise the *Argo* are: *Pyxis* or "compass," *Puppis* or "stern," *Vela* or "sail," and *Carina,* the "keel." Linguistics also preserves Jason's heroism in the limpid argonaut, a sea creature similar to the octopus, and in a shell named the nautilus of the order *Argonauta argo.*

A blended personality capable of both good and evil, Medea, the seductress, trod the paradoxical path of Pandora and the biblical Eve by both rescuing and damning Jason. A parallel to Clytemnestra, Medea paid dearly for her romance by giving up father, brother, and homeland to follow the Argonauts on their harrowing journey to Iolcus. Once married, Medea enjoyed only ten years of wedlock before she, like Clytemnestra, was forced to fend for herself against a faithless husband. Unlike Clytemnestra, however, Medea remained alive, perhaps the storyteller's acknowledgement of her supernatural powers, which rival the glamour of the Arab witch from *One Thousand and One Nights* and of Morgan le Fay in Arthurian lore.

Medea usually took the form of princess-witch in derivative lore and acted out notable themes. Her bold act of cutting all ties with Aeetes and Colchis symbolizes death; reestablishment in Colchis and later in Corinth and Athens represent multiple rebirths. A greater emphasis on destruction lay in Medea's sacrifice of Apsyrtus, a sibling murder. Not only did he die, but, like Osiris, he was shred into pieces, a foreshadowing of Pelias's fate in the boiling stockpot.

Heat and flame played an important role in Medea's magic, which she derived from devout adherence to the moon goddess, Hecate. On approach to Crete, Medea had no fear of the glowing robot Talus, which she transfixed with an unspoken spell. Pelias she boiled in a pot of herbed broth. Toward Glauce, Medea extended unbridled enmity in the flames that seared the young bride-to-be, a form of jealousy run amok. The story ended in fire as Medea, her hands reddened by her children's blood, departed in a fiery chariot, reminiscent of Phaethon's bolt into the heavens in the chariot of his father, the sun god. Nevertheless, Medea, as much a student of the occult as the witches in William Shakespeare's *Macbeth,* knew well the power she held in her hands.

Medea evolved into a cult figure associated with Hecate, the occult world's moon goddess, with the Roman Bona Dea, who was worshipped in a secret women's cult, and with Angitia or Anguitia, priestess of a Marrubian snake-charming cult. Like the stereotypical ogre's daughter, she performed the magic that enabled the hero to succeed, thus restoring symbolic potency to a failed male who plowed mother earth and quelled the dragon, an obvious phallic symbol rendered harmless by an empowered female. Her later escapades, including boiling the ram to rejuvenate it, appeared to have sprung from dissociated legends, one of which attaches her residence in Corinth to the town of Ephyra and another that allies her son, Medus, to the country named Media. Similar episodes of boiling a king appear in Celtic lore, in which the monarch is masked with a ram's head, hacked to bits, and cooked and served to votaries.

As conductress of a ship full of men, Medea the virago safely led the *Argo* back through the clashing rocks, interpreted by Joseph Campbell as a fierce vaginal passage or dangerous birth. By today's standards, Medea epitomizes the fear and repugnance generated by the superstitious public at the thought of a wise, healing female, such as a granny-woman, midwife, homeopath, medicine woman, or wiccan priestess. According to fearful males, such skill in medical lore, particularly birthing and poisons, places too much power in womanly hands. Yet, one thin thread of etymology connects the name Medea with the evolution of medicine.

Singers long before Homer created a Jason cycle, a body of adventure chanties that gathered material from numerous sailors. Like the mountain man tales that converged to form the Daniel Boone myth, and the woodsman's lore that formed the Paul Bunyan tales, Jason lore drew on numerous feats of oceangoing daring and piracy, even though the geography of the story stretches the imagination with its connection of the Rhine and Danube tributaries and the eastern shore of the Black Sea. Thus, songs and poems honoring the Argonauts reflect a universal regard for ocean-faring crews, who have been supplanted in the twentieth century by spaceships and astronauts.

Greek potters inscribed the *Argo's* adventures and Medea's sorcery on vases; Etruscan artistry pictured Jason as a Jonah figure, engulfed in the yawning mouth of a sea monster and surviving in its maw. Roman vase makers turned to Medea's murder of her children, as did Timanthes, the painter. Crafters dedicated wall panels, gem carvings, containers, and mosaic and pool floors to choice moments of the voyage and the high drama of Medea's sorcery, as exemplified on an urn now housed in the British Museum that shows the ram boiling in Medea's cauldron while Pelias looks on in anticipation of a second chance at youth, or the wall decorators of the basilica discovered in 1917 near Rome's Porta Maggiore revealing a fleeing youth and a veiled woman, probably Jason and Medea, hurrying toward deliverance from the dragon. In Renaissance Florence, Pesellino inscribed segments of marriage chests with the love story of Jason and Medea as well as the more adventuresome vignettes of the yoking of the bull and the defiance of Aeetes. Eugene Delacroix, also enamored of the Jason myth, painted Medea poised with blade above her doomed children.

Writers, especially students of Apollonius's *Argonautica,* have reproduced the Jason and Medea story from many angles, stretching from Ovid and Valerius Flaccus into the Victorian age, particularly John Gower's *Confessio Amantis;* Geoffrey Chaucer's *Legend of Good Women, Man of Law's Tale, House of Fame, Book of the Duchess,* and *Squire's Tale;* and Elizabeth Barrett Browning's *The Claim.* Various renderings of Ovid's version influenced Prospero's incantation in William Shakespeare's *The Tempest* as well as *The Merchant of Venice.* Other views of Jason are found in these sources: Christopher Marlowe's *Hero and Leander, Jew of Malta,* and *Tamburlaine;* Abraham Cowley's *On Dr. Harvey;* Sir John Denham's *On Abraham Cowley* and *Progress of Learning;* Matthew Prior's *Down Hall* and *On Beauty;* Ben Jonson's *The Alchemist;* Edmund Spenser's *Faerie Queene;* John Keats's *The Castle-Builder;* Alexander Pope's *Ode on St. Cecilia's Day;* Jonathan Swift's *A Motto* and *Verses on the Drying Up of St. Patrick's Well;* Algernon Swinburne's *Atalanta in Calydon* and *Ballad against the Enemies of France;* Countee Cullen's 1939 translation of *Medea;* and Louis MacNeice's *Autumn Sequel.*

The myth found its way into other European tributes, including *Médée,* an opera written by Maria Luigi Cherubini in 1797; Samuel Barber's musical opus *Medea's Meditation and Dance of Vengeance;* Robert Graves's mythology; *Médée,* Vincent D'Indy theater music and opus; Jean Anouilh's *Médée;* and Jan Six's play, *Medea,* illustrated with a sketch by Rembrandt. Into Pierre Corneille's times with his tragic *Médée,* the plot twists of Jason and Medea's relationship inspired the Victorian age with William Morris's *Life and Death of Jason.* A century later, Greek poet George Seferis reset the story in *Argonauts,* an existential probe of the soul's search for meaning.

Opera, dance, and cinema have also claimed the Jason myth as material. Francesco Cavalli, a pupil of Claudio Monteverdi, selected Jason as the focus of his opera *Giasone,* performed in 1649. Marc Antoine Charpentier's *Médée,* a neoclassic version, was first performed in 1693. Darius Milhaus produced an operatic *Médée* in 1938. Maria Callas, the austere-voiced diva, portrayed Medea in Pier Paolo Pasolini's 1970 color film *Medea,* a remake of Euripides's tragedy. A less artistic version appeared six years earlier entitled *Jason and the Argonauts,* starring Todd Armstrong and Honor Blackman. Martha Graham choreographed a modern rendition of the Jason and Medea love match in *Cave of the Heart.*

❦ See Also

Achilles, Herakles, Odysseus, Orpheus, Phaeton, Prometheus, Theseus.

❧ Ancient Sources

Aelian's *Varia Historia;* Aeschylus's *The Persian Women;* Antoninus Liberalis's *Metamorphoses;* Apollodorus's *Epitome;* Apollonius of Rhodes's *Argonautica;* Apuleius's *Argonautica Orphica* and *Golden Ass; Argonautica Orphica* (anonymous); Athenaeus's *The Learned Banquet;* Athenagoras's *Legatis pro Christianis;* Bacchylides's *Choral Lyric XVIII;* Callimachus's *Hecale* and *Hymn to Delos;* Carcinus's *Naupactica;* Cicero's *On Duties, On Old Age, On the Nature of the Gods,* and *Pro Lege Manilia;* Cinaethon of Lacedaemon's *Oedipodeia;* Diodorus Siculus's *Historical Library;* Eumelus's *Verse;* Euripides's *Atalanta* and *Medea;* First Vatican Mythographer; Herodotus's *Histories;* Hesiod's *Theogony;* Homer's *Iliad* and *Odyssey;* Hyginus's *Fables* and *Poetic Astronomy;* Justin's *Apology;* Lactantius on Statius's *Thebaid;* Lucian's *On the Dance;* Lycophron's *Alexandra;* Mimnermus's *Nanno* and *Naupactia;* Ovid's *Heroides, Metamorphoses,* and *Tristia;* Pausanias's *Description of Greece;* Pherecydes's *Heptamochos;* Philostratus's *Heroica;* Pindar's *Nemean Odes* and *Pythian Odes;* Plautus's *Pseudolus;* Pliny's *Natural History;* Plutarch's *On Rivers* and *Parallel Lives;* Pollux's *Onomasticon;* Ptolemy Hephaestion's *On Homer;* Scholiast on Apollonius of Rhodes's *Argonautica;* Scholiast on Dionysius's *Description of the Earth;* Scholiast on Euripides's *Knights* and *Medea;* Scholiast on Homer's *Odyssey;* Seneca's *Medea;* Servius on Virgil's *Aeneid;* Silius Italicus's *Verse;* Sophocles's lost plays; Statius's *Thebaid;* Stephanus Byzantium's *Hydissos;* Stesichorus's *Funeral Games of Peleas;* Strabo's *Geography;* Tacitus's *Annals;* Theocritus's *Idylls;* Timaeus's *History;* Johannes Tzetzes's *On Lycophron;* Valerius Flaccus's *Argonautica;* Xenophon's *Anabasis.*

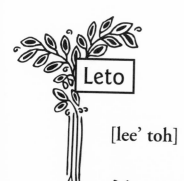

Leto

[lee' toh]

Genealogy and Background

A key maternal figure in Greek mythology, Leto, along with Ortygia and Asteria, were daughters of Titans Phoebe and Coeus and granddaughters of Uranus and Gaea, the brother and sister Titans who spawned much of creation. Before the marriage of her cousin Zeus to Hera, Leto was his first wife; because of Hera's festering enmity, Leto was maligned as Zeus's concubine rather than his wife. Nonetheless, Zeus and Leto produced bright-haired seven-month twins, both prodigies from birth: Apollo, the far-shooting archer and god of prophecy, creativity, and healing, and Artemis, also an archer, and the goddess of chastity, midwifery, and the hunt. Leto's lesser children may have included Hecate, Selene, and Britomartis, although their births are shrouded by numerous variations.

Journey

Leto was one of Zeus's many conquests and Hera's many victims. Heavy with child and exiled from human help, Leto moved at large over the lands and islands of the Aegean Sea. Before the birth of Artemis and Apollo, twins sired by Zeus, Leto wandered at Hera's direction in search of a resting spot and water to quench her thirst. Each time Leto chose a birthing place, Python, the serpentine monster of Delphi, chased her away. When human assistants intervened, Hera deluged them with epidemics, famine, and natural disasters.

On Ortygia (the metamorphosis of Leto's sister into a partially submerged islet bound to four posts), Leto prayed to Zeus, who had Boreas, the west wind, carry her to Poseidon. Because she was obliged to give birth in darkness, Poseidon sent dolphins to fetch her and, on the newly arisen island of Delos, on which Leto swore to raise a fragrant shrine, Poseidon sheltered her from sunlight by an arched wave of water droplets. To ease her nausea, he chained the floating isle to the Aegean Sea. Iris was dispatched to Olympus to bribe Eileithyia,

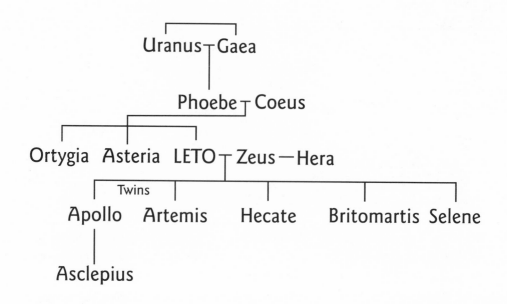

1. Delos 2. Lycia 3. Delphi 4. Thebes 5. Delphi

divine midwife, away from Hera with a gold and amber necklace, which was so large and flashy it impressed even Hera. Assisted by all Olympian goddesses except Hera, Leto clasped a palm or olive tree and strove for nine days to push the infants from her womb. In the *Homeric Hymn to Apollo,* Leto is praised for her beautiful ankles and for giving birth to such wise, skilled children. The arrival of the twins is described in this way:

> Rejoice, O blessed Leto, since you have borne splendid children,
> lord Apollo and Artemis who take delight in arrows; Artemis
> you bore in Ortygia and Apollo in rocky Delos as you leaned
> against the great and massive Cynthian hill, right next to the
> palm tree near the stream of the Inopus.

Artemis emerged first and reached for her brother, whom she helped deliver. At Apollo's birth, the earth cried out in joy.

All the goddesses helped bathe and swaddle the infant Apollo in white linen bound with gold braid. Themis fed him on nectar and ambrosia. In his honor, the islet was named Delos or "bright place," a gladsome hideaway where the Graces, Harmonia, Hebe, Aphrodite, and the Seasons danced as Artemis sang and Apollo plucked his lyre. Delos became the ancient world's holy of holies where no other children were permitted birth. Delian women were obliged to journey to nearby Rheneia before their delivery date.

After the birth of her babes, Leto still had to avoid Hera, who was known for holding a grudge. As a disguise against Hera's malice, Leto changed herself into a she-wolf. Still, Hera was able to drive Leto east to her homeland—Lycia on the shores of Asia Minor, the land of the Hyperboreans—where she tried to rinse her infants at a stream. So virulent was the local attitude against her that she was forced to turn inhospitable shepherds into frogs.

On the day of the twins birth, Leto set up Delphi in central Greece as Apollo's refuge and the center of prophecy. When Leto's children reached full godly power, they protected their mother from detractors and enemies. After Manto, Teiresias's daughter, went through Thebes urging women to worship Leto by lighting insense and twining their hair with laurel, the haughty, envious Niobe, wife of Amphion, the king of Thebes, refused and bid worshippers to throw down the laurel leaves and stop singing hymns of adoration. She flaunted her aristocratic lineage and family of seven sons and seven daughters as a means of belittling Leto.

In retaliation for such *hubris* and disrespect for their mother, Leto's twins slew all Niobe's family with arrows. Niobe, while trying to shield the last daughter, was turned into a weeping stone. As Book 6 of Ovid's *Metamorphoses* describes the transformation:

> Her very tongue is silent, frozen to her mouth's roof, and
> her veins can move no longer; her neck cannot bend nor her

arms move nor her feet go. Within also her vitals are stone.
But still she weeps.

Niobe's stony remains were whirled away to her homeland and situated on Mount Sipylus in Phrygia. The children were denied burial for ten days; on the eleventh, the gods relented and rid earth of the stinking corpses.

Another incident captures the devotion of the divine twins to their mother Leto. During performance of a sacred rite at Delphi, Leto was stalked by the monster Tityus, a would-be rapist who was mercilessly felled by Leto's children's arrows. In Homer's *Odyssey*, Odysseus toured the Underworld and saw Tityus stretched out on the ground. Odysseus reported that

> two vultures sitting on either side of [Tityus] tore into his body
> and ate at his liver and his hands could not keep them off.
> For he had assaulted Leto, the renowned consort of Zeus, as
> she was going through Panopeus, a city of beautiful dancing places,
> to [Delphi].

The severity of Tityus's punishments attests to the high position of Leto, which she attained through motherhood, and to Zeus's anger at so blatant an attack on his wife.

After Apollo and Artemis took their places among the Olympian gods, Leto remained active in their affairs. She intervened with Zeus when Apollo was remanded to Tartarus for slaying the Cyclopes, who were also Zeus's sons. Zeus agreed to commute his sentence to a year. Also, Leto hunted with Artemis and prayed to Zeus to turn the archer Orion into a constellation. During the Trojan War, Leto, Apollo, and Artemis supported the Trojans and supervised the successful treatment of Aeneas's wounds.

Alternate Versions A lesser version of the conception of Artemis and Apollo describes Zeus as changing himself and Leto into quails before attempting copulation. Some tellings name only Eileithyia and Dione as birthing assistants. Leto's delight in Apollo quickly cast Artemis into a secondary role as her brother took precedence. According to Callimachus's *Hymn to Artemis*, Artemis at age four sat on her father's knee and complained,

> I intended to live on the mountains most of the time.
> Unfortunately, women in labor will often be invoking
> me, since my mother Leto carried and bore me without
> pains, and the Fates have therefore made me patroness
> of childbirth.

Zeus was amused by her mature wisdom. In honor of so precocious a child, he ceded her thirty cities.

A minor version of Niobe's story numbers her offspring as ten sons and ten daughters or an even dozen, six of each sex. The youngest girl, a pale child named Chloris or Meliboea, remained alive because she prayed to Leto to spare her. Chloris, who was mother of Nestor, Agamemnon's adviser, turned to religious pursuits and erected an altar to Leto. An alternate telling of Tityus's death claims that Hera drove him to menace Leto. Justifiably, Zeus impaled him with lightning and drove him into the Underworld, where his liver was devoured by vultures.

Because Leto gave birth on Mount Cynthus, Apollo is sometimes known as Cynthius, and Artemis as Cynthia. Also, Apollo, who reflects the brightness of his grandmother, Phoebe, is also called Phoebus. The Roman name for Leto was Latona, Artemis was Diana, but Apollo, the favorite in both Greek and Latin lore, remained unchanged. Apollo is sometimes called the Delphian god because of his incarnation as a dolphin.

Symbolism

Leto, like Hera and Demeter, achieved the status of earth mother. Through the sacrifice of Ortygia, who became a sheltering island for her sister Leto, the birth of the divine twins was made possible. The name Leto implies darkness, the antithesis of her son, the golden-haired Apollo, a hopeful god. His home, Delos, was named the "place of light," thus connecting Leto's myth to sun worship.

Both Apollo and his sister demonstrated a mastery of the bow and arrow within days of their birth. When Apollo launched his arrows, they symbolized epidemic. To end the killing, worshippers prayed to Apollo for healing, which could be attained through Apollo's son Asclepius, known among Romans as Aesculapius, a doctor capable of resurrecting the dead, who was symbolized in a constellation as the serpent-holder. Another symbolic tie with Leto is the punishment of Tityus, whose liver represents naked passions, which threatened to defile Zeus's blameless mate.

Much of the Greek world paid tribute to Leto. The shrine on the island of Delos centered on the honor of Leto, as did the statue on the lofty city of Dreros atop Mount Cadistus, and far-flung shrines at Tegyre in Boeotia, Lete in Macedonia, Zoster in Attica, Abae in Phocis, Ephesus in Asia Minor, Cirrha on Delphi, and Amphigeneia in Pylus. At Phaestus in southern Crete, Leto earned the name Leto Phytia, or Leto the Creator for changing the sex of a girl child born to Galatea, whose mate, Lamprus, demanded that his daughters be killed at birth. The child, who had been disguised as a son named Leucippus, became the focus of Ecdysia, a festival commemorating his departure from girlish behavior and clothing. The term *ecdysiast,* or "stripteaser," evolved from this significant event.

Leto was the subject of two statues by Praxiteles and figures in Geoffrey Chaucer's *Troilus and Criseyde*, Sir Philip Sidney's *Arcadia*, Edmund Spenser's *Shepherd's Calendar* and *Faerie Queene*, Phineas Fletcher's *The Purple Island*, Christopher Marlowe's *Tamburlaine*, John Milton's *Sonnet* and *Arcades*, John Keats's *Endymion* and *Hyperion*, Jonathan Swift's *To Lord Harley*, and Robert Bridges's *Prometheus the Firegiver*.

❦ See Also
Agamemnon, Nestor.

❦ Ancient Sources
Aelian's *Varia Historia;* Antoninus Liberalis's *Metamorphoses;* Apollodorus's *Epitome;* Apollonius of Rhodes's *Argonautica;* Aristophanes's *The Birds;* Aristotle's *Historia Animalium;* Callimachus's *Hymn to Artemis* and *Hymn to Delos;* Hesiod's *Theogony;* Homer's *Hymn to Apollo, Iliad,* and *Odyssey;* Hyginus's *Fables* and *Poetic Astronomy;* Ovid's *Metamorphoses;* Pausanias's *Description of Greece;* Pindar's *Pythian Odes;* Plutarch's *Greek Questions,* and *Parallel Lives;* Servius on Virgil's *Aeneid;* Tacitus's *Annals.*

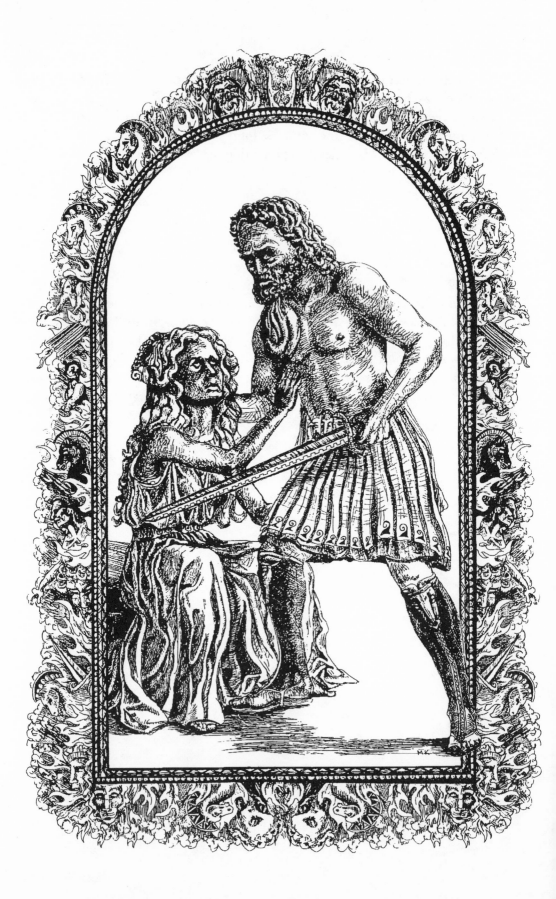

Menelaus

[mih · nuh · lay' · uhs]

Genealogy and Background

Descendant of Zeus, the great grandson of Tantalus, grandson of Pelops, and son of Atreus and Aerope, Menelaus—whose name means "the people's might"—and his more famous brother Agamemnon were known as the Atreidae, the most prominent Greek leaders of the Trojan War. During Atreus's family feud with his brother Thyestes, Menelaus was shuttled to King Polypheides's care in Sicyon on the northern Peloponnesus, then to Calydon and Oeneus in Aetolia. After journeying to Delphi for advice on locating Thyestes, Menelaus came under the protection of Tyndareus, the Spartan ruler who reestablished Atreus's sons in Mycenae. After Agamemnon ascended to the Mycenaean throne, he assisted his brother in wooing Helen, Tyndareus's divinely beautiful daughter sired by Zeus, and helped him assume rule in Sparta.

King Menelaus fathered a daughter, Hermione, by Helen. In Helen's absence, and before the start of the Trojan War, Menelaus sired two sons—Xenodamus by Cnossia, a sea nymph, and Megapenthes by his Aetolian slave, Tereis (or Pieris). Menelaus and Helen, after the conclusion of the Trojan War, apparently mollified of old hurts and animosities, produced a son, Nicostratus. Hermione, married for a short time to Neoptolemus, Achilles's brash son, was widowed. She married her cousin, Orestes, and produced Tisamenus, Menelaus's grandson who became Sparta's next ruler.

Journey

Menelaus met Paris, a Trojan prince, at Troy when he journeyed there to seek help concerning a famine afflicting Sparta. An oracle had promised that Sparta would not recover until an emissary journeyed to the Troad to sacrifice on a tomb of one of the sons of Prometheus. Menelaus made a pilgrimage to the graves of Lycus and Chimaereus. While Menelaus completed the task, he accepted the hospitality of Paris, a Trojan prince; the two men journeyed

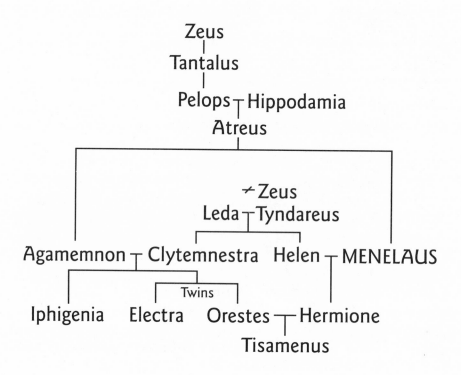

Zeus
|
Tantalus
|
Pelops ⊤ Hippodamia
Atreus

⤙ Zeus
Leda ⊤ Tyndareus

Agamemnon ⊤ Clytemnestra   Helen ⊤ MENELAUS

Twins

Iphigenia   Electra   Orestes ⊤ Hermione

Tisamenus

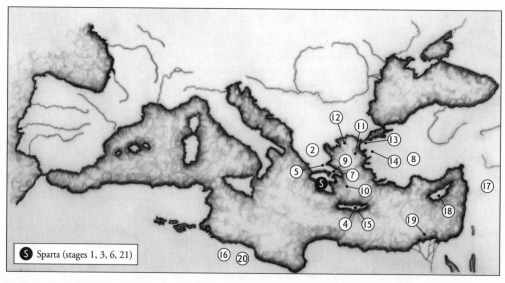

S Sparta (stages 1, 3, 6, 21)

1. Sparta 2. Aetolia 3. Sparta 4. Crete 5. Delphi 6. Sparta 7. Aulis 8. Mysia
9. Aulis 10. Delos 11. Tenedos 12. Lemnos 13. Hellespont 14. Troy 15. Crete
16. Libya 17. Phoenicia 18. Cyprus 19. Pharos 20. Libya 21. Sparta

together to Delphi. Receiving an unclear prophecy that Paris would cause him harm, Menelaus allowed Paris to accompany him back to Sparta. During Paris's visit, Menelaus was called to attendance at the funeral games of his maternal grandfather, Catreus, king of Crete. He left Helen to entertain their guest and had taken no action to prevent her seduction or rape—the main cause of the Trojan War, which was the focal point of Mediterranean life for a decade.

Agamemnon, the more influential of the two brothers, dispatched ambassadors to negotiate the return of his sister-in-law. One of the embassies brought Odysseus and Menelaus himself face to face with the Trojan hierarchy, who refused to relinquish either Helen or the treasure and household slaves she and Paris carried off from the Spartan treasury and palace. The Atreidae had little choice but to assemble a fighting force, composed in part by the many men who had courted Helen and who, at Odysseus's suggestion, had sworn to protect her. At the beginning of the war, Menelaus returned to Delphi to the shrine of Athena Pronaea before the temple of Apollo. In preparation for the war, he donated Helen's necklace to the goddess, then set forth on his mission to bring back his wife.

The Atreidae planned a strategy in Argos at Diomedes's palace, where a group voted Agamemnon as chief. Delayed eight years at Aulis until Agamemnon sacrificed his daughter Iphigenia, the fleet finally moved to Delos, among the Cyclades southeast of Greece, then northeast toward Tenedos, a small island, known today as Bozcaada, Turkey, due west of Troy's coastline. Heading west to the larger island of Lemnos, the Greeks finally beached their ships on the Troad, the northwestern promontory on Turkey's Asian shore.

While not as bold as Agamemnon, as intelligent as Odysseus, as handsome as Paris, or as invincible as Achilles, Menelaus nonetheless earned Homer's admiration for courage. In Book 10 of the *Iliad,* when Nestor complained that Menelaus slept and left the hard work to his older brother, Agamemnon justified Menelaus's subordinate role:

> Aged sir, other times I also would tell you to blame him, since often
> he hangs back and is not willing to work hard, nor that he shrinks
> from it and gives way, nor in the mind's dullness. But this time he
> woke far before me, and came to rouse me, and I sent him on to call
> those you ask after.

Most outstanding of Menelaus's field performance was his duel with Paris, despoiler of Menelaus's wife. Homer described the advancing Greek in epic terms as fair-haired, warlike, and wily. Cautious that the sons of Priam not cheat on the truce while Menelaus dueled with Paris, he called for a sacrifice of three lambs as binding rite against treachery.

Against a backdrop of cheering Greeks and Helen on the battlements pointing out notable warriors to Priam, Menelaus faced off against Paris, the seducer, and came close to losing the battle after his spear thrust failed to penetrate Paris's shield. Piously, Menelaus called on the heavens:

> Father Zeus, no God beside is more baleful than you
> are. Here I thought to punish [Paris] for his
> wickedness; and now my sword is broken in my hands, and the
> spear flew vainly out of my hands on the throw before, and I have
> not hit him.

(Homer's *Iliad*)

Bare-handed, Menelaus was in the act of dragging Paris by his chinstrap toward the Greek camp when Aphrodite intervened and removed Paris from imminent danger. Agamemnon declared the battle a victory for Menelaus. In the confusion that followed, in Book 4 of the *Iliad*, Pandarus fired off an arrow that nicked Menelaus in the belly. Menelaus shuddered at his close call and allowed Machaon to treat the wound. The war heated up once more, with Menelaus challenging Aeneas and slaying Scamandrius.

In Book 17, Menelaus reappeared in warlike vigor as he protected the corpse of Patroclus, Achilles's companion, from capture. More detailed than in earlier descriptions, Menelaus, "helmed in bright bronze," stalked among champions from both armies. In guardian pose he "stood over Patroclus and held the spear and the perfect circle of his shield before him, raging to cut down any man who might come forth against him." As in Book 3, he prayed, "Father Zeus, it is not well for the proud man to glory," yet Menelaus had little to glory about as he debated how he could stand up to Troy's best, who were squabbling over the god-made armor on Patroclus's corpse.

As Hector approached, Menelaus looked around for Ajax the Great, who managed for a short time to protect the fallen Greek. At Ajax's command, Menelaus called more Greeks to battle with a reminder of how shameful it would be if "Patroclus be given to the dogs of Troy to delight them." Most of the action pitted Ajax against Hector until Athena, in the form and voice of Phoenix, bolstered Menelaus, who struck Podes so hard that his spear penetrated the body through the gut. At the end of this pivotal scene, Menelaus, at Ajax's direction, sent Antilochus to fetch Achilles and near sunset helped drag Patroclus's body to safety.

In another crucial episode Menelaus disappointed his comrade by selecting Odysseus as recipient of the arms of Achilles. Following Ajax's ignoble suicide, Menelaus declared that the body should remain unhallowed by ritual as retribution for Ajax's treachery. In Sophocles's tragedy, *Ajax,* both the chorus and Teucer warred against Menelaus's bull-headedness until the authoritative voices of Odysseus and Agamemnon settled the matter and Odysseus helped Teucer dig Ajax's grave.

One of the most dramatic moments in Menelaus's lore is his first glimpse of Helen after her ten years' sojourn in Troy. Following Paris's death from a poisoned arrow shot from Philoctetes's bow, Helen had passed unceremoniously to Deiphobus, another of King Priam's sons who beat out Helenus and Idomeneus for the radiant daughter of Zeus. While the walls of Troy blazed with fires set by Greeks who had hidden themselves in the great hollow horse that Epeius built of fir planking, Menelaus climbed down from the horse, strode to Deiphobus's residence, slew him, and continued on his search for Helen. He found her, crouched beside Vesta's statue, unsure which side would offer her safe conduct.

Menelaus toyed with the idea of ending her life with a single swipe of his sword blade. The appeal of the astonishingly gorgeous woman who had shared ten years of his life defeated his dark urges. He removed her from her blood-spattered sanctuary and escorted her through angry Greek soldiers with fists upraised and rocks held ready for hurling. Over Hecuba's insistence that Helen pay with her life for the carnage, Menelaus chose to save his wife, whom he dragged by the hair to his ship.

More female-bashing clouded Menelaus's story. Euripides depicted Menelaus on Troy's battlements terrorizing Hecuba and Cassandra and in an unlikely setting in Thessaly menacing Andromache and her small son, Molossus, in order to assure Hermione's claim on Neoptolemus, who had won Andromache as a war prize. By threatening to slay the boy if Andromache refused to leave the shelter of Thetis's shrine, Menelaus, "hard as the rock and deaf as the wave," negated any heroic stature he gained at Troy by his unmanly bullying of a hapless war widow.

When the killing stopped and the Greeks divided the spoils, Menelaus joined Nestor and Diomedes in launching his fifty ships westward toward home. Eager to depart the killing fields, Menelaus disputed Agamemnon's order to sacrifice to Athena, whom Menelaus despised for protecting the Trojan citadel. The brothers departed over harsh words, Agamemnon to home and death, and Menelaus to a fitful voyage.

According to Book 4 of the *Odyssey*, over an eight-year period, only one-tenth of Menelaus's fleet survived the stormy seas and failed attempts to colonize the southern Mediterranean. The remaining five ships, forced south to Crete, then southwest to Libya and east to Phoenicia and Cyprus, at length, ragged and low on supplies, arrived at Egypt's Nile delta and the island of Pharos. Menelaus sought a glimpse of his future from Proteus, the Old Man of the Sea. On the advice of Eidothea, Proteus's daughter, Menelaus and his men suited up in smelly sealskins and awaited Proteus in his undersea cavern, where he corraled his herd of seals each night. Proteus eluded his captors by metamorphosing into a bearded lion, snake, leopard, boar, tree, and water. Worn down by Menelaus's warriors, he consented to forecast the Spartan king's future and divulged the fates of Odysseus, Ajax, and Agamemnon, who was already dead. Sadly, Menelaus paid tribute to his slaughtered brother by raising a cenotaph on the Egyptian shore.

At sea on the final leg of the journey to the Peloponnesus after a twenty-day layover, Menelaus slew a pair of Egyptian children and escaped local pursuers by sailing west to Libya. According to Euripides's *Orestes,* at Nauplia, a seaport on the Argolid bay, Menelaus again confronted cataclysm after Orestes killed his mother, Clytemnestra.

The day belonged to the bold, crazed Orestes, who menaced Hermione, Menelaus's treasured daughter. Finally, the danger was annulled by the gods, who removed Orestes and left Menelaus his victorious homecoming. Briefly snagged at the Malean promontory in southwest Greece, Menelaus lost more of his fleet, which was driven south to Crete. No poetry records the joyous welcome of king and queen. The smooth resumption of royal duties in Sparta and the birth of a son, Nicostratus, contrasted the lost years during which Menelaus may well have wondered if he would ever see his wife restored to her rightful place as consort.

As Homer describes him in Book 4 of the *Odyssey*, Menelaus retained much of his youth and vigor and demonstrated a valuable trait in epic literature—obedience to the guest code. His sympathetic treatment of Telemachus, Odysseus's son, and his manly behavior before his courtiers indicate that war had not depleted Menelaus's power or enthusiasm. To Telemachus, Menelaus offered fatherly advice and encouragement to hold out against his mother's suitors until his father could arrive safely at Pylos. A generous king, Menelaus presented royal gifts to Telemachus and sent him safely on his way.

Looking back over the events that marred the Greeks' homecoming, Menelaus regretted collecting a store of travel mementos from his lengthy voyages and losing so many men at Troy. He mourned that it took him and Odysseus nearly as long to return as to fight the war and that, before his brother could attain the honor worthy of a war hero, the seducer Aegisthus surprised him, and with Clytemnestra's aid, murdered the king. Thus the demise of Agamemnon at the hands of his wife and her lover set the tone for Menelaus's last years, when his nephew Orestes fought for sanity, and relieved of blood-guilt, married Menelaus's widowed daughter, Hermione. Menelaus died before Helen and was buried at Sparta or Phare, a smaller Laconian town that also claimed the honor. The couple reunited in the Elysian Fields, which Helen merited as daughter of Zeus.

Alternate Versions

Menelaus, sometimes called the son of Pleisthenes and Cleolla and the grandson of Atreus, appears in the questionably romantic recasting of the Trojan War, which describes a trick played on Paris by Hera, goddess of marriage and the family. Displeased that a royal guest would abduct the queen and dishonor Menelaus's hospitality, she drove Paris's ship by violent winds to Egypt, where King Proteus accepted Helen into the state's custody. Deluded by a wraith, Paris continued north to the Troad and fought a war over an imitation Helen, formed of smoke and illusion. At the end of the war, Menelaus reunited with his wife, who remained apart from the royal family in an Egyptian temple in order to avoid the lecherous grasp of Proteus's successor, King Theoclymenus.

Symbolism

Menelaus as epic hero lacks individuality and conviction. Shored up by his brother, he comes off as a victim determined to regain respect by whatever means necessary, including a role in the murder of Iphigenia, his niece, to obtain favorable winds to carry the Greek fleet northeast to Troy. During much of the fighting, Menelaus received only faint applause, even when he won the chariot race at the games honoring Patroclus, as Homer describes in Book 23 of the *Iliad*. A self-effacing champion, he gave up the prize—a mare—to Antilochus, whom he agreed was more deserving. Much of Menelaus's lore suggests a limp recasting of other myths, particularly the waylaying of Proteus in the cave, an uninspired version of Odysseus's meeting with the Cyclops. In toto, the myths including Menelaus usually star somebody else, particularly the irresistible Helen, smooth lover Paris, or authoritative Agamemnon.

In later years, the pattern remained the same: as an adjunct to Helen, Menelaus was worshipped at the Spartan altar at Therapne, where suppliants prayed for military strength, and in the Laconian town of Gythium, where he raised an icon of Praxidice, the goddess of justice, upon his safe return from Troy. Literature has given a small role to Menelaus, as found in William Shakespeare's *King Henry VI* (Part III), Michael Drayton's *The Owl*, Lord Byron's *Don Juan*, John Masefield's *A King's Daughter* and *Tale of Nireus*, Rupert Brooke's *Menelaus and Helen*, and Robert Graves's *Judgment of Paris*. Artists and musicians, also more interested in the adulterer than in the cuckolded husband, have scarcely noted Menelaus's role in the Trojan tragedy. One painting at Delphi, the work of Polygnotus, depicted Menelaus with round shield centered with a snake; another in Rome commemorated Menelaus's big moment—the fight over the corpse of Patroclus.

🐾 See Also

Achilles, Agamemnon, Ajax the Great, Epeius, Helen, Odysseus, Paris.

🐾 Ancient Sources

Acusilaus's *History;* Agias's *Returns of Heroes;* Apollodorus's *Epitome;* Dionysius Periegeta's *Periegesis;* Euripides's *Andromache, Cretan Women, Electra, Helen, Iphigenia in Aulis, Iphigenia in Tauris, Orestes,* and *Trojan Women;* Herodotus's *Histories;* Homer's *Iliad* and *Odyssey;* Hyginus's *Fables;* Lesches's *Little Iliad;* Lycophron's *Alexandra;* Pausanias's *Description of Greece;* Photius's *Library;* Proclus's *Chrestomathy;* Ptolemy Hephaestion's *On Homer;* Scholiast on Euripides's *Orestes;* Servius on Virgil's *Aeneid;* Sophocles's *Ajax, Capture of Troy,* and *Philoctetes;* Stasinus's *Cypria;* Stesichorus's *Helen* and *Recantation;* Strabo's *Geography* and *Historical Sketches;* Theocritus's *Idylls;* Virgil's *Aeneid* and *Georgics;* Xanthus's *Poems;* Zenobius's *Proverbs.*

Nauplius

[naw' plee · uhs]

Genealogy and Background

The Greek equivalent of a swash-buckling privateer, Nauplius (*nauplion* or "navigator" in Greek), the Argive captain of a band of Carian pirates and slavers and king of the island of Euboea, which lies due east of the Greek mainland, resides at the center of one of mythology's least comprehensible stories, which blends two heroes from different eras. He was the offspring of Egyptian ancestry who earned a sordid reputation for questionable dealings and later for stalking the wives of returning Greek war heroes. Born to Amynone, one of the most resourceful of the Danaides, Nauplius was Poseidon's son, husband of Clymene (sometimes given as Philyra or Hesione), and the father of Damastor, Proetus, and Polydectes. Nauplius's most famous son was the ill-fated hero of the Trojan War, Palamedes, who invented the lighthouse, dice, numbers, scales, the discus, a partial alphabet, and military pickets.

Journey

Remembered principally as a sea captain who discovered how to steer by the North Star in the constellation *Ursa Major* or "Big Bear," Nauplius aided King Aleus of Tegea in the southeastern Peloponnesus in getting rid of Auge, the unchaste votary of Athena and mother of Telephus, Herakles's son. He took her overland from Arcadia to the eponymous harbor of Nauplia, on the Argolid Bay of the Peloponnesus. Given the choice of drowning the girl or selling her into bondage, Nauplius—either for monetary reasons or out of pity—decided to keep her alive. He sailed east to the coast of Turkey and traded her to Carian pirates, who resold her to the king of Mysia in Asia Minor.

A later myth describes Nauplius's voyage south to Crete. There he gained possession of Catrius's two daughters, whom he was ordered

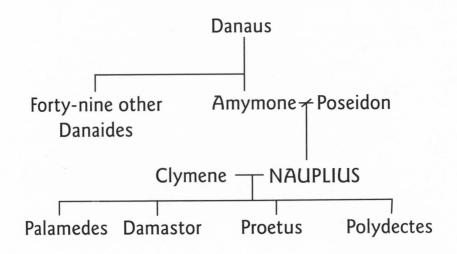

Danaus

Forty-nine other   Amymone ⚭ Poseidon
Danaides

Clymene ⚭ NAUPLIUS

Palamedes Damastor   Proetus   Polydectes

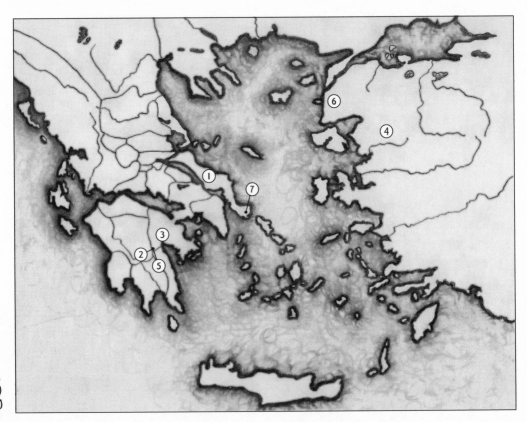

1. Euboea 2. Tegea 3. Nauplia 4. Mysia 5. Tegea 6. Troy 7. Cape Caphareus

to drown because a dire warning from an oracle indicated that the girls would bring about their father's downfall. Nauplius traded Aerope to King Atreus, who sired Menelaus and Agamemnon, leaders of the Greek force attacking Troy. According to one version, Nauplius chose to take Catreus's second daughter, Clymene, as his wife. They had three sons, Oeax, Nausimedon, and Palamedes, a promising lad educated by Chiron, the Centaur, and known for his ingenuity. Palamedes joined the Greek fleet and sailed to Troy. His ignoble death produced one of the most blatant examples of festering malcontent in mythology. According to numerous sources, including Aeneas's words in the second book of Virgil's Aeneas, Odysseus, whom Palamedes forced to join the Greek army, sent a phony letter, indicating that Palamedes was a spy in league with Troy's King Priam. In a fail-safe measure, Odysseus also suborned a slave to place a bag of coins in Palamedes's bedding. After Agamemnon arrested Palamedes, Greek soldiers lured him down a well and stoned him for these false charges. Palamedes's brother, Oeax, inscribed the details on an oar and tossed it into the ocean.

Nauplius intercepted Oeax's message and, from that time until his death, dedicated himself to vengeance. He immediately sailed to Troy to beg Agamemnon to bring the deceiver Odysseus to justice. Failing to gain the commander's sympathies, Nauplius sailed back to Greece to plot underhanded vengeance. Accompanied by Oeax, Nauplius, nursing his hatred of Odysseus and grief for Palamedes, sailed the eastern coast of Greece and struck up friendships with numerous anxious wives, spreading tales of Greek heroes returning with loving Trojan concubines, some already made mothers of Greek/Trojan offspring. Nauplius was successful in causing some wives to kill themselves. He lured Meda, Idomeneus's wife, and Aegialea, Diomedes's wife, into committing adultery, thus dishonoring the returning veterans and bringing shame to two noble houses.

The most virulent convert of Nauplius's ire was Clytemnestra, who plotted with her lover Aegisthus a bloody homecoming for the unsuspecting Agamemnon and Cassandra, his war bride. Ironically, Odysseus's wife, Penelope, proved the least amenable to manipulation and remained so faithful that she became a model of submissiveness. In one telling, Odysseus's mother, undeceived by Nauplius, repaid him in kind by telling him that his sons had died. Nauplius grew so despondent that he killed himself.

The final plot of the scheming Nauplius involved building a deceptive harbor light or a series of torches near the Gyroi, the round rocks of Cape Caphareus, south of Euboea. The Greek fleet, scattered by Athena's intervention, was at first unable to right its course. Then the sailors sighted Nauplius's lights. Joyous to be near home and believing themselves safely guided to harbor, they crashed their ships on the promontory. Ajax the Lesser, who was punished by Athena for raping her priestess and defiling the temple, died in the wreckage. Nauplius, meticulous in his spite, posted mariners on shore to kill all Greek soldiers who survived the wrecks.

Zeus, who disapproved of Nauplius's bogus harbor light, is said to have used the false beacon against the captain himself, who crashed his ship in the same spot, although there are no details to substantiate this subplot. A later descendant, also named Nauplius, served aboard Jason's *Argo* and gained an evil reputation as Nauplius the Wrecker, who lighted misleading harbor fires to lure unsuspecting enemy pilots toward certain death on the rocks. The characters have merged irretrievably, although at least five generations separate the two sea captains.

Alternate Versions

There are several versions of Nauplius's myth. The most prominent is that he made up a story of Odysseus's death and brought her close to suicide. An alternate telling of Nauplius's confrontation with Penelope describes him as trying to drown her. A third alternative is a story of Penelope's girlhood. Having run into Nauplius's treachery after her father had ordered her drowned, Penelope survived the sea after a block of purple-flecked ducks formed a rescue mission and brought her safely to shore. As a result, she was named Penelope, Greek for "duck." A vengeful ending to the Penelope story has Nauplius committing suicide after Anticleia, wife of Laertes and Odysseus's mother, convinced Nauplius that his other two sons had joined Palamedes in death. Her words caused him to kill himself.

An alternate ending of his son Palamedes's life depicts the Greeks as drowning him at sea in response of Odysseus's false accusation of complicity with the Trojans.

Nauplius's role in the wreck of ships returning from Troy is sometimes minimized. In one minor setting, Nauplius built huge bonfires to suggest welcoming beacons. Defeated in his attempt to wreak vengeance on the Greek survivors, he threw himself into the flames. In another, Ajax the Lesser met his death on the rocks after Athena beguiled him with a flash of lightning to avenge his sacrilege in dragging Cassandra from the goddess's sanctuary. As a result of this event, the craggy cape was named the Rocks of Ajax.

Symbolism

For victimizing worried wives of Greek military heroes, Nauplius carries one of the heaviest burdens of guilt in the aftermath of the Trojan War. On the positive side, Nauplius is said to have founded Nauplion or Nauplia, the chief port of Argos where a spring honored Hera with annual renewal of her virginity. His mother was memorialized by a spring that spouted after Poseidon seduced her. Nauplius's wife Clymene was honored with a statue and sacred grove on the island of Lesbos, directly opposite the coast of Asia Minor.

🌿 See Also

Aegisthus, Agamemnon, Ajax the Lesser, Auge, Cassandra, Diomedes, Odysseus.

🌿 Ancient Sources

Apollodorus's *Epitome;* Apollonius of Rhodes's *Argonautica;* Dictys Cretensis's *Trojan War Diary;* Didymus's *On Lyric Poets;* Diodorus Siculus's *Library of History;* Hyginus's *Fables;* Lactantius on Statius's *Thebaid;* Lucian's *Dialogues of Sailors;* Ovid's *Metamorphoses;* Pausanias's *Description of Greece;* Pindar's *Isthmian Odes;* Scholiast on Euripides's *Orestes* and *Helen;* Sophocles's *Ajax;* Strabo's *Geography;* Theon on Aratus's *Phenomena;* Johannes Tzetzes's *On Lycophron;* Valerius Flaccus's *Argonautica.*

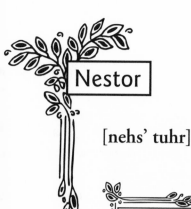

Nestor

[nehs' tuhr]

Genealogy and Background

The youngest child of the upstart Neleus, Nestor, sometimes called sweet-voiced, mellifluous, eloquent, and lucid, was born to Chloris, Amphion and Niobe's daughter, in Messenia, the southwestern province of the Peloponnesus. The family also claims a daughter, Pero, and eleven other sons, Taurus, Epilaus, Deimachus, Asterius, Pylaon, Eurybius, Phrasius, Eurymenes, Euagoras, Periclymenus, and Alastor. As a significant member of the Neleidae, Nestor was said to have been brought up in Gerenia, a town in Messenia in the southwestern quadrant of the Peloponnesus. Fortunately for him, he lived there at the time Herakles destroyed Pylos on the western shore of the Peloponnesus in revenge for Neleus's refusal to purify him for murder.

According to Book 11 of the *Iliad,* Nestor's accession to the Pylian throne was cataclysmic:

> For Herakles had come in his strength against us
> and beaten us in the years before, and all the
> bravest among us had been killed. For we who were
> sons of lordly Neleus had been twelve, and now I
> alone was left of these, and all the others had perished.

Out of the large number of possible heirs who preceded Nestor in line for the throne, he was surprised to inherit the throne of his self-made, autocratic father, who was buried in a secret tomb near Corinth on the northeastern Peloponnesus. Despite Herakles's contentious relationship with the rest of the family, Nestor is said to have loved the hero, who gave Nestor his father's place as king of Pylos in trust for Herakles's own descendants.

According to legend, Apollo promised Nestor the total number of years his relatives might have lived, thus guaranteeing him a long life. Around forty years of age, Nestor married Eurydice, mother of his two daughters, Polycaste and Peisidice, and seven sons, Autolychus

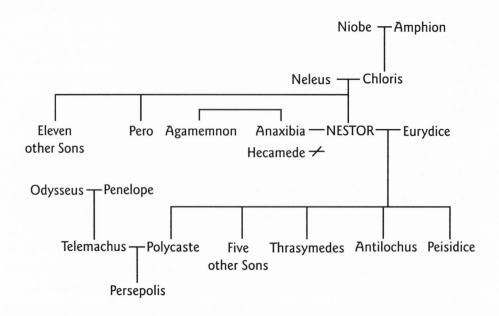

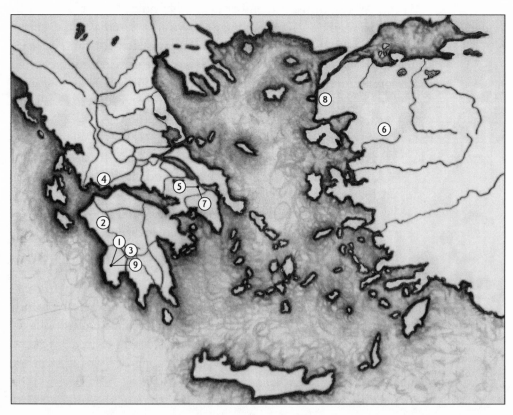

1. Messenia 2. Elis 3. Messenia 4. Calydon 5. Aulis 6. Mysia 7. Aulis 8. Troy
9. Messenia

or Antilochus, Peisistratus, Perseus, Stratius, Aretus, Echephron, and Thrasymedes. Peisidice, who disappeared from history at an early age with no offspring to her credit, may have died in childhood. Nestor ruled for three generations (i.e., three periods composed of three decades each) and married Anaxibia, Agamemnon's sister, after the death of his first wife. A rich man in land and goods, Nestor's perspicacious husbandry stemmed from a careful accounting of citizens, animals, and wine stores.

As king of Pylos, Nestor attained a respectful age of sixty during the Trojan War, to which he and his oldest sons, Antilochus and Thrasymedes, led a contingent of ninety ships. Unlike Agamemnon, Menelaus, Odysseus, and others, Nestor sailed safely back to Pylos and found his rule unopposed by usurpers. Before Odysseus returned home, Nestor hosted Telemachus, who wandered in search of information about his father. During the boy's stay, he was washed, massaged, and oiled by Princess Polycaste, who bore him a son, Persepolis or Perseptolis, Nestor's most illustrious grandson. After departing Nestor's hospitality, Telemachus was accompanied by Peisistratus, who escorted him safely to Menelaus's realm in Sparta. One source even lists Homer as Nestor's grandson by Polycaste. Nestor probably survived into his eighties, although legend accorded him 300 years and the blessing of Zeus.

Journey Nestor's name is connected with numerous exploits. In his own boasts, recorded in Book 11 of the *Iliad,* he completed successful cattle raids in Elis, northwest of Pylos. The young Nestor brought honor to his family by carrying off hundreds of swine, goats, mares, sheep, and cattle. As hero of the fight, he earned a major portion of the booty, from which he wisely chose the best to sacrifice to the gods.

Within three days, the Elians, led by King Augeas, struck back. Nestor's family was ready because Athena had warned them of the impending raid. Although Neleus penned up the boy's mount to keep him from daring too much, Nestor, eager to prove himself, stood his ground and was the first to draw blood. He smote the commander, Amarynceus, and killed Prince Mulius with a single spear thrust and, like a dark whirlwind, commandeered fifty chariots. Thus mobile, Nestor was able to slaughter 100 invaders and strip them of their splendid armor until Athena called a halt to the carnage. Poseidon led the Elians out of range of Nestor's troops, who pursued the departing army to the Olenian Rock. In Nestor's description of the event to Patroclus many years later, the old man savored his early victory with this hazy memory: "All glorified Zeus among the gods, but among men, Nestor. That was I, among men, if it ever happened." (Homer's *Iliad*)

Other events linked to Nestor's name received sketchy attention in ancient writings:

- He slew the giant Ereuthalion in Arcadia in hand-to-hand combat.
- His part in the war with the Lapiths and Centaurs earned him fame.

- He distinguished himself with a role in the expedition of the Argonauts to Colchis, a journey also undertaken by Nestor's brother, Periclymenus.
- At the funeral games honoring Amarynceus, Nestor bested contenders in wrestling, spear throwing, boxing, and running.

One of the participants at the Calydonian boar hunt, Nestor endangered himself by venturing too close and had to rescue himself with quick thinking and resourcefulness. As Ovid describes the close call in Book 8 of the *Metamorphoses:*

> [Nestor] leaped by his spear-pole into the branches of a tree which stood near by, and from this place of safety he looked down upon the foe he had escaped. The raging beast whetted his tusks on an oak-tree's trunk; and, threatening destruction and emboldened by his freshly sharpened tusks, ripped up the thigh of the mighty Hippasus with one sweeping blow.

This view of one of mythology's most spirited adventures indicates that Nestor fared well in comparison with other warriors, possibly by knowing when to strike as well as when to withdraw.

Nestor's most tedious journey was with Menelaus, who traveled Greece in search of warriors to make the long voyage to the Troad, on the northwestern promontory of Asian Turkey, to recover Helen. Nestor was particularly successful in recruiting followers at Aepy in Elis, and accompanied Odysseus and Ajax the Great to Scyros to uncover Achilles's hiding place. From Cyparissia, Dorium, Peleus, and Helus came more men, whom Nestor led to his ninety ships at Gerenia.

A surprise recruit arrived at Aulis as the fleet prepared for departure: Antilochus, Nestor's oldest son, who had in infancy been exposed and suckled by a dog and was, by the beginning of the Trojan War, barely old enough to volunteer. Achilles helped soothe Nestor's outburst against taking Antilochus into danger. In the end, Nestor proudly introduced the boy, the Greeks' youngest and fleetest soldier, to Agamemnon, the commander-in-chief. Before the fleet's arrival at the Troad, Nestor assisted in Achilles's capture of the nearby island of Tenedos and was rewarded with Hecamede, Arsinous's daughter, who served as Nestor's concubine during the war years.

As the oldest Achaian warrior and the only surviving Argonaut to fight at Troy, Nestor, who had already ruled two generations of Pylians, gave unstintingly of his wise council, particularly in the hot-tempered exchanges between Agamemnon and Achilles in the opening book of the *Iliad.* At a climactic moment in their estrangement over the return of a slave girl, Nestor shamed them both for dividing Greeks at a time when the army needed unity. He concluded even-handedly:

> You, Achilles, should not think that you can fight against a king. Although you are the mighty son of a goddess, Agamemnon is greater

than you are, for he is king over more people. As for you, Agamemnon, powerful as you are, do not take Briseis, for the Greeks gave her to Achilles as his prize of honor. Control your anger, for Achilles is the Greeks' great defense in this war.

Like Nathan facing a stubborn King David in the Bible or Merlin advising King Arthur's knights, Nestor accorded each man the respect due his office and the reproach due his bad behavior. In Book 4, Nestor again took the lead in settling the epic quarrel and suggested that Phoenix, Ajax the Great, and Odysseus should serve as the king's ambassadors to the sulking Achilles.

Nestor again distinguished himself during a tense moment in Book 3 when Odysseus stood alone to stop a rout of Greeks to their ships. A key strategist in both cavalry and infantry tactics, the Pylian king made his reputation for cool logic and the bold use of horses and men, whom he did not shrink from leading in battle. Odysseus, a worthy backup, usually concurred on every piece of advice that Nestor gave Agamemnon. In Book 7, it was Nestor who goaded a Greek champion to match arms in a private duel with Hector, Troy's strongman. After the drawing of lots from Agamemnon's helmet, Ajax was chosen. Later, Nestor himself experienced a taste of Hector's competence. Diomedes's quick action pulled the aged warrior from danger.

Much of Nestor's service is depicted through his relationship with Agamemnon. In Book 9 of the *Iliad*, Nestor brought up a difficult subject before the Greek assembly: the fact that Agamemnon and Achilles should not continue with their private war. During the night, as the Greeks rested from a daunting struggle against Hector in Book 10, Agamemnon personally sought out Nestor, "shepherd of the people." Finding him alongside his hut beside his ship with gear polished, honed, and lying in readiness, Agamemnon easily roused him.

Nestor asked, "Who are you, who walk alone through the ships and the army and through the darkness of night when other mortals sleep?" Realizing how troubled his commander had become over Hector's menace, Nestor reminded him that Zeus would not allow Hector a total victory. Nestor dressed quickly in the garb of a young warrior and awakened others of the inner council, including Ajax, Odysseus, and Diomedes. The latter, unwilling to give up his warm bed, snarled,

> Aged sir, you are a hard man. You are never finished with working.
> Now are there not others younger than you who could go about each
> of the princes and awaken them! But you, aged sir, are too much for us.
>
> (Homer's *Iliad*)

Taking the grumble as a compliment, Nestor reminded Diomedes that destruction could surely overwhelm Greek hopes if they failed to remain alert. At the late night conclave, Nestor sat in an open spot on the ground and formally addressed the others,

challenging them to select a champion. At length, Diomedes and Odysseus broke the silence to accept the dare and enter Trojan territory to spy on Hector.

In Book 11, Achilles, who was eager to learn the fate of the side he deserted, dispatched Patroclus to learn from Nestor how the Greeks were faring. Smoothly segueing into examples of courage from the illustrious past, Nestor used the occasion as a means of pricking Achilles's conscience. Nestor suggested that, if Achilles remained in his tent, Patroclus should don the famous armor and make a show of rallying the men.

Other isolated deeds attach to Nestor's wartime service. According to Lesches's *Little Iliad,* when Agamemnon tried to determine whether Ajax or Odysseus deserved Achilles's armor, Nestor made a sensible suggestion: send spies to the Trojan wars to eavesdrop and determine which of the two Greek warriors the enemy feared most. Also, Book 11 of the *Iliad* tells in detail how Nestor tended to Machaon, the healer, who sustained an arrow wound in the thigh. Nestor bore him to his hut, and summoned Hecamede, his captured serving woman, to lay out a meal. She responded by bringing a polished table and bronze basket, which Nestor easily lifted into place for her. She then set out onions, bread and honey, wine, cheese, and ale. Nestor oversaw Machaon's drinking of a curative potion and welcomed a visit from Patroclus, who honored the old man as friend, adviser, and patriot.

Even when strength deserted him, Nestor remained at the thick of battle, haranguing the Pylians to their best. The war brought grief to the old king, who witnessed Antilochus's death as the heir of the Pylian throne tried to save his father from Memnon, an Ethiopian ally of Priam. The battle began after Paris wounded one of Nestor's chariot horses. The fall of the horse addled its mate so that Nestor had to fight to keep the chariot from overturning. Memnon took advantage of his predicament and might have killed him. Antilochus fought off his father's attacker, then died in the fray. To honor his son, a brave sentinel and protector of the Greek horses, Nestor buried Antilochus in a plot near the unified graves of Achilles and Patroclus.

The funeral games for Patroclus, which occupy Book 23 of the *Iliad,* honored the strongest runners, hurlers, marksmen, and charioteers. Achilles, who revered Nestor as the Greek's great-hearted elder statesman, handed him fifth prize, a two-handled urn, and said:

> This, aged sir, is yours to lay away as a treasure in memory of the burial of Patroclus; since never again will you see him among the Argives. I give you this prize for the giving; since never again will you fight with your fists nor wrestle, nor enter again the field for the spear-throwing, nor race on your feet; since now the hardship of old age is upon you.

Nestor acknowledged that his limbs were slow and bent with age and that he wished he could again be young enough to box, wrestle, race, and hurl the spear. He concluded that Achilles made his heart happy and courteously wished him a similar contentment, knowing well that so contentious a heart as Achilles would never take satisfaction from old age.

Resettled on his throne along with Thrasymedes, his son who survived the Trojan War, Nestor restored the bones of Machaon the healer to Pylos. In an honored place near Asclepius's shrine at Gerenia, the relics healed sick pilgrims. A bronze statue of Machaon earned for the sanctuary the name *Rhodon,* meaning "the rose."

In the serenity of his court, Nestor, who was extolled widely for his age, courtesy, and wisdom, gratefully received Odysseus's son, Telemachus. In Book 3 of the *Odyssey,* the king and his family were sacrificing a bull to Poseidon as Telemachus arrived. Nestor took the occasion to reflect on the war years, particularly the cataclysmic end of Troy, which burned after hidden warriors escaped the wooden horse and opened the gates to attackers.

Nestor recalled his departure after ten years of battle. Setting sail with Diomedes and Odysseus, he had parted with Odysseus's fleet at Tenedos, where the famous wanderer had rejoined Agamemnon's ships. Nestor kept abreast of each warrior's fate and narrated the storm that blew Menelaus off course. He told of Aegisthus's murder of Agamemnon and the plight of Orestes, who was obliged by tradition to avenge his father's death and kill his mother, Clytemnestra. At length, Nestor sent Telemachus to Sparta to question Menelaus and Helen about more recent happenings and graciously offered the services of a chariot and his son Peisistratus as guide across the Peloponnesus.

Alternate Versions

Nestor's first wife is sometimes named as Anaxibia, Cratieus's daughter, and his second as Eurydice. Other analysts surmise that the two names applied to the same woman, although it seems likely that any man as long-lived as Nestor might have had several wives. An alternate telling of Nestor's recruitment of Achilles sets the event at Phthia, where Peleus gave his blessing to the young warrior's involvement in the Trojan War.

Symbolism

Nestor, an authoritative, although somewhat ineffectual man, whose name means "new speaker," derived fame from his advanced age, skill in logic, and experience. Like a windy Polonius advising Laertes, "To thine own self be true," the garrulous Nestor, sometimes viewed as a comic bore, spewed advice and rambling reminiscence for all occasions. A parallel to Merlin, Samuel Coleridge's ancient mariner, Obi-Wan Kenobi, the aged baseball coach in Bernard Malamud's *The Natural,* and other mentors of younger, less experienced men, Nestor, the sage, attempted to overcome loss of physical vigor with lengthy oratory, most of it didactic.

A foil to boastful adventurers, seducers of maidens, and self-satisfied favorites of the gods, Nestor stands out as an uncomplicated, worthy, and pious man, in part for his erection of a temple to Athena at Poeeessa on the island of Ceos while making his way to Troy. Few works of art depict Nestor among the more muscular of the Greek warriors. One planetoid or asteroid group honors him with a place among Achilles, Agamemnon, Hector, Patroclus, and Priam.

At least three sites have been claimed as Nestor's Pylos. An oversized, footed gold cup with dove wings creating four handles, which was located in a Mycenaean shaft grave and put on display in Athens, has been labeled the Cup of Nestor. Sir Arthur Evans's 1939 excavation of one possible Pylos site resulted in a cache of 600 tablets, but work on the dig was halted during World War II. In the 1950s, Michael Ventris pursued Evans's goal. Ventris was backed by American scientist Carl William Blegen, whose intense study of Nestor's palace at Epano Englianos five miles north of the Bay of Navarino on the road to Chora in Messenia produced the physical layout of the compound, including stairs, gateways, tombs, great room, hearth, courtyards, privies, and sleeping chambers. Blegen's book *The Palace of Nestor at Pylos in Western Messenia* (1966) gives strong insight into the evolution of the Greek language over a period of 3,300 years and describes a wealth of items excavated from tombs, including frescoes, tablets, celts, arrowheads, sword hilts and blades, tiaras, rosettes, crystal beads, sealing rings, pins, buttons, figurines, decorative urns, kitchenware and tableware, lamps, plaques, altars, and work-related objects, such as pestles, querns, rivets and studs, whetstones, balance beams with weighing pans, and loom weights.

Among locations linked with Nestor are the following:

- Pteleum, a town in Elis colonized by Thessalians.
- Amphigeneia, a town he claimed, which possibly lay in Messenia, although Strabo insists that it was built near the river Hypsoeis in Sicily and featured a temple honoring Leto.
- The harbor town of Coryphasium in Messenia is named as Pylos and also a shrine to Athena. North of this spot lies Nestor's Grotto, a small cave where the king may have hidden cattle from rustlers.
- Another questionable site is Arene, which Homer places on the Peloponnesus near the Minyeius River.
- Epitalium, a town south of the Alpheius River, has been mentioned in Homeric literature as a part of Nestor's dominion.
- The holy confines of Gerenia gave Nestor his name Gerenian, but no definite location in Messenia links the king with the city.

 Nestor's name survives in English as a synonym for adviser or wise man and is immortalized in these works: William Shakespeare's *King Henry VI* (Parts I and III), *Love's Labour's Lost, Troilus and Cressida,* and *Rape of Lucrece;* Edmund Spenser's *Faerie Queene;* Ben Jonson's *Volpone;* Sir Philip Sidney's *Arcadia* and *Astrophel and Stella;*

Michael Drayton's *Polyolbion;* Thomas Gray's *Extempore on Dr. Keene;* Thomas Hood's *Progress of Art;* John Keats's *King Stephen;* John Rochester's *On Drinking in a Bowl;* Elizabeth Barrett Browning's *Battle of Marathon;* and Algernon Swinburne's *Atalanta in Calydon* and *Song for the Centenary of Landor.*

❦ See Also

Achilles, Aegisthus, Agamemnon, Ajax the Great, Diomedes, Helen, Herakles, Menelaus, Odysseus.

❦ Ancient Sources

Apollodorus's *Epitome;* Apollonius of Rhodes's *Argonautica;* Aristophanes's *Knights; Chrestomathy* (anonymous); Dictys Cretensis's *Trojan War Diary;* Diodorus Siculus's *Library of History;* Eumelus's *Verse;* Eustathius on Homer's *Odyssey;* Herodotus's *Histories;* Hesiod's *Catalogue of Women* and *Theogony;* Homer's *Hymn to Apollo, Iliad,* and *Odyssey;* Hyginus's *Fables;* Lesches's *Little Iliad;* Ovid's *Metamorphoses;* Pausanias's *Description of Greece;* Philostratus's *Heroica;* Pindar's *Pythian Odes;* Scholiast on Euripides's *Alcestis;* Scholiast on Homer's *Iliad* and *Odyssey;* Scholiast on Pindar's *Olympian Odes;* Stasinus of Cyprus's *Cypria;* Stephanus Byzantium's *Nedo;* Strabo's *Historical Sketches.*

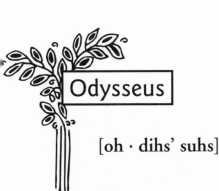

Odysseus

[oh · dihs' suhs]

Born on Mount Neriton, Ithaca, an island off the west coast of mainland Greece, the only child of Laertes and the kind, altruistic Anticleia, was Odysseus, one of Homer's favorite characters. As grandson of Arceisius and Aeolus, and great-grandson of Cephalus and Hermes as well as Jason's cousin, he claimed noble ancestry, from whom he earned the patronyms Aeolides and Arceisiades. Later, he learned that his skill in deception derived from Sisyphus, the violator of his mother and Odysseus's real father. His mother also bore a daughter, Ctimene, who married Eurylochus, Odysseus's second-in-command, and brought up Eumaeus, the foster child who eventually became Odysseus's loyal swineherd.

An intrepid navigator and mediator, Odysseus inherited the fertile Ithacan realm, at the western entrance to the Gulf of Corinth, over which his father in earlier years named him bailiff. This connection brought him the geographical name Ithacus. A comer from an early age, he was the prototypical well-rounded man, blessed with *arete,* or "excellence," able to box, wrestle, plow, hunt, skin, flay, and cook. In the affective domain, he attuned his spirit to gentleness and could be moved to tears by recitation and song. Like the heroes of Arthur's time, he embodied the best of chivalric heroism.

Finding a wife was one of Odysseus's easiest quests. Icarius was pleased to arrange so propitious a marriage as the one between Odysseus and Penelope, daughter of the Naiad Periboea, yet Icarius preferred that the couple settle in Sparta in the southern Peloponnesus. When Odysseus placed his bride in the chariot for the long journey over the Peloponnesus and across the Ionian Sea to Ithaca, Icarius followed at a trot, weeping and pleading for her to stay. Penelope signified her choice to obey her husband by drawing a veil over her face. Icarius, saddened by her departure, erected a shrine to modesty.

One of the Centaur Chiron's famous pupils, Odysseus was well educated. According to Ovid's *Metamorphoses,* "he was not beautiful,

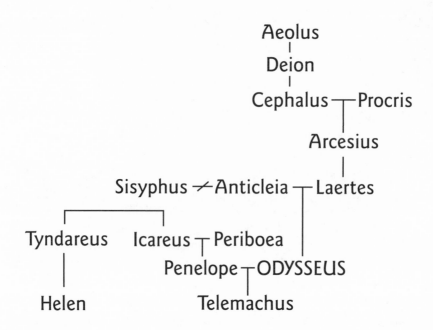

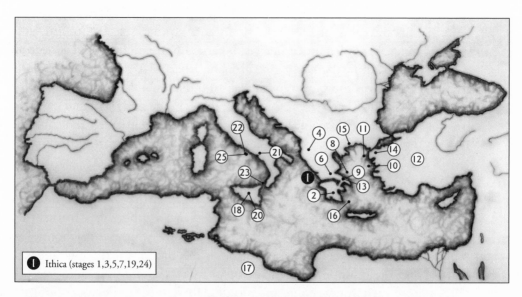

1. Ithaca 2. Sparta 3. Ithaca 4. Thesprotia 5. Ithaca 6. Delphi 7. Ithaca 8. Scyros
9. Aulis 10. Lesbos 11. Lemnos 12. Mysia 13. Aulis 14. Troy 15. Thrace
16. Cythera 17. Libya 18. Sicily 19. Ithaca 20. Sicily 21. Formiae 22. Aeaea
23. Strait of Messina 24. Ithaca 25. Aeaea

but he was eloquent." A short, stocky, auburn-haired man with pointed beard, he was deep of chest and broad in the shoulders, speaking boldly and logically with a ringing bass voice that convinced listeners of his honesty and forthrightness. Possibly, he limped a bit from a boar wound to his thigh and boasted of having escaped worse. Known for numerous romantic intrigues and for a brief hope of wedding Helen, Odysseus remained the faithful husband of Penelope, Helen's cousin, and the loving father of Telemachus and possibly a much younger son, Acusilaus, also known as Arcesilaus or Ptoliporthes, born to Penelope after Odysseus's return to Ithaca.

Journey No voyager compares with Odysseus, survivor of war, shipwreck, an angry goddess, sorcery, and treachery. From early times, Odysseus was a traveler. At the request of the boy's nurse, Eurycleia, Odysseus's maternal grandfather, Autolycus, named the child for the Greek *odion,* meaning "anger" or "hatred." The old man, who lived at Parnassus northeast of Delphi, requested that Odysseus visit him when he grew up. The boy did as his grandfather asked and earned many gifts. In the company of his uncles, he hunted a boar and received the glancing tusk wound that evolved into a striking scar across the thigh or knee.

Before reaching manhood, Odysseus answered his father's call to travel to Messenia in the southwest of the Peloponnesus to accost thieves who came by ship, rustled 300 sheep, and kidnapped the shepherds who guarded them. The story, which is incomplete, does not indicate how the young Odysseus fared in righting the injustices done to Ithaca. A version of the tale credits him with recovering mares in Pheneus, a town northeast of Arcadia.

As a guest at Ortilochus's home, Odysseus developed a friendship with Iphitus, prince of Oechalia, a land east of mainland Greece. Iphitus also sought stolen livestock. During their search, Iphitus presented Odysseus the bow of the fabled archer Eurytus; Odysseus reciprocated with a spear and sword. The gift bow was so valuable that Odysseus preserved it as an artifact, not taking it to Troy, but keeping it for use in Ithaca.

On a side trip to Ephyra, in Thesprotia, far up the western coast of Greece, Odysseus sought arrow poison from Medea's grandson, Ilus, an expert potion-maker. Ilus chose not to give Odysseus the concoction because he believed that the gods restrained him. Odysseus had to travel on to the island of Taphos, north of Ithaca, and get poison from Anchialus.

Odysseus joined a notable coterie of suitors for the favor of Tyndareus's beautiful daughter, Princess Helen of Sparta, sired by Zeus. Odysseus guessed from the beginning of his suit that Helen would choose Menelaus for his wealth, and struck a bargain with Tyndareus in the event that trouble should erupt from the famous courtship. In exchange for Odysseus's help in settling hostilities, Tyndareus would require every suitor to swear an oath to protect Helen and he would also arrange Odysseus's engagement to his niece Penelope, daughter of Icarius. Their marriage produced a fine son, Telemachus, who delighted both his parents.

Odysseus's advice to Tyndareus proved prophetic. After Paris abducted Helen, Menelaus and his brother Agamemnon launched a great fleet of warriors to return the unrivaled beauty to her rightful husband. When Menelaus and Palamedes, the commanders' ambassadors, approached Ithaca to recruit warriors, Odysseus, who was warned in advance that he would not return home for twenty years, donned a cone-shaped hat and mimicked eccentric behavior. In the guise of madness he yoked an ox to a horse or mule, then sowed salt in the furrow his plow made in the sand. To outwit the wily Ithacan, Palamedes placed the infant Telemachus in front of the plow point. Odysseus was unable to maintain the semblance of insanity if it cost him his son, so he diverted his mismated team and saved the baby from a grisly death. Laertes agreed to Odysseus's induction into the army and assigned Mysicus to guard him during the Trojan War. Likewise, Odysseus left Mentor behind as Telemachus's guardian and tutor.

One of the most valuable men on the Greek side, Odysseus chose to lead twelve Ithacan ships to Troy. He proved a worthy warrior and an even more respected adviser and strategist. He went with Menelaus to Delphi to seek advice on launching the war and accompanied Talthybius on an embassy far to the southeast to Cinyras, the home of the king of Cyprus, who promised to sponsor a segment of the growing fleet. Adept at trickery, Odysseus later saw through the ruse of Thetis, the sea nymph who hid her son, Achilles, among women on the island of Scyros east of Greece in the Aegean Sea. By sounding the attack, Odysseus discerned that only one child, who was dressed in girl's clothing, stripped and armed himself with shield and spear. Thus, Odysseus unmasked the imposter and enrolled the over-protected Achilles among Greece's warriors.

Leading fighters gleaned from the triad of western Greek islands—Cephallenia, Zacynthus, Leucas, and Ithaca—Odysseus suffered the same fate as Agamemnon and his fleet when the gods refused to send favorable winds at the Boeotian seaport of Aulis. Heeding the appeal of Calchas, Odysseus joined Diomedes in an embassy to Clytemnestra, Agamemnon's wife, whom they begged to send Iphigenia to marry Achilles. The entreaty was a wicked deception for which Iphigenia blamed Odysseus alone. Agamemnon, in order to gain the gods' assistance, slit the child's throat.

After another month's delay, the fleet set out for the final leg of its journey to the Troad. The Greeks passed Delos, among the Cyclades southeast of Greece, where they encountered the *Oenotropae* or "changers into wine," women who provided the fleet with amphorae of wine. Odysseus is said to have tried to kidnap the women, but Dionysus, god of wine, rescued them by changing them into doves. On Lesbos, in the northeast of the Aegean Sea, Odysseus demonstrated his skill in wrestling by pinning the king, Philomeleides.

At a stopover on the island of Chrysa near Lemnos off the Turkish shore, Philoctetes, the Malian captain, suffered a snakebite. The severity of the venom produced a foul-smelling wound that refused to heal. At Odysseus's request, Philoctetes was abandoned on Lemnos, but had to be retrieved before the Greeks could complete the destruction of Troy. Following the false landing at Mysia south of the Troad, Odysseus interpreted the oracle that explained how Achilles could heal a lingering wound, which Achilles had inflicted on Telephus, Herakles's son.

On reaching the Troad, a promontory at Hissarlik on the western shore of modern Turkey, Odysseus again took the role of spokesman and joined Menelaus and Palamedes, Nauplius's son, in an embassy to Priam. Their demand for the release of Helen failed. Only the intercession of Antenor prevented the Trojans from murdering the Greeks. Odysseus remained grateful to Antenor with the same fervor that fueled his hatred of Palamedes, who had disclosed Odysseus's feigned madness. Eventually, Odysseus forged a letter in King Priam's hand implicating Palamedes in a treacherous plot against the Greeks and urged Agamemnon to search Palamedes's tent for Trojan blood money. The Greeks, who found the evidence, which Odysseus probably planted, ignored Palamedes's claims of innocence and stoned him to death, an act that led to the victim's father's revenge on the wives of Greek leaders.

Some episodes demonstrate Odysseus's ability as a mediator. He succeeded in returning Chryseis to her father and also organized a short-lived truce while Paris fought Menelaus. When the quarrelsome Thersites interrupted councils of war, it was Odysseus's commanding presence that silenced him. In Book 2 of the *Iliad,* when the Greeks came close to abandoning their mission, Odysseus persuaded them to remain.

Not only did Odysseus demonstrate eloquence and brainpower, but he was also a mighty warrior and wielded a sword with skill, setting him apart from lesser men. In Book 9 of the *Iliad,* he volunteered to duel with Hector. In Book 10, when an occasion called for disguise, Odysseus also proved adept at theatrics, once disguising himself as a beggar so that he could accompany Diomedes to the Trojan camp. This jaunt resulted in the capture of Dolon, who provided significant allied troop information before Odysseus executed him. The foray ended with the murder of Thrace's King Rhesus and twelve of his warriors. Odysseus, along with the horses stolen from his victims, returned to camp triumphant.

In Book 11, Odysseus proved to be a tough competitor after finding himself alone on the field with Trojans crowding in. Homer describes him raging like a wild boar, "grinding to an edge the white fangs in the crook of the jawbones." Terrible to behold, the Ithacan stabbed man after man before Sokos's spear pierced both the circle centered on his shield and his protective vest and ripped the flesh from his ribs. Only Athena's protection kept the point from reaching a vital organ. With a yell, Odysseus summoned Menelaus and Ajax the Great to the spot where he lay fighting off the ravening Trojans with his spear.

By Book 14, Odysseus and Agamemnon had been removed to ships beached far down the shore, where both reposed for recovery. Upon hearing Agamemnon's wish to give up the war effort, Odysseus burst out in patriotic zeal: "I wish you directed some other unworthy army, and were not lord over us." The others heeded Odysseus's call to continue, and the slaughter recommenced.

At a crucial turn in the war, Achilles retired from the fray to pout in his tent. In Book 9, Odysseus was selected to head a party including Ajax the Great and Phoenix to pursuade the hot-headed warrior to remain loyal to Greece. For the first and only time, Odysseus failed Agamemnon. It took the death of the handsome, ill-fated Patroclus to roust Achilles out of his doldrums and back into armor. At the elaborate funeral games in Patroclus's honor, Odysseus won the footrace and tied Ajax in the wrestling ring. Later Odysseus persuaded Achilles to hold off a full-scale attack so the Greeks could rest from nonstop warfare.

After Achilles killed Hector and Paris slew Achilles, it was Odysseus who held off the jubilant Trojans as Ajax the Great recovered Achilles's body. The duo of Ajax and Odysseus turned into a fierce rivalry because both Greeks claimed the honor of Achilles's armaments. Much more suave at stating his case than the muscle-bound, inarticulate Ajax, Odysseus convinced the judges that he deserved the famed armor, made by Hephaestus at the request of the nymph, Thetis. Controversy surrounded the decision, causing Ajax to go mad with humiliation and commit suicide on his sword. Odysseus redeemed himself in part by convincing the Greeks to allow a suicide an honorable funeral. Later, he ceded Achilles's arms to Neoptolemus, Achilles's son, although an unlikely but more romantic telling describes the arms as lost overboard during the return voyage and washing up on the shore where Neoptolemus lived.

At no time was Odysseus more useful than at the end of the Trojan War. As the epic conflict reached its tenth year, the Trojans were at the end of their resources. Odysseus apprehended Priam's clairvoyant son, Helenus, the priest, and extracted information about how the miserable impasse could be ended. The essentials for a conclusion were the induction of Achilles's son, Neoptolemus, the recovery of Herakles's bow and arrows, and the theft of the Palladium, a statue of Athena housed in the Pergamum, Troy's citadel.

Odysseus immediately set about realizing these three goals. He sailed southeast with Phoenix to the island of Scyros and convinced twelve-year-old Neoptolemus to join the Greek force. On a shorter voyage east to Lemnos, Odysseus reclaimed Herakles's invincible bow and arrow from Philoctetes. Then Odysseus and Diomedes did the unthinkable: disguised as beggars and aided by Helen, they entered the enemy city and stole the Palladium, assassinating several Trojans on their way back to camp.

By thinking up the ruse of a handpicked party concealed in a hollow image in the shape of a horse, ostensibly as a propitiatory gift to Athena, Odysseus achieved lasting fame. In a later telling of his success, Odysseus claimed to have been mauled by Thoas and cloaked in rags to conceal his identity. He resurfaced in Troy, pretending to have deserted the Greek army. To assure the mission's success, he persuaded Helen to agree to the plot, to imitate the voices of Trojan wives, and to convince Hecuba to keep their strategy a secret. On his way back to camp, he cut down the Trojan gatekeepers.

Presentation of his Trojan Horse, constructed of fir planking by Epeius and drawn on logs to the city gate, implied that the Greeks were making a peace offering and sailing back to their homes without retrieving Helen. Although Laocoon warned his countrymen that Odysseus was an accomplished liar, the scheme, calling for Odysseus and a select band of mercenaries to steal out of the horse by night, open the gates, and initiate a fatal night attack on the unsuspecting populace, succeeded like no other plot in military history. Still grateful for Antenor's favor, Odysseus crept to the old man's door and stretched out a panther skin to indicate that no harm should come to him or his sons.

The bloodbath that followed, as described by Aeneas in Virgil's *Aeneid,* spared few Trojans, male or female, old or young. Odysseus helped exterminate the royal line of Priam by calling for the execution of Hector's son, Astyanax, who was only a small boy. According to Seneca in *Trojan Women,* Andromache, the boy's mother, begged:

> So may you see again your faithful wife; so may Laertes live to greet you again; so may your son behold your face, and ... excel his father's valor and the years of old Laertes. Pity my distress: the only comfort left me in my woe is this my son.

After she spoke the words, she realized their futility. Odysseus's wish to end the Trojan threat to Greek power overrode his pity for a single boy. Andromache cursed Odysseus by wishing a similar fate for his son. With no thought to her anguish, he stonily led the child away, complaining that her delay to the fleet was a mere annoyance. Then he or one of his men tossed Astyanax over the battlements to his death on the rocks below.

Other views of Odysseus depict him as unusually civilized, as demonstrated by his insistence that Menelaus not kill Helen. Never shying from bloody involvement, Odysseus also demanded that Polyxena be murdered on Achilles's grave to assure favorable winds, and that Ajax the Lesser be executed for raping the priestess, Cassandra, before the statue of Athena. As Odysseus predicted, Ajax, who escaped killing, brought down the wrath of the goddess, who allowed the wrecking of the Greek fleet on its return to the mainland.

No wanderer in Western literature suffered the implacable hatred of Poseidon that Odysseus endured. The Ithacan's state of mind appeared unstable as he accepted Queen Hecuba, his grumbling war prize, joined Nestor and Diomedes, and put to sea apart from Agamemnon's ships. Shortly, a quarrel erupted at Tenedos, where Odysseus parted with his comrades and rejoined Agamemnon. Had he remained with Nestor or Diomedes, he might have saved himself ten years of homeless wandering.

On setting sail from the Troad through the Hellespont, the narrow strait that separates European Turkey from its Asian half, and north to Chersonese on the Thracian coast far to the north edge of the Black Sea, his twelve shiploads of loyal Ithacans witnessed the virulent cruelty of his concubine, Hecuba, who plotted revenge on King Polymestor, murderer of Polydorus, the only surviving Trojan prince, for maligning

Odysseus. To avenge Polydorus's death, Hecuba had Polymestor's children killed and his eyes plucked out. Having endured the extremes of war, loss of family and kingdom, and the brutal deaths of everyone she loved, Hecuba was incapable of serving Odysseus as a war prize. The gods changed her into a hellish monster, and she disappeared into the Mediterranean. In another telling, Hecuba was stoned to death, with Odysseus hurling the first stone. The place in which she was buried was named "bitch's tomb."

The fleet sailed on to Ismarus, a Ciconian city on the northern Aegean shore of Thrace, which the Greeks looted, leaving only Apollo's priest, Maron, and his wife alive. The Ithacan crew dallied in victory while sampling twelve jars of Maron's sweet wine, and were waylaid by area nations, who slaughtered seventy-two of Odysseus's crew. Storm-driven across the Aegean Sea toward Cythera and Cape Malea on the southern end of the Peloponnesus, an area connected with the worship of Aphrodite, the crew caromed north toward Ithaca for nine days, then were forced far to the south-west to the shores of Libya on Africa's northern coast.

Odysseus halted on the promontory to take on fresh water. The three scouts whom Odysseus dispatched failed to return. He went in search of them and discovered that a tribe of dreamy Lotophagi, or lotus-eaters, had shared with the trio their honeyed fruit clusters of *cordia myxa,* a kind of crabapple, and the sweet, intoxicating mead derived from its pulp, which quelled their will to go on. Odysseus escorted his scouts back to the ship and ignored their tears as he tied them down before departing.

Odysseus sailed west to Sicily, arriving in a few days at the island of the one-eyed Cyclopes, giants who did no work and lived off the land in scattered caves. By slipping into the calm waters of a neighboring island, the crew managed to observe the area from a distance for two days. The third day, Odysseus, laden with wineskins as gifts for the locals, lowered his tender and rowed close enough to inspect the larger island. In Euripides's version of the story, Silenus, a slave, warned Odysseus of the cannibalistic Cyclopes, but the wanderer allowed curiosity to overcome his judgment. Accompanied by twelve mariners, he investigated the giant's cave. The party found no inhabitants, but a wealth of cheese, curds, milk, and livestock.

Instead of taking his men's advice about stealing supplies and returning to the fleet, Odysseus opted to eat a hearty meal and lie in wait of the cave dweller, Polyphemus, son of Poseidon and the nymph, Thoosa. The burly Cyclops returned at sunset with his herds of goats and sheep, sealed the cave entrance with a stone, then turned on the intruders who had boldly helped themselves to his stores. Odysseus appealed to the universal guest code by reminding him that the gods commanded all to do no harm to travelers. The impious Cyclops sneered at deities and laws and snatched up two sailors, whom he brained and devoured raw.

After Polyphemus settled down to sleep, Odysseus and his remaining ten men discussed their predicament. By dawn, they had arrived at no solution and watched helplessly as Polyphemus milked his flock, gulped down two more victims, opened the cave entrance, and replaced the stone. Immured in the cave with his eight remaining crewmen, Odysseus had time to devise a plan of escape. When Polyphemus returned at sunset, he again opened and resealed the entrance, then ate two more sailors. Odysseus, left with only half his original scouting party, asserted himself by sharing some of Maron's Ismarian dessert wine. Polyphemus was so pleased with the vintage that he and Odysseus struck up a conversation. Odysseus, who claimed his name was Oudeis, Greek for *No-Man,* merited a gift in return for the wine. Polyphemus made what he considered a generous offer—he would eat the remaining crew and save No-Man for last.

His gut stretched with too much food, Polyphemus passed out and spewed up some of his meal. The horrific sight of bloody limbs in a stream of vomit spurred Odysseus to action. He heated a pointed green olive-wood stick in the fire, then ground its sharpened end into Polyphemus's single eye. The giant yelled through his door that No-Man had blinded him. The other Cyclopes, unable to make sense of his distress cries, urged him to thank his father Poseidon and left him to his ravings.

The next morning, without vision, Polyphemus had to use his hands to prevent the Greeks from slipping away. He opened the stone door and let his woolly flock slip under his fingers on their way to pasture. Odysseus, who had anticipated this change of method, had tied his six mariners to the underbellies of trios of sheep. Clinging precariously to the underside of the lead ram, Odysseus escaped with his party and stole Polyphemus's sheep.

Unable to depart Sicily without boasting of his clever deception, Odysseus divulged his identity and shouted:

> Cyclops, in the end it was no weak man's companions you were to eat by violence and force in your hollow cave, and your evil deeds were to catch up with you and be too strong for you, hard one, who dared to eat your own guests in your own house, so Zeus and the rest of the gods have punished you.

> (Homer's *Odyssey*)

Polyphemus yelled back that their encounter had long been foretold and prophesied correctly that Odysseus would wander far and return by foreign vessel after his mariners were all dead. Though blind, the Cyclops ripped away the mountain top and hurled it toward the sound of Odysseus's taunts. The force of the projectile drove Odysseus's ships back toward the beach. Again he pushed off and urged his men to row mightily so that they could escape the monster.

Odysseus's fleet moved north, directly toward Aeolus's realm, the island of Aeolia, where the winds were anchored. Odysseus received the courtesy of the king and queen and their twelve children, especially Polymela, who offered him sexual favors. At the end of a great feast, Aeolus presented Odysseus an ox-hide sack tied tightly at the neck. He explained that the fiercest winds were bound inside, and that the remaining zephyrs would waft him west over the Ionian Sea toward Ithaca.

On the tenth day out of port, Odysseus came so close to Ithaca that he could see herdsmen's fires on the mainland. Relaxed and secure at last, the war-weary captain fell asleep. His crew, suspicious that Aeolus's gift held riches, opened the sack and let out the strong winds, which forced the fleet back to Aeolia. Odysseus, grieved to have been so close to the end of his journey, pleaded for additional help from Aeolus, but the king, possibly angry that Odysseus took advantage of Polymela's innocence, feared that Odysseus was being punished by a deity and forced Odysseus and his mariners away from his shores.

A week out of Aeolia, the fleet arrived at Telepylus, the Laestrygonian city, which probably lay near Formiae, Italy. Within the high-banked harbor, Odysseus dropped anchor and sent out a three-man party. His scouts found a giant woman fetching water from a spring. She came from a noble lineage; her father was Antiphates and her grandfather Lamus, once the king of the realm. She escorted the scouts to the royal compound, where King Antiphates devoured one of the trio. The remaining crewmen fled back to Odysseus, who chopped the anchor cable and roared for his oarsmen to pull for their lives. Only his ship escaped. The remaining vessels were inundated with boulders that the savage Laestrygonians showered down on them from above. What mariners escaped overboard, the giants skewered with tridents and saved for dinner.

Deeply saddened by the plight of the Ithacan veterans, Odysseus moved hastily to the island of Aeaea, the "island of the dawn," off Italy's west coast, an area now called Cape Circeo. The men, traumatized by two encounters with cannibalistic giants, remained on board ship for two days. On the third day, Odysseus scaled a high place and spotted a forest dwelling, the home of the enchantress, Circe, the "concealer," granddaughter of the sea god, Oceanus, and daughter of Perse and the sun god, Helios. Against the warnings of his mariners, Odysseus formed two parties and drew lots to select the group who would move inland. Eurylochus, captain of the selected party, departed through tall oaks toward the palace.

Within hours, Eurylochus reported alarming developments. The scouting party had discovered docile wolves and lions around the lone residence. From the windows came sounds of a woman's voice inviting them inside. Eurylochus remained on guard as the woman, adept at magic potions, plied the men with wine, then touched them with her wand. The men, whom she immediately altered into pigs, were immured in a muddy sty and fed on slops. Eurylochus was forced to abandon the luckless men and report the loss to Odysseus.

The remaining half of Odysseus's men were too frightened to rescue the scouting party, so Odysseus made the trip alone. Along the way, he encountered Hermes, who was disguised as a striking youth. Hermes schooled Odysseus in Circe's wiles and explained how a divine white-flowered, black-rooted moly, a form of the aromatic plant rue, cyclamen, garlic, or squill, could change them back into human shape. After the god withdrew into the forest, Odysseus encountered the sorceress and willingly sipped her wine. When the moly kept Circe's evil powers from altering him into a beast, he held the startled witch at sword point and made her promise to do him no harm.

Because his visit had been foretold, Circe lay with Odysseus and in her tender moments agreed to free the scouting party from their bestial forms. She hurled a potion at them, then watched as they grew back into human males. Odysseus felt sure enough of his power over Circe to summon the remainder of the crew to Circe's lair. Surrounded by her nymphs, the men spent a year in bliss before urging Odysseus to return to sea.

As Odysseus separated from his bewitching lover, she directed him to journey to the shades of the dead and to seek the advice of the blind seer, Teiresias. On the way out of Circe's home, the men were dismayed by the accidental death of Elpenor, the youngest of their group, who had climbed to the roof in a drunken escapade, tripped, and fallen, breaking his neck. Filled with dread at their next trial, as was Orpheus before and Aeneas after them, the men left Elpenor unburied and sailed from Aeaea.

By nightfall, the ship, blown by a northerly wind, reached Oceanus's stream, which girdled the earth. The sailors stepped out into Persephone's Grove, Cimmerian territory, which is obscured from the sun, and followed the way to the juncture of the rivers Periphlegethon and Cocytus with the Acheron in the far northwest of Greece. Near a crag at the Fields of Asphodel, they dug a deep hole and filled it with milk, honey, wine, water, and a sprinkling of barley meal. Lured by this libation, the wraiths accepted the sacrifice of a black ewe and sturdy ram in honor of the king and queen of the dead. The animal's blood gushed into the pit as spirits pressed for a drink to restock their bloodless veins. Odysseus adamantly forced them back with his sword and waited until Teiresias's ghost could drink its fill.

Before the seer arrived, Elpenor's spirit pleaded for a ritual burial on Circe's island. The spirit of Anticleia, Odysseus's mother, also pushed forward, surprising him with the news of her passing, which occurred after he left for Troy. At length, Teiresias, leaning on a gold cane, greeted Odysseus and warned that the last leg of the journey would be fraught with danger because Odysseus had angered Poseidon, god of the waves, by blinding his son, Polyphemus.

Teiresias assured Odysseus that he could reach Ithaca if he and his crew avoided harming Helios's livestock, pastured on the island of Thrinacia. If anyone threatened these sacred flocks, Odysseus would lose every crewman and return to his kingdom aboard a borrowed vessel. Once in Ithaca, he would face the hangers-on who hovered about Penelope, awaiting news of her husband's arrival so that they could kill him and marry the rich queen. The remainder of Odysseus's life would offer no quarter from wandering. He would arm himself with an oar and search out a nation of people who ate no salt. When Odysseus located people so far from the sea that they incorrectly identified the oar as a winnowing fan, he would know that his quest had ended. Then he would live out his old age and die by the sea.

Odysseus completed his interview with Teiresias, then turned to his mother for news of his father, son, and wife. Anticleia reported:

All too much with enduring heart she does wait for you
there in your own palace, and always with her the wretched nights
and the days also waste her away with weeping.

(Homer's *Odyssey*)

Anticleia added that Telemachus oversaw his father's investments and Laertes, who was old and sorrowful, stayed indoors. Anticleia herself had grieved herself to death. Three times Odysseus tried to embrace his mother, but she slipped away from his grasp.

More familiar shades pressed to the pit to drink blood and address their friend. Among them were Agamemnon, who, having been murdered by a jealous wife, warned Odysseus to tread carefully at the entrance of his own home. Achilles's shade heard news of his son, Neoptolemus, but Ajax the Great's ghost, still angry that Odysseus won Achilles's armor, averted his face from his old comrade. Other inhabitants of Hades—the judge Minos; the hunter Orion; the tortured souls of Sisyphus, Tantalus, and Tityus; Herakles; and famous women, including Phaedra, Jocasta, Leda, Antiope, Chloris, Pero, Iphimedeia, Procris, Maera, Clymene, Eriphyle, and Ariadne—appeared before a deluge of spirits forced their way to the blood-filled pit. Odysseus withdrew in haste.

Odysseus and his crew sailed back to Circe's isle, burned Elpenor's remains, and interred the ashes alongside his oar, which served as a gravestone. Circe offered more advice to her former lover, particularly how to avoid the Sirens, enticing girl-faced birds who coaxed sailors to their deaths on treacherous rocks with ethereal song. After the Sirens came the Symplegades or clashing rocks, and Scylla and Charybdis, the double-threated Strait of Messina in the deadly pass between Italy and Sicily. With a final warning of the dangers of slaughtering Helios's herds, she sent the Ithacans forth at dawn.

As the ship neared the Sirens' shores, linked historically with Faro, Sicily, or possibly Naples, Italy, Odysseus blocked his mariners' ears with wax. He had them tie him to the mast so that he could enjoy the exotic music and made them promise not to release him, even if he commanded them. When the deadly singers were long behind their wake, the sailors removed the wax from their ears and freed Odysseus. The Sirens, outwitted for the first time, killed themselves. Unaware, of the Sirens' fate, the Ithacan ship sailed past the Planctes, volcanic islands known today as the Lipari Islands, north of Sicily.

Immediately, Odysseus drew near the treacherous suck and regurgitation of the deadly whirlpool, personified as the female Charybdis. The ships hugged the coast, imperiling the crew by drawing near the twelve-foot, six-headed monster Scylla, who bared sharp teeth, barked like a dog, and menaced from a cavern atop a crag on the Sicilian coast. Against Circe's advice, Odysseus armed himself and challenged Scylla as she gobbled men with each of her six heads. Unable to battle both Scylla and

Charybdis, the captain could not save the men, who called out to him and stretched their hands in supplication. Grim-faced, he sailed south.

At last near Helios's meadows on Thrinacia in Sicily, Odysseus discovered the sun god's daughters, Lampetie and Phaethusa, supervising 350 sheep and 350 white cattle. Despite double warnings of the disaster awaiting rustlers, Odysseus's men rebelled at the inhuman pace they had followed and forced the captain to beach his ship. The crew ate from their stores for a month as south winds impeded their departure. When they had consumed all that Circe had provided, they had to forage for game and fish.

Odysseus, fearing the worst, knelt in prayer. He succumbed to sleep, leaving the men to do as they dared. Led by Eurylochus, the mariners slew Helios's cattle. Lampetie alerted Helios, who summoned Olympian gods and threatened to light up Hades if they refused to bring the rustlers to justice. On the seventh day, the Ithacans ended their feasting and pushed their ship into the foam. As soon as they reached the deep, Zeus stirred up a storm that shredded the ship with a single thunderclap and drowned the crew. Out of twelve shiploads of Ithacan veterans, only Odysseus remained alive.

To save himself from drowning, Odysseus fashioned a crude raft by tying the recovered mast to keel planking. Drifting northward, at dawn he again entered the Strait of Messina and was pulled into Charybdis. He grabbed hold of an overhanging fig branch just as his raft was pulled to the ocean floor. At evening, the whirlpool tossed up the raft and Odysseus once more rowed his craft out of perilous waters. The misadventure gave rise to the phrase *between Scylla and Charybdis,* a metaphoric statement of a dilemma like the one that had taxed Odysseus.

For nine days, Odysseus clung to life, then washed ashore at Ogygia, Calypso's tree-shaded isle known as the *sea's navel.* With nymphs as her only companions, Calypso, herself a domesticated sea nymph and possibly a sister to Circe, wheedled Odysseus to remain in her charming, violet-scented cave as her lover and become immortal. The alder and poplar wood and fragrant cypress enticed the weary seaman, who had had his fill of salt air; the clustering vines and clear streams eased his wanderlust, but dreams of his wife in Ithaca saddened him beyond the temptations of the exotic islander.

Meanwhile, on Olympus, the gods took notice of Odysseus's plight. Athena, a champion of the wily hero, persuaded Zeus to hearken to Odysseus's devout offerings and to end the protracted sufferings by conveying him home to Ithaca. To quicken the process and assist with the homecoming, Athena joined Telemachus, who was attempting to hold off the plague of suitors who thronged the Ithacan court.

After Odysseus's lengthy stay at Ogygia (one to ten years, depending on the source), Hermes, dispatched from Olympus, gave the final word: Calypso had to let Odysseus depart for home. Before agreeing to leave, Odysseus sat on the shore, teary-eyed, and groaned aloud at the difficult decision to put to sea once more. The weary captain borrowed Calypso's adze, saw, and plane and crafted a boat from native trees, stocked it with Ogygian meal, meat, wine, and water, and pushed it into the waves. He left behind the twin boys, Nausithous and Nausinous, whom he had sired, and possibly others, sometimes given as Latinus, Telegonus, and Auson, and sailed for two and a half weeks.

Sighting Scheria off the west coast of Greece and northwest of Ithaca, Odysseus found himself once more the object of Poseidon's spite. A storm thrust him onto the Phaeacian land and nearly sank him. The sea goddess, Leucothea, in the form of a bird, urged Odysseus to remove his clothes, wrap himself in her veil, and swim toward shore, leaving his boat to the elements. Protected from danger, for two days he made his way to the rocky shingle of Scheria on the island of Drepane, now called Corfu, and took refuge at a river. Worn past caring, he tossed the veil aside and slept under a bush beneath a heap of leaves.

With Athena's help, the princess, Nausicaa, preparing for betrothal, appeared at the riverbank to superintend the palace laundry. The serving women made a holiday of the event, shared their lunch, and tossed a ball while their clothing dried in the sea breeze. Their conversation awakened Odysseus, who covered his nakedness with a branch and presented himself to the princess as a suppliant. Unafraid of the brine-crusted survivor, she tended his hurts, clothed and fed him, then escorted him to the idyllic palace of King Alcinous and Queen Arete. The royal household promised to help him return to Ithaca.

Alcinous invited Odysseus to remain and marry Nausicaa and hosted a banquet to mark the occasion. The chanting of Demodocus, a blind minstrel, caused Odysseus to fall into cadence and utter the story of his harrowing misadventures. The Phaeacians, realizing how determined the Greek veteran was to reunite with his family, placed him aboard a ship the next morning and returned him to Ithaca before the rise of the morning star. Odysseus, fast asleep with his exertions and the catharsis of his narration of the previous night, lay amid a heap of Phaeacian gifts. Poseidon, angered at the Phaeacians' intervention in his punishment of Odysseus, turned their ship to stone, and walled off their city from the harbor.

Great-hearted Odysseus, whom Athena enveloped in a cloud, awoke with no memory of how he came to the unidentified beach. The goddess welcomed him home and warned him that he faced a great trial: freeing his court from the 108 ravenous suitors, who came from Ithaca and the colonies of Samos, Dulichium, and Zacynthus, to squander his wealth as they pursued his wife. Athena cast a spell over Odysseus that disguised him as a wandering beggar. He sought Eumaeus, the royal swineherd, who failed to recognize his king, but treated him kindly.

Telemachus, returning from a journey to Menelaus's palace, joined the pair and promised to aid the old beggar. Odysseus announced his true identity and embraced his son, whom he had not seen since babyhood but who bore a strong resemblance to his father in face and mannerisms. They formulated a strategy to free the hall of the parasitic suitors: as Odysseus made his way into the court, Telemachus would surreptitiously gather the suitors' weapons and lock them in the armory.

Passing Melantheus, the disloyal goatherd, Odysseus, accompanied by the loyal swineherd, arrived home at last, where Argus, Odysseus's favorite dog, collapsed and died at sight of his returning master. The wanderer shed a tear at Argus's passing. Stuffing themselves on delicacies, the discourteous suitors offered Odysseus a plate. Only Eurymachus, an unprincipled lout, degraded the old beggar by tossing a stool in his direction. Irus, a rival suppliant, challenged the newcomer. Odysseus stripped to reveal a surprisingly well muscled body, struck Irus a single blow, and smashed his jaw.

Queen Penelope entered the hall to announce that, since Telemachus was old enough to inherit the throne, she would choose a husband, since no news of Odysseus could justify a longer wait. She berated the interlopers for their lengthy tenure at her banquet table, then withdrew to her room to avoid their loathsome boasting and wrangling. Melantho, a disloyal servant girl, treated Odysseus rudely; her lover Eurymachus also insulted him. The undercurrent rose to a dangerous level until Amphinomus suggested that the suitors end their night's revels.

After the weapons were locked in underground chambers, the servant, Eurycleia, bolted the serving women's rooms. Odysseus joined his wife and pretended that he was a former companion of her long-lost husband. She revealed that for three years she had been stalling the suitors by pretending to weave a winding sheet for Laertes. Each night she pulled out the latest rows until a serving woman divulged her trickery. In the guise of Idomeneus's brother, Odysseus made up more stories of himself and proclaimed that Ithaca's king would soon reach home.

However, hopeful of Odysseus's return and heartsick that she was fated to marry another in place of her much beloved husband, Penelope was doubtful of the news. She put the stranger in Eurycleia's care and retired to her empty bed to weep for her husband. The old servant, while bathing his feet, glimpsed the scar on his thigh and knew for certain that the beggar was her king. He pledged her to silence. The next morning began with an ominous rumble of thunder. At Penelope's suggestion, the suitors competed in a contest of strength with the winner to receive the queen in marriage.

Following Odysseus's directions, Telemachus set up a row of twelve axes as a target. Penelope produced the bow that Iphitus had given Odysseus and opened the contest. The contenders, including Telemachus, tried in vain to string the king's bow. Odysseus, having recruited the help of Eumaeus and Philoetius, the herdsman, prepared to take his turn at the targets. After Penelope withdrew with her attendants, Odysseus, without even rising from his seat, succeeded in stringing the bow and shooting through the rings in the twelve targets. Meanwhile, Philoetius barred the door. With his son as assistant, Odysseus started executing suitors, beginning with the insulting Antinous and Eurymachus. Telemachus speared Amphinomus. The pair reloaded their quivers; their helpers prevented Melantheus from arming the remaining suitors, trussed him, and suspended him from a beam.

Athena, disguised as Mentor, Ithaca's resident graybeard, appeared to help Odysseus with the slaughter. The killing continued until all were dead except Phemius, the singer, and Medon, the messenger. Phemius implored,

I am at your knees, Odysseus. Respect me, have mercy. You will be sorry in time to come if you kill the singer of songs. I sing to the gods and to human people, and I am taught by myself, but the god has inspired in me the song-ways of every kind.

(Homer's *Odyssey*)

Odysseus chose to spare him as well as Medon, who cared for Odysseus in boyhood. Next, the king turned his wrath on twelve disloyal servants and ordered the room cleansed of the carnage. After the women completed the task, Telemachus hanged them with cable from a ship and cut off the hands, feet, nose, ears, and genitals of Melantheus for siding with the suitors. The house was purified with burning sulfur.

When the banquet hall was ready for Odysseus's reunion with his wife, Eurycleia summoned her from her nap. At first, Penelope, a wily equal to her husband, doubted the identity of a grizzled old man in rags drenched in gore. To prove himself, he described how their bed was created from the trunk of a rooted olive tree, a fact only Penelope's true mate would know. At these words,

her knees and the heart within her went slack as she recognized the clear proofs that Odysseus had given; but then she burst into tears and ran straight to him, throwing her arms around the neck of Odysseus, and kissed his head.

(Homer's *Odyssey*)

Odysseus bathed and robed himself royally. Athena, who had restored Odysseus's manly beauty, lengthened the night for their enjoyment.

In Book 24 of Homer's *Odyssey,* the day after the arrival of the suitors in Hades, Odysseus met Laertes on his rural acreage and conferred about how they could restore order to Ithaca after Odysseus's lengthy absence. Eupeithes, smarting at the murder of his son, Antinous, led the majority of the city's people against the king. Laertes cut down Eupeithes with a single spear shot. Athena halted a second bloodbath and dispersed the citizens. A lightning bolt from Zeus ended Odysseus's vengeance. Athena, still posing as Mentor, smoothed over local differences and brought peace.

Once more in control of Ithaca, Odysseus faced the last of his trials. As Teiresias had predicted, he sailed southeast to Elis on the Peloponnesus to meet with King Polyxenus, then traveled north to Thesprotia to sacrifice to Hades, Persephone, and Teiresias, to marry Queen Callidice, and to conduct a war against the Brygi, whom Ares led. Odysseus suffered defeat. Callidice died, leaving Odysseus's son, Polypoetes, to rule Thesprotia. Odysseus ended his final pilgrimage and returned to Penelope in Ithaca to enjoy his declining years and to rule in European style, more like an enlightened lord of the manor than the omnipotent king.

The wanderer's death seems almost an afterthought. Odysseus's son, Telegonus, arrived with his warriors from Circe's isle. The Ithacans fought off his warriors, but Telegonus killed his father with a spear point hewn from a stingray. As Teiresias had foretold, Odysseus's end came from the sea. The king's body was interred on Aeaea. According to Plato, in Hades Odysseus was given a choice of reincarnations. His former life had been so fraught with misery that he chose to return to earth as an ordinary man. Odysseus's demise brought unusual pairings. Penelope, by then an old woman, married her stepchild, Telegonus. Circe, an immortal, took Telemachus as husband.

A host of historians, archaeologists, writers, and adventurers have attempted to establish the route that Homer has Odysseus follow on his way home from the Trojan War, although the sixth-century writer's geographical conceptions may be so self-limiting that any paper and pencil map is impossible. The way east was relatively clear, following the path that Agamemnon's fleet took to the Troad: from Aulis past Delos, among the Cyclades southeast of Greece, in a northeasterly direction to Lesbos. Strabo adds that Odysseus, disguised as Aithon, grandson of King Minos, landed at a treacherous spot near Amnissos on Crete and took refuge in the cave of Eleithyia, site of a Minoan cult. He then moved up the coast of Asia Minor to Tenedos, a small island due west of Troy's coastline, then farther west to Chrysa and the larger island of Lemnos, where Agamemnon marooned Philoctetes before proceeding to the Troad, on the coast of modern-day Turkey, and camping along the Hellespont.

The return of the Ithacan fleet is more difficult to pinpoint. The first leg of the journey passed through the Hellespont into the Black Sea to the northern coast, where Odysseus ended his brief possession of the slave Hecuba. His ships returned by the same route, then traveled north to Thrace before being blown south toward his extensive Mediterranean wanderings. From there they headed west, to an area where Greek colonists eventually settled. The nebulous quality of semibarbaric peoples along the periphery of the more civilized Greek world suggests a poet's imaginative recreation of the wanderer's curiosity about what lay beyond home. Samuel Butler conjectured that the journey centered on Sicily and Italy's west coast and was described, not by Homer, but by Nausicaa, pseudonym of a Sicilian author from Eryx who had limited knowledge of sea lanes, winds, and landfalls.

In the twentieth century, the debate as to the physical existence of a route continued. Writer Ernle Bradford, a member of the Royal Navy and reader of Homer during World War II, used simple logic to retrace Odysseus's voyage in Homer's *Odyssey*—he matched poetic clues with existing landmarks. Bradford boldly listed distinct spots that fit Homer's poetic descriptions:

- Leaving Troy on twelve ships, ten oars per side, Odysseus sailed north to Ismarus on the Thracian coast to what is now Alexandropolis, then south and southwest through the Cyclades and around Cape Malea, a windblown pinnacle of land at the southern tip of the Peloponnesus.

- Due west to the island of Jerba off Tunisia, Odysseus landed ten days later at the lotus-eaters' realm.
- Sailing north by northeast, the fleet reached Favignana or Goat Island, called Aegusa in ancient times, where they encountered fog.
- Across the depths Odysseus could see Mount Eryx in Erice, Sicily, where the Cyclopes ruled and demanded human flesh.
- Odysseus halted at Ustica, an island north of Sicily, the home of Aeolus and the winds. He was blown by storm almost to Ithaca, then returned to Erice, sorrowing that he came so near to home only to be blown away again.
- From there, he made safe passage in six days to southern Corsica or Bonifacio, Sardinia, the Laestrygonian stronghold.
- Departing in haste, Odysseus pressed due east to Monte Circeo, Circe's welcoming lair, on Italy's shore near Terracina.
- A side trip to the Pillars of Herakles, the rocky tor that separates Spain and Morocco, brought him to the entrance of Hades. Without delay, he returned the same route.
- Hugging Italy's coast, he skirted the Sirens at the Gulf of Salerno, then past the volcanic isle of Stromboli, he threaded the unpredictable Strait of Messina, surviving Scylla and Charybdis by clinging to the Italian coast.
- The fleet arrived safely at Taormina, a hillside town on Sicily's eastern shore where Helios pastured his cattle.
- Curving south and west, Odysseus reached Malta, which he called Ogygia, Calypso's isle, where he lay by night in the enchantress's arms and by day mourned his marooning.
- He then moved directly to Corfu, home of Nausicaa, in a makeshift raft, and from there down the Greek coast homeward to the Ithacan port of Vathi.

In similar manner did Vincente Bérard, author of *Dans le sillage d'Ulysse*, create a hypothetical route. According to Bérard, from Thrace, Odysseus, like Aeneas, was blown southwest to the area around Tripoli on the north coast of Africa. From there he moved northeast to Sicily's coast, where he encountered Circe, the Cyclopes, and the Underworld. Pushed dramatically west to Gibraltar, the dividing point between Spain and Morocco, Odysseus accepted the hospitality of Calypso before returning to Sicily, rounding the southern shore, which he identified with Helios's isle, then north to the Strait of Messina.

Uncertainty clouds an analysis of much of the trip home. Local legends vary: Odysseus may have beached his ship off Italy at Ischia near Cumae, off Yugoslavia at Mljet or Lastovo, or off Greece at Corfu. In many of these places, local insistence on their part in the myth has resulted in a myriad of Hotel Odysseuses and many possible harbors. He may have passed through the Aeolians, a seven-island chain, and encountered the blustery scirocco. Whatever his zigzag route, the final leg of the journey impelled Odysseus to Scheria, which Bérard places off western Greece in the vicinity of Ithaca. Considerable debate arises over the actual location of Ithaca, which is usually linked to modern Thiaki, since little physical evidence can be linked to Odysseus's palace, which resembles in verse the splendor of Mycenae's House of Columns. A cult thrives at Polis Bay, linked by the tenuous proof of Tris Langadas, a site that may have been Homer's Ithaca.

Rhys Carpenter, an open-minded scholar who wrote *Folk Tale: Fiction and Saga in the Homeric Epics,* proposed a blended route, noting that the realistic elements of the early stages of Odysseus's journey fade to fantasy in the segment covering Scylla, the island of Helios, Charybdis, Oceanus, Hades, and the foggy land of the Cimmerians. It is this portion of the poem that suggests the author's acquaintance with old salts who superimposed the ends of the known world over their own imaginings, much as science fiction writers create mythic planets and galaxies far beyond the telescopic and satellite journeys of mortals.

Whatever the critics' conjectural paths, most of the action occurs in the area between Sicily and Italy. Circe's isle may lie near Terracina, Italy, not far from her father Helios's home on Thrinacia; Calypso, who may have been Circe's sister, is linked to Ogygia, also named as Aeaea in the strait between Sicily and western Italy. The Sirens, equally difficult to place on a map, lived on a rocky outcrop somewhere between Aeaea and Scylla's abode. Wherever these mythic sites lie, Odysseus became the single most traveled heroic figure in ancient literature, with Aeneas playing a close second and Dionysus, Herakles, Jason, and the Indian Rama not far behind.

Alternate Versions

According to the tradition that claims that Sisyphus sired Odysseus, he was born in Alalcomenae in Boeotia, when Anticleia was passing through on her way to her fiancé, Laertes. At his birth, his mother named him, then gave him the nickname Hypsipylon, Greek for "high gate," possibly to honor a moon goddess. Another telling describes how Anticleia set her infant on her father Autolycus's knee and bade him give the boy a name. The old brigand scowled and muttered,

> In the course of my life I have antagonized many princes, and I shall therefore name this grandson Odysseus, meaning "The Angry One," because he will be the victim of my enmities. Yet if he ever comes to Mount Parnassus to reproach me, I shall give him a share of my possessions, and assuage his anger.

(Robert Graves's *Mythology*)

It was on this journey to meet his grandfather that Odysseus was wounded by the boar.

An alternate telling of Odysseus's engagement to Tyndareus's niece depicts a footrace down a street in Sparta called the Apheta. Odysseus won the race and gained the prize, the hand of Penelope, formerly called Arnacia or Arnaea. Variations on the complex Odyssean cycle suggest that Odysseus slew Penelope for committing adultery with Antinous or Amphinomus. Another account has her returning to Sparta to her father's home, and from there to Mantineia, where she gave birth to Pan, sired by Hermes. Her burial mound lies in Arcadia in Mantineia.

Variations on the Trojan War describe how Odysseus accompanied Nestor to Phthia to draft Achilles, the promising fifteen-year-old student of Phoenix, the scholar. A listing of Agamemnon's staff names Odysseus, Diomedes, and Palamedes as commanders of the land troops and Achilles, Phoenix, and Ajax the Great as fleet commanders. At council meetings held in the Ithacan ships, Odysseus usually sided with Nestor, the oldest among the Greeks and Agamemnon's chief adviser.

Retellings of Odysseus's feud with Palamedes describe a variety of retaliatory plots. One plot has Odysseus's servant planting Trojan gold in Palamedes's tent. A second story reports Diomedes joining Odysseus in a faked discovery of treasure in a deep shaft. The plotters held a rope for Palamedes to climb down, then hurled boulders on him. A third variation describes how Odysseus and Diomedes took Palamedes fishing and drowned him. The savagery of Odysseus's vengeful plots help place the myth in the Iron Age, before the civility of the Bronze Age lessened support for unbridled acts of violence.

The Roman version of the theft of the Palladium claims that Odysseus found only a copy of the Palladium and that the original remained safe until Aeneas could rescue it from the burning citadel. A late addition to the story describes how Diomedes strapped the Palladium to his shoulders and set off toward camp. Odysseus, walking behind, grew jealous of the glory Diomedes would receive and attempted to murder his companion. Diomedes, catching the glint of Odysseus's unsheathed weapon in the moonlight, leaped aside to avoid a blade in the back.

The families that Odysseus is said to have sired vary dramatically. During his residence with Circe, he is said to have fathered sons Telegonus, Agrius, Ardeas, Romus, Antius, and Latinus and a daughter, Cassiphone; by Calypso he sired the twins Nausinous and Nausithous as well as Auson and Telegonus. In his later years, he agreed to a ritual marriage with Callidice, queen of Thesprotia, and sired Polypoetes, her successor on the throne. A variation on his fatherhood of Ptoliporthus has Telemachus journeying to Scheria to marry Nausicaa. This source gives Ptoliporthus or Perseptolis as Telemachus's son and Odysseus's grandson.

Another setting describes a journey to Epirus, where Odysseus is said to have ravished Euippe, King Tyrimmas's daughter, and sired Euryalus, whom Odysseus later slew without recognizing him. Odysseus endured a lengthy tribunal before Neoptolemus in Epirus. The judge, corrupted by his desire for Cephallenia, ruled against Odysseus and in favor of the suitors' families. The penalty was exile. Telemachus, having

suffered enough, received damages from the plaintiffs. The old wanderer is said to have traveled as far as Thoas's realm in Aetolia or west to Italy.

Another version states that late in his life, Odysseus was exiled to Aetolia in the south of mainland Greece, where he married King Thoas's daughter and fathered Leontophonus.

Symbolism

Many secondary exploits are attached to Odysseus's lore, which, like the Hebrew Bible or Islamic Koran was taught to school children throughout the ancient world, particularly the budding Alexander of Macedonia. Odysseus, called by the Romans Ulysses or Ulixes, is the prototypical misadventurer of Western literature, the first Greek hero to combine brawn with wit and intelligence and to sacrifice passion to character.

Like the Norse Sigurd, the Arabian sailor, Sinbad, and William Shakespeare's Prospero, Odysseus is courageous, pragmatic, and enterprising and has come to symbolize survival through self-sufficiency. Evoking images of Orpheus, Aeneas, Herakles, Theseus, Pirithous, Beowulf, the Babylonian Gilgamesh, and the Nyangan epic hero Mwindo, he braved the world of the dead and Charybdis, a parallel to the Grimm brothers' *Frau Holle,* a forbidding, bottomless hellhole. Like Rama, Odysseus is pitted against mighty, farseeing deities, and like Hansel and Gretel, he enters the house of a witch. His appearance as the mad plowman has been interpreted as a visual representation of war's inconsistencies and futility, sowing salt as corrosive seed that corrupts the ground. The trick to summon Achilles from his hiding place among women replicates Welsh lore in which Gwydion or Odin incites Llew Llaw Gyffes to battle to free him from his mother Arianrhod's overprotectiveness.

Odysseus proved equal to the temptation of the lotus-eaters. Avoiding the conflict Adam engendered by tasting the fruit of the Tree of Knowledge and the despair of the speaker in John Keats's mesmerizing "La Belle Dame Sans Merci," he recognized the release inherent in a restful, anxiety-soothing drug, yet chose not to partake. Other mythical figures have known similar temptation, such as the Scottish ballad of Thoms the Rhymer, who heeds Queen Elphame's warning not to taste the apples of Paradise. Likewise, Odysseus bested Polyphemus, the Greek equivalent of Baal, Tesup, or Moloch, atavistic sun gods. Freed from doom in the Cyclops's cavern, he returned to the true light of Helios and made his escape, just as mythic cave dwellers seek the light in Plato's *Allegory of the Cave.* In similar fashion, Odysseus parallels the Babylonian Marduk in using a holy herb to counter the death-bearing charms of Circe, an equivalent of Tiamat.

Other death plots, such as Calypso's youth-giving iris, the seductive Sirens, and the fiendish Scylla, failed to snare the wily, god-favored Odysseus. His meticulous voyage between the downward sucking Charybdis and the nine-headed shore monster suggests other literary dangers, particularly the mythological Harpies, Gorgons, and

Hydra and the iridescent dogs in Sir Arthur Conan Doyle's "Hound of the Baskervilles" or of seafarers' embroidered sea monsters, reflective of real sea creatures such as octopi, jellyfish, or entangling sea vines.

The romantic intrigues connected to Odysseus can be divided into two types. With Circe and Calypso, he had no mortal ability to resist divinity, but with the fetchingly pubescent Nausicaa, he courteously declined. Without doubt, his loyalty to Penelope symbolizes folk concurrence in the wisdom of monogamy. However, sociologists point out that Odysseus was the first ancient hero to violate the matriarchal hierarchy by demanding that Penelope follow him home to Ithaca. Still, mythographer Donna Rosenberg points out the strength of the women in Odysseus's world, from the magicians Calypso and Circe, to the monstrous Scylla and the Sirens, to Penelope herself, as crafty in her own way as her husband.

Unlike his Hebrew parallel, Jacob, most literary Odysseuses are picaresque characters who live by their wits and diplomacy and give full range to their sexual appetites and curiosity. They lie and deceive, yet commit no unforgiveable sins. In the Roman perception, Odysseus, like Turkish Greeks, could be trusted to commit rascalities of minor proportions. Virgil depicts him as the unscrupulously light-fingered thief of the holy Palladium and the framer of Palamedes, whose execution Odysseus engineered out of spite. Virgil's Aeneas, on the other hand, makes use of Odysseus's confrontations with Scylla and Charybdis and skirts Circe's isle. Aeneas's triumphal entry into Dido's banquet hall parallels Odysseus's honored place at Alcinous's court, where he, like Aeneas, recounts his adventures.

Later writers developed Odysseus's lore to suit their needs. Tacitus describes the dauntless wanderer moving north to the Rhine, where his altar remained during the Roman occupation. Under Christian influence, Dante Alighieri in the *Inferno* pictures Odysseus in similar form—as a prototypical wandering Jew, like the Celtic Saint Brendan, perpetually seeking his quest and punished in hell for his uncontrollable curiosity. Local people concocted stories of visits made by Odysseus, and of the children sired during his stay with Circe, so they could name cities such as Ardea and Agria after these mythic offspring. Other geographical landmarks linked with the Odysseus myth include the Horse's Tomb, the spot where Tyndareus forced Helen's suitors to pledge to defend her.

Revivals and transformations of the Homeric Odysseus play a part in the works of notable French poets such as Jean Giraudoux's *La guerre de Troie n'aura pas lieu,* Hilaire Belloc's *In Praise of Wine,* Andre Gide's *Philoctète,* and Joachim du Bellay's sonnet on "Ulysse." English poetic references appear in the following works: John Gower's *Confessio Amantis;* Edmund Spenser's *Faerie Queene;* William Shakespeare's *King Henry VI* (Part III), *Titus Andronicus,* and *Rape of Lucrece;* Ben Jonson's *On the Famous Voyage;* John Cleveland's *Upon an Hermaphrodite;* Sir John Davies's *Nosce Te Ipsum;* Matthew Prior's *Down Hall;* John Keats's *Endymion* and *Acrostic;* Lord Byron's *Don Juan;* George Crabbe's *The Library;* John Milton's "Comus," *At a Vacation Exercise,* and *Paradise Lost;* Percy Shelley's *Hellas;* Alexander Pope's *Dunciad* and *Argus;*

Alfred Noyes's *Forty Singing Seamen;* C. Day Lewis's *The Antique Heroes;* Alfred Lord Tennyson's "Lotus-Eaters" and "Ulysses;" Dante Gabriel Rossetti's *Death's Songsters;* Elizabeth Barrett Browning's *The Fourfold Aspect;* Robert Browning's *The Ring and the Book;* and Louis MacNeice's *Day of Returning.*

More exotic representations fill James Joyce's reinvention in the novel *Ulysses;* Jean Giono's *Naissance de l'Odyssée;* Book 26 of Dante Alighieri's *Inferno;* Johann Goethe's *Nausikaa;* Giovanni Pascoli's *Ultimo Viaggio;* William Shakespeare's *Troilus and Cressida;* Hilda Doolittle's *At Ithaca;* Samuel Butler's *Authoress of the Odyssey;* Robert Graves's fanciful novel *Homer's Daughter;* and Nikos Kazantzakis's *Odyssey* and *Zorba the Greek.* The 1992 Nobel Prize honored an even more farfetched Odysseus figure, Derek Walcott's Achille, the fisherman hero of *Omeros,* a Caribbean epic named by the Greek spelling of Homer. Academia as well has pondered the Odysseus myth, as demonstrated by W. B. Stanford's scholarly *The Ulysses Theme,* Lord Carlisle's *Diary in the Turkish and Greek Waters,* and Ernle Bradford's travel book and film *Ulysses Found.*

Visual representations demonstrate the figured fantasies Homer's words inspire in artists. Re-creations of the most vivid of Odysseus's wanderings appeared throughout the Mediterranean world—on Aegean funerary urns, Pompeian frescoes, Athenian and Roman statuary, Tanagran terra cottas, and in Polygnotus's frescoes in the Lesche or Club House of Delphi, which depict the fall of Troy and Odysseus's journey through the Underworld. From more recent times come tapestries by Jacob Jordaens, Renaissance paintings by Piero di Cosimo, Giovanni Battista Tiepolo, Dosso Dossi, and Pinturicchio, and later European works by E. M. W. Turner, Sir Edward Coley Burne-Jones, Charles Gleyre, Jean Raoux, and Bartholomew Spranger. In many glimpses of the old sailor, he is identified by the jaunty oval sailor's cap that became his trademark. Not a traditional theme in music, Odysseus received attention in Claudio Monteverdi's theater music, *Il ritorno d'Ulisse,* and two operas, Luigi Dallapiccola's *Ulysses* and Gioacchino Albertini's *Circe.*

❦ See Also

Achilles, Aeetes, Aeneas, Agamemnon, Epeius, Herakles, Jason and Medea, Menelaus, Nauplius, Nestor, Orpheus, Theseus.

❦ Ancient Sources

Aelian's *On the Nature of Animals;* Aeschylus's *Philoctetes;* Apollodorus's *Epitome;* Apollonius of Rhodes's *Argonautica;* Arctinus of Miletus's *Sack of Troy;* Aristotle's *Poetics;* Cicero's *Against Atticus* and *On the Nature of the Gods;* Conon's *Narrations;* Cratinos's *Odysses;* Dares of Phrygia's *Trojan War;* Dictys Cretensis's *Trojan War Diary;* Didymus's *On Lyric Poets;* Duris the Samian's *Histories and Criticisms;* Eugammon of Cyrene's *Epicorum Graecorum Fragmenta* and *Telegony;* Euripides's *Cyclops, Hecuba,* and *Trojan*

Women; Eustathius on Homer's *Iliad;* Homer's *Iliad* and *Odyssey;* Horace's *Odes;* Hyginus's *Fables* and *Preface;* Lesches's *Little Iliad;* Livius Andronicus's *Odyssia Latina;* Johannes Malalas's *Chronographica;* Ovid's *Metamorphoses;* Parthenius's *Love Stories;* Pausanias's *Description of Greece;* Petronius's *Satyricon;* Pindar's *Nemean Odes;* Plato's *Republic;* Pliny the Elder's *Natural History;* Plutarch's *Table Talk* and *On the Life and Poetry of Homer;* Polyaenus's *Strategems;* Scholiast on Apollonius of Rhodes's *Argonautica;* Scholiast on Aristophanes's *Clouds;* Scholiast on Sophocles's *Philoctetes;* Seneca's *Trojan Women;* Servius on Virgil's *Aeneid;* Silius Italicus's *Verse;* Sophocles's *Ajax, Odysseus,* and *Philoctetes;* Stasinus of Cyprus's *Cypria;* Suidas; Johannes Tacitus's *Dialogue on Orators;* Theocritus's *Poems;* Theophrastus's *History of Plants;* Johannes Tzetzes's *On Lycophron.*

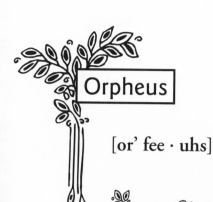

Orpheus

[or' fee · uhs]

Genealogy and Background

An anomaly among human heroes, Orpheus, the semidivine son of Calliope, the chief Muse who presided over epic poetry, and Oeagrus, king of Thrace and a river god, grew up on the outskirts of Olympus. Orpheus is said to have had two brothers: Linus, who became Orpheus's and Herakles's music teacher, and Rhesus, king of Thrace and a veteran of the Trojan War. From the Dactyls, the daemonic caretakers who guarded the infant Zeus, Orpheus learned occult rituals passed down by the goddess Rhea. According to Ovid's *Metamorphoses,* Orpheus taught music to King Midas.

Master of songs based on the thirteen-consonant scale, the lyre, and the lute, which his patron and possibly his father, Apollo, gave him in childhood, Orpheus, who was believed to have invented the nine-stringed cithara, was a tender, contemplative visionary capable of divine melody that charmed savage men, wild and tame beasts, the surf, rivers, trees, and winds, and even softened stones. As Apollonius of Rhodes describes him in *Argonautica:*

> And wild oaks, memorials yet of his singing, which
> he had led right on from Pieria by the spell of his lyre,
> marched in ordered ranks, each behind his fellow, to
> range themselves, with all their leaves, upon the fringe
> of the Thracian shore.

So powerful was the musical spell of Orpheus's melody that fishers encouraged him to accompany them so that he could sit on deck, sing songs, and charm the fish.

Journey

Like Odysseus, Aeneas, Herakles, Dionysus, and Theseus and Pirithous, Orpheus earned fame for daring to journey to Hades. Orpheus sailed aboard the *Argo* as a handpicked

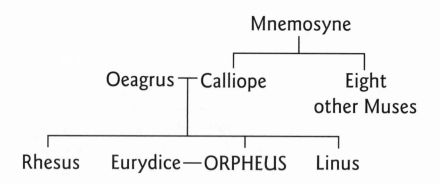

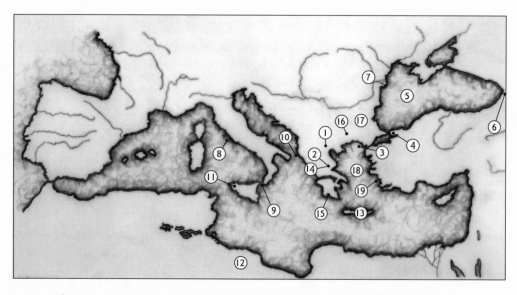

1. Mt. Olympus 2. Pagasae 3. Samothrace 4. Bosporus 5. Black Sea
6. Colchis 7. Danube River 8. Aeaea 9. Strait of Messina 10. Corcyra
11. Drepane 12. Libya 13. Crete 14. Pagasae 15. Taenarum 16. Thrace
17. Hebrus River 18. Aegean Sea 19. Lesbos

member of Jason's crew. Although Orpheus is not credited with superhuman strength or prowess, at the harbor of Pagasae in Thessaly on Greece's northeast shore, he moved the beached *Argo* down to the water by the magic of music and exhorted Jason's mariners with lusty sea chanties, soothing their squabbles and the raging seas with gentle tones. So entrancing were his improvisations that Apollonius reports:

> as he ceased, still leant their heads towards him with
> eager ears, one and all hushed but hungry still by his
> enchantment, so strong a spell of music had he left
> within their hearts.

(Apollonius of Rhodes's *Argonautica*)

When the *Argo* strayed off course, it was Orpheus's music that righted it.

To assure Jason's success in retrieving the Golden Fleece, Orpheus served as much more than singer. He sat in the coxswain's seat and directed rowing. When the *Argo* strayed off course, it was Orpeus's music that righted it. When prophecy and interpretation were necessary to keep Jason in tune with the divine, Orpheus joined Mopsus, the chief soothsayer on the *Argo,* in advising the captain of necessary obeisances.

Because of his skill with the lyre, in minor versions of his myth Orpheus mesmerized the clashing rocks and the guardian dragon of the Golden Fleece and influenced the crew to stop long enough at Samothrace south of Thrace to become initiates of the Cabeiri or Samothracian mysteries. Thus protected by the cult, he was able to drown out the alluring Sirens, who enticed the Argonauts to steer their vessel onto rocky shoals. Poets say the Sirens were turned to stone by his powerful melodies. He also provided romantic music for Jason's marriage to Medea. Some mythographers add that he could calm waves, and during a storm, called down tongues of fire to light over the heads of Castor and Pollux as symbols of grace. For his loyalty and skill on the long voyage to the Black Sea, Jason awarded Orpheus a wife, Eurydice, whom he courted with ballads. By the time the ship had reached the Bosporus and headed for safe harbor in the city of Adresteia in Mysia, it was Orpheus who led his fellow sailors in a vigorous ritual dance. According to Apollonius, fully armed, the men "danced a measured step in full harness, smiting swords and bucklers" to ward off evil.

Orpheus's marriage to the beautiful daughter of Apollo, the dark-haired, dark-eyed Naiad, Eurydice, a nuptial presided over by Hymen himself, is the most congenial glimpse of Orpheus depicted in Greek and Roman mythology. However, despite Orpheus's sincere devotion to the nymph, omens for the newlyweds boded ill as wedding torches sputtered and smoked, bringing tears to the celebrants' eyes. The bride and groom, with eyes for each other alone, failed to notice the portent.

In the early months of the union between Orpheus and Eurydice, the omens proved true: Eurydice, who roamed a meadow gathering spring blossoms, died from the bite of a poisonous snake that struck her foot. By the time her husband found her, Eurydice's spirit, led by Hermes, had already made its fearful journey into Hades. Bereft of his love, Orpheus intoned the bitterest of all his songs, moving the spirits of upper earth to mourn. But these earthly sprites were powerless to intervene in the doom issued from the king of the dead. With no one to aid his fallen wife, Orpheus resolved to risk death and make the grim descent to the Underworld to return Eurydice to earth so that she could live out a normal allotment of years.

Entering the Underworld at Taenarum on the southern tip of Laconia in southern Greece, Orpheus passed unharmed along the downward path, to the River Styx, where his sweet songs about boyhood boats cajoled a teary-eyed Charon into allowing him passage over the dark waters. So moved was the ferryman that he forgot to collect his rightful toll. Orpheus strode onward through the dismal confines of Tartarus, strumming and singing poignant melodies to influence the hardened denizens of Hades. While he was passing through the Field of Asphodel, Orpheus's plaintive notes caused the damned—Sisyphus, Ixion, the Danaides, Tityus, and Tantalus—to halt their toils to listen. The bloodless shades, three-headed Cerberus, and raging Erinyes wept. Even the stern judges—Minos, Aeacus, and Rhadamanthys—fell into a reverie as he strummed and sang.

His passage to the throne of Hades complete, Orpheus entreated the gods to return Eurydice or else let him die and join her. Remembering their own romance, Hades and Persephone, rulers of the Underworld, were so moved by Orpheus's thwarted passion that they took compassion on him and summoned Eurydice from the assembled shades. She limped toward her husband, still crippled by the wound to her foot. Before the throne of the Underworld, she heard the pronouncement of the king and queen of the dead: she could return to life on the condition that the couple not look back on the way up the shadowy path. If Orpheus disobeyed, as did the Hebrew Lot who could not look back at Sodom and Gomorrah as he escaped their destruction, Eurydice would return to unending residence among the departed as rapidly as Lot's wife turned to salt.

Through the Field of Asphodel, across the sleeping form of Cerberus, and through the gates of murky Tartarus, Orpheus followed Persephone's instructions and trod the craggy path in silence, listening the while for Eurydice's footsteps behind him. On he strode, into Charon's boat, across the Styx, and back to Avernus. Near the great gates at the cave entrance, filled with longing to embrace his beloved, he stepped into the light and turned to reassure himself that Eurydice was indeed following. Because she had not yet taken the final step from the passageway, with a single cry of dismay, she dissolved into an impalpable shade and, like mist, vanished from his outstretched hands.

Heart-stricken at losing her a second time, Orpheus tried to retrace his pilgrimage to the throne of Hades and lay inconsolable for seven days on the Stygian shore, castigating the Fates for his torment. Charon, who was not to be charmed a second time, refused him a return passage. Grimly, the old man ferried his passenger back to the craggy shores. Orpheus, scarcely aware of his actions, stumbled up the slope to fresh air and sunlight.

Blaming himself for his haste, Orpheus, refusing food and sleep, wandered Thrace (where his trauma turned to madness), and took up residence in a cave; his musical gift quelled by grief and self-accusation, he withdrew from human contact and sang no more. When rabid Thracian Maenads, the crazed worshippers of Dionysus, pursued him, he spurned their amorous overtures. Enraged by Orpheus's rejection, or possibly incited by Dionysus, they threw stones and abandoned Orpheus's bloody form in the dust. They returned to him, demanding once more that he make merry music. At his continued silence, they leaped on him, tore the singer to bits, and tossed his remains and his lyre into the Hebrus River, which lies on the European side of modern Turkey. For their savagery to the gentle poet, their mates tattooed the Maenads with a netted pattern.

While floating to the Aegean Sea, Orpheus's head, still possessing the lyric voice, called to Eurydice; the verdant banks echoed his plaintive cry. Drifting southeast in the Aegean Sea to the island of Lesbos, Orpheus's dismembered body washed ashore. The Muses lovingly gathered each segment and buried them at Leibethra, where a nightingale honored him with the sweetest trills heard in all of Greece. His soul, freed from its mortal entanglement, drifted down the path once more to join the ghost of his bride, where Aristaeus, one of Eurydice's former suitors, found him on his sojourn in the Underworld. The gods, mindful of Orpheus's singular talent, placed his lyre in the night sky to remind humankind of the depth of Orpheus's love for Eurydice.

Alternate Versions

There are various accounts of Orpheus's parentage. Alternate legends name Apollo, the god of sunlight and creativity, as his father, whose paternity joined with the influence of a Muse—sometimes named as Calliope or Polyhymnia or Menippe, daughter of Orion. Other versions say the Muses bestowed unearthly gifts of music and poetry on their infant, who some say grew up on Mount Parnassus. One account credits Hephaestus with designing the first lyre, which Apollo gave his son.

According to some accounts, Orpheus and Eurydice lived a year together on the banks of a river. In other tellings, Orpheus's beloved Eurydice was bitten moments after the wedding ceremony while strolling the meadow with her bridal attendants or while fleeing the lustful clutches of Aristaeus, one of her former suitors who believed her to be an enchantress and chased her into a nest of venomous snakes. She died instantly of multiple bites and lay in the wild until evening, when her husband found her.

Orpheus, driven out of his mind with grief, climbed Olympus to beg Zeus to intercede with his brother Hades, the god of the dead. In other versions of Orpheus's journey to the royal court of Hades, he traveled through an entrance on Mount Avernus straight to Hades's throne, where only Persephone took pity on him. Another setting credits Hades with softening the harsh penalty of death and allowing Eurydice to return to life. Differing explanations of Orpheus's motivation for disobeying the gods' requirement not to look at his wife blame the poet for impatience, weakness, and a rejection of reality in causing Eurydice's return to the Underworld. One unusual account faults Eurydice's tender wound, which impeded her advance into the upper world.

Other versions of the myth claim that Orpheus was a false husband who loved only men and young boys, particularly Boreas's winged son, Calais, who, along with his twin brother, Zetes, accompanied the Argonauts. An eastern setting describes Orpheus as suffering seven months of mourning by the river Strymon east of Macedonia and in the frozen caves of Tanais on the modern day Don River in southern Russia; this Turkish myth credits local women with the singer's violent death because he was no longer able to accompany their merrymaking with sprightly music, and because he condemned the Maenads' lascivious behavior, because he preferred the embrace of his own sex, or because he organized an Underworld cult that excluded females. One source claims that Orpheus committed suicide and that his remains were buried at the location of an oracle on Lesbos. A particularly savage version depicts a quarrel between Aphrodite and Persephone. In anger that Calliope, the judge, had ruled in Persephone's favor, Aphrodite had all local women fall in love with Orpheus and dismember him in their lust to possess him.

In some versions, only Orpheus's head and lyre—the source of his song—survived the ordeal and arrived on the island of Lesbos, where local cultists of lyric poetry honored his memory and consulted the oracle at his shrine. His remains, according to one account, were buried at the base of Mount Olympus in Leibethra, on the southern border of Macedonia, and were honored by poets, singers, and lovers. In two markedly different accounts, Zeus struck him with a thunderbolt, possibly to punish him for the sin of pride or to elevate him to the fields of the blessed. Alternate points of interment include Leibethra in Thessaly, Pieria south of Olympus, and the river Meles. One piece of lore claims that fishers located Orpheus's remains in order to stem a plague that ravaged Thrace and that they found the head still singing.

Lodged among the blessed in the Elysian Fields, Orpheus's shade, clothed in flowing white raiment, sang for the other spirits. In Book 10 of Plato's *Republic,* Orpheus appeared before the throne of the Fates and was allowed to select a new incarnation. He chose to become a swan. Mentioned as forebear of both Homer and Hesiod, he continued to surface in discussion of the afterlife and the Eleusinian mysteries. In his honor, orphic verses encouraging the soul to overreach mortal limitations were inscribed on tombstones and plaques and sung as dirges.

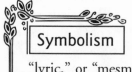

Symbolism An ever-fresh artistic motif, Orpheus's story, an allegory of longing and grief, preserves his name in the adjectives *orphean,* meaning "lyric," or "mesmerizing," *orphic,* implying mysticism, and in the nouns *orpheum,* a name often applied to theaters and music halls, and *orphics,* the moral teachings ascribed to Orpheus. Pursued in Sicily and Italy in the sixth century B.C., Orphic cults developed the myth, abandoning wild processions and adding conservative traditions. Followers were expected to display loyalty, obedience, and devotion to mates. The alternative for disobeying the cult was a forbidding reminder of the netherworld, from which mortals never return. In 520 B.C., Hipparchus hired Onomacritus, an Athenian poet of the sixth century B.C., to edit Orpheus's hymn collection. A century later, the group of songs were sung as a sacred psalter, rich in morality, humanistic doctrine, and ritual.

One mystical offshoot of Orphic worship had supplicants devour raw hunks of a slain bull as a gesture toward Dionysus, the god of rejuvenation. Ultimately, the cult mellowed to a tendency toward white-robed followers pledging to adhere to Orphic celibacy, ascetic lifestyles, and vegetarianism, a philosophy that prefigured Christian monasticism and later puritanism. The gentler humanistic strains of the worship of Orpheus replaced subjugation to the bellicose Zeus in the same way that blood sacrifice in the worship of Yahweh gave way to the symbolic communion service in honor of Christ, a deity tormented with much the same savagery that killed Orpheus.

In artistic re-creations, Orpheus's tortuous journey to Hades epitomizes the soul's striving for its mate; his wife's name, Eurydice, in Sanskrit means "dawning light." She was killed by a serpent, symbol of dark and menacing evils. Willing to pit his life in a struggle with the perpetual darkness from which no sojourner is allowed return, Orpheus impressed the gods with his daring and his transcendent music, which caused them to suspend the unremitting laws of death that foreshorten earthly love. Orpheus was depicted as the prototypical widower and represents the extremes of passion, which fluctuate from ecstasy to the depths of remorse. Immortalized in astronomy, Orpheus's lyre lives among the stars as the constellation Lyra, which features Vega, the brightest star in the northern hemisphere, and an annual meteor shower, the Lyrids, which are visible each April.

An alternate interpretation of the Orpheus myth warns of the awesome responsibility of godlike talents, which become too great a burden for mortal grasp. This view of the myth faults Orpheus for *ate,* or insane obsession, and *hubris,* the overweening pride that was the deadliest of sins in the ancient world. Because he allowed his emotions to overrule his head and insisted that Eurydice escape her mortal lot, he overstepped human bounds and challenged the will of the gods. For so deadly a crime, his punishment—a false renewal of hope and a second death for Eurydice—brought him to the edge of despair and a savage death, much as Daedalus's use of engineering skills cost him his son.

Linked to a martyred cult figure in eastern Mediterranean lore, Orpheus, who, like Dionysus, the Egyptian Osiris, and the Welsh alder god Bran of the *Mabinogion,* undergoes dismemberment and resurrection into godhood, resembles other religious figures who overcome death. His name is connected with the alder and his lore with the willow, which, like Dionysus's vine, is annually pruned to encourage new growth. The Orphic cycle, characterized by its escape from the mortal confines of death through piety, also stresses the sublime powers of poetry, which are capable of moving even the gods. Onomacritus composed the *Orphia*, a metaphysical world view supposedly based on the verses of Orpheus. The worship of Orpheus through verse and song permeated the ancient world. One Orphic cult extended all the way into Roman times and influenced Catullus, Virgil, and the Alexandrian poets.

A similar motif of Orpheus's character also exists in American Indian lore. The journey to retrieve the dead was accomplished by any family member, usually with the help of a wise crone who supplied a pipe to summon the spirit, or a strong potion to serve as inducement. Just as Orpheus was forbidden to look back at Eurydice, the Indian retriever was instructed not to touch the spirit or look at it. If the injunction was broken, the spirit returned irretrievably to the land of the dead. In the Blackfoot setting of the story, the rulers of the netherworld warned a grieving husband that his wife might return to him if he brought her to earth and underwent a ritual cleansing in the sweat lodge, then accepted her with kindness. In time, he mistreated his mate, who instantly disappeared.

Among Pawnee storytellers, the Orpheus myth parallels their whistle dance. In the pantomime, a young widower journeyed to the Underworld to find his wife. He carried with him four wads of mud, given him by the wise old crone to toss at his wife as evidence of the human link to the earth. For the trek home, the aged sage provided red beans, a rattle, and a whistle whittled from elk bone as a source of communion with the deceased. The man used his amulets to transform himself into a powerful warrior. As such, he took a second wife. His neglect of the first wife reduced her to a skeleton, which he buried a second time. In vain he danced the whistle dance to revive her once more.

The singer's touching story has had many artistic interpretations. It enriches Attic vase drawings such as *Orpheus among the Thracians*, housed in the Berlin Museum, Roman mosaics, sculpture by Auguste Rodin, paintings by Polygnotus, Nicolas Poussin, Gustave Moreau, Padovanino, Vecillio, Titian, Delville, Swan, Camille Corot, and Odilon Redon. European and American writers, particularly Jean Anouilh, Elizabeth Madox Roberts, Tennessee Williams, Robert Lowell, Oskar Kokoschka, Johann Goethe, Hilaire Belloc, and Rainer Maria Rilke, have found inspiration in the Orpheus myth. Plays by Angelo Poliziano and Giacomo Torelli capture the poignance of Orpheus's loss, as does *Orpheus*, a ballet choreographed in 1948 by George Balanchine.

Musical tributes include these: Franz Liszt's melodic symphony *Orpheus;* Franz Schubert's *Orpheus;* William Schuman's fantasy, *A Song of Orpheus;* Igor Stravinsky's *Orpheus;* Benjamin Britten's *Orpheus Britannicus Suite;* Hector Berlioz's *La Mort d'Orphée,* an opus for voice and orchestra; Claudio Monteverdi's famed opera *Orfeo,* which influenced later interpretations; Franz Josef Haydn's *Orfeo ed Euridice;* Christoph Gluck's *Orfeo et Euridice;* and others by Ottorino Respighi, Salomone Rossi, Darius

Milhaus, Gian Francesco Malipiero, and Jacques Offenbach. Additional operas by Giulio Caccini, Jacopo Peri, and Ottavo Rinuccini focus on Eurydice alone. English melodist John Dowland was honored as the English Orpheus; a twentieth-century male chorus from Uppsala, Sweden, is called the Sons of Orpheus.

An unprecedented list of references in English literature include the following: Geoffrey Chaucer's *Book of the Duchess, House of Fame, Merchant's Tale,* and *Troilus and Criseyde;* Thomas Moore's *Genius of Harmony* and *Vision of Philosophy;* Robert Henryson's *Orpheus and Eurydice;* Phineas Fletcher's *The Purple Island;* Giles Fletcher's *Christ's Triumph over Death;* Sir Philip Sidney's *Astrophel and Stella;* John Skelton's *Garland of Laurel;* Sir John Denham's *Progress of Learning;* Edmund Spenser's *Epithalamion, Hymn in Honour of Love, Shepherd's Calendar, Faerie Queene,* and *Ruins of Time;* Thomas Vaughan's *Olor Iscanus;* William Shakespeare's *Rape of Lucrece, King Henry VIII, Merchant of Venice, Two Gentlemen of Verona,* and *Titus Andronicus;* Abraham Cowley's *The Spring;* John Milton's *Il Penseroso, Paradise Lost,* and *Lycidas;* William Shenstone's *Love and Music;* Edward Young's *Ocean;* Robert Herrick's *His Farewell to Poetry* and *Orpheus and Pluto;* Thomas Carew's *Elegy on the Death of John Donne;* Alexander Pope's *Ode for Musick;* Michael Drayton's *The Muses' Elizium* and *To Himself and the Harp;* William Collins's *On the Use and Abuse of Poetry;* William Cowper's *On the Death of Mrs. Throckmorton's Bullfinch;* William Wordsworth's *Power of Music* and *Written in a Blank Leaf of Ossian;* Robert Southey's *Thalaba;* John Keats's *Endymion* and *Lamia;* Percy Shelley's *Orpheus, Prometheus Unbound,* and *Hellas;* Lord Byron's *Hints from Horace;* Alfred Lord Tennyson's *Idylls* and *The Last Tournament;* Dante Gabriel Rossetti's *The Kiss;* Charles Lamb's *The Ballad-Singers;* George Chapman's *Shadow of Night;* Algernon Swinburne's *Eurydice;* Matthew Arnold's *Thyrsis;* D. H. Lawrence's *Medlars and Sorbapples;* W. H. Auden's *Orpheus;* and C. Day Lewis's *A Time to Dance.*

Films based on the Orpheus myth include Jean Cocteau's 1949 masterpiece, *Orphée,* set in France. Featuring a poet as Orpheus, the plot has the personification of Death, in the form of a princess, fall in love with him and offer to guide him through a looking glass to the Underworld to retrieve his deceased lover. A melange of poetic imagery swells this fantasy into ecstasy as Death, the loser, condemns herself to extinction to save Orpheus.

The sequel to *Orphée,* Jean Thullier's *Le Testament d'Orphée,* filmed in 1959, depicts the mythic character as a poet of the Age of Enlightenment who dies, moves into a timeless landscape, then returns to life to reestablish an identity. A puzzling fantasy, *Le Testament d'Orphée* departs so earnestly from the Orpheus myth that it received little acclaim, despite its cast glittering with notables such as Jean Cocteau, Yul Brynner, Jean Marais, Pablo Picasso, and Charles Aznavour. A 1993 *Orphée,* an opera by Philip Glass, drew more on the Jean Cocteau version of the myth than on antiquity.

A famous effort, Marcel Camus's *Orfeu Negro* or Black Orpheus, a tense, explosive remake set in the 1959 carnival atmosphere of Rio de Janeiro, was a 1958 Cannes Film Festival favorite. The film has earned a cult following for its portrayal of Orpheus, a poor tram conductor and sometime dancer and guitarist, who, like a South American

Pied Piper, entices children and animals as well as women with his native charisma and pulsating music. The arrival of Euridice, a waif escaping an unspecified death threat at the home of her cousin, Seraphina, relieves Orpheus from a moribund marriage to the shrewish Mira.

The chemistry between the black musician and Euridice mixes with the frenzied preparations for Carnivale, a pre-Lenten festival that is the Brazilian equivalent of Mardi Gras. Celebrants don garish wings and masks; Orpheus appears as a Greek warrior. Mira, aided by a symbolic character named Death, stabs Euridice to death. Orpheus, grieved at the loss of his fragile love, descends thirteen floors past Cerberus, the watchdog of Hades, to a voodoo ritual that requires him to reenact the myth by singing to his dead love, but to avoid looking at her.

He supports his lover from the hellish pit to a mountaintop. A swirling melee engulfs the pair. Someone throws a stone that hurls the doomed pair to their deaths. The coda of the piece is a prophecy of reincarnation and mythic perpetuation: young male singers imitate Orpheus's guitar playing and, propriating the rising sun, lead a young girl away. The film, which is marred by obscure motivation and lack of control, earned an Academy Award nomination for best foreign film.

Poets too have devoted thought to the myth. In 1980, poet Elaine Feinstein noted how scantily the lore of Orpheus depicts the wife, who blossoms only in verses strummed to her husband's lyre. The 1983 setting of the poem "Eurydice," by imagist Hilda Doolittle, reverses the usual order of the myth by letting the twice-doomed wife, a mirror for Orpheus's self-love, confront a narcissistic husband: "for your arrogance and your ruthlessness I am swept back where dead lichens drip dead cinders upon moss of ash." In 1992, an off-Broadway opera by Craig Lucas featured Gerald Busby's music in *Orpheus in Love,* a modern setting that places the main characters in high school, with dream sequences recreating hell.

🌿 See Also

Aeneas, Daedalus and Icarus, Dionysus, Herakles, Jason and Medea, Odysseus, Theseus.

🌿 Ancient Sources

Aeschylus's *Agamemnon* and *Bassarae;* Apollonius of Rhodes's *Argonautica;* Apollonius of Tyana's *Autobiography;* Aristophanes's *Frogs;* Athenaeus's *The Learned Banquet;* Cicero's *On Divination;* Clement of Alexandria's *Protrepticus* and *Stromateis;* Conon's *Narrations;* Diodorus Siculus's *Library of History* and *Orphic Hymn;* Diogenes Laertius's *Prooemium;* Epigenes's *Tragedies;* Eratosthenes's *Star Placements;* Euripides's *Alcestis* and *Bacchants;* Hesiod's *Theogony;* Homer's *Iliad;* Hyginus's *Fables* and *Poetic Astronomy;* Ibycus's *Calydonian Boar Hunt; Lithica* (anonymous); Lucian's *Against the*

Unlearned; Onomacritus's *Orphica;* Ovid's *Metamorphoses;* Pausanias's *Description of Greece;* Philostratus's *Heroica* and *Life of Apollonius of Tyana;* Pindar's *Pythian Odes;* Plato's *Republic* and *Symposium;* Plutarch's *On the Slowness of Divine Vengeance;* Servius on Virgil's *Georgics;* Sophocles's *Deaf Satyrs;* Strabo's *Historical Sketches;* Valerius Maximus's *Handbook;* Virgil's *Aeneid* and *Georgics.*

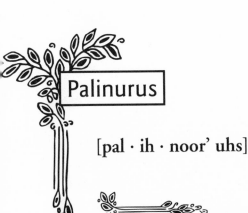

Palinurus

[pal · ih · noor' uhs]

Genealogy and Background

Like Menelaus's Canopus and Odysseus's Elpenor in Greek lore, Palinurus, son of Iasus, served Aeneas, Rome's founder, as helmsman on the flight from the fallen Troy to the new Troy after the Trojan War. Palinurus's berth as pilot on a chancy adventure based on directions from the gods may have given him the anonymity he craved. More likely, he was so minor a figure in Rome's epic that no family tree exists. Whatever the nature of his former home and family, Palinurus, known only by his patronym, did not die a sailor's death. After falling into the sea, he swam to land, but was murdered and tossed into the dark waters southwest of Italy by savage locals, fulfilling Venus's warning that he and his followers would complete their voyage, but at the cost of one life.

Journey

Palinurus earned no interest from ancient poets on the first segment of the epic voyage, which apparently took him over the same wayward carom from Troy to Crete toward Hesperia, the mythic promised land in Italy. With the other Trojan stalwarts, Palinurus must have taken his turn at the watch on the way past Cythera, Laconia on the southern tip of the Peloponnesus, and the Strophades, where the remains of once-proud Troy straggled through the stormy Ionian Sea. Up the western coast of Greece to Actium, Buthrotum, and Dodona, he wintered with the nameless crew while his skipper visited with Andromache and Helenus. Jogged from thoughts of home to duty, the fleet once more set out for the west, beached at Drepanum, Sicily, steered clear of the deadly isle of Aeaea—Odysseus's undoing—and through the doom-laden Scylla and Charybdis off Italy's boot. They stopped at Mt. Eryx in Sicily to pay their respects to Anchises, Aeneas's deceased father. A lengthy pause

Iasus
|
PALINURUS

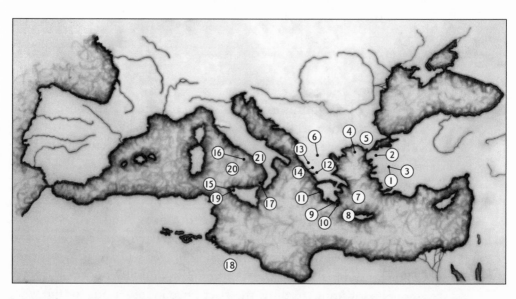

1. Mt. Ida 2. Troy 3. Mt. Ida 4. Samothrace 5. Aeneadae, Thrace 6. Macedonia
7. Delos 8. Pergamum, Crete 9. Boeae 10. Cythera 11. Strophades 12. Actium
13. Buthrotum 14. Dodona 15. Drepanum, Sicily 16. Aeaea 17. Scylla and Charybdis
18. Libya 19. Drepanum 20. Tyrrhenian Sea 21. Cape Misenum

in Libya on Africa's north shore followed a storm that removed Aeneas from his original route and drove him due south to beached wreckage, rest, and a lengthy dalliance with Queen Dido. The royal delay ended, the gods turned them once more to Drepanum toward their goal—the Tyrrhenian coast. Palinurus was unaware of the divine recompense and looming peril as the ships appeared, for once, to sail smoothly with the gods' unanimous blessings. He rejected his captain's suggestion that he take a well-deserved rest in the final leg of the sail toward the land that would one day be Rome. An experienced sailor he replied,

> Would you have me ignorant of the sea's calm face and the still waves? Shall I trust this perilous thing? How shall I trust Aeneas to fickle breezes and sky, when I am so often tricked by the treachery of calm waters?
>
> (Virgil's *Aeneid*)

The idealistic pilot gripped the tiller, turned toward the Libyan coast, and watched the stars off Cape Misenum.

Morpheus, intent on destroying the hapless man, sprinkled his eyes with a bough soaked in the waters of Lethe, the River of Forgetfulness, and the powers of the river Styx, the watery moat that girdled the Underworld. Lost to the god, Palinurus tumbled overboard, his hands so tight on the stern and steering oar that he ripped them from their moorings. While Aeneas's ship went its uncharted way without steering mechanism or steersman, Morpheus, his aim satisfied, slipped back into the upper air.

Palinurus cried to his crewmates for assistance in the hope of being rescued from the cold water but no one heard him and so he swam east in the dark Tyrrhenian Sea with only a vague hope of reaching shore. Realizing that the ship was adrift and rudderless, Aeneas took over the task of sailing as his vessel approached the Sirens' rocks. He searched for his steersman and grieved for Palinurus because his gullible pilot trusted the calm night and lay unburied at Velia, "naked on an alien sand."

After Aeneas journeyed to Hades to confer with his father's spirit, he met the helmsman's ghost, which wandered the far shore of the river Styx. In Book 6 of Virgil's *Aeneid*, Aeneas was so moved by the unexplained departure that he asked,

> What god, O Palinurus, reft you from us and sank you amid the sea? forth and tell. For in this single answer Apollo deceived me, never found false before, when he prophesied you safety on ocean and arrival on the Ausonian coasts. Lo, is this his promise-keeping?

Palinurus replied that the gods were not to blame; he suffered a mishap at the tiller, and rough wintry seas bore him away. Four days later, after swimming with all his might, he stumbled onto land and tried to climb the rocky headlands of southern Italy, where the fiercely territorial Lucanians murdered him.

Because his body lacked proper burial ritual, including the obolus on the tongue to pay Charon to ferry him to Hades, Palinurus begged his captain for succor:

> By heaven's pleasant light and breezes I beg you
> by your father, by Iulus your rising hope
> rescue me from these distresses, O unconquered one!

Aeneas, who was choked with emotion, allowed the Cumaean Sibyl to intervene. She promised a hunt for Palinurus's remains, a worthy resting place, and an annual tribute from the Lucanians at a grotto, which would immortalize the hapless sailor.

Symbolism

Palinurus epitomizes several factors in voyage lore: the vulnerable crew members who bore Jason, Odysseus, and Aeneas over unfamiliar waters, and the *quid pro quo* attitude of anthropomorphic gods, who heartlessly demanded a sacrifice in exchange for Aeneas's success. With no warning, Palinurus was forced to give his life so that Rome might be founded and the gods of Troy resituated in a new shrine. As he described his tenuous hold on life, "I caught with crooked fingers at the jagged mountain-headlands, the barbarous people attacked me in arms and ignorantly deemed me a prize." Weary from his three-day swim, Palinurus was unable to ward off his attackers and died, ironically escaping death by drowning only to be killed on unfriendly shores.

Like some wayward animal lost from the herd, the corpse of Palinurus was wave- and wind-tossed, a perpetual vagabond in the afterlife. Similar to dogfaces, labeled "cannon fodder" in modern warfare, sailors from times past have performed similar deeds of dedication and honor and have died from a single unguarded moment. Many lie in unmarked graves in distant lands or at the bottom of the sea. Other aspects of Palinurus's fate accentuate acquiescence to duty to a superior officer, particularly one so god-driven as Aeneas, and the lack of appropriate funeral rites, an essential ritual that releases souls from their wanderings on the Stygian shores so that they can find rest from earthly toils in Hades's dwelling.

In honor of Palinurus, Cape Palinuro on a jut of land in the Tyrrhenian Sea in Campania, Italy, bears his name. Geoffrey Chaucer mentioned Palinurus's mishap in *The House of Fame*. Robert Naumann immortalized him in *Palinuro*. In 1944, novelist, editor, and critic Cyril Connolly resurrected the name as a pseudonym, under which he wrote a dismal autobiography, *The Unquiet Grave*. The work, replete with the cynicism born of the trauma of World War II, ascribes to Palinurus a symbolic disenchantment with Aeneas's messianic mission to reestablish Troy. Connolly depicts Aeneas's loss of his pilot as the epitome of frustraton and a subconscious hint that Virgil himself was growing weary with his task of providing Augustus and the newly created Roman Empire with a suitable epic.

❦ See Also
Aeneas, Canopus, Odysseus, Sthenelus.

❦ Ancient Sources
Strabo's *Geography;* Virgil's *Aeneid.*

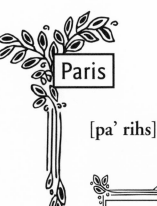

Paris

[pa' rihs]

Genealogy and Background The second son of King Priam and Queen Hecuba of Troy, Paris, the world's most handsome male, took second place to his mighty brother, Hector, leader of the Greek forces during the Trojan War. The grandson of Laomedon and a descendant of Dardanus, Paris was also brother to Cassandra, the prophetess, and her twin, Helenus, a prophet; Deiphobus; and Creusa, wife of Aeneas. Before Paris's birth, a dream warned Hecuba that her child would be a torch that would burn Troy to the ground. This phantasm was interpreted by Priam's illegitimate son Aesacus, also a seer, who feared that the omen proved that the infant should be destroyed immediately after birth. The Sibyl, Herophile, one of Apollo's votaries, seconded his opinion. Thus, the king handed over the child to Agelaus, a king's man or shepherd, who left Paris to die of starvation or animal attack on Mount Ida.

In standard mythic motif, Agelaus returned five days later to find that Paris, whom a female bear had tended, was unharmed. Taking the boy's grit and stamina as an omen, the shepherd wrapped the un-named child in a money belt—the origin of the name Paris—brought him to his cottage and reared him as a foster son. To convince Priam that he had slain the child, Agelaus presented the king a dog's tongue.

In time, Paris's noble heritage asserted itself through boyish glimmers of the handsome, sturdy, daring man he would become. While still a shepherd, Paris left his first wife, Arisbe, who was probably much older than he, to marry the nymph, Oenone, whose name he carved on rocks and birch bark and with whom he had a son, Corythus.

Paris earned the name Alexandros or Alexander, meaning "de-fender," by serving his foster father well in guarding the flocks against beasts and rustlers. One of his chief amusements was training his most promising bull to fight and pitting it against bulls in other herdsmen's pastures. When Priam's servants stole Agelaus's best bull to use as a funeral offering honoring the king's second-born, Paris journeyed to Troy to compete against other athletes, including his royal brothers,

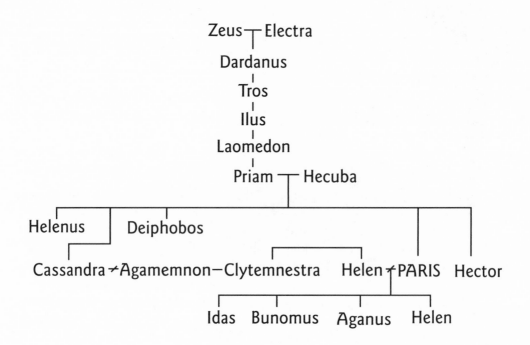

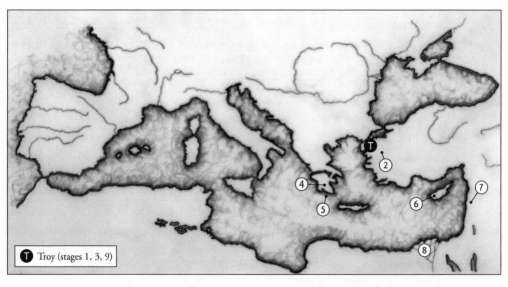

Troy (stages 1, 3, 9)

1. Troy   2. Mt. Ida   3. Troy   4. Sparta   5. Cranae   6. Cyprus   7. Sidon   8. Nile River
9. Troy

to win back the valuable bull. So outstanding was his performance that he won all the events—boxing, running, and chariot racing. Aristocratic contenders, belittled by a common herdsman, spurred Hector and Deiphobus to challenge the upstart, who hid at Zeus's shrine in the citadel. At this holy spot, Cassandra recognized that the astounding athlete was her brother and warned the court that Paris brought certain death to the house of Priam. Paris produced his swaddling garments as added proof. The royal household, forgetful of the prophecy of doom, repatriated him.

While Paris was reestablishing himself as a prince, the Olympian deities were gathering in Phthia at the wedding of Thetis and Peleus. Eris, the goddess of strife, who had been deliberately excluded from the nuptials, threw a golden apple into the court. Three goddesses—Aphrodite, Hera, and Athena—snatched it up and began quarreling over the inscription, *For the Fairest,* a designation each claimed. Zeus wisely refused to settle the matter and dispatched the trio across the Aegean Sea to the Troad, where Paris, a comely youth, would choose the rightful owner.

Accompanied by Hermes and Apollo, the goddesses appeared on Mount Ida and disrobed for the judging. Athena, who was eager to win, promised Paris that he would be skillful and cunning and would always win in battle if he chose her. Hera, the Queen of Olympus, offered him world power and wealth. Aphrodite, the cleverest of the three, knew well what a young man would desire most: she vowed to mate him with Helen, a Spartan queen and the world's loveliest woman, even though Aphrodite knew that Helen was already wed to Menelaus. Without a second thought, Paris selected Aphrodite. As an Egyptian epic poet described the exchange, Paris thrust the glowing fruit into her palm before she stopped speaking, thus setting in motion a string of deadly events. So Helen was won—without even knowing she was the prize. Both Helenus and Cassandra and his wife, Oenone, warned that a mating with the married queen of Sparta would bring disaster, but youthful fervor and rashness won out over portents.

Journey   Abandoning Oenone, who fled to her home on Mount Ida with their infant son and promised to return if she were needed, Paris, accompanied by his cousin, Aeneas, set sail for Sparta in the south-central Peloponnesus. A more ironic version has Paris meet Menelaus and accept an invitation to Sparta's royal court. In the style of the Mediterranean world, he was well received by Helen's brothers, Castor and Pollux, and by King Menelaus. The queen, inflamed by Aphrodite and lured by lavish gifts appropriate for a state visit, was enamored of the young prince on first glance.

At the Spartan court, Paris behaved unseemly by casting sheep's eyes on the queen, scribbling her name on a dusty table, and drinking from the segment of her goblet rim where her mouth had touched. Meanwhile, Menelaus failed to notice that his wife was encouraging the flirtatious Trojan prince. Nine days after Paris's arrival, the king had to leave his guest in order to attend the funeral of Catrius, his grandfather, in Crete. During Menelaus's absence, Paris stole art objects and kidnapped the queen, leaving behind her small children—her daughter, Hermione, and sons, Maraphius and Pleisthenes. The question of Helen's compliance is one of mythology's heavily debated subjects. A more damning version declares that she made her choice and looted the palace, Apollo's altar, and the royal slave quarters on her way south to the harbor.

On the journey east, the couple were said to have consummated their union on the island of Cranae in the Gulf of Laconia, the southernmost tip of Greece, although the island of Salamis off the east coast of Greece also claims that honor. The shrine of Aphrodite Migonitis remains as Paris's thanks to the goddess. Sailing for the Troad, Paris called into a Cyprian port on the far eastern coast of the Mediterranean so that he would not cross paths with Menelaus. Hera, who disapproved of the pair's illicit relationship, forced the Trojan ship to a Phoenician landfall at Sidon, an ancient port that Paris overran.

For a brief time, the couple, blown south to the mouth of the Nile River, hid in Egypt, then completed the voyage to Troy, where the Spartan queen enjoyed a hearty welcome. Determined that her sojourn would last, Helen employed a powerful love potion to secure Paris's attentions. She noted that a magic stone of the city battlements bled when chafed, and she collected the droplets to use as an aphrodisiac; she kept Paris by her side as though in the heady moments of first love.

Helen and Paris were happy for a time in Troy before the war began, following unsuccessful negotiations by Menelaus and Agmemnon for Helen's return. They produced three sons—Bunomus, Aganus, and Idas—and a daughter, Helen. Nothing good accrued to Paris for this adultery. A single event taught him an unpleasant truism about unfaithfulness. Oenone sent Corythus to assist the Greeks in their long siege. Instead of obeying, the youth insinuated his way into Helen's favor. When Paris realized the son shared his father's vices, he killed him. Thus, Paris learned the hard way that the woman who cuckolded Menelaus was capable of doing the same thing to Paris.

For ten years, the Greeks battled the Trojans for the return of Sparta's queen. Paris, a skilled archer who looked dashing in uniform, took an active part. As Homer describes him in Book 3 of the *Iliad:*

> The godlike Paris vaulted from the ranks of the Trojans, as challenger
> wearing a leopard hide, across his shoulders bearing bow and sword;
> while brandishing in his hands two spears honed to a fine point, he
> challenged the best of the Greeks to fight hand-to-hand to the death.

This episode altered rapidly when Menelaus leaped from his chariot and frightened the guilty Paris so terribly that he flinched as though he had seen a snake and turned a greenish color.

Hector was sickened by Paris's cowardice and chastised his brother as "woman-crazy, cajoling, better had you never been born, or killed unwedded." (Homer's *Iliad*) Hector spared no invective in blaming Paris for violating the guest code and stealing a queen, thereby calling down the wrath of Greece on Troy. He sneered, "The lyre will not aid you, nor Aphrodite's favor, nor your curls or handsome profile when you fall to the dust." He wished that the Trojans had stoned Paris long before.

At a later duel fought with Menelaus, both contenders made a good showing by striking the other's shield dead center. Zeus prevented Menelaus from killing Paris by breaking Menelaus's sword four times. Menelaus was throttling Paris and dragging him by his helmet to the Greek side when Aphrodite saved him from choking by concealing him in vapor and carrying him safely to his perfumed bedroom. The goddess summoned Helen, who watched the battle from a tower, and left her to attend the prince.

In Book 6, Hector, who was peeved at his brother's blatant dalliance and the cost to his nation, strode into Paris's house and found him busy taking stock of his shield, bow, armor, and vest. With angry words, Hector goaded Paris to leave his shirking and take part in the war that threatened Troy. Paris hastened to involve himself in the fighting and caught up with Hector before he said farewell to his wife and son. Hector imparted a grievous rumor—that Trojans resented being forced into battle for a crime committed by Paris.

By Book 7, Paris had mellowed somewhat and was willing to return the goods he looted from the palace plus some of his own possessions, still he refused to end the carnage by giving Helen back to her husband. Four books later, Paris endured the taunts of Diomedes, whom he shot in the foot. Diomedes was nettled at being wounded by a "foul fighter, lovely in your locks, eyer of young girls." The incident presaged Achilles's death, which Hector predicted in Book 22, with his dying words, "For I might be made into the gods' curse upon you, on that day when Paris and Phoebus Apollo destroy you."

Shortly before Troy's fall, Paris had already killed Euchenor, Deiocur, and Menestheus and wounded Diomedes, Eurypylus, and Machaon. Aided by Apollo, Paris, just as Hector had prophesied, sent a wild shot toward Achilles and fatally wounded him in the heel. Ironically, Euripides describes Paris as a member of the special detachment of Trojans sent to fetch Philoctetes to join the Trojan side because Philoctetes, owner of Herakles's bow, was prophesied to play a major role in ending the war.

The predestined shot from Philoctetes with Herakles's bow caught Paris unaware. Philoctetes first missed his target, then caught Paris's right hand. The third shot put out Paris's right eye. The fourth and most deadly wounded him in the groin, although some sources claim the ankle. Menelaus attempted to finish off his enemy, but Paris managed to drag himself back to the city gates.

Paris summoned Oenone, a healer. Still angry by his disavowal of their marriage, she declined to come to Troy. Mortally ill, he had himself borne on a litter to Mount Ida, only to find Oenone as adamantly opposed to him as ever. He was carried back to Troy to die. Oenone, watching his departure, recaptured a glimmer of love for her wayward husband and ran to catch up. Paris died before she could reach his bedside.

Ironically, the death of the man whose actions caused the war made no ripple in the concluding chapters. More carnage followed Paris's death. The sight of his corpse threw Oenone into such a frenzy that she hanged herself. Menelaus, on entry to the fallen city, dishonored Paris's remains. None of Paris's and Helen's offspring survived: their boys died during the collapse of burning roof beams, and Hecuba killed little Helen.

Later, Trojans recovered his mutilated body and gave it a princely burial. Euripides's *Trojan Women* depicts Cassandra as happy for her brother, who enjoyed the love of Helen, a "child of heaven."

Alternate Versions The interpretation of Hecuba's prophetic dream is sometimes attributed to Herophile or to Cassandra, Paris's older sister. Another version of the omen mentioned a child of doom born on a particular day. Priam, who dismissed the possibility that the firebrand was his own Paris, executed Munippus and his mother Cilla, Priam's sister, who bore her son the same day that Hecuba gave birth to Paris. One myth credits Hecuba with bribing the shepherd to deceive Priam by raising the boy far from the palace.

Other alterations give added color to the romantic tale of Paris:

- Agelaus identified Paris, who cowered behind the statue of Zeus in the courtyard, and dug out a rattle as evidence of the youth's claim to royal status.
- The Judgment of Paris (the beauty contest between the three goddesses, Aphrodite, Hera, and Athena) occurred while Paris was still a herdsman. He remembered it only as a vision.
- Paris was originally dispatched to Greece to reclaim Hesione, Priam's sister, whom Herakles had betrothed to his friend, Telamon. Paris accepted the journey with the ulterior motive of kidnapping Helen.
- At the moment of kidnap, Hera, still angry that she did not merit the golden apple and the title of most beautiful goddess, substituted a vision in place of the real Helen.
- Aphrodite wafted their ship back to Troy in only three days.
- One unlikely telling claims that Paris, changed into the shape of Menelaus, deceived her by pretending to be her husband.
- In Herodotus's version, Hermes guided Helen to Egypt's King Proteus, who restored her to Menelaus after the war. In the meantime, the gods placated Paris with a phantasm of Helen, who sailed with him to Troy.

- Paris was a skilled archer, although Homer describes him as dressed in heavy armor more suited to a swordsman.
- Paris joined with Deiphobus in ambushing Achilles when he ventured toward the Trojan gate to woo Polyxena.
- Oenone stabbed herself and collapsed over her unfaithful husband's corpse. Other tellings describe her leaping from Troy's battlements, or onto Paris's funeral pyre.

Symbolism Not a favorite of Homer, Paris, dubbed the "hero of the dancing floor," was rarely depicted as a victim of fate. Usually cast as a spineless, characterless coward, or Helen's fawning lapdog, he became a piteous dupe who only performed manly duties after Hector gave him a scathing tongue-lashing and dragged him to the field. Paris's peers repudiated him for his glib rhetoric and fancy manners, both attributes of a lady's man. Like the Mississippi gambler or the self-absorbed, over-dressed fop, Paris, garbed in gorgeous outfits with appropriate coif and scent, won no respect from the Trojan warriors.

In art, pottery, music, and fresco, Paris's myth receives much attention. The symbols used to identify Paris are usually a red Phrygian cap, a boyish, peach-fuzzed face, and the golden apple of discord in his outstretched hand, as shown in a fresco on the Aegean island of Cos which depicts the Judgment of Paris; a fourth-century B.C. statue by Euphranor; a statue in the Vatican Museum; and a public bath in Xanthus, an ancient city south of Troy on the southern tip of Lycia. A basilica unearthed near Rome's Porta Maggiore in 1917 contains a painted panel showing Paris carrying away his love prize. In more ornate form, a paneled room in the Baths of Trajan, discovered near the Colosseum in 1907, retells most of the Trojan War, including the pairing of Helen and Paris. Christoph Gluck captured a similar setting with his opera, *Paride ed Elena.*

Famous canvases, spanning diverse styles from the Renaissance works of Raphael to Antoine Watteau's impressionism, detail Paris's importance to mythology and generally show him as a lover, not a warrior. Lucas Cranach's *Judgment of Paris* dresses Paris in medieval armor and the three goddesses in Florentine gold necklaces. Peter-Paul Rubens's *Judgment of Paris,* which hangs in the Dresden Museum, aligns three naked goddesses in tempting poses and surrounded by cupids. To the right sits Paris, a ruddy, muscular shepherd boy assisted by Hermes in finalizing the Olympian beauty contest. Likewise, Jacques-Louis David's *Paris and Helen,* which hangs in the Louvre in France, accentuates a lascivious pose with a two-horned lyre in Paris's left hand and, atop winsome curls, the Phrygian cap, shaped into an obvious phallic knob. More active is *The Rape of Helen,* an early Renaissance panel painted by either Benozzo Gozzoli or Fra Angelico and housed in London's National Gallery. The panel stresses the consternation of Spartan courtiers as Paris violates the ancient guest code and spirits away the queen.

The number of literary references to Paris rivals most other mythic characters, even Herakles. Balanced throughout the Renaissance, Romantic, Victorian, and Modern ages, the references include these: Geoffrey Chaucer's *Book of the Duchess, Troilus and Criseyde, Parliament of Fowls, House of Fame,* and *Squire's Tale;* Sir Philip Sidney's *Astrophel and Stella* and *Arcadia;* Edmund Spenser's *Faerie Queene* and *The Shepherd's Calendar;* Christopher Marlowe's *Tamburlaine;* William Shakespeare's *Troilus and Cressida* and *Rape of Lucrece;* Ben Jonson's *Charis;* John Suckling's *His Dream;* George Chapman's *Ovid's Banquet of Sense;* Phineas Fletcher's *The Purple Island;* John Milton's *Paradise Lost;* Abraham Cowley's *On the Death of Mrs. K. Philips;* Samuel Daniel's *Civil Wars;* James Thomson's *Summer;* Alexander Pope's *Dunciad;* Matthew Prior's *On Beauty, Cupid and Ganymede, Pallas and Venus,* and *Alma;* Lord Byron's *Childe Harold* and *Don Juan;* Alfred Lord Tennyson's *Oenone, The Death of Oenone,* and *Lucretius;* Robert Browning's *The Ring and the Book;* Dante Gabriel Rossetti's *Troy Town* and *Cassandra;* Gerard Manley Hopkins's *Escorial;* William Butler Yeats's *Lullaby* and *When Helen Lived;* Rupert Brooke's *It's Not Going to Happen Again;* John Masefield's *Clytemnestra, Tale of Nireus,* and *The Spear Man;* and Robert Graves's *Judgment of Paris.*

One of the most interesting of modern descriptions of Paris's role in the Trojan War appears in George Seferis's *Helen,* in which the prince, deceived by godly trickery, "lay with a shadow as though it were solid flesh: and we were slaughtered for Helen ten long years." The poem replicates *Die Aegyptische Helena,* an opera with music by Richard Strauss and a libretto by Hugo von Hofmannsthal, which re-creates the double deceit of Paris, the seducer, contenting himself with a duplicate of the real Helen.

❦ See Also

Achilles, Aeneas, Agamemnon, Cassandra, Helen, Menelaus.

❦ Ancient Sources

Aelian's *Varia Historia;* Agias of Troezen's *Returns of Heroes;* Antoninus Liberalis's *Metamorphoses;* Apollodorus's *Epitome;* Arctinus of Miletus's *Aethiopis* and *Sack of Troy;* Colluthus's *Rape of Helen;* Conon's *Narrations;* Cratinos's *Dionysalexandros;* Dares of Phrygia's *Trojan War;* Dictys Cretensis's *Trojan War Diary;* Eugammon's *Telegony;* Euripides's *Andromache, Electra, Helen, Philoctetes, Rhesus,* and *Trojan Women;* Eustathius on Homer's *Iliad* and *Odyssey;* Herodotus's *Histories* and *Persian Wars;* Homer's *Iliad* and *Odyssey;* Hyginus's *Fables;* Lesches's *Little Iliad;* Lucian's *Dialogue of the Gods;*

Lycophron's *Alexandra;* Ovid's *Heroides;* Parthenius's *Love Stories;* Pausanias's *Description of Greece;* Plato's *Phaedrus;* Proclus's *Chrestomathy;* Ptolemy Hephaestion's *On Homer;* Quintus Smyrnaeus's *Post-Homerica;* Scholiast on Euripides's *Andromache* and *Iphigenia in Aulis;* Servius on Virgil's *Aeneid;* Sophocles's *Philoctetes;* Stasinus of Cyprus's *Cypria;* Stephanus Byzantium's *Arisbe;* Suidas's *Herophila;* Tryphiodorus's *Sack of Troy;* Johannes Tzetzes's *On Lycophron;* Virgil's *Aeneid.*

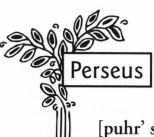

Perseus

[puhr' see · uhs]

| Genealogy and Background | The romantic blond-haired figure born in Tiryns in Argos, immured in an underground cell, the child of Danae, sired by Zeus and conceived in a shower of golden light, was prophetically called Perseus, "the destroyer," and Eurymydon, "he who rules widely." Perseus, a world-famous hero, married Andromeda, princess of Ethiopia, who bore two daughters, Authochthe, of whom nothing is known beyond her marriage to Aegeus, and Gorgophone, who earned fame as the mother of Icarius, Tyndareus, and Leucippus. Of Perseus's sons, Alcaeus, Mestor, Electryon, Sthenelus, Heleius, and Perses, the last earned fame as the progenitor of the Persian nation. Alcaeus and Electryon fathered the Heraclidean line and Mestor the Taphian. The house of Perseus, though well supplied with male heirs, ended with the death of his grandson Eurystheus, the cowardly king who tormented Herakles by assigning twelve difficult labors.

Perseus was an heir to the Argive throne through his great-grandfather, Abas, and Queen Aglaia and his grandfather, Acrisius. At Acrisius's command, both Perseus and Danae were forced into a wooden box and set afloat because Acrisius feared an oracle that predicted that Perseus would bring about his downfall.

The brass-edged box proved sturdy against the buffeting of wave and wind. As an untitled fragment of lyric verse by Simonides describes the terrifying passage:

> The mother round her infant gently twined
> her tender arm, and cried, "Ah me! my child!
> what sufferings I endure! thou sleepest the while,
> inhaling in thy milky-breathing breast
> the balm of slumber."

With Zeus's assistance, the chest beached itself on the island of Seriphos, one of the Cyclades in the Aegean Sea. Dictys, a well-

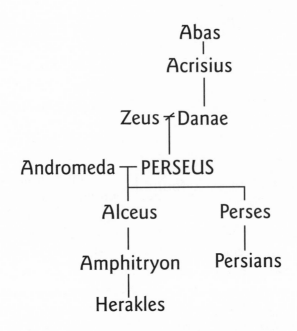

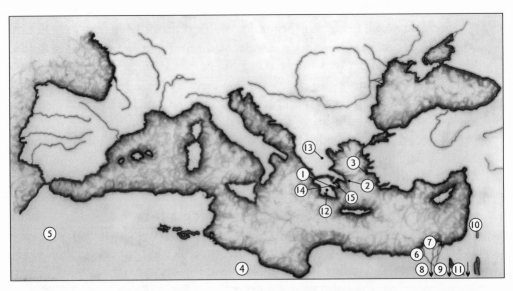

1. Tiryns 2. Seriphos 3. Samos 4. Libya 5. Mt. Atlas 6. Egypt 7. Nile River
8. to Chemmis 9. to Ethiopia 10. Joppa 11. to Philistia 12. Argos 13. Larissa
14. Tiryns 15. Mycenae

intentioned fisher, caught the floating ark in his nets, broke the lock, and freed mother and infant, for whom he provided a home.

As Perseus neared manhood, he protected his foreign-born mother from aggressors. Polydectes, a local king, attempted to force her into marriage, but withdrew his suit when Perseus declared his mother off limits. To circumvent the growing menace of Perseus, Polydectes concocted a fake betrothal to Hippodameia, a Pisan princess and daughter of Pelops, Poseidon's cupbearer, and exacted a tribute of horses as part of her dowry so that Seriphos would not be ridiculed as a poor island. Because he had no stock to contribute, Perseus vowed to bring any gift Polydectes could demand, even the head of Medusa, the snaky-haired Libyan Gorgon whose name means "the cunning one" and who was turned into a monster by Athena for engaging in intercourse on the goddess's sacred ground. The king, certain that Perseus would die on so rash a mission, held him to his word to travel to North Africa to fetch the head of the evil beast.

Journey On the expedition to decapitate Medusa, Perseus pondered how to accomplish the impossible: to overpower one Gorgon, then elude her lethal, brass-handed sisters, Euryale, and Stheno or Stheino, the sight of whom turned mortals to stone. Fortunately for Perseus, the goddess Athena wanted Medusa dead and championed Perseus's mission, however ill-advised. She led him to Deicterion on Samos off the shores of Asia Minor and taught him how to identify Medusa, whose likeness was displayed there. According to her method, Perseus, armed with the goddess's brilliant shield, was to journey southwest to Libya in North Africa, where Atlas bore the world on his shoulders. Athena told Perseus to then locate the grotto of the Graeae, a trio of swan-shaped crones named Enyo, Pemphredo or Pephredo, and Deino, who shared one tooth and one eye. Perseus completed the journey and wrested the precious eye as the Graeae exchanged it, one to the other. He extorted information concerning some nymphs who possessed the special armaments he needed to fight the Gorgons. After obtaining directions to the nymphs, Perseus kept his word and handed over the eye.

Perseus continued on his way to Hades and located the Stygian nymphs, who owned the cap of invisibility, a pair of winged sandals, and a special sack. He accepted these necessary tools, then received from Hermes, the gods' messenger, an adamantine sickle or sword, hard as diamonds and sharp as honed steel. Thus obscured, capable of flight, and possessing Hermes's weapon, Perseus was ready to face the Gorgons in their den.

The westward route leading to the home of the Gorgons in the land of the Hyperboreans, beyond human cartography, filled most men with fear because the plain lay strewn with petrified shapes of beings who had gazed on the Gorgons and had been instantly transformed into statues where they stood. To expedite his own passage, Perseus used his shield as a mirror and followed the reflected path to the Gorgons. The sight of the monstrous beings appalled him—they bore golden wings, panting canine tongues, and boarlike tusks. To escape their vengeance, he waited until they were asleep, and then, with Athena guiding his arm, lopped off Medusa's head with a single swipe of the sickle.

Euryale and Stheno heard the attack and hurried aloft to search for interlopers. Because Perseus wore the cap of invisibility and concealed Medusa's head in the sack, they could not avenge their sister's death. As Perseus's winged shoes bore him out of their reach, they slunk back to their lair to gather up the headless remains of their beloved Medusa.

Perseus moved rapidly toward Atlas's home among the Hesperides. Because the goddess Themis had predicted that a son of Zeus would steal the golden apples, Atlas gave Perseus a rude send-off. Perseus retaliated by snatching the dripping head of Medusa from its pouch and flashing the transfixing visage in front of Atlas, who immediately solidified into Mount Atlas. (Note that this account is chronologically impossible, since Herakles, a later kinsman of Perseus, held the earth on his shoulders while Atlas fetched the golden apples of the Hesperides.)

Perseus was content with Atlas's comeuppance and continued his flight over Libya, dropping Gorgon's blood, which turned into a tangle of snakes still slithering about the desert. He made a leisurely detour east to Egypt to view Chemmis (alternately spelled Chemnis or Chennis), later called Panopolis, on the Nile River northwest of Thebes, the home of Danaus and Lynceus, his ancestors. The gathered Egyptians were so impressed with Perseus's exploits that they initiated a shrine to him.

Farther south in Ethiopia, Perseus encountered the seacoast kingdom of Cepheus, his distant kinsman, who also ruled Joppa on the west coast of lower Asia Minor. The situation at that moment was dire: Queen Cassiopeia had offended the Nereids, or sea nymphs, by claiming to be more beautiful than they. Poseidon, in defense, sent a female sea monster or whale inland to terrify the kingdom. Cepheus discovered from the oracle of Ammon that he must sacrifice Princess Andromeda or else lose all. His subjects demanded that the girl be clothed only in jewels and bound to a coastal crag off Philistia.

From Perseus's vantage point, the lovely Andromeda looked small, naked, and vulnerable as she awaited an unspeakable death in the jaws of the monster. As it approached the bait, Perseus quickly demanded that King Cepheus and Queen Cassiopeia pledge to give him Andromeda for his wife if he could stave off the monster and save the princess. From their tearful watch at the shore, they called out their promise and sent Perseus on his winged way.

Perseus dashed skyward, swooped down on the scaly villain, plunged a blade into its heart, hacked it to bits, and so rescued Andromeda. In Ovid's more lyric *Metamorphoses:*

Perseus, light-winged, evades his jaws, and where
the shell-crustation gapes and leaves him bare,
on back, on bony flanks, the sword-strokes hack,
or where the fish-flukes end the tapering tail.

So heinous was the carnage that the sea ran red with the monster's blood. He had armed himself with Medusa's head in case the monster eluded him. To hold Andromeda in his arms, he laid the monster's head face down on a reef of sea plants, which were hardened into coral.

The hero followed the ancient custom of sacrificing to the deities who benefited an endeavor and purified his hands of blood. Thus cleansed, he raised three shrines. The first shrine was to Hermes and smoked with the sweet fragrance of calf. The second shrine, to Athena, was laden with a cow, and the last one, to Zeus, bore the carcass of a slaughtered bull. That night, honored at King Cepheus's table, Perseus looked longingly at Andromeda, his future bride. His hopes were dashed, however, when Cepheus ceded rights to Andromeda to a previous suitor, her uncle, Phineus. The two men faced off as Cepheus took cover.

Phineus hurled a single javelin before Perseus had time for one command, "Shield your eyes!" His enemies, who ignored the warning, looked on the head of Medusa, which Perseus dangled before them, and instantly froze into statues. Phineus tried to elude instant death by lurking behind a screen, but Perseus flushed him out to face the inevitable. Phineus died with tears petrified on his stony cheeks. Perseus, freed of his rival, clapped the deadly burden back into its package and joyously clasped Andromeda.

After a year of happiness in Ethiopia as Andromeda's husband and Perses's father, Perseus prepared to return northwest to Seriphos. Cepheus and Cassiopeia were upset over their daughter's departure. Perseus easily overrode their objections by leaving them Perses to raise as Ethiopia's future king. Andromeda and Perseus continued on their way to Argos on the Peloponnesus to meet Danae.

Return to Seriphos plunged Perseus into a second confrontation with Polydectes, who was again pursuing Danae. To hold him at bay, Danae, championed by the fisherman Dictys, took refuge in a holy shrine, which Polydectes respected and left undefiled. Perseus saw to Danae's safety and introduced her to her daughter-in-law, Andromeda. Then, in his usual take-charge fashion, he strode to the banquet hall to challenge Polydectes. Before the startled king could defend himself, Perseus held aloft Medusa's head and turned king and courtiers to stone.

Perseus's unorthodox search for a bride-gift ended with the return of the Gorgon's head to Athena, who anchored it in the center of her shield. To Hermes, Perseus returned the sandals, cap, shield, sword, and pouch. Dictys, rewarded with the rule of Seriphos, remained behind as Perseus set out with wife and mother and a band of Cyclopes for Argos.

Perseus returned to his grandfather's house without animosity, but Acrisius, who had remained informed about his grandson's feats, took refuge at Larissa in Thessaly. Perseus left his wife and mother at the Argive court and followed Acrisius. As Perseus neared the town, games to honor the passing of King Teutamides's (or Teutamas's) father were being organized. Perseus signed up for the pentathlon, which included discus hurling, his best skill. The whim of the breeze, and possibly the will of the gods as well, launched the projectile toward Acrisius's head. Just as the oracle had predicted, the king was killed by his grandson. Perseus gathered his grandfather's remains for a royal funeral and interred them with full honor at the Argive shrine of Athena at the city's highest point, although the people of Larissa claim an alternate burial spot in their city limits.

Because of the unusual circumstances of his accession to the Argive throne, Perseus chose to depart to Tiryns, southeast of Argos on the Argolid bay, and exchange realms with Megapenthes, Proetus's son and Perseus's cousin, who would rule Argos in Perseus's stead. Thriving from a change of scenery and the absence of stigma attached to Acrisius's death, Andromeda and Perseus enjoyed a peaceful reign. With the help of the muscular Cyclopes, single-eyed giants who were the sons of Poseidon, the king fortified Midea in Argolis, said to be his son Electryon's birthplace, and founded and colonized Mycenae to the north, which became the greatest city in prehistoric Greece. Perseus named the city for the mushroom or *mycos* that sprang forth by a magical brook because one sip from the mushroom cap quenched his thirst.

Alternate Versions

Many facts about the Perseus myth vary from source to source, particularly in the Roman version, which depicts the child Perseus and his mother washing ashore at Latium near Rome, where Danae married King Pilumnus and fathered Turnus, Aeneas's rival. In one telling, Perseus tossed the Graeae's eye into Lake Tritonis; he may also have robbed them of their communal tooth, thus rendering them helpless. Another variation describes Hermes as the giver of the armament that protected Perseus from the Gorgons. The route that Perseus covered may have taken him to Joppa in Syria, an alternate possibility for Cepheus's kingdom. In one version, Cassiopeia boasts not of her own beauty, but that of Andromeda. Other settings of the myth feature Agenor, Cassiopeia's pick for a son-in-law, as Perseus's rival for Andromeda.

Variances concerning the Acrisius story add interest to the myth. One major alteration is the fact that Perseus invented the discus throw and taught it to the people of Larissa. Another view of Acrisius's death has him injured in the foot, a motif that affected many mythic characters from Achilles, who was killed by Paris's arrow, to Herakles, who was bitten in the foot by a crab as the hero sliced away at the Hydra's nine heads.

According to Ovid, Proetus, Acrisius's brother, drove Perseus out of the kingdom, so Perseus employed the head of Medusa once more and turned Proetus to stone. Polydectes married Danae and Perseus withdrew from the palace to live in Athena's temple. Acrisius attempted to reconcile himself with his grandson, even though an oracle predicted that the boy would bring about his downfall. At the funeral games for Polydectes, who perished in a storm at sea, Perseus made the fateful toss, accidentally killing Acrisius. Megapenthes, Proetus's son, then killed Perseus to avenge the death of Proetus. The Athenians set up a sacred grove to honor Perseus and side altars to Dictys and the Nereid, Clymene, who assisted him.

Perseus receives mention in several lesser myths. When a band of *haliae* or "sea women" followed Dionysus from the Aegean Sea to Argos, the wine god inflicted a terrible plague on Perseus's kingdom by causing the women to fall into fits of cannibalistic rage and eat their young. In another account, Perseus made peace by atoning for his murder and raising a temple to Cretan Dionysus. The god felt enough at home there to inter his wife, Ariadne, on the site.

A third view of Perseus describes how he opposed the worship of Dionysus and quelled Dionysian cults from Argos. Perseus became so opposed to Dionysian cults that one source claims he attacked the god and drowned him in a fight at a Lernian lake. The same episode caused Perseus to kill Ariadne.

| Symbolism | The ancient story of Perseus is often interpreted, like John Bunyan's *Pilgrim's Progress* and Herman Melville's *Moby Dick*, as an allegory of darkness and light or goodness and evil. The myth was already well ingrained in Mediterranean lore by the time of Hesiod and Homer. The golden-haired child, sired by Zeus's sunbeams on Danae or "burned earth," who was immured in a dark cell, grew to wholesome manhood. Against Acrisius or "darkness" and the dim forces of the grizzled Graeae and forbidding Medusa, Perseus triumphed by directing healthful rays into Athena's shield and thus avoiding doom. During the battle with the sea monster Perseus, like Antaeus, gained strength by affixing his weight against earth for leverage and by relying on a strong sword arm to plumb to the heart of the snarling, slippery attacker. Thus, he avoided the woeful demise of Phaethon and Icarus, who depended too heavily on the gift of flight, a deadly freedom from earth's gravitational pull that conflicts with the order of the universe. A temperate hero in the vein of Aeneas and Theseus, Perseus avoided the lure of *hubris* by curbing his desire and by containing his list of enemies to two monstrous vermin, both subdued by skill and wit. That done, in response to a human love for a fair damsel, he gave up his supernatural gifts (wings, sword, and the head of Medusa) and, after putting up a good fight, embraced a worthy bride. His reward suited his deeds—he formed a worthy alliance with Andromeda, "ruler of men," who becomes his trusty consort and lifetime

partner. Unlike Herakles, a Perseid offshoot and legendary womanizer, Perseus remained fixed in one household, content with one wife and one family.

Perseus's miserable childhood, marked by the threat of drowning, reflects a standard motif illustrated by the exposure of Paris, Asclepius, Aegisthus, Linus, Oedipus, and Herakles and the watery exodus of Romulus and Remus, Horus, Semele, and Moses. The evolution of a champion from such ignoble beginnings links Bellerophon and Perseus in the killing of the Chimaera and Medusa, respectively, and recalls other slayers of monsters, such as Herakles, Saint George, and Beowulf. The stories of beings petrified by one glance at Medusa's head parallel the use of masks by temple officials, who kept local doubters in subjection by judicious applications of superstition. Most likely, the historical Perseus merely beheaded a Libyan ruler and buried the head at Argos as a military trophy.

Although classed in company with such demigods as Theseus, Achilles, and Herakles, Perseus, whose death was not memorable enough to form a significant mythic episode, merely faded from literature. However, Athena honored him and his wife with star clusters alongside Cassiopeia, Cepheus, and Cetus, the whale or sea monster that once threatened Andromeda. Perseus's constellation, located near Taurus, contains the Demon Star, also called the *Beta Persei*. In addition, the famed August meteor shower, the *Perseids,* honors Perseus. To inject a note of heavenly humor, Poseidon is credited with stuffing Cassiopeia's celestial likeness in a vegetable basket with her feet turned skyward as a fitting reward for her vanity.

Medusa's death, a service to humankind, reflects the monster-ridding services of Herakles, although on a much smaller scale. The story, obviously arises from savage times and concludes with either the head of Medusa on Athena's aegis or the skin of the monster peeled and dried to form the aegis itself. Another telling describes how Perseus buried the fiendish head in the center of Argos near his own daughter, Gorgophone. From the monster's corpse sprang two children sired by Poseidon, Chrysaor, a monster linked to moon worship, and Pegasus, the winged horse who bore Bellerophon up Mount Olympus. Because Perseus felt no antagonism toward these offspring of Poseidon, he allowed them to escape.

The people of Joppa (now called Jaffa), grateful to be rid of a sea monster, displayed the rock where Andromeda was chained and pulled so hard on her chains that she grazed the surface. The monster itself, turned to a stony skeleton, adorned the marketplace until the aedile Marcus Aemilius Scaurus transported them to Rome in 115 B.C. The island of Seriphos, one of the Cyclades, also contains its evidence of Medusa's power in the circle of rocks that locals claim to be the petrified guests at Polydectes's table. An oblique reference to Perseus occurs at Mount Apesas in Cleonae on the Peloponnesus, where the hero set up a shrine to Zeus. The island itself, Perseus's landing place, was so poor that Roman emperors marooned incorrigibles there.

The arts feature Perseus on painted vases, an ivory carving from Hera's shrine at Samos, a wine jug painted by Amasis and displayed in the British Museum, and the metopes of a sixth-century B.C. Sicilian temple at Selinus, now located in the Museum of Palermo. In the museum at Eleusis an oversized amphora dating to the seventh century B.C. depicts Perseus's triumph over the Gorgon. Wall paintings at Pompeii feature Perseus's love for Andromeda and probably echo works by the Greek Praxiteles. A fifth-century Attic vase, now housed in Leningrad's Hermitage Museum, depicts Danae at the moment of Perseus's conception.

Many artists, notably Peter-Paul Rubens, Guido Reni, Albrecht Durer, Piero di Cosimo, Rembrandt van Rijn, Sir Edward Coley, Edward Burne-Jones, Titian, and Eugène Delacroix, have focused on the love angle. Other works—especially Benvenuto Cellini's bronze statue at Florence depicting Perseus lifting Medusa's grisly head, Michelangelo de Caravaggio's painting of her snaky head, and Paolo Veronese's painting of Perseus protecting Andromeda from a yawning dragon mouth which catches the mythic hero in midair, sword aimed at the coils below—focus on violence and horror. Likewise, modern dance pioneer Martha Graham choreographed a twentieth-century work, *Errand into the Maze,* a re-creation of Perseus's courage in the dank Cretan cell.

Writers and philosophers, from Xerxes to Sigmund Freud's psychoanalytic analysis, to Iris Murdoch's 1961 novel *The Severed Head,* have found worthy symbolic grist in Perseus. Francis Bacon's *Wisdom of the Ancients* allegorized the tale into an attack on war, which Perseus defeats by annihilating the Gorgon, the personification of war. In 1855, Charles Kingsley's *Heroes* pictured Perseus as the epitome of the man of action.

Other European versifiers have drawn on Perseus's lore, including these: Matthew Prior's *Prologue, Spoken at Court;* John Cleveland's *To Prince Rupert;* Phineas Fletcher's *The Purple Island;* George Chapman's *Andromeda Liberata;* Edmund Spenser's *Ruins of Time;* William Shakespeare's *King Henry V* and *Troilus and Cressida;* Alexander Pope's *Temple of Fame;* Pierre Corneille's *Andromeda;* John Keats's *Endymion;* Robert Browning's *Sordello;* Dante Gabriel Rossetti's *Aspecta Medusa;* Charles Kingsley's *Andromeda;* and Gerard Manley Hopkins's *Andromeda.*

Later Christian interpretations of the rescue of Andromeda from the sea monster reissued the myth in didactic form: as the missionary's salvaging of a soul menaced by sin. The story of Medusa receives similar treatment as the triumph of virtue over sin.

❦ See Also

Acrisius, Aeneas, Bellerophon, Dionysus, Herakles.

❦ Ancient Sources

Aeschylus's *Bassarae;* Apollodorus's *Library;* Apollonius of Rhode's *Argonautica;* Aratus's *Phenomena;* Clement of Alexandria's *Address to the Greeks;* Diodorus Siculus's *Library of History;* Eratosthenes's *Star Placements;* Euripides's *Electra* and *Ion;* Herodotus's *Histories;* Hesiod's *Shield of Herakles* and *Theogony;* Homer's *Iliad;* Horace's *Odes;* Hyginus's *Fables* and *Poetic Astronomy;* Josephus's *Jewish Wars;* Manilius's *Astronomica;* Ovid's *Metamorphoses;* Pausanias's *Description of Greece;* Pindar's *Pythian Odes;* Pliny's *Natural History;* Scholiast on Apollonius of Rhodes's *Argonautica;* Scholiast on Euripides's *Orestes;* Servius on Virgil's *Aeneid;* Simonides of Ceos's *Verse;* Sophocles's lost plays; Stephanus Byzantium's *Iope;* Strabo's *Geography;* Johannes Tzetzes's *Chiliades* and *On Lycophron.*

Phaethon

[fay' uh · tuhn]

According to the works of Plutarch, Phaethon's myth has its roots in a real king of the Molossians of Epirus, who studied the stars. The mythic child of the Titan Helios and the sea nymph, Clymene, Phaethon and his sisters, the Heliadae or Heliades (Merope, Helia, Phoebe, Aetheria, and Dioxippe or Lampetia), were the grandchildren of Tethys and Oceanus on Clymene's side and of Hyperion and Theia on Helios's side. Helios, the magisterial, purple-robed sun god and charioteer of the heavens, was worshipped on the island of Rhodes, which took its name from Rhodos, an alternate name for Helios's mother and Phaethon's grandmother.

This illustrious family produced more notables: Phaethon's two half-sisters, the sorceresses Circe and Pasiphae, and his half-brother, Aeetes, the father of Medea, also a magician. Spoiled as the only male child in a household of females, Phaethon grew up under the care of his mother and her husband, King Merops of Ethiopia, and knew nothing of his real father's fame and glory until adolescence, when Clymene revealed the truth.

Journey

Phaethon brought grief on himself by becoming arrogant. He quickly alienated his friends, some of whom doubted his boasts that he was the son of Helios. Epaphus, the Egyptian king, sneered "You are a fool to believe all your mother tells you, and are swelled up with false notions about your father." (Ovid's *Metamorphoses*) Phaethon took great pride in his patrimony, however tenuous the evidence, and lied that his father had allowed him control of the sun chariot. Epaphus doubted his story; Phaethon promised that the next time he held the reins, he would guide the chariot close to Epaphus's village.

At his mother's suggestion, Phaethon set out to satisfy his curiosity by acquainting himself with Helios. The energetic Phaethon traveled

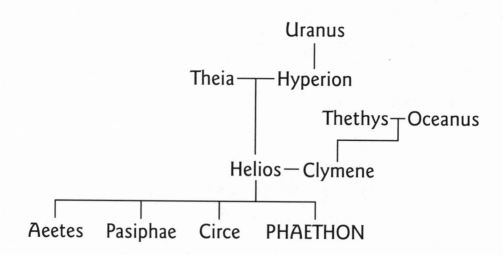

```
                              Uranus
                                |
                 Theia ——————— Hyperion
                                          Thethys ┬ Oceanus
                                                  |
                 Helios — Clymene

    ┌──────────┬──────────┬──────────┐
  Aeetes   Pasiphae    Circe     PHAETHON
```

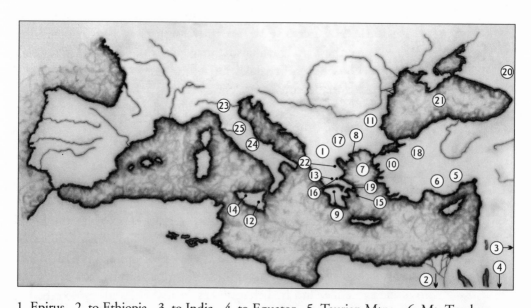

1. Epirus 2. to Ethiopia 3. to India 4. to Equator 5. Taurian Mtns. 6. Mt. Tmolus
7. Aegean Sea 8. Mt. Athos 9. Mt. Oete 10. Mt. Ida 11. Mt. Haemus 12. Mt. Aetna
13. Mt. Parnassus 14. Mt. Eryx 15. Cynthus, Delos 16. Mt. Othrys 17. Rhodope
18. Mt. Dindyma 19. Mt. Cithaeron 20. Caucasus Mtns. 21. Black Sea 22. Mt. Ossa
23. Alps 24. Apennines 25. Po River

uninvited to the east across Ethiopia and India, expecting to find his father where the sun appeared at the horizon. He located his father on the equator, flanked by twelve constellations, six to the right—Aries, Taurus, Gemini, Cancer, Leo, and Virgo—and six to the left—Libra, Scorpio, Sagittarius, Capricorn, Pisces, and Aquarius. Together they formed the Zodiac. Attending Helios were Hours, Days, Months, Years, Ages, and Seasons. Climbing the incline to the royal palace, the boy was awed by architectural embellishments—the ivory roof, silver double doors, precious jewels, and ornate craftsmanship, all the work of Hephaestus, blacksmith of the gods.

Phaethon quavered before the bright aura of the throne, his self-esteem shaken by misgivings, and he begged Helios for a favor to prove that he was really his parent. Helios, generous to a fault toward his comely son, removed his glittering crown so that the boy could look at him, then granted the request before learning the nature of the boon: Phaethon yearned to steer the radiant chariot of the sun through one daily course to prove to the world that he sprang from a mighty Titan. Immediately, Helios recalled that his son was mortal and subject to a willful covetousness of godlike powers. He shook his head and wished that he could withdraw the dire pledge.

Though the boy displayed no apprehensions, Helios remained fearful, recognizing that he risked certain death by grasping godlike powers. To himself he commented:

> Aware that I could not trust the chariot to his
> guidance, I resisted his importunity a long time; but
> at last, adding tears to his entreaties, and his mother Clymene
> leagueing with him so impetuously in the attack, they extorted my
> consent.

> (Ovid's *Metamorphoses*)

He warned Phaethon of the steep climb, the horses' size and power, and the steep incline through the signs of the zodiac. He begged Phaethon to reconsider the request from a father's perspective and delayed the chariot's departure, but the boy remained adamant in his wish to drive the sun.

With Diana, the moon goddess, Aurora, the dawn, and Lucifer, the morning star, looking on, Helios paid Phaethon the honor of personally leading out the equipage, protecting the boy's skin with holy ointment, and crowning him with the royal rays, formed of silver and pearls. In his heart, Helios countered grim forebodings. His final words were a reminder to spare the whip and follow a clear route paralleling the Zodiac rather than a line linking Arctic, Antarctic, Tropic of Cancer, Tropic of Capricorn, and Equinox. In Helios's words,

> I gave him especial instructions for his government, how he should
> fix himself so as to keep a steady command, how far he might give
> the rein in ascending, and how he then should tend downwards, and

how he was to manage so as always to keep master of the bridle, and
to direct such fiery courses; I told him likewise the danger of not driving constantly straight forward.

Helios concluded that Phaethon should be gentle and, as the Romans were fond of
quoting, *medio tutissimus,* or "remain safe in the middle path," neither too high nor
too low.

According to Ovid, before mounting the chariot, the impatient boy paused long
enough to admire Hephaestus's handiwork: its golden wheels, ridge pole, and axles,
its silver spokes, its jingling bridles and chrysolite yoke set with gems, reflecting the
sun's radiance. Helios settled him into place and tied the heavy reins about his son's
waist. Setting out from east to west, Phaethon gathered the traces, and signaled to
the wing-footed, fire-exhaling white horses—Pyreis, Eous, Aethon, and Phlegon, four
abreast—to thunder across the well-worn tracks in the sky, just as they did each day
for Helios. In Euripides's *Hippolytus:*

> He starts; the coursers, whom the lashing whip excites, outstrip
> the winds, and whirl the car high through the airy void. Behind the
> sire, borne on his planetary steed, pursues with eye intent, and
> warns him with his voice, Drive there! now here!-here!
> turn the chariot here!

Clucking like any worried parent, Helios excused Phaethon's poor performance as a
normal response to power and blamed the horses for being skittish under the hand
of an inexperienced driver.

Fear of the Zodiac terrified the boy, causing him to depart from the standard
east-to-west path. Too weak to control the heavenly team, Phaethon felt the chariot
jolt out of control, dipping close enough to set fields aflame and dry up earthly mois-
ture. Driving a westward arc, he grazed the Taurian Mountains in Cilicia, headed
northwest over Mount Tmolus in Lydia, and around the curve of the Aegean Sea
over Mount Athos in Macedonia. Moving erratically over the region, he brushed
roughly against Oete in Corinth, the foothills of Boeotia, and Mount Ida south of
Troy. His wheels bruised Haemus northeast in Thrace and Etna far to the southwest
in Sicily.

On he caromed over the ancient world's key mountains—Parnassus, Eryx, Cynthus in Delos, Othrys, Rhodope, and Mimas in Ionia on Greece's western shore, Dindymus in Phrygia, as well as Mount Cithaeron north of Athens, the Caucasus
Mountains rimming the east end of the Black Sea, Ossa north of Thessaly, the Alps
north of Italy, and the Apennines, Italy's rocky spine. Overcorrecting, the youthful
charioteer singed the clouds and stars, enraging them. In panic, Phaethon dropped
the reins and held on to the framework. Unaccustomed to having their freedom, the

horses galloped far from their customary path. In Lucian's *Dialogue of the Gods,* the chariot rolled "now up, now down, now to the right, now to the left, now even in the most contrary directions."

The nymphs bewailed their waterless springs. The river gods of the Meander, Eurotas, Orontes, Nile, Rhine, Rhone, Po, Tiber, and Ganges clenched their fists in rage. To Poseidon's dismay, the seas contracted; the earth cracked open, revealing the secrets of Hades. Gaea became so incensed that she hid in Hades's realm. Zeus, who was disturbed by the outcries of earthlings, deities, and stars, blamed Helios for nearly destroying the earth by setting a mere boy in charge of the sun chariot. Zeus was so angered because of the danger to humanity that he halted Phaethon with a single thunderbolt to ward off a worldwide catastrophe.

For his folly, Phaethon died instantly. Ovid describes the foolish boy's body aflame, turning, turning in a cindery spiral toward earth. In *Hippolytus,* Euripides claims that "his blood fell on the earth; his hands, his feet, rolled whirling like Ixion's wheel." Helios quickly righted his team and continued on course to the stable.

Phaethon's pitiful remains fell into the Eridanus, a river in northern Italy currently known as the Po. The boy's remains lay on foreign soil, far from the comfort of a home burial. Clymene and the Naiads gathered his bones and interred them with the honor befitting a son of Helios. They marked his grave with a suitable epitaph honoring his daring. Phaethon's sisters wept so unceasingly that four months later, the gods turned them into poplar trees. The newly formed bark hushed their cries, and their tears changed into amber. In Book 6 of his *Eclogues,* Virgil describes their bitter bark as ringed with moss. The doting girls were later known as *Phaethontiades,* in honor of their brother.

Another mourner, Cycnus, the musically adept king of Liguria near modern-day Genoa, a cousin and possible lover of Phaethon, was so grief-stricken that he was changed into a swan, which Apollo blessed with a lovely call. In Book 10 of the *Aeneid,* Virgil states that

> Cycnus, in grief for his beloved Phaethon, while he sings and
> soothes his woeful love with music amid the shady sisterhood
> of poplar boughs, drew over him the soft plumage of white old
> age; and left earth and passed crying through the sky.

The term *swan song* derives from the fact that the swan is allowed its song only at the point of death.

Zeus was slow to pardon Helios for his parental indulgence and warned him that another transgression would result in forfeiture of the rights to drive the sun. In a commanding voice, Zeus thundered that the Titan had to repair the pole and one wheel of the sun chariot and continue driving. He concluded with an ominous reminder that there would be no second chance.

Alternate Versions

Phaethon's parents are sometimes given as Eos and Cephalus. Helios has been named as Phaethon's grandfather, with Clymenus and Merope as his actual parents. Alternate mothers from this poorly delineated period of mythology include Rhode and Prote. The sun god is also named Phoebus Apollo, Sol, or Hyperion. Other settings list Selene and Eos as Phaethon's sisters and Electryone as his half-brother. A third list of the Heliadae include only three—Phaethusa, Lampetia, and Pasiphae. According to Hesiod's *Theogony,* Aphrodite was so taken with Phaethon that she abducted him and set him up as temple guard. An alternate version of Phaethon's journey casts a different light on the boy, whom the story describes as nagging his father until he wore down his resolve to refuse access to the sun chariot. Hyginus declares a bolder version: that Phaethon took the chariot without asking.

The Heliadae, risking the sin of *hubris* with their delight in their brother's precocity, fastened the magnificent steeds to the leader poles. One version numbers nine steeds: Lampon, Phaethon, Chronos, Aethon, Astrope, Bronte, Pyreis, Eous, and Phlegon. Their pride turned to terror as they realized that Phaethon was unequal to the task and Zeus, ruler of heaven, had no choice but to end the abortive flight with a death-dealing blast, although one version depicts Phaethon as drowning in the Eridanus River. Ovid's telling describes the chariot in ruins, the horses in disarray and loosed from the chariot tongue. A resetting of the funeral dirge for Phaethon depicts the Heliadae as confederates. A poetic version describes Cycnus as collector of Phaethon's remains. For their crime of supplying Phaethon with the sun's holy chariot without first obtaining his permission, the five sisters were changed into trees.

One account of the burial site lists the Ilissus, a river near Athens. Herodotus casts doubt that such a river exists except in the poet's imagination. Apollonius of Rhodes not only concurs with the Italian location of the Eridanus, but insists that the Argonauts were offended by the noxious steam arising after Phaethon's smoky remains vaporized the waters. So vile and poisonous was the sulfurous stench that it killed the birds above it.

Symbolism

Pointedly named "the shining one" by his father, Phaethon was the son of fire and water, suggesting an ungovernable tension born into the boy. Although literature and art temper blame with pity, Phaethon's name became synonymous with rash, presumptuous, unbridled immaturity as well as conceit, boastfulness, imprudence, the perils of coming-of-age, and as with teenagers of all eras, deadly high jinks on roads and highways. The structure of the myth is a classic example of *hubris* or "pride" leading to *ate* or "temporary madness" concluding in pride's antithesis, *nemesis,* or "retribution." The story, filled with the morning-to-evening colors of heaven, and the mysticism connected with the passage of time, inspired a painting by Nicolas Poussin and verse by numerous poets, particularly Joseph

Addison. The word *phaethon* came to designate a rapid, easily maneuvered open carriage, called a *phaeton*.

The grief inspired by Phaethon's violent death forms a mythic explanation of amber, a resin that exudes from Baltic pines, sometimes entrapping insects, leaves, and blossoms in its sticky globules. Amber has been used in jewelry and its fragrant oil added to medicines. Phaethon's death also reflects a primitive explanation of meteors. Other connections with nature and topography are a mythic explanation of the Sahara Desert and its black-skinned natives, polar icecaps, the scarred blur known as the Milky Way, and volcanic mountains, all supposedly caused by Phaethon's careening voyage. According to the Cretans, Phaethon was both morning and evening star; he was also identified with the planet Saturn, while Cycnus was linked with the constellation *Cygnus*.

Phaethon, or Pheton, is remembered in a symphony by Camille Saint-Saens and paintings by Peter-Paul Rubens and Michelangelo as well as notable works of English verse, including: Geoffrey Chaucer's *House of Fame* and *Troilus and Criseyde;* Giles Fletcher's *Christ's Triumph over Death;* Richard Lovelace's *Triumphs of Philamore;* Christopher Marlowe's *Tamburlaine* and *Hero and Leander;* William Shakespeare's *Romeo and Juliet, Two Gentlemen of Verona, King Richard II,* and *King Henry VI* (Part III); John Donne's *Eclogue;* George Meredith's *Phaethon;* Matthew Prior's *To the Lord Bishop of Rochester;* Edmund Spenser's *Faerie Queene;* John Rochester's *Could I But Make My Wishes;* Michael Drayton's *Barons' Wars;* Richard Crashaw's *Sospetto d'Herode;* George Chapman's *Ovid's Banquet of Sense;* Thomas Carew's *A Fly That Flew;* Alexander Pope's *Weeping;* Lord Byron's *Don Juan;* Robert Browning's *Paracelsus;* and Algernon Swinburne's *Tristram of Lyonesse.*

❦ Ancient Sources

Apollodorus's *Epitome;* Apollonius of Rhodes's *Argonautica;* Diodorus Siculus's *Library of History;* Eratosthenes's *Star Placements;* Euripides's *Hippolytus;* Herodotus's *Histories;* Hesiod's *Theogony;* Hyginus's *Fables* and *Poetic Astronomy;* Lucian's *Dialogue of the Dead* and *Dialogue of the Gods;* Lucretius's *On the Nature of Things;* Nonnus's *Dionysiaca;* Ovid's *Metamorphoses* and *Tristia;* Plutarch's *On the Slowness of Divine Vengeance;* Scholiast on Pindar's *Olympian Odes;* Solinus's *Collectanea Rerum Memorabilium;* Johannes Tzetzes's *Chiliades;* Virgil's *Aeneid* and *Bucolics.*

Pirithous

[py · ree' thoos]

Genealogy and Background

The Thessalian adventurer from Larissa in Thessaly, Pirithous (or Peirithous), son of Ixion and Dia, grew up to lead the Magnetes, local heroes from northeastern Greece; the Lapiths, a rowdy mountain tribe from Thessaly famous for carousing; and the Centaurs, Pirithous's half-brothers on his father's side, whom Ixion is said to have sired by his wife's ghost. At his home near the Peneus River, Pirithous married Hippodameia (or Deidameia), mother of his son Polypoetes, a warrior in the Trojan War and leader of troops from five *demes.*

Journey

A minor king and lesser hero when compared with the great warriors—Herakles, Achilles, Perseus, and Theseus—Pirithous took part in the Calydonian boar hunt and Jason's search for the Golden Fleece. One of his first daring exploits involved testing the herdsmen of Marathon by rustling their cattle, in part to rival the widespread reputation of Theseus. When Theseus pursued him, the two men dropped their weapons, embraced, and became immediate friends, drawn to each other by mutual respect as well as physical attraction. Pirithous, in his enthusiasm for their friendship, offered to return the cattle he had stolen.

When Pirithous wearied of his youthful exploits, he settled the bride price for Butes's daughter, Hippodameia. The wedding, which was attended by all the Olympians except Eris and Ares, was set in a shady, rustic cavern, where, according to Ovid, the guests were singing at the time that the bridesmaids escorted Hippodameia to her place at the table. At this dramatic point, the excluded gods sought revenge for the slight by arranging a mid-wedding brawl, complete with flying utensils and crockery, broken candelabra, and smashed flasks. The nuptials erupted into a day-long battle with the Centaurs, residents

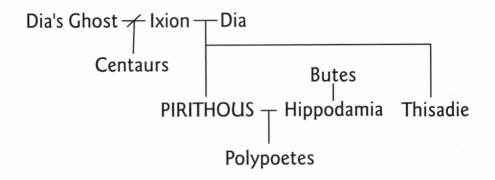

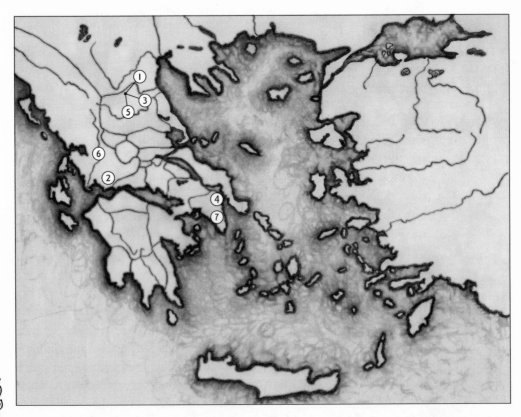

1. Larissa 2. Calydon 3. Larissa 4. Marathon 5. Larissa 6. Aetolia 7. Aphidna

of Mount Pelion on the Magnesian peninsula who were known for their inability to tolerate unmixed wine.

The drunken Centaurs, who attempted to drag the bride away by her hair, met with the Lapiths, a two-fisted cadre living in Pirithous's kingdom. Eurytion made advances to Hippodameia while other Centaurs were making obscene gestures and postures to female guests and youths. Most of the losses of this ignoble scuffle were suffered by the Centaurs. Pirithous docked Eurytion's nose and ears, then forced the Centaurs out of his realm to Mount Pindus, the rocky spine that ran from north to south through Greece. The day's set-to resulted in a protracted war between the Lapiths and Centaurs.

Wedded life formed a negligible part of Pirithous's lore, although his warrior son, Polypoetes, brought honor to his parents by heading five bands of Thessalians during the Trojan War and by serving on the handpicked squad who entered Troy in the belly of the wooden horse. In late middle age, possibly after his wife's death, Pirithous aided Theseus in the war against the Amazons and in a search for mates sired by Zeus. They settled on the mutual abduction of Helen. The two, having taken a blood oath at the shrine of Serapis, kidnapped Helen, who was only ten or twelve years old at the time. They carried her from her home in Aetolia to Aphidna, a suburb of Athens, along with Pirithous's sister, Thisadie, Helen's companion, and Aethra, Theseus's mother, as chaperon. By a toss of the dice, Theseus received Helen.

Against his will, but true to the oath to seek a daughter of Zeus, Theseus joined Pirithous on a clumsy stunt to Tartarus, the dark region of the Underworld, in search of Persephone. Venturing through Taenarum toward murky depths, Pirithous and Theseus made their way to the throne of Hades, who offered them seating in the Chairs of Forgetfulness. At Persephone's direction, the supernatural powers of the benches locked the two wanderers into place. Four years later, Herakles was able to gain the release of Theseus, but an ominous rumble warned Herakles not to transgress the hospitality of Hades. Thus, Pirithous remained in Hades, where he battled the combined menace of Cerberus, the Erinyes, and poisonous snakes.

Alternate Versions

The Pirithous myth sometimes labels him as the son of Dia and Zeus, or of Ixion and Perimela. The etymology of Pirithous's name, "the one who turns in a circle," suggests Dia's attempt to elude Zeus, who pranced around her like a horse. A variation on the wedding day combat described Pirithous's battle with the drunken Centaurs as ending with Hippodameia's death, although this version does not account for the birth of Polypoetes, their worthy son whom Homer describes in the *Iliad*. The loss of Hippodameia supposedly paved the way for Pirithous's least heroic quest, the search for a daughter of Zeus as second wife. A historical retelling of the journey to Hades has Theseus and Pirithous stealing Cora or Core, Persephone's playmate, from King Aidoneus of Epirus. The king discovered the plot and set his dog Cerberus on Pirithous, who was chewed to death. Other variations of the mythic journey to Tartarus relieve Pirithous of torment after Herakles gains his release by negotiating with Hades.

Symbolism

One of the minor figures who visited the Underworld, Pirithous, unlike Aeneas, Odysseus, Orpheus, Dionysus, and Theseus, his friend and companion, did not elude Hades or return to the upper air. For this reason, Pirithous, like Bellerophon, Icarus, and Phaethon in the sun chariot, symbolizes the rash, sophomoric human adventurer who attempts more than the gods will tolerate. Left to sit out eternity in the Chair of Forgetfulness, Pirithous, whom critic Philip Slater describes as a scapegoat for Theseus's share of the crime of *hubris,* is tidily dismissed from mythology after serving his ignoble purpose.

More significant than daring in the Pirithous myth is the deeply committed friendship to Theseus, his honorary brother and possible lover. Like Achilles and Patroclus, Aeneas and Achates, or David and Jonathan, the two men, who epitomize the *doppelganger* motif, enjoyed each other's company, particularly when their exploits carried a hint of danger. Their vigorous defeat of the Centaurs symbolizes the triumph of civilization over barbarous atavism and the sybaritic promiscuity of earlier times.

Pirithous is not without honor. A shrine was erected to the hero at Colonus and at sanctuaries sacred to Theseus, his blood brother. Vase paintings, seventh- and sixth-century B.C. bronzes, Pompeiian wallpaintings, friezes at the temple of Apollo at Bassae, sculptures and pediments at Zeus's temple at Olympia, metopes of the Parthenon, the Elgin Marbles in the British Museum, Micon's painting at the Theseum in Athens, works by Polygnotus, and reliefs by Michelangelo and Piero di Cosimo, detail the fight between the Centaurs and Lapiths. Yet, Pirithous receives scant mention in English verse, named only in Edmund Spenser's *Faerie Queene* and Algernon Swinburne's *Atalanta in Calydon.* Geoffrey Chaucer's *The Knight's Tale,* which gives a more complete accounting of the camaraderie between Theseus and Pirithous, records that Pirithous was

> a worthy duke...that was a friend to Duke Theseus since the days of their childhood and who came to Athens to visit his friend because he was always looking for amusement; for no one in the world did he love as much as he admired [Theseus].

Chaucer concludes that, when one of the pair died, the other sought him in Hades. This poetic version does not detail of the search for the dead friend.

❦ See Also

Herakles, Jason and Medea, Theseus.

❦ Ancient Sources

Aelian's *Varia Historia;* Antoninus Liberalis's *Metamorphoses;* Apollodorus's *Epitome;* Athenaeus's *The Learned Banquet;* Bion's *Poetic Fragments;* Callimachus's *Hymn to Artemis;* Dares of Phrygia's *Trojan War;* Diodorus Siculus's *Library of History;* Eustathius on Homer's *Iliad* and *Odyssey;* Hesiod's *Descent of Theseus into Hades;* Homer's *Iliad* and *Odyssey;* Hyginus's *Fables;* Menecrates's *History of Lycia;* Ovid's *Metamorphoses;* Panyasis's *Heraclea;* Pausanias's *Description of Greece;* Pherecydes's *Heptamochos;* Pindar's *Nemean Odes;* Plutarch's *Parallel Lives;* Proclus's *Chrestomathy;* Scholiast on Aristophanes's *Knights;* Seneca's *Hippolytus;* Servius on Virgil's *Aeneid;* Stasinus of Cyprus's *Cypria;* Stephanus Byzantium's *Atrax;* Strabo's *Historical Sketches;* Johannes Tzetzes's *Chiliades* and *On Lycophron;* Virgil's *Aeneid.*

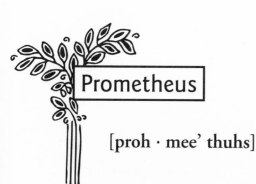

Prometheus

[proh · mee' thuhs]

Genealogy and Background

Prometheus, mythology's doomed traveler, spent a dismal jail sentence on the fringes of the known world. His name, meaning "foresight" in contrast to his brother Epimetheus or "hindsight," Prometheus, bore a paradoxical pair of titles: thief of fire and saviour of humanity. A cunning, resourceful Titan of the earliest layer of Greek mythology, Prometheus claimed Uranus, the sky god, and Gaea, mother earth herself, as grandparents. The son of Iapetus and either Asia or Clymene, a daughter of Oceanus, Prometheus, also called Acacesius or "the god who harms no one," had three brothers—Atlas, Typhon, and Menoetius—each of whom Zeus doomed, the first to bear the heavens on his shoulders, the second impaled under Mount Etna, and the third hurled into Tartarus.

The gods played a major role in Prometheus's story; because he could foresee the coming face-off between Zeus and his father Cronus, Prometheus wisely backed Zeus, the eventual ruler of all creation. Zeus's daughter, Athena, was Prometheus's tutor in math, sailing, architecture, astronomy, medicine, and the art of metalwork.

In contrast to Prometheus's wise manipulation or godly power, Epimetheus, a somewhat oafish dupe of Zeus, was easily fooled by bribes. Prometheus, his antithesis, was endowed with prophetic power and foretold that Atlas would provide Herakles with the golden apples of the Hesperides and that a cataclysmic flood would cover the earth.

Both Prometheus and Epimetheus established famous and influential families. Prometheus's marriage to Calaeno received little notoriety, but their son, King Deucalion of Phthia, arose to greater prominence than did his brother, Hellen, or sister, Thebe, for whom Thebes is named. In the meantime, Epimetheus married Pandora, a robotic woman fashioned at Hephaestus's forge under Zeus's direction. Born to this couple was Pyrrha, the first mortal female, who married Deucalion. Because Zeus despaired of human behavior during the Bronze Age, he decided to obliterate the first humans from the earth.

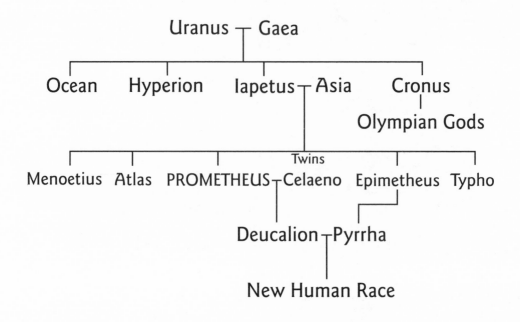

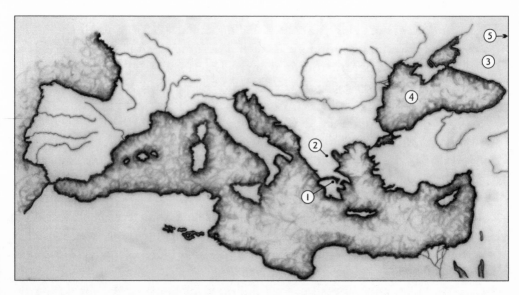

1. Sicyon 2. Mt. Olympus 3. Caucasus Mts. 4. Black Sea 5. to Caspian Sea

To preserve the best in humankind, he chose Deucalion and Pyrrha as the worthiest examples of earthly beings. After Prometheus warned Deucalion to build a great ark or chest in which to protect his family, Zeus flooded the earth and drowned the remainder of humanity and all beasts. From Deucalion and Pyrrha, parallels of Noah and of Gilgamesh, came Prometheus's grandchildren, a large family of human beings handcrafted from clay and water to inhabit the earth.

With the help of Athena and Eros, Prometheus fashioned human forms, which he modeled in the shape of the gods out of material left over from the earth's formation. He gave human forms an upright position so that they could contemplate the heavens rather than face the mud from which they sprang. Because the animals had used up stingers, hooves, tusks, fins, fur, fangs, claws, shells, wings, and horns, humans lacked an innate protection, so he gave them reason and a thumb by which to manipulate weapons and tools. Thus, Prometheus was the progenitor and benefactor of all human life.

Prometheus often challenged Zeus, the testy, sometimes vindictive Olympian authority who overcame the Titans' tyranny. Zeus then established his own authoritarian regime, sapping human progress by demanding constant subservience and the best of the flock. At Sicyon, near Corinth, Prometheus evolved a scheme to rob Zeus of the best meat. He dismembered a bull for the Hellenic sacrifices and separated the parts into two packets. In one he placed the muscles and organ meats in a covering of skin and topped the whole with the foul-smelling stomach and intestines. In the second bundle he wrapped the skeleton in layers of juicy, tempting fat. When given a choice of sacrificial gifts, Zeus selected the second, then discovered that he had been tricked into leaving meat as human sustenance. From that moment on, Zeus stoked a perpetual enmity against Prometheus and his human creatures by reclaiming fire and hiding it on Olympus so that humans had to eat raw meat.

Journey When Prometheus saw the pathetic humans trying to fend for themselves against savage animals, unpalatable food, and an ill-tempered god, he felt impelled to intervene in the balance of power, an act construed by the gods as the most serious form of blasphemy and *hubris*. Journeying to Olympus by the dark of the moon with Athena, his cohort, he stole a glowing coal from Apollo's chariot wheels as they began the daily journey across the sky. Prometheus concealed the feeble spark in a hollow fennel stalk and tucked it into his clothing. In retribution for this impiety, Zeus dispatched Pandora to earth to unleash miseries on humanity.

For the crime of theft and for refusing to reveal the secret that Thetis's son Achilles would eventually outdistance the prominence of his father, Prometheus received a more direct reprimand. Zeus had Hephaestus, supervised by the daemons Might and Violence, chain the over-confident Titan to a pillar or windy crag on Mount Caucasus, the extreme eastern end of the world overlooking the Black and Caspian seas, and

swore by the river Styx that Prometheus would never regain his freedom. According to Aeschylus's *Prometheus Bound,* Zeus thundered:

> I shall nail you in bonds of indissoluble bronze on this crag far from men. Here you shall hear no voice of any mortal; here you shall see no form of mortal.... For you, a god, feared not the anger of the gods, but gave honors to mortals beyond what was just. Wherefore you shall mount guard on this unlovely rock, upright, sleepless, not bending the knee.

To account for his excessive penalty, Zeus concocted a lie about Prometheus's unholy desire for Athena, with whom he allegedly sought to couple on Olympus.

Hephaestus and all humanity and nature, too, sympathized with Prometheus, whose awkward position brought perpetual torment and no protection from the elements. Each day, a hellish eagle, the offspring of Typhon and Echidna and Zeus's personal emblem, pecked out Prometheus's liver. Each morning, the liver regenerated for another day of torment. Alone in misery, yet adamant in his defiance, Prometheus called to the four elements—wind, water, earth, and sun—to witness the cruelty of his sentence and regretted that he had not received capital punishment and a sojourn in Tartarus. His pitiable cries were heard by Jason's Argonauts on their way to Colchis. Oceanus's daughters, flying in on silken wings, wept at his predicament. Prometheus assuaged himself with a single fact: the knowledge that Zeus would one day be brought low.

After 30—or 30,000—years, Herakles, Zeus's son, skewered the eagle with an arrow and snapped Prometheus's chains with his bare hands. Caught between admiration for his son Herakles's strength and daring and loathing for Prometheus, Zeus compromised by making Prometheus wear a steel ring forged from his chains. Like Jacob Marley's ghost manacled to his ledgers and strongbox in Charles Dickens's *A Christmas Carol,* Prometheus had to drag a piece of the crag, which was linked to him by a steel binder.

Prometheus performed a mutually gratifying service for Chiron, the immortal Centaur who was nicked by one of Herakles's venom-dipped arrows. Condemned to a life of agony, Chiron pleaded for a volunteer to trade deathlessness for mortality so he could die and end the pain. Prometheus accepted the swap, thus alleviating Chiron and decking himself in immortality.

Alternate Versions

Alternates given for Prometheus's mother were Asopis or Themis; for his father, Eurymedon; and for his wife, Axiothea, Hesione, Clymene, or Pronoea. These variations alter the story very little, since at this remote stage of narrative, males and their mates rarely shared any kind of partnership or mutual endeavor. A second telling of the theft of fire describes Prometheus as boldly robbing Hephaestus's forge. The bird that tormented him is sometimes identified as a vulture.

| Symbolism | Prometheus, whose name may have evolved from the Sanskrit for *firedrill,* symbolized the intellectual, pro-human influence that challenged the patriarchal Olympian authority. A generous life force, he accepted torture as the consequence of rebellion. The myth, dating to Paleolithic blood sacrifices, reverbrates about the eastern Mediterranean, where Zeus was said to have chained the defiant Titan. In remote villages of the Caucasus and farther east in India, nature lore connects his struggles with earth tremors. Like Tantalus, he reaches in vain for food and water; like Tityus, he is incapable of avoiding the beak of a vulture that pecks his vital organs.

Promethean lore contains a blend of blame and praise. Like Loki, Coyote, and the serpent that tempted Eve, Prometheus has been labeled the prototypical trickster or outwitter of the gods. A blend of strength and weakness, he also epitomized the most egregious and least tolerable of ancient sins, *hubris,* or "pride," which proved his undoing, and like Job, Jonah, Jeremiah, the Wandering Jew, and Christ, became a universal symbol of suffering, or like Ixion, Sisyphus, and Faust, a model of emotional extremes resulting in damnation.

As a balance to Prometheus's idealism stand his accomplishments. Among his beneficent innovations are healing drugs, a number system, veterinary medicine, shipbuilding, reading, the interpretation of ritual sacrifice as well as dreams and omens, and the discovery and shaping of metals. Aeschylus claimed that Prometheus withdrew prophecy from among human talents and replaced it with the more elusive gift of hope. The stoics applied allegory by naming him the first philosopher, who developed forethought at the expense of gut-wrenching anxiety, the vulture of modern times.

Prometheus's most significant deed, the gift of fire, offended Zeus at the same time that it elevated life on earth from a cold, hardscrabble subsistence to an agreeable existence with some semblance of comfort. In honor of this audacious deed and its predictable consequence, Prometheus's theft of fire was reenacted by the torch-bearer who began Olympic games by running into the arena to touch off the eternal flame that guards truth. Other honoraria preserved the Promethean myth. The blood that dropped to earth from Prometheus's wounds formed the fragrant crocus, valued in the ancient world for the yellow dye extracted from its stamen and for the spice called saffron. In Attica, he, like Hermes and Daedalus, was worshiped by craftsmen, especially potters: a shrine honored him at Colonus; the Prometheia, a torch race in which participants try to carry a flame in a fennel stalk to the finish, originated at the Academy, where a sanctuary honored the Titan.

Prometheus's gifts to humanity include the formation of human bodies from clay and the creation of the arts, from which the rare earth metal *promethium* and the adjective *promethean,* indicating daring originality, are derived. In Panopeus, a town

in Phocis near the Boeotian border, peasants claim that a large boulder smelling like flesh remains from the time that human beings were modeled from clay. The Talmud compares Prometheus to the archangel Michael, creator of Adam from the dust of the earth. Second century Christian prelates translated Promethean suffering into godly passion, a parallel to Christ's crucifixion.

Early literary references include verse by Marsilio Ficino and Pierre de Ronsard, essays by Francis Bacon, Sir John Davies's *Orchestra*, Edmund Spenser's *Mutability Cantos* and *Faerie Queene*, Vincenzo Monti's comparison of Prometheus with Napoleon in *Prometeo*, Samuel Daniel's *Civil Wars*, Sir John Denham's *To His Mistress*, Johann von Schiller's *Gods of Greece*, John Milton's *Paradise Lost*, William Diaper's *Callipaedia*, Michael Drayton's *Idea*, Jonathan Swift's *Prometheus* and *Apollo to the Dean*, as well as discussion by Voltaire and Johann Gottfried von Herder. An idyllic interest of the Romantic poets, Prometheus appears in Henry Wadsworth Longfellow's *Epimetheus* and *Prometheus*, William Wordsworth's *The Excursion*, Samuel Coleridge's *The Nose*, Lord Byron's *Age of Bronze, Don Juan, Childe Harold*, and *Prophecy of Dante*, as well as Herman Melville's *Moby Dick*, and *Hyperion*, the epistolary novel of German poet Friedrich Holderlin, all paeans to liberty, daring, suffering, and creativity.

The work containing the most renowned grandeur and pathos, Percy Shelley's four-act verse drama, *Prometheus Unbound*, concludes triumphantly:

> To suffer woes which Hope thinks infinite;
> To forgive wrongs darker than death or night;
> To defy Power, which seems omnipotent;
> To love, and bear; to hope till Hope creates
> From its own neck the thing it contemplates;
> Neither to change, nor falter, nor repent;
> This, like thy glory, Titan, is to be
> Good, great and joyous, beautiful and free;
> This is alone Life, Joy, Empire, and Victory.

Thus Shelley set Prometheus in the crown of the Romantic era as the ornament of its credo—freedom is worth the price it exacts.

The Victorians and post-Victorians too were influenced by Prometheus's example, as revealed by Robert Browning's *Death in the Desert* and *With Bernard de Mandeville*, and works by Elizabeth Barrett Browning, Arthur Rimbaud, Friedrich Nietzsche, and Thomas Hardy. Modern verse depictions, including Robert Bridges's *Prometheus the Firegiver* and Robert Lowell's *Prometheus*, continue the tradition of honor to a noble champion of human rights over tyranny. André Gide, in an iconoclastic view, depicts the Titan in *Le Prométhée mal enchaîné*, a modernized study of masochism. Modern mythographers continue to apply Promethean lore to the human situation, as demonstrated by Louis Séchan's *Le mythe de Prométhée* and C. Kerényi's *Prometheus, Archetypal Image of Human Existence*. Johann Goethe, too, chose Prometheus as the focus of *Prometheus,* his drama on suffering, which Arthur Honegger, Franz Schubert, Franz Liszt, and Hugo Wolf set to music. Ludwig van Beethoven's ballet, *The Creatures of Prometheus,* Aleksandr Nikolayavich Scriabin's *Poem of Fire,* operas such as Carl Orff's *Prometheus* and Gabriel Fauré's *Prométhée,* and Franz Liszt's symphonic *Prometheus* stress the tension between Titanic might and creativity.

Early drawings and carvings of Prometheus, found on a third-century B.C. sarcophagus and in Panaenus's paintings and Attic vases featuring Satyrs lighting firebrands from Prometheus's smoldering stalk and the Titan's hands working clay to create humanity, reflect the mythic episodes as feats of daring and benevolence. Astronomers find Prometheus among celestial constellations in the humbled pose of the Kneeler. In contrast, artistic renderings from Renaissance times center on Prometheus's altruism. Painters, notably Jacob Jordaens and Michelangelo, were drawn to the nature of brutality and its effect on noble character. Peter-Paul Rubens's *Fall of the Titans* shows the collapse of the Titans under massive boulders; his *Prometheus Bound,* like Titian's *Prometheus,* and Gustave Moreau's *The Torture of Prometheus,* captures the twisted, agonized body of Prometheus, head down, as an eagle picks at his torso. The swirling grace of Fritz Zuber-Bühler's *Prometheus and the Sea Nymphs* surrounds the imprisoned Titan with eight nymphs, who offer their loveliness as a diversion to his pain. The twentieth-century sculptor Jacques Lipchitz dwelled on vindication by creating a scene in which Prometheus strangles the bird that pecks his liver.

See Also

Herakles, Jason and Medea.

Ancient Sources

Aeschylus's *Prometheus Bound, Prometheus the Firebearer,* and *Prometheus Unbound,* Apollodorus's *Epitome;* Aristophanes's *The Birds;* Euhemerus's *Sacred Scripture;* Eustathius's on Homer's *Iliad* and *Odyssey;* Hesiod's *Theogony* and *Works and Days;* Horace's *Odes;* Hyginus's *Fables, Preface,* and *Poetic Astronomy;* Lucian's *Dialogue of the Gods* and *Prometheus on Caucasus;* Ovid's *Metamorphoses;* Pausanias's *Description of Greece;* Philostratus's *Life of Apollonius of Tyana;* Pindar's *Isthmian Odes;* Plutarch's *Which Animals Are Craftier?;* Scholiast on Apollonius of Rhodes's *Argonautica;* Scholiast on Euripides's *Orestes;* Scholiast on Pindar's *Olympian Odes;* Servius on Virgil's *Eclogues;* Stephanus Byzantium's *Thebe;* Strabo's *Historical Sketches;* Tertullian's *Essays;* Johannes Tzetzes's *On Lycophron.*

Sisyphus

[sih' sih · fuhs']

Genealogy and Background

No other mythological character earned the kind of left-handed fame that belongs to Sisyphus, the man who talked his way out of hell. Named "the super-smart," the evil, doomed Sisyphus came of good stock; his genealogy, which arose immediately after Deucalion survived the flood that drowned the first humans, established a major Greek dynasty, which was honored by Homer in Book 6 of the *Iliad*.

The great-grandson of Deucalion, grandson of Hellen, son of Aeolus, King of Thessaly, and his illustrious wife Aenarete, Sisyphus had seven brothers: Cretheus, Athmas, Deion, Magnes, Perieres, Macareus, and Salmoneus, the insane brother whom he despised. Sisyphus's five sisters included Calyce, Perimede, Canace, Alcyone, and Peisidice. The extended family contained notables such as Cretheus's grandson, Jason, leader of the Argonauts; Nestor, sage descendant of Salmoneus; Trojan War heroes Protesilaus and Podarces; and the adventurers Dictys and Polydectes, companions of Perseus. A major blot on the family name was the incestuous mating of Sisyphus's brother and sister, Macareus and Canace, whose offspring Aeolus relegated to ravenous dogs. Aeolus sent Canace a ritual sword with which to end her shame; Macareus seized the same weapon and killed himself.

Sisyphus is credited with founding the ancient Argive city of Ephyra, which he accomplished with the aid of Medea. A devious plotter and wheeler-dealer, he earned fame as a cattleman, entrepreneur, and promoter of Corinth at the southern base of the isthmus, the slender, strategic spit of land joining the Peloponnesus to mainland Greece, which he inherited after the death of Creon and the departure of Jason and Medea. Sisyphus married Merope, one of the Pleiades, the daughters of Atlas and Pleione. Their children included Ornytion, Sinon, Thersander, Almus, and Glaucus, whom Sisyphus taught the charioteer's art.

One episode of the family lore describes Sisyphus's discovery of his nephew Melicertes's remains, which were gently deposited on the

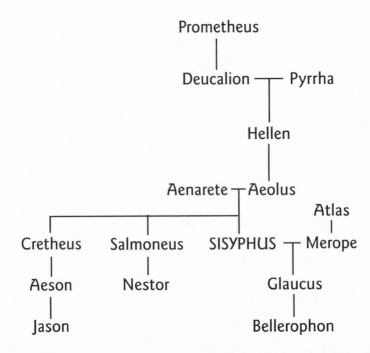

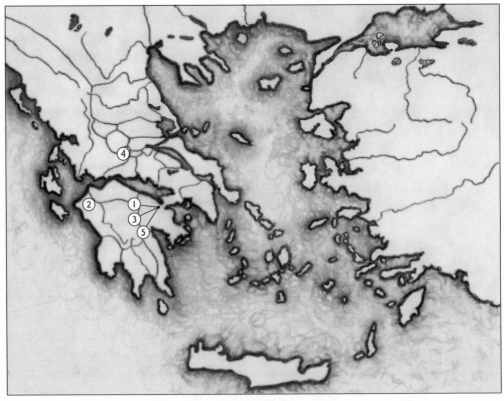

1. Ephyra   2. Salmone   3. Ephyra   4. Mt. Parnassus   5. Ephyra   6. Hades

Corinthian shore by a kind dolphin. At the command of the Nereids, Sisyphus buried him on the spot and established the Isthmian Games, celebrated to honor the drowned boy every four years. Melicertes's name was changed to Palaemon. The Palaemonion, a double sanctuary and the most sacred point on the isthmus, was the sacrificial altar of black bulls. Artworks depicted this rite as well as the tender return of the boy's corpse on a dolphin's back. Because Glaucus's horses, maddened by a drug fed to them by the goddess Aphrodite, turned on their master and devoured him, the Isthmian Games were supposedly haunted by Taraxippus, the horse-terrifier, a visitation of Glaucus's spirit. Glaucus's son, Bellerophon, rider of the winged Pegasus, is also connected with failed attempts at animal control and resulting crippling and death.

According to Hyginus's *Fables,* at the urging of Pythia, Apollo's priestess at Delphi, Sisyphus also fathered twin sons by his niece, Tyro, to retaliate against her father, Salmoneus. Salmoneus had seized power in Thessaly and humiliated the family by driving his chariot through town, banging pots on a trailer attached to the rear of the car in a frail imitation of thundering Zeus. Even though Tyro murdered the twins rather than expose them, Sisyphus used their corpses against Salmoneus by claiming that they were the victims of incest. After seeing the tiny corpses displayed in Salmone's plaza, angry locals drove Salmoneus from the throne. Zeus responded by obliterating the city with one powerful bolt of lightning.

Sisyphus earned the nickname Hypsipylon or "high gate," the masculine form of the moon goddess Hypsipyle, and a reputation for vindictiveness, cruelty, and exploitiveness. He established his thriving herd on land given him by Medea, populated with beings grown from toadstools. Beset by cattle rustlers, he scratched the initials *SS* inside his herd's hooves and trailed stolen animals to the barn of his neighbor, Autolycus. Sisyphus was indignant about the steady depletion of his herd by Autolycus's thievery and followed the trail up Mount Parnassus and ravished the thief's daughter, Anticleia, Laertes's wife, thereby siring Odysseus, who inherited a notable share of his father's wily underhandedness.

Journey A noted self-promoter and con man, Sisyphus was privileged to observe the god Zeus in the form of an eagle abducting Aegina, a mortal maid, to a nearby island. To assure water to the arid citadel at Corinth, Sisyphus refused to help the river god, Asopus, search for his missing daughter or identify her captor until Asopus supplied the city with a spring. Only after the Perenian fount bubbled forth from the courtyard behind Aphrodite's altar did Sisyphus divulge where Zeus had taken Aegina.

In punishment for intervening in godly amours, Zeus had Hades devise cruel and everlasting torture for Sisyphus. The deceptive Corinthian outwitted Hades by having him demonstrate a new pair of handcuffs designed by Hephaestus, which Sisyphus locked. For days, Hades languished in chains in Sisyphus's residence. Because no one performed his duties, souls could not report to the Underworld for judgment. At length, Ares freed Hades and turned over the devious host to the giver of divine penalty.

Transported toward the Underworld, Sisyphus employed a second ruse: he bade Merope to leave his corpse unburied and to pour no ritual libation nor place the token obolus on his tongue. On arrival before the throne of Persephone, Sisyphus pleaded a logical case: an uninterred victim had no right to cross the river Styx. Sisyphus reasoned that he should correct this oversight by returning to Corinth, living out a full mortal life, then receiving formal burial. He lied to the trusting Underworld queen that he would tidy his affairs and return. Since he had no intention of keeping his word, the gods sent Hermes to gather him up and send him off to meet his fate. His actual burial mound was never disclosed.

The judges of the dead, Minos and Rhadamanthys, took no chances with Sisyphus's second arrival at their tribunal. To prevent further escape plans, Sisyphus was assigned an immense stone. Sisyphus's task was to roll it up a hill, over the top, and down the opposite slope. The charge, which he never fulfilled, kept him bathed in sweat and dust throughout eternity. So shameful an onus forced Merope to abandon her relationship with Sisyphus and the other Pleiades to hide their association with a flagrantly unscrupulous mortal.

When Odysseus journeyed into Hades in Book 11 of the *Odyssey,* he reported seeing, alongside Tityus, whose vital organs are picked by vultures, and Tantalus, betrayer of Zeus, the toiling figure of Sisyphus:

> He was suffering strong pains, and with both arms embracing
> the monstrous stone, struggling with hands and feet alike, he
> would try to push the stone upward to the crest of the hill, but
> when it was on the point of going over the top, the force of
> gravity turned it backward, and the pitiless stone rolled back
> down to the level. He then tried once more to push it up,
> straining hard, and sweat ran all down his body, and over his
> head a cloud of dust rose.

As Odysseus departed, he wondered whether Sisyphus was even aware that the task could never be completed. In contrast, Book 6 of Virgil's *Aeneid* makes passing reference to the doomed rock hoister, placing him close by Ixion, forever fixed on a burning wheel, and Pirithous, bound to the stone chair of Forgetfulness. Book 4 of Ovid's *Metamorphoses* creates a similar pairing of Sisyphus and Ixion. Other descriptions of the Underworld depict Sisyphus with the Titans and the Danaides, who suffered a similar fate of being condemned to fill sieves with water and transfer it to a leaky water jar for eternity.

Most versions describe Sisyphus's grave as unmarked. Pausanias lists it as a sacred Corinthian landmark. The historian and geographer Strabo comments that a shrine, the Sisypheion, survives on the hill of Corinth to honor the king who brought prosperity to the region.

Alternate Versions

Two alternate tellings of Odysseus's birth reduce the violence inherent in Sisyphean lore. One has Autolycus offering Anticleia to her uncle, Sisyphus, so that she might preserve his propensity for trickery in the resulting grandchild. The other version depicts the love-starved Anticleia, although betrothed to Laertes, giving herself to the first eye-catching male to arrive at her isolated mountain home. To cover her carnal sin, she married soon enough to pass off Odysseus as Laertes's son.

The hero Theseus is said to have ended Sisyphus's notorious career as robber and assassin of unwitting travelers, who had to pass over the Gulf of Corinth when coming and going from the Greek mainland to the Peloponnesus. A retelling of Sisyphus's condemnation to Hades has Zeus piercing him with lightning and sending him directly to perdition. Rather than Hades, king of the dead, the Homeric version pictures Zeus dispatching Thanatos, the personification of death, to lead Sisyphus down the path to the Underworld. A minor version of the story depicts Sispyhus's punishment as an everlasting version of his own style of executing travelers by dropping boulders on them.

Symbolism

An accursed mortal whose name is synonymous with the torments of hell, Sisyphus, alternately spelled Sesephus, was derived from the Hittite Tesup, a sun deity, whose symbol may have been Sisyphus's stone, a form of sun disc. Captured in the verb *sisyphize,* meaning "to cheat or deceive," and the adjective *sisyphean,* the tortuous fate of the trickster, Sisyphus echoes other failed sun heroes, notably his proud grandson, Bellerophon, who tried to ride the winged horse Pegasus up Olympus, and Phaethon, Helios's offspring, who tried to drive the sun's chariot. The name of Sisyphus's niece, Tyro, derives from *tyranny,* or "walled city," and links her directly with the Tyrians, who revered her as patron goddess. Sisyphus's likeness, rolling the stone uphill in a tableau of the sun's daily path across the heavens, adorns bronze statues and bas-reliefs. A Hebrew parallel to Autolycus's theft of Sisyphus's cattle occurs in Genesis 29–30, which describes how Jacob defrauded Laban of spotted sheep by clever use of animal husbandry.

The emblem inscribed on the hooves of Sisyphus's cattle has earned convoluted explanations. One possibility is the opposing halves of the lunar cycle, thus linking Sisyphus to growth and shrinkage or benediction and malediction. Like the connection to the solar disc, the symbol allies Sisyphus's myth with heavenly light, a characteristic of the sun worship common to Corinthian lore. An unrelated bit of celestial lore describes Merope as the weakest star of the Pleiades because she mated with a mortal of ill repute.

Many mythologies contain a Sisyphean figure. By the Middle Ages, the baleful fate of Sisyphus and his Tartarean companions, Tantalus and Ixion, came to symbolize the Christian sins of pride, greed, and lust. Known in African lore as the trickster, the Sisyphean character reappears in benign form in Joel Chandler Harris's *Uncle Remus* and his tales of Br'er Rabbit. Similar curious, mischief-making man-animals permeate American Indian lore, for example Old Man or Old Man Coyote or the raven, rabbit, bluejay, or mink. Marked by reprehensible character traits, such as stubbornness, cruelty, and gluttony, the Native American trickster Coyote foiled the Creator's plans or pulled pranks on human beings. He also amused an audience by outwitting himself and causing himself pain or embarrassment, such as yanking off his own tail or getting his head or paw caught in a jar. To the Micmac, Wabanaki, and Nova Scotia Indians, the trickster Glooskap was a wily rascal who pulled pranks on the unsuspecting; to the Penobscot of Maine he was Gluscabi, a similar joker and deflator of the pompous. In Ojibwa legends, the trickster, Nanabozho or Wenabozho, assisted Indians by outwitting forces in nature. The ever-present Fon of Dahomey was both tricky and clairvoyant.

American literature contains Sisyphean tales of Daniel Webster, spin-off of the Faust legend, who outwitted Satan much as Sisyphus outflanked Thanatos or Death. In modern French literature, Albert Camus, the famed existentialist writer and philosopher, gave the story a more forbidding twist by contemplating *Le mythe de Sisyphe* for its depiction of futility, fruitlessness, and absurdity. Published in 1942, the brilliant essay focuses on the human condition, which suffers an indiscriminate, unforeseen death lacking either earthly meaning or divine significance. Albert Camus's stress on the irrationality of fate develops a nonclassical side of the Sisyphus myth, which tends toward the ancient concept of divine punishment for specific fault or frailty. Numerous other poetic tributes to Sesephus/Sisyphus appear in Geoffrey Chaucer's *Book of the Duchess,* Edmund Spenser's *Faerie Queene,* Christopher Marlowe's *Hero and Leander,* Phineas Fletcher's *The Purple Island,* Abraham Cowley's *To Dr. Scarborough,* Jonathan Swift's *Ode to the King,* John Dryden's *Conquest of Granada,* Lord Byron's *English Bards and Scots Reviewers,* Charles Lamb's *The Ballad-Singers,* and Robert Browning's *Ixion.*

 ❧ See Also

Bellerophon, Jason and Medea, Nestor, Odysseus, Perseus, Phaethon, Pirithous, Theseus.

🌿 Ancient Sources

Apollodorus's *Epitome;* Apollonius of Rhodes's *Argonautica;* Cicero's *Tuscan Debates;* Eumelus's *Verse;* Eustathius on Homer's *Iliad* and *Odyssey;* Hesychius's *Lexicon;* Homer's *Iliad* and *Odyssey;* Horaces's *Odes* and *Satires II;* Hyginus's *Fables;* Lucretius's *On the Nature of Things;* Ovid's *Fasti, Heroides, Ibis, Metamorphoses,* and *Tristia;* Pausanias's *Description of Greece;* Philostratus's *Imagines;* Phrynichus's *Plays;* Polyaenus's *Stratagems;* Scholiast on Aristophanes's *Acharnians;* Scholiast on Homer's *Iliad;* Scholiast on Sophocles's *Ajax* and *Philoctetes;* Scholiast on Statius's *Thebaid;* Servius on Virgil's *Aeneid* and *Georgics;* Sophocles's *Ajax;* Strabo's *Geography;* Theognis's *Verse;* Johannes Tzetzes's *On Lycophron;* Virgil's *Aeneid.*

Sthenelus

[sthihn' uh · luhs]

Like Aeneas's faithful cohort Achates and Menelaus's pilot Canopus, Sthenelus, a member of the colorful Danaid line, served in a secondary role with the Argive forces at Troy. As Diomedes's driver, he performed worthy service, yet because Homer makes little mention of him in the *Iliad*, he fell into the also-ran category of mythic voyagers. The son of Capaneus and Evadne, Sthenelus, one of the Anaxagoridae whose name indicates the ability to thrust back the enemy, was a grandson and great-grandson of Iphis and a descendant of Stheneboea, the lustful queen who fell to her death from Pegasus after trying to seduce Bellerophon, and Proetus, the king of Tiryns who seduced Danae, his niece.

Sthenelus's family suffered an unusual blend of loss and honor during the war of the Seven against Thebes, when Sthenelus was a youngster. Capaneus, guardian of the Ogygian gate, was hit by Zeus's thunderbolt as he defied the god and mounted a scaling ladder to the top of the fortification. Although this death rendered the corpse sacred and worthy of a dignified burial under a monument, his remains were shoved into a pile of corpses and ignobly burned with the rest. Evadne became so distraught at the loss that she sacrificed herself on the same pyre. This double tragedy left Sthenelus an orphan. An unlikely telling of the story of Capaneus insists that after Zeus pierced him with a lightning bolt he was brought back to life by Asclepius, Apollo's son, and honored with a statue at Delphi. For Asclepius's sacrilege, he was hit by one of Zeus's thunderbolts: Apollo avenged him by changing him into a constellation.

Journey With no adult to inherit Capaneus's scepter, Sthenelus ruled Argos for fourteen years until he was old enough to continue his father's war on Thebes as a member of the Epigoni,

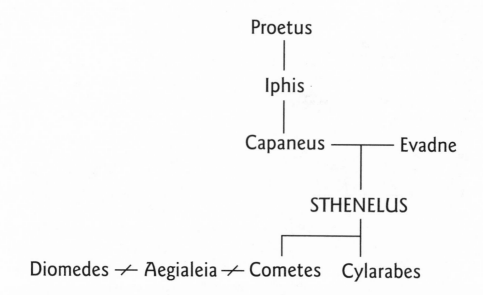

Proetus
|
Iphis
|
Capaneus ——————— Evadne
|
STHENELUS
|
Diomedes ⚭ Aegialeia ⚭ Cometes   Cylarabes

1. Argos   2. Thebes   3. Argos   4. Aetolia

or "After-Born," the second generation to join forces and march to Thebes to liberate it from usurpation and avenge the deaths of their fathers. This second wave—which allied Sthenelus with Alcmaeon, Amphilochus, Aegialeus, Diomedes, Polydorus, Hippomedon, Promachus, and Thersander—succeeded in quelling the Cadmeians at the Glisas River. With Alcmaeon in the lead, the Epigoni ultimately took Thebes and destroyed it, a cataclysm which prefigured the Trojan War.

Twenty years later, Sthenelus, who had traveled to Aetolia as one of Helen's suitors and a career soldier, traveled northeast with the Greek forces to Troy. Like the Three Musketeers in Homer's description, the triad make their brief debut in Book 2 of the *Iliad*:

> the leader was Diomedes of the great war cry with Sthenelus, own son
> to the high-renowned Capeneus, and with them as a third went Eu-
> ryalus, a man godlike, a son of Mecisteus the king and scion of Talaos;
> but the leader of all was Diomedes.

The final line explains why Sthenelus and Euryalus receive little attention—they were overshadowed by Diomedes, one of the stars of the Greek fighting force. In Sthenelus's absence, his young son, Cylarabes, substituted on the Argive throne. The assembling of leaders for the Trojan War put Sthenelus and fellow companion Euryalus in the vanguard of the Argive contingent among eighty black warships under the leadership of Diomedes, his wartime friend. In Book 23 of Homer's *Iliad*, Sthenelus is described in action as Diomedes's charioteer at the horse races honoring Patroclus:

> [Diomedes] vaulted down to the ground from his shining
> chariot and leaned his whip against the yoke. Nor did
> strong Sthenelus delay, but made haste to take up prizes
> and gave the woman to his high-hearted companions to
> lead away and the tripod with ears to carry, while Diomides set
> free the horses.

On the night of Troy's fall, Sthenelus distinguished himself by volunteering for the assault party that boarded the wooden horse, a group of between twenty-five and fifty of Greece's bravest warriors, including Neoptolemus, Menelaus, Diomedes, Epeius, the craftsman who had made the horse, and Odysseus, the clever designer of the famous ruse.

Meanwhile, Sthenelus's son Cometes brought shame to his family and strained Sthenelus's relationship with Diomedes. Because the troublemaker Nauplius spread rumors that Greek husbands were returning home with concubines, he was able to punish the Greeks for stoning his son Palamedes to death for treason as a result of false information from Odysseus. Some wives believed the story. One of them, Aegialea, wife of Diomedes, retaliated against the supposed wrong by luring

Sthenelus's less noble son Cometes into cohabiting with her and asked his assistance in murdering Diomedes. The plot failed because Diomedes, forewarned, departed for a colony in Italy.

Alternate Versions

Sthenelus's mother is alternately named Euadne or Ianeira; some claimed she was the daughter of Iphis. A variance on this relationship names Iphis as Capaneus's brother. Iphis was a childless king who served as interim regent until Sthenelus was old enough to reign in Argos. A small detail concerning Capaneus's death has him stationed at the Electrian gate of Thebes when he was killed.

The genealogy of Argis indicates that Diomedes, a member of the newer line of kings, had less claim to the Argive throne than that of Sthenelus, who was sired to an earlier sept. Thus, Diomedes and Sthenelus appear to be distant cousins of the ruling class. Although Sthenelus may have come from a more illustrious parentage, Diomedes outranked him in bravery, coming second to Achilles on Homer's list of the bravest at Troy. Sthenelus's mother is alternately listed as Ianeira. Another description of his lineage names Iphis as his uncle.

Symbolism

When war prizes were distributed, Sthenelus, whose service did not warrant a Trojan woman as reward for gallantry, obtained the statue of the three-eyed Zeus, which he bore back to Argos and set up in a place of honor. Sthenelus's royal line ended with Cylarabes, the childless king who had reunited the tripartate realm of Argos. Ironically, Orestes, son of Agamemnon and one of the most pathetic of secondary victims of the Trojan War, married Hermione and assumed rule in Argos. According to Pausanias's *Description of Greece,* Sthenelus was buried beneath a magnificent monument. He is featured in Elizabeth Barrett Browning's *Battle of Marathon.*

See Also

Diomedes, Helen, Menelaus, Nauplius, Odysseus.

🌿 Ancient Sources

Aeschylus's *Seven against Thebes;* Apollodorus's *Epitome* and *Library;* Apollonius of Rhodes's *Argonautica;* Dictys Cretensis's *Trojan War Diary;* Diodorus Siculus's *Library of History;* Euripides's *Suppliants;* Eustathius's on Homer's *Iliad* and *Odyssey;* Hesiod's *Catalogue of Women;* Homer's *Iliad;* Hyginus's *Fables;* Justin's *Apology;* Lesches's *Little Iliad;* Ovid's *Art of Love;* Pausanias's *Description of Greece;* Plutarch's *Parallel Lives;* Quintus Smyrnaeus's *Post-Homerica;* Johannes Tzetzes's *On Lycophron* and *Posthomerica.*

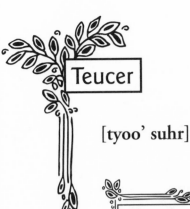

Teucer

[tyoo' suhr]

Genealogy and Background

Like Agamemnon, Odysseus, and Menelaus, Teucer, a decorated Trojan War veteran, was forced to wander the eastern Mediterranean before reestablishing himself with his family. Teucer was the illegitimate offspring of Hesione and Telamon, who received Hesione as war prize during his sojourn with Herakles against Troy. Teucer, whose nickname, "the Trojan," honors Troy's founder, also named Teucer, lived in an adverse atmosphere on the island of Salamis south of Athens in the Bay of Eleusis. His mother, deeply aggrieved by her enslavement, gave birth to Teucer, then, during a second pregnancy, escaped Telamon's surveillance and took refuge in Miletus, Crete, where Trambelus, Teucer's brother, was brought up by Hesione's second husband, King Arion. Reared by Periboea, his stepmother, Teucer was the younger half-brother of Ajax the Great and likewise a Greek hero, despite kinship with the Trojan royal family. By serving as foster father to his nephew Eurysaces, Teucer honored Ajax, his much admired sibling.

Journey

Among the suitors who traveled to Aetolia to court Helen, Teucer, armed with backstrung bow and quiver of arrows, joined the Greek force that besieged Troy. As the Achaians' best archer, he was the Greek parallel of Paris, who was also reputed for his skill with the bow. Teucer was frequently paired with his spear-wielding half-brother; he ducked behind Ajax's legendary eight-ply shield, then darted out to aim deadly shots. Homer captures Teucer's unusual relationship with Ajax in Agamemnon's words from Book 8 of the *Iliad:*

> Telamonian Teucer, dear heart, o lord of your
> people, strike so; thus you may be a light given to
> the Danaans, and to Telamon your father, who

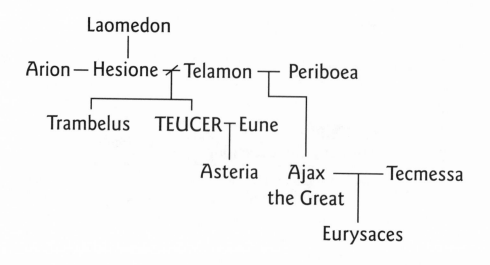

Laomedon
|
Arion — Hesione ⊣ Telamon ⊤ Periboea

Trambelus   TEUCER ⊤ Eune

Asteria   Ajax ⊤ Tecmessa
the Great |

Eurysaces

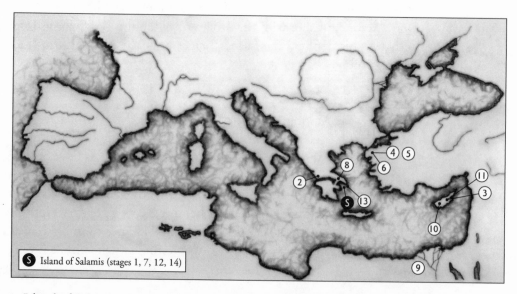

S Island of Salamis (stages 1, 7, 12, 14)

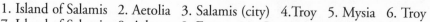

1. Island of Salamis 2. Aetolia 3. Salamis (city) 4. Troy 5. Mysia 6. Troy
7. Island of Salamis 8. Athens 9. Egypt 10. Cyprus 11. Salamis (city)
12. Island of Salamis 13. Aegina 14. Island of Salamis

cherished you when you were little, and, bastard as you were, looked
after you in his own house.

Agamemnon promised that, if Teucer continued to fight well, he could expect a worthy gift, such as a tripod or horses and a chariot.

As Greece's best archer, Teucer saw considerable action on the battlefield, wounding Glaucus, Bellerophon's grandson, in the arm and Sarpedon in the chest, and killing a worthy number of adversaries, including Hector's charioteer, Archeptolemos, and Gorgythion, Priam's son. Hector was so angered by his driver's death that he aimed his arrow at an exposed area of Teucer's neck. The blow caused temporary paralysis in Teucer's arm, but Ajax sprang to his aid and covered him with his shield. Teucer was relayed by two warriors to his ship, where he recovered.

In an episode from Book 13 of the *Iliad*, Teucer speared Imbrios and rushed to strip the Trojan's armor. Hector, quick on the defense, hurled in vain at Teucer. As before, Ajax rushed onto the scene and distracted Hector. In a failed shot described in Book 14, Zeus, in order to protect the Trojan leader, broke Teucer's bowstring. Undaunted, Teucer, obeying Ajax's orders, dropped his bow, armed himself with shield, helmet, and spear, and drove harder against the advancing Trojans.

At Patroclus's funeral games, Teucer participated in the archery contest. Because he neglected to honor Apollo, Teucer missed his shot. Instead, he pierced the string that held the targeted pigeon and allowed it to fly harmlessly away. Even then, the Greeks honored the archer with thunderous applause. For his prowess, Teucer, losing to Meriones, took second prize—ten single axes.

According to Sophocles's *Ajax,* following Ajax's suicide, Teucer, recently returned to Troy from Mysia, south of the Troad, blamed the gods "who plan these things and all things ever for mankind." Teucer rebuked Menelaus for threatening to leave the corpse on the shore for seabirds to peck. With backing from Odysseus, Teucer won over King Agamemnon, dug the grave himself, and rejecting Odysseus's offer of assistance, single-handedly interred his fallen half-brother. When the final siege of Troy was planned, Teucer took a place inside the wooden horse. At the end of the war, sailing aboard the Greek fleet from the Troad to Salamis, Teucer placed Eurysaces on a separate vessel.

King Telamon's excoriation of Teucer led to his exile among the Athenians. After Eurysaces gained the throne of Salamis, Teucer tried to ingratiate himself, but Eurysaces rejected his overtures. In desperation, Teucer consulted an oracle and welcomed Apollo's advice to reestablish himself far from Salamis. According to Euripides's *Helen,* during his wanderings, seven years after the Trojan War, Teucer was startled to find Helen living under Proteus's protection in Egypt. He vowed that, if she had been on Greek soil, he would have killed her for all the grief she had caused both Greeks and Trojans.

While conversing with Helen in Egypt, Teucer requested that the seer Theonoe show him the way to Cyprus, which was destined to be his new home. After journeying northeast to Cyprus, a major island off the coast of Asia Minor to the west of Syria, Teucer was accepted by Belus, the Sidonian king in Syria and father of Queen Dido, and took up residence in a Syrian colony on the island. There, at the bidding of Apollo, he established a second Salamis on the east coast, which Constantine the Great later renamed Constantia. Teucer married Belus's daughter, Eune, and fathered Asteria.

Late in his life, Teucer returned to Greece to the original Salamis. Telamon forced him out a second time, causing Teucer to live for a short time south of Salamis on the gulf island of Aegina. Reconciled at last with his father, Teucer returned once again to Salamis and assumed kingship of the realm. In retaliation for Teucer's act of distancing himself from Ajax's son, Telamon offered a hostile reception, implying that Teucer was weak and blaming him for failing to protect Ajax. Teucer fell into despair and killed himself, thus failing to avenge Ajax's ignoble demise. From the deck of his ship in the Bay of Salamis, Teucer, in vain, delivered a formal rebuttal of Telamon's accusations.

Alternate Versions

An alternate version of this myth has Teucer returning to Greece and leaving his nephew, Eurysaces, and Tecmessa behind in Troy. In this Teucer settled on Cyprus and married the daughter of King Cinyras. Different tellings also insist that Teucer remained on Cyprus, never returning to his family or the Salaminian throne to which he held a legitimate claim. Another variation relates that Teucer did not attempt his return until Telamon's death, but that Eurysaces blocked Teucer's political ambitions by driving him away from Salamis.

Symbolism

According to tradition, the Bay of Salamis became a departure point for exiles, who often emulated Teucer by justifying the actions that provoked their departure. Cypriot kings claim to have descended from Teucer. The herb *teucrium* is named for Teucer, and the Latin word *teucrioides* describes plants that resemble teucrium.

See Also

Ajax the Great, Helen, Menelaus, Odysseus.

❦ Ancient Sources

Aeschylus's *The Persian Women;* Apollodorus's *Epitome;* Arctinus of Miletus's *Aethiopis* and *Sack of Troy;* Euripides's *Helen;* Eustathius's on Homer's *Iliad* and *Odyssey;* Homer's *Iliad;* Horace's *Odes;* Pausanias's *Description of Greece;* Philostratus's *Heroica;* Pindar's *Nemean Odes;* Scholiast on Homer's *Iliad;* Scholiast on Pindar's *Isthmian Odes;* Scholiast on Sophocles's *Ajax;* Servius on Virgil's *Aeneid;* Sophocles's *Ajax;* Johannes Tzetzes's *On Lycophron;* Virgil's *Aeneid.*

Theseus

[thee' suhs]

Genealogy and Background

Founder of Athens and Attica's most illustrious hero in the age before the Trojan warriors, Theseus, whose lineage links him with Pelops, Tantalus, and Zeus, was lauded, according to Plutarch's *Lives of the Noble Greeks,* "as high as to Erechtheus and the first inhabitants of Attica." Sometimes labeled the "second Herakles" for his courage, strength, and alertness, Theseus was ostensibly the son of Aegeus and Aethra, a princess of Troezen in the southwest corner of Argolis on the Peloponnesus. However, on the night Theseus was conceived, Athena sent a dream to Aethra instructing her to visit the tomb of Sphaerus. While she carried out appropriate ritual, Poseidon overpowered and raped her, thus negating Aegeus's claim to Theseus.

Aegeus departed from Aethra, leaving instructions to conceal the birth of a son, whom Pallas's heirs would kill to assure their hold on the Attic throne. As Aegeus departed, he presented Aethra with a sword and sandals, which he buried under a boulder. He made her promise that, if their lovemaking produced a son, she should send the boy to Athens with the items he had left behind. Because Aethra was certain that a god was responsible for her pregnancy, she founded a shrine to Athena Apaturia on the island of Sphaeria, and having been abandoned by her husband, took refuge there. At the time that Theseus was born at Genethlium, a village near Troezen's harbor, Aegeus had married his third wife, the sorceress Medea.

Theseus, who was reared by his grandfather, Pittheus, a learned philosopher and king, to protect him from Pallas's envious sons, grew up at Troezen, where Connidas tutored him. A favorite story indicates the boy's early display of *arete,* or "excellence." Herakles had removed his lion skin in front of gathered courtiers. The other children fled, but seven-year-old Theseus snatched up a sword and threatened the fearsome fur. Forever afterward, the boy took Herakles as his model and emulated his exploits.

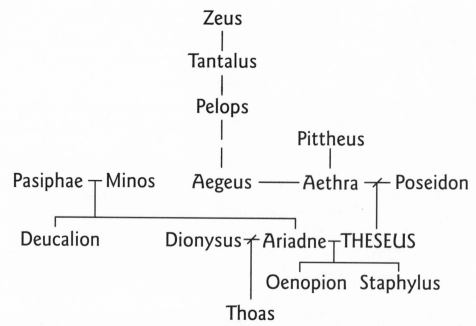

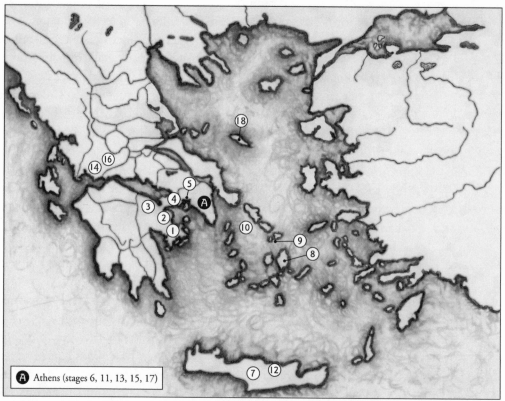

1. Troezen 2. Epidaurus 3. Corinth 4. Megera 5. Eleusis 6. Athens 7. Crete 8. Naxos
9. Delos 10. Aegean Sea 11. Athens 12. Knossos 13. Athens 14. Calydon 15. Athens
16. Aetolia 17. Athens 18. Scyros

Many young women are intimately linked with the heroic Theseus, who is said to have sired numerous illegitimate offspring:

- On his journey from Troezen to Athens, Theseus walked along the Isthmus of Corinth, where he encountered Perigoune or Perigune, daughter of the outlaw, Sinis, and sired a son, Melanippus, who became a great athlete.
- Theseus is called the seducer of Alope, daughter of the villain Cercyon.
- Oenopion, Thoas, and Staphylus are listed among Theseus's sons by Ariadne, although Thoas was probably sired by Dionysus.
- To cement political alliance with Athens, Deucalion, Ariadne's brother, may have arranged for Theseus to leave Ariadne, Minos's daughter, and marry Phaedra, also Minos's daughter, who bore two sons, Acamas and Demophon.
- On the sea voyage from Athens to Crete, Theseus was also linked with Eriboea (or Periboea or Phereboea), the Megaran princess whom the ship captain tried to rape.
- The journey home brought him on a side trip to Troezen, where he seduced Anaxo and her daughters and slew her sons.
- Another mythic mate is the Amazon Antiope, whom Herakles is said to have given Theseus for his part in capturing Hippolyta's belt. From their union came Hippolytus, who, on the day Theseus wed Phaedra, attacked Athens to avenge his mother's disgrace.
- Other women linked with Theseus include Aegle, Hippe, Iope, Meliboeia, and Helen, who is said to have borne Iphigenia, who was adopted and reared by Clytemnestra.

Theseus's ignoble death at the hands of his brother-in-law Deucalion left sons Acamus and Demophon in jeopardy. Both youths honored their father by fighting at Troy and releasing their grandmother from bondage to the spiteful Helen. When the usurper Menestheus died, the boys returned home to reclaim the Attic throne. Demophon survived his brother and guided Athens through an illustrious period of history.

Journey At sixteen years of age, Theseus revealed his readiness to rejoin his father in Athens by locating the sword of Cecrops, founder of Athens, and a pair of sandals that Aegeus had hidden beneath a boulder at the shrine of Zeus Sthenius near Hermione. With his mother's help, Theseus armed himself and secretly set out for Athens. He rejected his grandfather's advice to cross the Saronic gulf. Plutarch's *Parallel Lives* claims that Theseus repudiated a safe journey:

> He thought it therefore a dishonourable thing and not to be endured, that Herakles should go out everywhere, and purge both land and sea

from wicked men, and he himself should fly from the like adventures that actually came in his way; disgracing his reputed father by a mean flight by sea, and not showing his true one as good evidence of the greatness of his birth by noble and worthy actions, as by the token that he brought with him the shoes and the sword.

Instead, he traveled to the Isthmus of Corinth on foot, deliberately pitting himself against fierce pirates and cutthroats.

His journey involved an incident that underscored his mettle. At Epidaurus on the Peloponnesus overlooking the Saronic gulf, he killed Hephaestus's son, Periphetes, a crippled spoiler called "trouncer" for his love of cracking skulls with his bronze club. As a war prize, Theseus seized the notorious club and carried it along. At Cenchraea on the southwestern end of the Isthmus of Corinth, Theseus slew the brigand Sinis or Sinnis, nicknamed "bender of pines," the sadistic torturer who tied his victims to bowed pine trees, then loosened the trunks to rip their bodies in two. His other method of killing the unsuspecting was to toss them high into the air so that they would smash onto boulders below. With the death of Sinis, Theseus began adding to his stature as altruistic defender of travelers.

Like Herakles, his monster-quelling hero, Theseus continued on his way northeast, ridding the area of an assortment of evils. He overcame Phaea, the wild sow of Crommyon, with a single sword thrust. At the Scironian Rocks near Megara on the north coast of the Saronic gulf, Theseus battled Sciron, the lurking waylayer of travelers who required travelers to bend down and wash his feet, then pushed them into the sea and into the lair of a giant flesh-eating sea turtle. In like fashion, Theseus reached downward, grabbed Sciron's ankles, and yanked him off balance before hurling him into the sea.

From this successful battle, Theseus moved on toward Cercyon, called the "grappler," a second villain on the route to Eleusis who challenged all strangers to a wrestling match. Theseus defeated Cercyon by tossing him upward, then down to his death on the rocks below. Before setting out once more for Athens, Theseus established Cercyon's grandson, Hippothoon, as ruler of Eleusis.

The last and most beneficial in Theseus's series of killings was Procrustes, nicknamed "stretcher" and also called Polypemon or Damastes, who ruled the road from Megara to Athens. A treacherous savage, Procrustes invited guests to spend the night, then trimmed their bodies to fit his short bed or, if the traveler was short, stretched his guest's limbs to conform to the dimensions of the bedframe. Theseus ended Procrustes's terrorism by tying him to the bed and hacking off all overhanging parts. The conclusion of this pilgrimage came at the Cephissus River, where the Phytalides, the first to offer genuine hospitality, cleansed Theseus of the killings at the altar of Zeus.

Arriving at the Acropolis, Theseus, dressed in long formal chiton rather than the more familiar short tunic, was ridiculed by carpenters perched on the roof of the shrine of Apollo Delphinius. Because he was labeled a sissy for his ankle-length garment, Theseus snatched up a yoke of oxen and tossed them over the temple roof. The workers quickly returned to their roofing and ceased their taunting of Theseus.

As a result of the lengthy journey and numerous tests of courage and strength, Theseus found that his reputation as a slayer of evil-doers had preceded him. His father, Aegeus, then bewitched by his third wife, Medea, was unable to identify Theseus, even though the youth bore Aegeus's heirloom sword and sandals. At a banquet at the Dolphin Temple, Medea, with Aegeus's concurrence, plotted to poison Theseus because he represented a threat to the accession of Medus, her son by Aegeus. Just as he lifted his sword to cut a slice of meat, Aegeus recognized the weapon, carved with the intricate serpents of Erechtheus, and thrust the chalice laden with aconite, or wolfsbane, from his son's hand. Below the table, a court hound lapped up the spilled liquid and instantly fell into fatal paroxysms. Before Attica's lords, Aegeus clasped his son and heir and welcomed him home with a citywide celebration and multiple sacrifices to the gods.

Thus declared the heir to Athens, Theseus faced two evils: his stepmother Medea, who vanished in a cloud, and his fifty contentious cousins, who launched an immediate rebellion. The cabal divided into two companies, one marching from Sphettus toward Athens with Pallas and the other lying in wait for Theseus at the village of Gargettus. Again, in *Parallel Lives,* Plutarch preserves the particulars of the one-sided clash arising from their jealousy:

> They had with them a crier of the township of Agnus, named Leos, who discovered to Theseus all the designs of the Pallantidae. He immediately fell upon those that lay in ambuscade, and cut them all off; upon tidings of which Pallas and his company fled and were dispersed.

For killing Pallas's sons, Theseus spent a year in Troezen working off his sin. He was later tried at the Court of Apollo the Dolphin and found innocent on grounds of justifiable homicide.

Of all his trials, Theseus worked hardest and risked the most to end the shameful dilemma of Athens—the tribute of seven youths and seven maidens to be sacrificed to the Minotaur, an unspeakable Cretan monster also called Asterius—a blood price to compensate Minos for his son, Androgeus, who was killed while hunting a bull there. As a counter move to halt the cycle of fourteen Athenian victims every nine years, and to end a plague of droughts, famine, and pestilence, Athenians pressured Aegeus to offer his own son, who was both illegitimate and foreign, as a member of the chosen. Instead, Theseus volunteered to join the third contingent bound for sacrifice in Crete. Aegeus begged him to alter his decision, but Theseus would not be dissuaded.

In April, Theseus himself supervised the casting of lots for selection of the remaining thirteen youths. To assure enough warriors, he had two males replace two maidens and dressed the men in women's clothes so that Minos would not realize his

trickery. At the end of the ceremony, he offered to Delphinium Apollo an olive branch tied up with white wool, the Greek gesture of peace. As he departed, he carried a set of white (or red) sails so that, if he bested the Minotaur, the crew could replace their black sails to announce the victory of their champion and the end of Athens's bloody tribute to Minos.

For this grim voyage, the Attic fleet set sail from the secret harbor at Thymoetadae on the Bay of Salamis. Along the way, Theseus obeyed the Pythia, Apollo's priestess, by calling Aphrodite to be his conductor. As he sacrificed a nanny goat to the goddess, the animal changed into a buck.

Upon arrival on the island, Theseus and the others were forced down the cold, foul-smelling tunnels of the Labyrinth, the chamber designed by Daedalus to confine the Minotaur. Before Theseus passed through the entrance, the princess Ariadne, who loved Theseus on sight and had consulted Daedalus on the best way to traverse the warren of hallways, slipped him a ball of twine and advised him to tie one end of the thread to the entrance so that he could find his way out of the confusing passages. After locating the Minotaur and wrenching its throat with his bare hands, Theseus returned to Minos's court, crippled the Cretan navy by boring holes in the hulls, killed Minos's son, Asterius, and the jailer, Taurus, in a late evening sea battle, and, under cover of an October night, carried Ariadne and the thirteen young Athenians back to Attica.

Beaching his fleet at the harbor of Dia or Naxos, the largest of the Cyclades, Theseus, at the command of Dionysus, abandoned Ariadne so that the god might have her for himself. On the island of Delos, Theseus honored Aphrodite, the goddess of love, with a statue provided by Ariadne. His ritual crane dance, a ceremonial reenactment of the journey through the Labyrinth, involved the other young Athenians, who joyously celebrated around the sacred altar their liberation from a grisly death. So involved was Theseus with his festival that he forgot that his beached ship still bore black sails. Upon his arrival to the port of Phalerum, his inadvertent signal caused Aegeus to leap to his death into the sea that later bore his name. Thus a triumphal entry to Athens was tempered by grief for the unforeseen loss of Theseus's father.

As Athens' king, Theseus—displaying an amalgam of foresight and authority—proved himself a worthy politician and administrator. He set up a centralized government, annexed Megara and eleven other *demes,* which he bound into a tight commonwealth, wrote a constitution, issued coins, established the Pan Athens festival to honor Poseidon, and Federation Day as a national holiday, and created a workable class system of landowners, farm laborers, and craftsmen. In lieu of a monarchy, Theseus championed a republic, although he continued to head the court and the military. To delineate Attica from the Peloponnese, he set up a column at the southwestern border with the Ionian and Peloponnesian boundaries clearly marked.

To the demands from Deucalion that he return the escaped inventor, Daedalus, to Crete, Theseus smoothly replied that Daedalus, his kinsman, must remain in Athens. In secret, Theseus gathered a Cretan fleet at Thymoetadae and staffed it with

Daedalus and other exiles from Crete. He made a successful foray against the island from Knossus and slew Deucalion and his men. Theseus then installed Ariadne as regent, with his sons Oenopion and Staphylus set to inherit after her. The conclusion of this bloody reprisal was an unbreakable truce under which no Cretan could ever breach the peace with Athens. As a rest from his labors, Theseus joined the Calydonian boar hunt, but tossed his spear in vain.

Theseus is noted for his humanitarianism in granting asylum to Oedipus, whose daughter Antigone led him to Colonus shortly before his death. Theseus also rescued Antigone and her sister, Ismene, from Creon's kidnappers and assisted at the burial of the Seven against Thebes. When Herakles went mad and murdered his family, Theseus brought him comfort. Another side of Theseus's altruistic nature was his alliance with Pirithous, who stole from Theseus's flocks, then returned the animals so that the two men could be friends. Together, they took part in the war between the Centaurs and the Lapiths, a clash arising on Pirithous's wedding day from the Centaurs' attempt to abduct Hippodameia from her bridegroom.

Because of an ill-advised plan to marry women conceived by Zeus, Theseus, at age fifty, journeyed to Aetolia and kidnapped Helen, who was only ten at the time, reputedly raped her, and then assisted Pirithous in passing through the gate at Taenarum to stalk Hades in search of Persephone. Helen's brothers, Castor and Pollux, marched on Athens to rescue her from house arrest at Aphidna and captured the aged Aethra to serve her as nursemaid. The rescuers, with the help of turncoat Athenians, placed Menestheus, a seedy demagogue, in power. Meanwhile, Theseus and Pirithous, still in the Underworld, were tricked by Hades to take seats in the stone Chairs of Forgetfulness, which locked them in place for four years. Only Theseus, with Herakles's help, was able to flee eternal confinement. He returned to earth, leaving Pirithous forever seated in Hades.

Back in Athens, Theseus discovered his throne usurped and his children in peril. He dispatched them north to Elephenor's care in Euboea and sought a self-imposed exile. Sailing at first toward Crete, Theseus was beaten back by a storm to Scyros, one of the Sporades in the Aegean Sea off Euboea's eastern shore, where he lost his footing and fell from an escarpment. Possibly, King Lycomedes of Scyros pretended to extend hospitality, then, at the command of Menestheus, Theseus's rival for Athens, pushed Theseus from a cliff.

Alternate Versions

So much of Theseus's lore suffers variations or interpolated events that scholars have proposed the theory that, like Daniel Boone and Paul Bunyan, Theseus may have been an amalgam of three heroes from Marathon, Troezen, and Attica. One of the most ribald tales connected with Theseus describes his father Aegeus's trip to Delphi, where he received inexplicable advice. In Plutarch's *Parallel Lives,* Pythia warned, "Loose not the wineskin foot, you chief of men, until to Athens you see again." On his way past Troezen, Aegeus, veteran of two childless marriages, accepted the hospitality of Pittheus and recounted Pythia's strange command. Pittheus, who perceived the sexual meaning of the wine-skins, plied Aegeus with wine, then steered him to the bed of his daughter, Aethra.

An alternate telling of Medea's malice describes her attempt to defeat the youth by pitting him against a fire-breathing bull that Herakles had unleashed in the plain of Marathon and which was terrifying the people of Tetrapolis. On the way, Theseus spent the evening as guest of Hecale, a righteous old woman who prayed to Zeus to protect the youth. Her prayers were answered. Theseus subdued the animal and was preparing to slice its throat at the altar of Apollo Delphinius when Aegeus recognized his sword. On the way past Hecale's cottage, Theseus stopped to thank her and discovered that she had died. In her honor, he erected an altar to Zeus Hecaleius, where annual rites honored her piety.

Plutarch offers a variation on the creature Phaea, whom he claims was a human female. Because she robbed with lasciviousness and brutality, she was named the sow. For her swinish behavior, Theseus killed her, thus ridding the Corinthian isthmus of one of its numerous hazards. Another telling reduces the nobility attached to Theseus's volunteer duty as one of the sacrificial fourteen youths bound for Crete. According to Hellanicus, Minos came to Athens in person to select the best young people present. These victims were immured in an underground prison and ruled over by a savage jailer named Taurus rather than by the half-man, half-bull called the Minotaur. Plutarch notes that this version elevates Crete's end of the story from feral savagery to a more civilized settling of the score between rival cities.

A resetting of Theseus's mating with Eriboea describes a contest with Minos, who insisted that Theseus was not the son of Poseidon. To boast his own divine paternity, Minos called down lightning from Zeus, his father. Then Minos tossed a gold ring overboard and demanded that Theseus prove that he was sired by the god of the sea. Theseus immediately dived to the bottom of the sea, where a school of dolphins guided him to the Nereids' cave. They handed over the ring. To add to Theseus's feat, Thetis (or Amphitrite) gave him the jeweled coronet she had worn at her wedding to Peleus. Theseus surfaced and climbed aboard the ship. He grandly presented the ring to Minos and placed the crown on himself.

A romanticized version of Theseus's adventures describes how Ariadne offered him a luminous tiara. By the light shed from its glittering points, he was to make his way into the Labyrinth, kill the Minotaur, and return to wed her. However, he did not remain forever in Ariadne's debt, as she had hoped. One version describes Theseus as true to Aegle, who may have been one of the seven maidens waiting to be fed to the Minotaur. Another telling says that a storm separated Theseus from Ariadne at Cyprus, where local women admired her so warmly that they sent her counterfeit love letters to carry on the charade of Theseus's love for her. Even with their tender ministrations, Ariadne died giving birth to a child sired by Theseus. In her honor, he returned, set up a bronze and a silver statue, and initiated a cult dedicated to his Cretan princess in the grove of Aphrodite Ariadne.

The questionable tale of Theseus's part in Herakles's battle with the Amazons describes how Theseus sailed to the southwestern shore of the Black Sea and lured Antiope, the queen's sister (also identified as Melanippe or Queen Hippolyta herself) aboard his ship, then prevented her from disembarking. After sailing for Greece, Theseus incurred the wrath of the Amazons. Led by the Queen's sister, Oreithyia, they allied with the Scythians, followed him all the way home, and for four months battered him before the Pnyx (the knoll) at the gate of the Acropolis, where Theseus killed Molpadia, one of the Amazons, as she attempted to rescue Antiope. The Athenians, aided by Antiope, were so successful at holding off the Amazons that the female warriors agreed to a truce. Antiope, however, died in battle, leaving Theseus loveless until his union with Phaedra.

Phaedra's adultery with Hippolytus confuses the story of Theseus's marriage to the Cretan princess. A favorite story in music, cinema, and art, the doomed passion of stepmother and stepson was ignited when Hippolytus visited Athens to be initiated into the Eleusinian mysteries. While Theseus made a state journey to Delphi (or accompanied Pirithous to Thessaly), Phaedra was so torn by her lust for her husband's son that she built an altar to Aphrodite on the corner of the Acropolis that looked toward Troezen and which she fed a perpetual flame while starving herself pitiably.

A meddling serving woman, keen to the melting looks Phaedra cast at the outdoorsy young man, warned Hippolytus, who scorned the love of women. Phaedra inscribed her damnable emotion on a suicide note and swallowed poison. On his return, Theseus found the note, which falsely accused Hippolytus of making carnal overtures. The angry king, like Potiphar defending his wife from Joseph in Genesis in the Hebrew Bible, banished the innocent youth and called down Poseidon's curse. Instantly a bull rose from the waves, terrified Hippolytus's horses, and caused his chariot to tumble over the cliffs at the narrowest part of the Isthmus of Corinth. Hippolytus, tangled in the traces, was dragged over jagged rocks. Theseus later discovered that Aphrodite, who had felt slighted by Hippolytus's refusal of young females, had concocted the tragic scenario as an antidote to her wounded pride.

Even more disturbing to fastidious Athenians was the myth linking their hero with Hades. A rewriter of myth cast the story as an earthly adventure that took Theseus to Epirus in search of a wife for Pirithous. Among the Molossians, Theseus ran afoul of King Hades, who imprisoned him and fed Pirithous to the three-headed guard dog Cerberus. Theseus gained release after Herakles arrived and intimidated Hades.

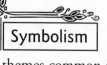

Symbolism   Although more anchored in the human sphere than the coarser myths of Herakles, Theseus's lore parallels traditional heroic themes common to European literature:

- Like King Arthur cleansing Britain of thieves and blackguards, or Robin Hood ridding Sherwood Forest of villains, Theseus rid much of lower

Greece of its most heinous highwaymen. As Plutarch described his service to the area, "I found none so fit as him that peopled the beautiful and far-famed city of Athens...."

- Theseus's lore parallels Herakles, the hero who rid the world of human and animal menace. Also, emulating Herakles, Orpheus, Aeneas, Dionysus, the Babylonian Bel and Marduk, the Irish Cuchulain, the French Ogier le Danois, Christ, and the British heroes Arthur, Gwydion, and Amathaon, Theseus braved Hades.
- The conference of royalty by the lifting of the Rock of Theseus suggests the myth of Jason, whose sandals helped identify him, as well as similar legitimizing events in the lives of Christ, Galahad, and Arthur, the bastard sired by Uther Pendragon, who proved his claim to the throne by pulling a sword from a stone.
- In the style of Romulus, Rome's founder, and the Hebrew David, King of Israel, Theseus united the warring factions around Athens into a strong, unified nation, which survived unchallenged until Castor and Pollux, the Dioscuri, waged war to return Helen to her family.
- In harmony with the lines "Give me your tired, your poor, your huddled masses yearning to breathe free" of Emma Lazarus's "The New Colossus," which are inscribed on the Statue of Liberty, Theseus, a lover of democracy and despiser of autocracy, proclaimed, "Come hither, all ye people," thus opening the city to migrations of foreigners.

Notable traditions and themes cluster about Theseus, in particular, the following:

- Named after the deposit of items under a boulder, some say that Theseus was not formally named (i.e., tied to a patronymic) until he arrived at his father's court in Athens.
- Like a warrior giving his opponent no handhold, Theseus is credited with shaving his forelock Homeric style, to honor the Delphic oracle, thus introducing a new style to Greece, the Thesian tonsure.
- In honor of Sinis, Theseus is said to have organized the Isthmian games and to have begun the custom of awarding palm leaves to victors.
- The lifting of the boulder from the sword and sandals, the fight with the Minotaur, and the journey to the Underworld suggest a dual role for Theseus: as youthful initiate who is equal to the unraveling of mature complexities and as late-in-life defier of death. In both extremes, Theseus achieved redemption from ghastly fates that symbolize the extinction of life.
- The lengthy friendship with Pirithous suggests a kind of Achilles/Patroclus, David/Jonathan, Aeneas/Achates, and Damon/Pytheus relationship.
- The epic fall of Theseus parallels other victims of *hubris,* notably Herakles, Oedipus, Bellerophon, Phaethon, and Ajax the Great. Literally tumbling

to his death and slipping from public notoriety, Theseus, who overreached by battling the Amazons and attempting to outwit Hades, earned a lengthy period of disaffection during which Athenians ceased honoring his accomplishments.

The most moving of lore attached to his name is the purported appearance of an oversized benevolent spirit at the Battle of Marathon. In *Parallel Lives* Plutarch describes the omen, "many of the soldiers believed they saw an apparition of Theseus in arms, rushing on at the head of them against the barbarians."

Just as King Arthur anticipated when England needed him most, Theseus remained in attendance over his chosen city. Under advisement from Pythia, Phaedo, Athens's archon, set out to find Theseus's bones and again inter them in a sacred place. Cimon scoured Scyros in search of Theseus's burial cairn. He found it with the aid of an eagle, which clawed the earth over Theseus's remains. The coffin, bones, and bronze spear and sword, borne with military honors to Athens, were met with great rejoicing by thankful Athenians, who attributed their victory to the ghost of Theseus. In the fourth century B.C., he was buried in a covered shrine called the Theseum near the gymnasium of Ptolemy in the center of Athens at the southern end of the Agora. In memory of his devotion to the distressed, his tomb became a refuge for the lowly and the hunted. The rites in honor of the mythical king occur annually on the eighth of Pyanepsion, the day he rescued Athenian youth from the Cretan bull.

Art has found a universal hero in Theseus. The Stoa of Athens contains a bas-relief of Theseus's battle against Sciron; Rome's Villa Albani has a bas-relief depicting Aegeus's recognition of his son. Theseus's love for Pirithous, crowning at Athens, meeting with the sea nymphs, abduction of Helen, battle with the Minotaur, role in the Calydonian boar hunt, and governance of Attica adorn urns, wine cups, statuary, and painted vases dating from the fifth century B.C., one by the potter Glaucytes and another credited to Exekias. A fresco at Herculaneum re-creates the battle with the Minotaur; another depicts Ariadne, sunk in grief as Theseus rows away from Naxos, his face turned from her prostrate form. Nicolas Poussin painted *Theseus Finding His Father's Arms;* Antonio Canova chose *Theseus and the Dead Minotaur* for the subject of a neoclassic statue. Peripheral aspects of the Theseus myth figure in the *Chant de Minos,* a painting by Henry de Montherlant, and in Henri Matisse's colorful canvases *Minotaur* and *Pasiphae.*

Literature contains many references to Theseus. Boccaccio honored him in *Teseida* and Geoffrey Chaucer in *The Knight's Tale.* The French playwright Jean Racine chose romantic scenes for *Phèdre;* André Gide preferred symbolism for *Thésée.* Mary Renault's novels, *The Bull from the Sea* (1962) and *The King Must Die* (1958), revive for twentieth-century readers the intrigue of Theseus's youthful voyage to Crete. Poetry, particularly that of the English Victorians, has dwelled on numerous facets of Theseus's career, as immortalized in Algernon Swinburne's *Phaedra,* Elizabeth Barrett Browning's *Queen Anelida,* and Robert Browning's *Artemis Prologises.* Other glimpses of Theseus's story include these: Geoffrey Chaucer's *House of Fame, Anelida and Arcite,* and *The Legend of Good Women;* Phineas Fletcher's *The Purple Island;* Edmund Spenser's *Faerie Queene;* William Shakespeare's *Midsummer Night's Dream* and *Two Gentlemen of Verona;* Pierre Corneille's *Phèdre;* Richard Lovelace's *Princess Louisa Painting;* Matthew Prior's *On Beauty;* Oliver Goldsmith's *Theseus;* John Keats's *Isabella;* Lord Byron's *The Corsair;* C. Day Lewis's *Ariadne on Naxos;* Thomas Hood's *Hero and Leander;* George Santayana's *Odes;* and Louis MacNeice's *Autumn Sequel.*

Musical and cinematic Theseus spin-offs are less numerous than works based on other myths, particularly Jason, Antigone, Orpheus, and Herakles. Ildebrando Pizzetti and Arthur Honegger chose Phaedra as the theme of their musical tragedies; Richard Strauss's *Ariadne auf Naxos,* a comic opera, deemphasizes Theseus in favor of the cast-off Cretan princess. In 1961, Greek and U.S. moviemakers collaborated on an erotic *Phaedra,* starring Melina Mercouri and Anthony Perkins, that stressed the doomed love between Theseus's wife and her diffident stepson.

🌿 See Also

Daedalus, Herakles, Jason and Medea.

🌿 Ancient Sources

Aelian's *Varia Historia;* Aeschylus's *Eumenides;* Agias of Troezen's *Returns of Heroes;* Antoninus Liberalis's *Metamorphoses;* Anticlides's *Nostoi;* Apollodorus's *Epitome* and *Poetic Astronomy;* Aristophanes's *The Wasps;* Aristotle's *Constitution of Athens, Constitution of the Bottiaeans,* and *Politics;* Athenaeus's *The Learned Banquet;* Aulus Gellius's *Attic Nights;* Bacchylides's *Choral Lyric XVIII* and *Dithyrambs;* Bion's *Poetic Fragments;* Callimachus's *Hecale, Hymn to Apollo,* and *Hymn to Delos;* Catullus's *Poems to Lesbia;* Clidemus's *Atthis;* Demon's *History;* Dicaearchus's *Hypotheses;* Diodorus Siculus's *Library of History;* Diogenes Laertius's *Prooemium;* Euripides's *Children of Herakles, Hippolytus, Suppliants,* and *The Mad Herakles;* Eustathius on Homer's *Odyssey;* First Vatican Mythographer; Hellanicus's *Atthis;* Herodorus; Herodotus's *Histories;* Hesiod's *Catalogue of Women* and *Descent of Theseus into Hades;* Hesychius's *Lexicon;* Homer's *Iliad* and *Odyssey;* Hyginus's *Fables;* Ibycus's *Calydonian Boar Hunt;* Ion of Chios's *Fragments;* Isocrates's *Panathenaicus* and *Panegyric;* Justin's *Apology;* Lactantius on Statius's *Thebaid;* Lycophron's *Alexandra;* Lysias's *Funeral Oration;* Menecrates's *History of Lycia; Minyas* (anonymous); Ovid's *Heroides, Ibis, Metamorphoses,* and *Remedies of Love;* Paeon the Amathusian's *Essay;* Panyasis's *Heraclea; Parian Marble* (anonymous); Pausanias's *Description of Greece;* Pherecydes's *Heptamochos;* Philochorus's *Atthis;* Photius's *Etymologicum Magnum* and *Library;* Pindar's *Nemean Odes;* Plato's *Republic* and *Symposium;* Pliny the Elder's *Natural History;* Plutarch's *Greek Questions, Parallel Lives,* and *Which Animals Are the Craftier?;* Proclus's *Chrestomathy;* Scholiast on Aristophanes's *Knights, Parliament of Women,* and *Peace;* Scholiast on Euripides's *Medea;* Scholiast on Homer's *Iliad;* Scholiast on Pindar's *Nemean Odes;* Scholiast on Statius's

Thebiad; Scholiast on Theocritus's *Idylls;* Seneca's *Hippolytus, The Mad Hercules,* and *Phaedra;* Servius on Virgil's *Aeneid;* Simonides of Ceos's *Verse;* Sophocles's *Oedipus at Colonus;* Stasinus' of Cyprus's *Cypria;* Strabo's *Historical Sketches;* Thucydides's *History;* Johannes Tzetzes's *Chiliades and On Lycophron;* Virgil's *Aeneid;* Xenophon's *Anabasis.*

Glossary

Acheron
[ak' uh • rahn]
A dismal river of the underworld named for a partially submerged river in Epirus. The Acheron and the Styx are both named as the dividing line that souls must cross to pass into Hades.

aegis
[ee' juhs]
Athena's protective skin shield or breastplate, originally carried by Zeus or Apollo. The aegis, which Athena brandished before enemies, is centered with the Gorgon's head and an edging of snakes, meant to inspire awe or fear.

amphora
[am' for uh] pl. amphorae
A large-bodied, two-handled, oval clay container or jar flaring outward from a stopper or seal above the slender neck to a broad middle and receding to a sharp tip or knob at the bottom. The amphora was used to store liquids, primarily wine, but also oil. The shape, meant to facilitate pouring, was seated in a cradle or support for storage or transportation. Port authorities stamped amphorae with identification, such as vintage, grade, vintner, tax, and date of seal.

apotheosis
[uh pah' the oh' sihs]
A transformation from mortal to immortal, such as in Dionysus's removal from earthly life to a divine position among the Olympian gods. The person apotheosized passed from a human state to godhood without dying or being reincarnated.

arete
[ah ray' tay]
A state of excellence or fineness of performance or skill, such as competence with a sword or on the speaker's platform. The goal of perfection, which often led to the sin

of *hubris* or overweening pride or pomposity, brought about the downfall of Achilles, who longed for a short, illustrious life rather than a normal span of years marked by mediocrity.

    See hubris

ate
[ah' tay]
Ruinous, foolhardy behavior; blindness to reason; madness. Personified as a goddess, a state of *ate,* such as the insanity that plagued Herakles and inspired Bellerophon's flight up Olympus on the back of Pegasus and Phaethon's gallop aboard Helios's chariot, usually preceded a cataclysmic and/or ignoble demise.

augur
[aw' guhr] pl. augures
In Roman times, a prognosticator or diviner who discerned the course of international policy, the source of a plague or run of ill fortune, or the outcome of a military campaign or election by making certain ritual observations, such as the pattern of smoke from a ceremonial fire or the behavior of sacred birds. An interpretation of an augury or auspices involved observing and/or recording prophetic signs or omens, which could be read by a priest or priestess trained in presaging the future.

Bacchante
[bah' kuhnt ay] pl. Bacchantes
A female follower of Bacchus, the Roman name for Dionysus, the god of wine; a reveler or drunken celebrant. Crazed with the presence and majesty of the god, these ecstatic women decked themselves in wild animal skins, snakes, ivy, and grape leaves or oak or fir branches, and bore a scepter formed of fennel stalk topped with a pine cone and draped in vines as they processed or danced a ritual celebration. Husbands, fathers, and local peacekeepers often apprehended and restrained bacchantes for lewd performances, destruction of property, or harm to infants.

    See Maenad, thyrsus

bassarid
[bas' suh rihd] pl. bassarids
Female worshippers or celebrants from Thrace who followed Dionysus with ecstatic dance and joyful procession. A Bacchante; a Maenad.

bull-roarer
[bool' rohr • uhr]

A ritual noisemaker composed of a flat wooden, bone, or clay circular disk attached at the center to a length of cowhide or rope and swung over the head in rapid circles to create a humming sound. Bull-roarers were used in Cretan worship services as a method of acknowledging the power and majesty of the bull, symbol of Poseidon.

Calydonian boar hunt
[ka' lih doh' nee • uhn]
The effort of an illustrious band of heroes to rid the area of Calydon in Aetolia of a ravaging boar. Oeneus, king of Calydon, suffered the displeasure of Artemis, whom he had slighted, and faced the fierce beast alone. To rid the country of deadly menace, he chose Meleager as leader and summoned the best hunters in Greece, including Acastus, Admetus, Amphiaraus, Amyntor, Ancaeus, Atalanta, Caeneus, Castor, Cepheus, Deucalion, Dryas, Echeon, Eurytion, Herakles, Hippasus, Hippothous, Hyleus, Idas, Iolaus, Iphicles, Laertes, Lelex, Leucippus, Lynceus, Nestor, Panopeus, Peleus, Phoenix, Pirithous, Polydeuces, Telamon, and Theseus. Having enjoyed a nine-day banquet, the party set out on the tenth day. Mishaps caused the accidental piercing of Eurytion with Peleus's javelin as well as lethal gorings of Anceus and Hyleus. Atalanta made the first mark on the boar, followed by a shot to the eye by Amphiaraus; Meleager made the kill. To honor Atalanta, his love, he gave her the dressed meat and valuable hide. The event served as a touchstone of courage and camaraderie and prefigured the Trojan War, the central event of ancient Greek history.

catharsis
[kuh • thar' sis]
An emotional release, cleansing, or purification of sinful thoughts, behaviors, or habits, despair, or depression. Attendees at ancient Greek theater performances welcomed a purgation of pity and fear and a subsequent renewal of hope and expectation of good through identification with staged scenes depicting characters in dire situations. These experiences equated with the emotional emptying of guilt and perception of salvation at modern evangelical worship services.

Centaur
[sihn' tahr]
A wild, unruly mythological being composed of a horse body and the torso, head, and arms of a man. These barbarous beings, native to the mountains of Thessaly in ancient Greek mythology, were notorious for lechery, connivance, and the inability to tolerate alcohol. Drunkenness often led the centaurs to fight, steal, and rape, as demonstrated by the crafty Nessus, who sought to despoil Deianira, the wife of Herakles, while ostensibly offering her passage across a river. The centaurs named Pholus and Chiron, on the other hand, demonstrated humanity and learning by studying the arts and natural methods of healing and by teaching their wisdom to human pupils such as Jason, Achilles, and Asculepius.

Cercopes
[suhr • koh' puhs]
Two apish, uncivilized dwarves who robbed passersby. The Cercopes met their match in Herakles, who suspended them from the end of a stick tied to their feet and swung

them over his shoulders so that they faced his posterior. The Cercopes eventually over-taxed Zeus's patience. He banished them to Ischia and Proscida, two islands west of Naples, Italy.

Charon
[kar' uhn]
The dismal, elderly ferryman who bore souls across the Acheron and the Styx rivers and into the land of the dead. Only individual souls who were provided with ritual libations of wine and an obol or coin in the mouth were allowed entrance into Hades. Others wandered the opposite shore and begged Charon to end their tenure in limbo.
See Acheron, Styx

Cocytus
[kahk' sih • tuhs]
A chill river of the underworld; a branch of the Acheron that bounded one side of Hades.

crater
[kray' tuhr]
A ceremonial wine bowl, often fitted with handles and decorated with a circular frieze.

Cyclops
[sy' klahps] pl. Cyclopes
A mythological giant bearing a single eye in the middle of his forehead and known for cannibalism, uncivilized behavior, and disrespect to the gods. These pastoral beings lived on isolated crags and tended flocks of sheep and goats or worked at forges. The most famous Cyclops, Polyphemus, attempted to devour Odysseus's party, whom he immured behind a huge stone in his cave. In death, the Cyclopes were immured in Tartarus, the lowest level of the underworld.

cynic
[sih' nihk]
Any philosopher or sage who followed the teachings of Diogenes (c. 400–323 B.C.) by living a simple, unadorned existence, shunning acquisitiveness or worldly displays of possessions and prestige, and enduring misfortune and civil turmoil by ignoring it. Through wisdom, the cynic sought a pure, peaceful, sinless life.

dactyls

[dak' tihlz]
Supernatural beings or daemons endowed with mysterious powers of creativity and communion with the divine.

daemon or daimon
[day' mahn] pl. daemones
A nonspecific term for god or divinity. The Romans translated the Greek concept of daemones into the Lares and Penates, who watched over individual families and were propitiated at family altars, especially at mealtime and on feast days.

Dardanelles
[dahr' duh • nelz']
A narrow salt-water strait leading northeast from the Aegean Sea to the Sea of Marmara; the Hellespont. Named for the city built by Dardanus, the mythical founder of Troy, the area separates the modern nation of Turkey into two segments, one in Europe and one in Asia.
See Hellespont

deme
[deem] pl. demes
The Attic name for a governmental unit or hereditary parish or county, 170 of which formed Attica.

dig
Scientific slang for an area staked out for archaeological excavation and study. During the nineteenth century, ancient Troy was Heinrich Schliemann's dig at Hissarlik, Turkey, as was Mycenae on the Peloponnesus.

Dioscuri
[dy' uhs • koo' ree]
Castor and Pollux (or Polydeuces), the twin sons of Leda, fathered by Tyndareus and Zeus, and brothers of Helen and Clytemnestra. Because Pollux claimed immortality from Zeus, he shared his powers with Castor by living alternately on Mount Olympus among the gods and among mortals in Hades. The Dioscuri figure in several myths, particularly the recovery of Helen in childhood from Pirithous and Theseus, the Calydonian boar hunt, and the voyage of the *Argo*. In astrology, the Dioscuri became the Zodiac figure of Gemini, the celestial twins. They were worshipped as gods in the Peloponnese. Their cult spread to Sicily, Italy, and other Greek colonies.

dithyramb
[dihth' ram]
A ritual chant or hymn used for worship sung by a soloist, such as Orpheus, or by a single or antiphonal choir. Choirmasters in the ancient world competed for prizes by composing dithyrambs suited to special occasions. A significant portion of the Pythian games was devoted to the creation and performance of dithyrambs.

411

doppelganger

[dahp' puhl • gang' uhr]

A literary motif that pairs two characters, usually opposites, such as the Dioscuri, one of whom was mortal and one immortal.

Dryad

[dry' ad]

A nymph inhabiting a tree, particularly the oak. These winsome, timid creatures depended on their residence for life and, therefore, stayed in close contact with the sheltering tree. At the death of the tree, the Dryad inevitably died.

See Nymph

Eleusinian mysteries

[eh' lyoo • sih' nee uhn]

Secret religious ceremonies performed each fall at the shrines of Persephone and Demeter in Eleusis, near Athens. The cult allowed only formally initiated members (i.e., pure, shameless participants), to take part in sacred drinks, hymn singing, and sacrifice. A significant role in the Eleusinian mysteries conferred great honor and respect on the worshipper.

Elysian Fields

[eh • lee' zhun] or Elysium

The fields of the blessed, where heroes and favorites of the gods passed from life to an untroubled afterlife. Virgil describes Aeneas as a visitor to the Elysian Fields, where he enjoyed a poignant reunion with his father's spirit and saw a vision of the greatness of Rome.

See Tartarus

Epigoni

[ih • pih' guh • nee]

The male offspring or successors of the Seven against Thebes, who followed Adrastus in a second assault against the city to avenge their fathers, who died in the first assault ten years before.

Erinyes

[ih rihn' yeez]

The Furies or Eumenides, vengeful spirits who hounded wrongdoers into frenzied madness or suicide. Orestes, the most pitiable victim of their spite, faced the dilemma of having to murder his mother to repay her killing of her husband Agamemnon, Orestes's father. At length, he completed his task, escaped the Erinyes's curse, and returned to sanity.

guest code
A binding social relationship requiring hosts or locals to be charitable to strangers and to do no harm to visitors who ate at their table or slept under their roof. Likewise, guests were expected to behave civilly and to do no harm or take no object from a host. Paris violated the guest code by taking advantage of Menelaus's absence at his grandfather's funeral and by abducting Helen, Queen of Sparta, to Troy. This violation of courtesy and honor led to ten years of war and extensive disruption of families and nations.

Hades
[hay' deez]
The god of the Underworld, as well as the Underworld itself, ruled over by Pluto or Dis and his queen, Persephone or Proserpina. Hades was divided into the Elysian Fields, or home of the blessed, a royal court, and Tartarus, the punishment center for the most heinous of mortals. The three-headed dog, Cerberus, guarded the entrance to the Underworld, through which souls passed to be judged by Minos, Aeacus, and Rhadamanthys. The Underworld was coursed by rivers: the Styx, which spirits had to cross in the ferryman's boat; Lethe, the river of forgetfulness, in which reincarnated souls were dipped to rid them of memories of their past lives; Acheron, the river of sorrow; Cocytus, the river of regret or remorse; and Phlegethon, a terrifying fiery current. Ancient sources list numerous entrances to Hades; most common was Taenarum in southwestern Greece.

Harpy
[har' pee]
One of several winged creatures whose name, meaning "snatchers," indicate their predatory nature. The daughters of Tharma and Electra, they lived in the Strophades, islands in the Aegean Sea, and carried off children. Another description has them fetching souls to Hades.

Hecatombaeum
[hehk' uh • tohm' bee uhm]
July on the Greek calendar, the month in which a hundred oxen were sacrificed and the civil year began.

Hellespont
[hehl' luhs • pont]
The early name for the narrow salt-water strait leading northeast from the Aegean Sea to the Sea of Marmara; the Dardanelles.
See Dardanelles

hubris or *hybris*
[hyoo' brihs]
Vaunted pride, insolence, conceit, ambition, or over-confidence—the deadliest sin in Greek lore because it put humans in competition with divinity. Such lack of restraint brought severe penalties from the gods, such as the hanging death of Arachne, the weaver who challenged Athena. Because she bested the goddess, Arachne was severely punished and hanged herself in despair. In drama, *hubris* or the "tragic flaw" causes a protagonist to violate morality by trying to surpass human limitations. In most cases, death or a calamity strikes the central figure, as with Oedipus's loss of his kingdom, prestige, wife, and eyesight.

Isthmian games
[isth' mee • uhn]
The athletic contests that celebrated Greek unity began in the eighth century B.C. To honor Poseidon, Corinth, under the leadership of Sisyphus or Theseus, initiated the Isthmian games, held on the first and third years of the Olympiad or quadrennial. Dating to 580 B.C., winners received monetary awards from their sponsors as well as victory odes and celebratory wreaths.
See Nemean games, Olympian games, Pythian games

Lethe
[lee' thee] adj. Lethean
The river of oblivion; a river of Hades that was tasted by or splashed over souls to release them from past memories and events and outfit them with new identities. Aeneas saw the future of Rome depicted in souls being bathed in Lethe and readied for an illustrious rebirth in Rome. Thus, Virgil was able to utilize a mythological phenomenon as a method of glorifying Augustus Caesar, the poet's patron.

libation
[ly • bay' shuhn]
A liquid offering of wine, honey, blood, milk, or mead poured at a shrine, altar, or funeral pyre to symbolize fealty, obedience, respect, or veneration. Catullus, the Roman lyricist, traveled over land and sea to deliver a ritual libation over the tomb of his brother.

Maenad
[may' nad] pl. Maenads or Maenades
A frenzied nymph or female worshipper of Dionysus; a Bacchante. These ecstatic cult followers led local converts in a passionate procession through the countryside and engaged in extreme dances and sexual rites with satyrs. The Maenads' assault on Orpheus indicates their power over mortals; because he slighted their importance and hinted that he preferred young males to maidens, the Maenads tore him to bits.

metopesc

[meht' uh • peez]

The carved or decorated space separating the side-by-side segments of a triptych or three-part mural or altarpiece. These adornments filled in panels beneath ceiling beams in Greek temples and often contained significant symbols and motifs, such as magical plants, ships, monsters, and characters.

Minotaur

[mihn' uh • tawr]

A monster with the body of a man and the head of a bull, named Asterius or Asterion; the shameful offspring of a white bull given by Poseidon to King Minos of Crete, and born of the king's wife, Pasiphae. Minos hired Daedalus, the chief inventor of the ancient world, to construct a labyrinth in which to hide the bull and to imprison the inventor and his son so that they could not divulge the secret of the winding passageways. Annually, the Minotaur was fed seven young men and seven maidens, a grim tribute extracted from Athens.

Naiad

[nay' ad]

A delicate fresh-water nymph sired by Zeus and inhabiting a river, spring, lake, or fountain. So dependent was the Naiad on her aquatic residence that she died if it dried up. Her presence was nurtured by local people who drank or bathed in the waters to improve health and depended on the Naiad's power over fertility, growth, and prosperity.

Nemean games

[nuh • mee' uhn]

The athletic contests that celebrated Greek unity began in the eighth century B.C. To honor Zeus and commemorate the death of the infant Opheltes, Argolis, under the leadership of Herakles or the Seven against Thebes, initiated the Nemean games, held on the second and fourth years of the Olympiad or quadrennial. Dating from around 573 B.C., winners received celebratory crowns of wild celery and the prestige of having brought honor to their sponsoring cities.

    See Isthmian games, Olympian games, Pythian games

Nemesis

[nihm' uh • sihs]

The daughter of Nyx (Night), Oceanus, or Erebus (Darkness) and the personification of retribution, chastisement, discipline, or justice. As a goddess, Nemesis, seated at her shrine at Rhamnus near Athens, assisted Zeus in maintaining earthly order. The ultimate enforcer, she inflicted vengeance for malfeasance, impeded the victorious or wealthy from an overbalance of blessings, and curbed excesses of human emotion, such as arrogance or anger. Likewise, Nemesis acquired a crucial role in drama, in which she represents poetic justice or fate.

nymph
[nihmf]
A minor nature divinity or mortal sired by Zeus and who dwelled in forests, groves, mountains, grottoes, and streams in the form of a lovely girl. These lithe, blissful beings sang, spun, and attended important goddesses, especially Artemis and also Calypso and Circe. Individual nymphs, particularly Echo and Daphne, led individual lives, loved mortals and gods, and had their own myths.

See Dryads, Naiads

obolus or obol
[oh' buh • luhs]
A small silver coin of ancient Greece valued at one-sixth of a drachma. An obolus was placed in the mouth of a corpse to pay Charon for passage over the river Styx into the Underworld. Unmourned souls like those of Palinurus and Elpenor were forced to wander the earthly side of the Styx and plead for passage until a living person performed ritual honor and paid the toll for the crossing into Hades.

Olympian games
[oh • lihm' pee • uhn]
The athletic contests that celebrated Greek unity began in the eighth century B.C. and was held under a multinational truce, which extended safe conduct for all participants. To honor Zeus, Elis initiated the Olympian games, held the fourth year of the Olympiad or quadrennial. The games were the most prestigious of the four cycles—Isthmian, Nemean, Olympian, and Pythian—and set the tone and style of performance as well as the rules governing competition. Dating to 776 B.C., the events included pentathlon, foot races, wrestling, chariot racing, horse racing, colt racing, mule racing, trotting, boxing, and the pancration, a combination of boxing and wrestling. Winners received monetary awards from their sponsors as well as victory odes and celebratory olive wreaths woven of branches from a sacred grove.

Palladium
[puhl • lay' dee • uhm]
The statue of Pallas Athena carved from wood or the shoulder blade of Pelops. Approximately sixty inches tall, the figure stood upright with feet together, left hand holding a distaff or spindle and right hand clutching a spear, thus symbolizing the peacetime and wartime dominions of the goddess. The Palladium reportedly fell from the sky or from Mount Olympus into Dardanus's hands. As the Troad's chief talisman, it was prophesied to be the deciding factor in the downfall of Troy. The prophecy proved true after Diomedes and Odysseus crept into the city in the tenth year of the

Trojan War and stole the sacred icon. According to Roman lore, the Trojans kept a dummy statue and preserved the original in a separate place. After the Greeks gained entrance through the Scaean gate in their wooden horse and set fire to the city, Ajax the Lesser defiled the image with his touch and was drowned. Aeneas then took possession of the real Palladium and bore it to Italy. His descendents enshrined the Palladium in the Temple of Vesta, where it provided similar protection over Rome.

parthenos
[pahr' thih • nohs]
The Greek word for maiden or virgin. The Parthenon in Athens took its name from the word *parthenos,* a synonym for Athena, a virgin goddess.

patronym
[pat' roh nym]
The surname derived from a father's name. For example, Aeneas was also called Peleides or "son of Peleus." The patronym was essential to delineate characters whose names were borne by more than one person, such as Ajax, Cleopatra, Helen, and Diomedes. Some characters, such as the Danaides and the Heraclids, were better known by their patronyms than by their given names.

Peloponnesus or Peloponnese
[peh' loh puhn neh' suhs]
The southern segment or peninsula of Greece, separated from the northern portion by the Gulf of Corinth and joined on the eastern shore by a slender isthmus. Peloponnesian political regions include Arcadia or Arcady, Argos or the Argolid, Elis, Laconia or Lacedaemonia, and Messenia. The Peloponnesus is the scene of important events in ancient Greek history, particularly the labors of Herakles and the abduction of Helen from Sparta.

phallus
[fal' luhs]
A symbolic penis; a fertility symbol adorning a worshipper of Dionysus and carried or venerated during a ritual encouraging a good harvest, healthy human offspring, and the future of a tribe or nation.
   See Priapus

Phlegethon River
[fleh' guh thahn]
One of the rivers of Hades; the fiery perimeter of the underworld. The Phlegethon joined Cocytus in a great cataract, which flowed into the Acheron.

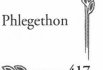

Priapus

[pry' uh puhs]

A fertility god symbolized by an oversized phallus or male sex organ; a good luck deity born of Dionysus and Aphrodite or Adonis and Aphrodite. In Roman gardens, Priapic figures presided over groves, orchards, and flower and vegetable beds.

Pythia

[pih' thee uh]

A title borne by a succession of prophetesses of Apollo at Delphi. From her perch on a stool over a deep cleft in the rock, the Pythia fell into a deep trance and muttered loose, ambiguous phrases in answer to petitioners' questions. She was greatly venerated for assisting rulers in solving difficult problems and for helping sufferers regain their health.

Pythian games

[pih' thee uhn]

The athletic contests that celebrated Greek unity began in the eighth century B.C. To honor Apollo, Delphians initiated the Pythian games, second in importance to the Olympian games. Dating from around 582 B.C. and held the third year of the Olympian or quadrennial, the games featured hymn-writing contests, held at the theater at Delphi, as well as horse racing and other athletic events. Winners received celebratory crowns of laurel cut from the valley of Tempe, the sacred meadow of Apollo which lay between Mount Ossa and Mount Olympus.

See Isthmian games, Nemean games, Olympian games

Satyr

[say' tuhr]

A bestial, frolicsome woods deity or daemon characterized by protruding penis and the ears, hips, tail, and legs of a goat or horse. The Satyrs, who were key participants in Dionysus's worship, were noted for drunken, lecherous behavior. In art, Satyrs are frequently depicted as rapists. The promiscuity and salacious wit of the Satyr gave rise to Satyr plays or Satire, which ridiculed local events and dignitaries with pointed, humorous skits.

Sibyl

[sih' buhl]

A local or itinerant seer who fell into ecstatic trances, tore her hair, scribbled indecipherable writings, and writhed in the grip of Apollo, who spoke prophecy through the Sibyl's fervid babblings. Aeneas visited the Cumaean Sibyl at Campania in order to learn the way into the Fields of the Blessed.

See Pythia

Sileni
[sy lee' nih]
A synonym for satyrs.

Stoic
[stoh' ihk]
A follower of a philosophy that encouraged a passionless life in which neither joy nor sorrow altered basic behavior. The purpose of Stoic wisdom was the furtherance of a rational acceptance of extremes and the search for goodness. As delineated by Marcus Aurelius, the Stoic writer and Roman emperor, "Live each day as though it were your last."

Styx River
[stihks] adj. Stygian
The chief waterway through Hades; a synonym for Acheron, the river souls crossed by paying a toll to Charon the ferryman.

Tartarus
[tahr' tuh ruhs]
The center of torment in Hades; the final destination of the wicked in the Underworld, where punishments were made to suit the crimes committed on earth.
   See Elysian Fields

thyrsus
[thuhr' suhs]
The fennel stalk or scepter topped with a pine cone and wound with ivy, grape vines, and branches that Bacchantes or Dionysus himself carried in procession.

Titan
[ty' tuhn]
One of six giant pre-Olympian deities born to Uranus and Gaia; a member of the oldest generation of Greek gods.

trickster
[tihk' stuhr]
A mischievous, sometimes humorous male deity or sprite who defrauds humans through illusion, deception, and outright theft. The trickster is identifiable in most of world mythology, particularly African and native American lore, in which he takes the form of a small animal, such as a rabbit, raven, or squirrel.

Troad
[troh' ad]
A jut of land on the northwestern shore of what is now the Asian side of Turkey. As the site of the Trojan War, epic poetry romanticizes the two major aspects of this valuable land—its access to major shipping lanes and its ties to Greece to the west, and eastern powers that rivaled the Mediterranean periphery.

votary or votress
[voh' tuh • ree]
An adherent or devotee of a deity or cult. Usually a female, the votary pledges fealty and advocacy to the divinity, whom she serves as a temple watcher, keeper of a sacred flame or shrine, or local priestess. Votaries, who may be orphans or jilted brides or lovers, often take up residence at altars because they have no other place to go.

Ancient Sources by Author

Acusilaus (5th century B.C.)
    History – Menelaus

Aelian (A.D. 170–235)
    Varia Historia – Aegisthus, Dionysus, Helen, Herakles, Jason, Leto, Medea,
        Paris, Pirithous, Theseus
    On the Nature of Animals – Arion, Herakles, Odysseus

Aeschylus (524?–456 B.C.)
    The Persian Women (March, 472 B.C.) – Jason, Medea, Teucer
    Seven against Thebes (468 or 467 B.C.) – Adrastus, Sthenelus
    The Suppliants (463 B.C.) – Aegisthus
    Prometheus Bound – Prometheus
    Prometheus Unbound – Prometheus
    Prometheus the Firebearer – Prometheus
    Eumenides – Cassandra, Theseus
    Agamemnon (458 B.C.) – Aegisthus, Agamemnon, Cassandra, Helen,
        Orpheus
    Bassarae – Orpheus, Perseus
    Epigoni – Adrastus
    Edonians – Dionysus
    Philoctetes – Diomedes, Odysseus
    Danaides – Danaides
    Amymone – Danaides
    Orphic Hymns – Dionysus

Agias of Troezen (8th century B.C.)
    Returns of Heroes – Achilles, Agamemnon, Helen, Herakles, Menelaus, Paris,
        Theseus

Alcaeus (7th century B.C.)
    Hymn to Dionysus – Dionysus

Alcidamas (4th century B.C.)
    Odysseus – Auge

Alexis (375–275 B.C.)
    Plays – Auge

Amphis (5th century B.C.)
    Government by Women – Auge

anonymous (8th–6th century B.C. Cyclic Poets)
    Argonautica Orphica – Jason, Medea
    Chrestomathy – Nestor
    Coins of Gortyna – Cadmus
    Danais – Danaides
    Epigoni – Adrastus
    Lithica – Orpheus
    Minyas – Theseus
    Parian Marble (3rd century B.C.) – Theseus
    Nostoi – Theseus

Antoninus Liberalis (2nd century A.D.)
    Metamorphoses – Achilles, Bellerophon, Diomedes, Dionysus, Helen, Herakles, Jason, Leto, Medea, Paris, Pirithous, Theseus

Apollodorus (c. 180–140 B.C.)
    Epitome – Achilles, Acrisius, Admete, Adrastus, Aeetes, Aegeus, Aegisthus, Aeneas, Agamemnon, Ajax the Great, Ajax the Lesser, Andromache, Auge, Bellerophon, Cadmus, Cassandra, Daedalus, Danaides, Dardanus, Diomedes, Dionysus, Epeius, Helen, Herakles, Icarus, Jason, Leto, Medea, Menelaus, Nauplius, Nestor, Odysseus, Paris, Phaethon, Pirithous, Prometheus, Sisyphus, Sthenelus, Teucer, Theseus
    Library – Alcaeus, Dionysus, Herakles, Perseus, Sthenelus
    Poetic Astronomy – Theseus

Apollonius of Rhodes (c. 300–225 B.C.)
    Argonautica (c. 260 B.C.) – Achilles, Acrisius, Aeetes, Auge, Cadmus, Danaides, Dionysus, Herakles, Jason, Medea, Nauplius, Nestor, Odysseus, Orpheus, Perseus, Phaethon, Sisyphus

Apollonius of Tyana (1st century A.D.)
    Autobiography – Orpheus

Apuleius (c. A.D. 125–c. 171)
    The Golden Ass – Jason, Medea

Aratus (315–239 B.C.)
  Phenomena – Perseus

Arctinus of Miletus (8th century B.C.)
  Aethiopis – Achilles, Ajax the Great, Helen, Paris, Teucer
  Sack of Troy – Achilles, Aeneas, Cassandra, Helen, Odysseus, Paris, Teucer

Arian (A.D.95–175)
  Indica – Dionysus, Herakles

Arion (fl. 628–625 B.C.)
  Hymn to Poseidon – Arion

Aristophanes (c. 450–c. 385 B.C.)
  Knights (424) – Nestor
  The Wasps (422) – Theseus
  The Birds (414) – Leto, Prometheus
  Thesmophoriazusae (411) – Canopus
  Frogs (405) – Dionysus, Orpheus

Aristotle (384–322 B.C.)
  Constitution of the Bottiaeans – Theseus
  Constitution of Athens – Theseus
  Politics – Aegisthus, Theseus
  Poetics – Auge, Dionysus, Odysseus
  Historia Animalium – Leto

Athenaeus (fl. A.D. 200)
  The Learned Banquet – Admete, Aegeus, Agamemnon, Ajax the Great,
    Dionysus, Epeius, Helen, Herakles, Jason, Medea, Orpheus, Pirithous,
    Theseus

Athenagoras (A.D. 177)
  Legatis pro Christianis – Jason, Medea

Aulus Gellius (c.123–165)
  Attic Nights – Arion, Theseus

Bacchylides (fl. 5th century B.C.)
  Choral Lyric XVIII – Aegeus, Herakles, Jason, Medea, Theseus
  Dithyrambs – Dionysus, Theseus

Bion (fl. c. 100 B.C.)
  Poetic Fragments – Pirithous, Theseus

Callimachus (305–241 B.C.)
Hymn to Delos – Auge, Herakles, Jason, Leto, Medea, Theseus
Hecale – Jason, Medea, Theseus
Hymn to Apollo – Theseus
Hymn to Artemis – Helen, Herakles, Leto, Pirithous
Epithalamion for Helen – Helen
Iambi – Epeius

Carcinus (? 7th–6th century B.C.)
Naupactia – Jason, Medea

Catullus (c. 84–c. 54 B.C.)
Poems to Lesbia (published posthumously) – Aegeus, Aeneas, Dionysus, Theseus

Cicero (106–43 B.C.)
On Old Age (44 B.C.) – Jason, Medea
Against Atticus (68–44 B.C.) – Odysseus
On the Nature of the Gods – Daedalus, Dionysus, Herakles, Icarus, Jason, Medea, Odysseus
Pro Lege Manilia – Jason, Medea
On Divination (60 B.C.) – Orpheus
Tuscan Debates – Epeius, Sisyphus
On Duties (44 B.C.) – Herakles, Jason, Medea

Cinaethon of Lacedaemon (8th century B.C.)
Oedipodeia – Aegisthus, Jason, Medea

Clement of Alexandria (b. A.D. 150)
Address to the Greeks – Dionysus, Perseus
Protrepticus – Orpheus
Stromateis – Orpheus

Clidemus (c. 350 B.C.)
Atthis – Theseus

Colluthus (5th century A.D.)
Rape of Helen – Helen, Paris

Conon (3rd century B.C.)
Narrations – Dardanus, Diomedes, Dionysus, Helen, Herakles, Odysseus, Orpheus, Paris

Cratinus (484–419 B.C.)
    Dionysalexandros – Helen, Paris
    Nemesis – Helen
    Odysses – Odysseus

Cyclic Poets. See anonymous.

Dares of Phrygia (? 5th century A.D.)
    Trojan War – Achilles, Helen, Odysseus, Paris, Pirithous

Demodocus (? 6th century B.C.)
    History of Herakles – Herakles

Demon (c. 300 B.C.)
    History – Theseus

Dicaearchus (4th century B.C.)
    Hypotheses – Theseus

Dictys Cretensis (? 2nd or 3rd century A.D.)
    Trojan War Diary – Achilles, Aegisthus, Agamemnon, Ajax the Great,
        Andromache, Auge, Cassandra, Diomedes, Epeius, Helen, Nauplius,
        Nestor, Odysseus, Paris, Sthenelus

Didymus (c. 80–10 B.C.)
    On Lyric Poets – Nauplius, Odysseus

Dio Chrysostomus (A.D. 40–112)
    Orationes – Aegisthus

Diodorus Siculus (fl. 60–21 B.C.)
    Library of History (21 B.C.) – Acrisius, Adrastus, Aeetes, Aegeus, Alcaeus,
        Auge, Cadmus, Daedalus, Danaides, Dardanus, Herakles, Icarus, Jason,
        Medea, Nauplius, Nestor, Orpheus, Perseus, Phaethon, Pirithous,
        Sthenelus, Theseus
    Orphic Hymn – Dionysus, Orpheus

Diogenes Laertius (3rd century A.D.)
    Verse – Orpheus, Theseus

Dionysius of Halicarnassus (c. 30 B.C.)
    Roman Antiquities – Aeneas, Dardanus, Herakles

Dionysius Periegeta (? 2nd century A.D.)
    Periegesis – Menelaus

Diotimus (fl. 3rd century B.C.)
Heraclea – Herakles

Duris the Samian (340–260 B.C.)
Histories and Criticisms – Odysseus

Ennius (239–169 B.C.)
Annales (c. 170 B.C.) – Aeneas

Epigenes (6th century B.C.)
Tragedies – Orpheus

Eratosthenes (c. 275–194 B.C.)
Star Placements – Dionysus, Helen, Herakles, Orpheus, Perseus, Phaethon

Eugammon of Cyrene (8th century B.C.)
Telegony – Helen, Odysseus, Paris
Epicorum Graecorum Fragmenta – Odysseus

Euhemerus (fl. 316 B.C.)
Sacred Scripture – Prometheus

Eumelus (fl. c. 730 B.C.)
Verse – Jason, Medea, Nestor, Sisyphus

Euripides (c. 484–c. 406 B.C.)
Auge – Auge
Telephus – Auge
Cretan Women – Menelaus
Cyclops (438) – Odysseus
Alcestis (438) – Herakles, Orpheus
Medea (431) – Aeetes, Aegeus, Jason, Medea
Children of Herakles (c. 428) – Herakles, Theseus
Hippolytus (428) – Aegeus, Herakles, Phaethon, Theseus
Andromache (c. 427) – Achilles, Aeneas, Andromache, Cassandra, Helen,
    Menelaus, Paris
Hecuba (425) – Achilles, Aeneas, Agamemnon, Andromache, Daedalus,
    Icarus, Odysseus
The Mad Herakles (c. 422) – Admete, Herakles, Theseus
Suppliants (421) – Adrastus, Sthenelus, Theseus
Ion (c. 417) – Admete, Herakles, Perseus
Antigone – Adrastus
Trojan Women (415) – Agamemnon, Ajax the Lesser, Andromache,
    Cassandra, Epeius, Helen, Menelaus, Odysseus, Paris

Electra (413) – Aegisthus, Agamemnon, Cassandra, Daedalus, Helen, Icarus, Menelaus, Paris, Perseus
Iphigenia in Tauris (c. 413) – Achilles, Agamemnon, Menelaus
Helen (412) – Agamemnon, Canopus, Helen, Menelaus, Paris, Teucer
Phoenician Women (c. 410) – Adrastus, Cadmus
Orestes (408) – Aegisthus, Agamemnon, Cassandra, Helen, Menelaus
Bacchants (405) – Cadmus, Dionysus, Orpheus
Iphigenia in Aulis (405) – Achilles, Agamemnon, Cassandra, Helen, Menelaus
Stheneboea – Bellerophon
Philoctetes – Helen, Paris
Rhesus – Diomedes, Helen, Paris
Bellerophon – Bellerophon
Atalanta – Jason, Medea
Oineus – Diomedes, Dionysus

Eusebius (A.D. 260–340)
Preparation for the Gospel (A.D. 312) – Herakles

Eustathius (12th century A.D.)
On Homer's *Iliad* and *Odyssey* – Achilles, Aegeus, Aegisthus, Agamemnon, Bellerophon, Cassandra, Danaides, Dardanus, Dionysus, Epeius, Helen, Herakles, Nestor, Odysseus, Paris, Pirithous, Prometheus, Sisyphus, Sthenelus, Teucer, Theseus

Fabius Pictor (A.D. 200)
History of Rome – Aeneas

First Vatican Mythographer (?) – Aegeus, Helen, Herakles, Jason, Medea, Theseus

Gorgias (483–376 B.C.)
Encomium of Helen – Helen

Hecataeus (c. 500 B.C.)
Mythologic History – Auge

Hegius of Troezen. *See Agias.*

Hellanicus (5th century B.C.)
Roman Antiquities – Aeneas, Herakles
Atthis – Theseus
Troica – Aeneas

Herodotus (fl. 450–428 B.C.)
　　Histories – Aegeus, Ajax the Great, Arion, Cadmus, Danaides, Helen,
　　　　Herakles, Jason, Medea, Menelaus, Nestor, Paris, Perseus, Phaethon,
　　　　Theseus
　　Persian Wars – Helen, Paris

Hesiod (8th–7th centuries B.C.)
　　Histories – Achilles, Acrisius, Agamemnon, Theseus
　　Theogony – Aeetes, Bellerophon, Cadmus, Dardanus, Dionysus, Herakles,
　　　　Jason, Leto, Medea, Nestor, Orpheus, Perseus, Phaethon, Prometheus
　　Works and Days – Prometheus
　　Shield of Herakles – Herakles, Perseus
　　Catalogue of Women – Aegisthus, Ajax the Great, Alcaeus, Antigone, Helen,
　　　　Herakles, Nestor, Sthenelus, Theseus
　　Oxyrhynchus Papyrus – Auge
　　Descent of Theseus into Hades – Pirithous, Theseus

Hesychius (5th century A.D.)
　　Lexicon – Aeetes, Aegeus, Diomedes, Sisyphus, Theseus
　　Antheia – Dionysus
　　Lenai – Dionysus
　　Bassarai – Dionysus
　　Epeius – Epeius
　　Hippeion – Danaides

Homer (9th–8th centuries B.C.)
　　Iliad – Achilles, Acrisius, Adrastus, Aeneas, Agamemnon, Ajax the Great,
　　　　Ajax the Lesser, Andromache, Bellerophon, Cassandra, Dardanus,
　　　　Diomedes, Dionysus, Epeius, Helen, Herakles, Jason, Leto, Medea,
　　　　Menelaus, Nestor, Odysseus, Orpheus, Paris, Perseus, Pirithous, Sisyphus,
　　　　Sthenelus, Teucer, Theseus
　　Odyssey – Achilles, Adrastus, Aegisthus, Agamemnon, Ajax the Great, Ajax
　　　　the Lesser, Antigone, Cadmus, Canopus, Cassandra, Diomedes, Dionysus,
　　　　Epeius, Helen, Herakles, Jason, Leto, Medea, Menelaus, Nestor, Odysseus,
　　　　Paris, Pirithous, Sisyphus, Theseus
　　Hymn to Aphrodite – Aeneas
　　Hymn to Apollo – Leto, Nestor
　　Hymn to Dionysus – Dionysus
　　Kerkopes (?) – Herakles

Horace (65–8 B.C.)
　　Satires II (30 B.C.) – Sisyphus

Odes (23 B.C.) – Acrisius, Daedalus, Danaides, Herakles, Icarus, Odysseus, Perseus, Prometheus, Sisyphus, Teucer
Ars Poetica (20 B.C.) – Helen
Carmina (19 B.C.) – Agamemnon, Bellerophon, Daedalus, Danaides, Dionysus, Icarus,

Hyginus (64 B.C.–A.D. 17)

Fables – Achilles, Acrisius, Adrastus, Aeetes, Aegeus, Aegisthus, Agamemnon, Ajax the Lesser, Andromache, Arion, Auge, Bellerophon, Cadmus, Cassandra, Danaides, Dionysus, Epeius, Helen, Herakles, Jason, Leto, Medea, Menelaus, Nauplius, Nestor, Odysseus, Orpheus, Paris, Perseus, Phaethon, Pirithous, Prometheus, Sisyphus, Sthenelus, Theseus
Poetic Astronomy – Acrisius, Arion, Dionysus, Helen, Herakles, Jason, Leto, Medea, Orpheus, Perseus, Phaethon, Prometheus
Preface – Odysseus, Prometheus

Ibycus (6th century B.C.)

Calydonian Boar Hunt – Orpheus, Theseus

Ion of Chios (5th century B.C.)

Fragments – Theseus

Isidore of Seville (A.D. 560–636)

Origins – Cadmus

Isocrates (436–338 B.C.)

Panegyric – Adrastus, Theseus
Panathenaicus – Theseus
Encomium of Helen – Helen

Josephus (A.D. 37–c. 100)

Jewish Wars (A.D. 76) – Perseus

Juba (25 B.C.–A.D. 23)

Roman Questions – Cadmus

Justin (c. A.D. 100–165)

Apology – Admete, Aeetes, Alcaeus, Jason, Medea, Sthenelus, Theseus

Lactantius (A.D. 240–324)

On Statius's *Thebaid* – Aegeus, Helen, Herakles, Jason, Medea, Nauplius, Theseus

Divine Institutions (?)

Lesches of Mytilene (8th century B.C.)
   Little Iliad – Achilles, Aeneas, Ajax the Great, Andromache, Cassandra, Diomedes, Helen, Menelaus, Nestor, Odysseus, Paris, Sthenelus

Livius Andronicus (3rd century B.C.)
   Odyssia Latina – Odysseus

Livy (c. 59 B.C.–A.D.17)
   From the Foundations of the City (c. A.D. 14) – Aeneas, Dionysus, Herakles

Lucian (b. A.D. 120)
   Prometheus on Caucasus – Prometheus
   Dialogues of Sailors – Danaides, Nauplius
   Against the Unlearned – Orpheus
   Dialogue of the Dead – Helen, Herakles, Phaethon
   Dialogue of the Gods – Helen, Herakles, Paris, Phaethon, Prometheus
   On the Dance – Jason, Medea

Lucretius (96–55 B.C.)
   On the Nature of Things (60 B.C.) – Aeneas, Phaethon, Sisyphus

Lycophron (c. 320 B.C.)
   Cassandreis – Achilles
   Alexandra – Aeneas, Cassandra, Dardanus, Dionysus, Helen, Herakles, Jason, Medea, Menelaus, Paris, Theseus
   Aethiopis – Ajax the Great

Lysias (458–380 B.C.)
   Funeral Oration – Theseus

Lysimachus (360–281 B.C.) – Adrastus, Herakles

Macrobius (fl. A.D. 400)
   On Pisander – Aeneas
   Saturnalia – Herakles

Johannes Malalas (A.D. 491–578)
   Chronographica – Odysseus

Manilius (fl. 1st century A.D.)
   Astronomica – Perseus

Megasthenes (350–290 B.C.)
  Indica – Dionysus

Menecrates (4th century A.D.)
  History of Lycia – Pirithous, Theseus

Meursius (?)
  On Lycophron – Adrastus

Mimnermus (fl. 632–629 B.C.)
  Nanno – Jason, Medea

Mnaseas (3rd century B.C.)
  Travels – Herakles

Moschus (c. 150 B.C.)
  Idylls – Cadmus

Naevius (c. 264–261 B.C.)
  The Punic Wars – Aeneas

Nonnus (5th century A.D.)
  Dionysiaca – Cadmus, Dionysus, Phaethon

Onomacritus (c. 520 B.C.)
  Orphica (520 B.C.) – Dionysus, Orpheus

Ovid (43 B.C.–A.D. 18)
  Amores (22–15 B.C.) – Danaides
  Ibis – Adrastus, Aegisthus, Helen, Sisyphus, Theseus
  Heroides (15 B.C.) – Achilles, Aeetes, Aegeus, Danaides, Helen, Herakles,
    Jason, Medea, Paris, Sisyphus, Theseus
  Art of Love (c. 1 B.C.) – Cassandra, Sthenelus
  Remedies of Love (c. A.D. 2) – Theseus
  Metamorphoses (A.D. 8) – Achilles, Acrisius, Aeetes, Aegeus, Aeneas, Ajax the
    Great, Andromache, Bellerophon, Cadmus, Daedalus, Danaides,
    Diomedes, Dionysus, Helen, Herakles, Icarus, Jason, Leto, Medea,
    Nauplius, Nestor, Odysseus, Orpheus, Perseus, Phaethon, Pirithous,
    Prometheus, Sisyphus, Theseus
  Tristia (A.D. 11) – Jason, Medea, Phaethon, Sisyphus
  Fasti (posthumous, c. A.D. 18) – Aeneas, Arion, Cadmus, Dionysus, Helen,
    Herakles, Sisyphus

Paeon the Amathusian (?)
  Essay – Theseus

Panyasis (5th century B.C.)
  Heraclea – Pirithous, Theseus

Parthenius (c. 1st century B.C.)
  Love Stories – Achilles, Helen, Odysseus, Paris

Pausanias (fl. A.D. 150)
  Description of Greece – Achilles, Acrisius, Admete, Adrastus, Aeetes, Aegeus,
    Aegisthus, Aeneas, Agamemnon, Ajax the Great, Ajax the Lesser, Alcaeus,
    Andromache, Arion, Auge, Bellerophon, Cadmus, Cassandra, Daedalus,
    Danaides, Diomedes, Dionysus, Epeius, Helen, Herakles, Icarus, Jason,
    Leto, Medea, Menelaus, Nauplius, Nestor, Odysseus, Orpheus, Paris,
    Perseus, Pirithous, Prometheus, Sisyphus, Sthenelus, Teucer, Theseus

Petronius (1st century A.D.)
  Satyricon – Odysseus

Pherecydes (fl. 550 B.C.)
  Heptamochos – Aegeus, Cadmus, Daedalus, Herakles, Icarus, Jason, Medea,
    Pirithous, Theseus

Philochorus (fl. 340–306 B.C.)
  Atthis – Admete, Herakles, Theseus

Philostratus (b. A.D. 170)
  Heroica – Achilles, Ajax the Lesser, Cadmus, Diomedes, Helen, Jason,
    Medea, Nestor, Orpheus, Teucer
  Imagines – Diomedes, Herakles, Sisyphus
  Life of Apollonius of Tyana – Dionysus, Helen, Herakles, Orpheus, Prometheus

Photius (9th century A.D.)
  Library – Achilles, Aegisthus, Helen, Herakles, Menelaus, Theseus
  Etymologicum Magnum – Theseus

Phrynichus (6th and 5th centuries B.C.)
  Plays – Sisyphus

Pindar (518–446 B.C.)
  Pythian Odes (446 B.C.) – Acrisius, Aeetes, Aegisthus, Agamemnon,
    Cadmus, Cassandra, Danaides, Dionysus, Herakles, Jason, Leto, Medea,
    Nestor, Orpheus, Perseus

Nemean Odes – Admete, Adrastus, Andromache, Helen, Herakles, Jason, Medea, Odysseus, Pirithous, Teucer, Theseus

Olympian Odes – Bellerophon, Daedalus, Herakles, Icarus

Isthmian Odes – Ajax the Great, Bellerophon, Herakles, Nauplius, Prometheus

Pisander of Rhodes (?)
Exploits of Herakles – Herakles

Plato (428–347 B.C.)
Phaedo – Dionysus
Phaedrus – Helen, Paris
Meno – Daedalus, Icarus
Republic – Odysseus, Orpheus, Theseus
Symposium – Orpheus, Theseus
Cratylus – Canopus
Ion – Epeius
Axiochus – Danaides

Plautus (c. 254–184 B.C.)
Amphitryon – Herakles
Pseudolus (191 B.C.) – Jason, Medea

Pliny the Elder (A.D. 23–79)
Natural History (A.D. 77) – Cadmus, Daedalus, Diomedes, Herakles, Icarus, Jason, Medea, Odysseus, Perseus, Theseus

Plutarch (c. A.D. 45–c. 120)
Table Talk – Dionysus, Odysseus
De E apud Delphos – Dionysus
On Rivers – Aeetes, Dionysus, Herakles, Jason, Medea
Parallel Lives – Adrastus, Aegeus, Ajax the Great, Daedalus, Herakles, Icarus, Jason, Leto, Medea, Odysseus, Pirithous, Sthenelus, Theseus
Greek Questions – Achilles, Admete, Diomedes, Dionysus, Leto, Odysseus, Theseus
Roman Questions – Diomedes, Herakles
On the Virtues of Women – Bellerophon
On the Life and Poetry of Homer – Odysseus
On the Slowness of Divine Vengeance – Orpheus, Phaethon
On Love – Herakles
On the Face Appearing in the Orb of the Moon – Herakles
Symposium – Cadmus, Helen, Orpheus
Which Animals Are Craftier? – Prometheus, Theseus

On the Malice of Herodotus – Danaides

Pollux (2nd century A.D.)
Onomasticon – Herakles, Jason, Medea

Polyaenus (c. A.D. 162)
Stratagems – Herakles, Odysseus, Sisyphus

Praxilla (5th century B.C.)
drinking songs – Herakles

Proclus (2nd or 1st century B.C.)
Chrestomathy – Helen, Menelaus, Paris, Pirithous, Theseus

Ptolemy Hephaestion (6th–5th century B.C.)
On Homer's *Iliad* – Achilles, Aeetes, Aegisthus, Cadmus, Helen, Herakles, Jason, Medea, Menelaus, Paris

Quintus Smyrnaeus (c. 400 A.D.)
Post-Homerica – Achilles, Ajax the Great, Andromache, Diomedes, Helen, Paris, Sthenelus

Sappho (7th century B.C.)
Fragments – Helen

Scholiast (a body of notes from either the Greek or Latin commentaries)
On Apollonius of Rhodes's *Argonautica* – Aeetes, Alcaeus, Dionysus, Herakles, Jason, Medea, Odysseus, Perseus, Prometheus, Sthenelus
On Aristophanes's *Acharnians* – Sisyphus
On Aristophanes's *Frogs* – Herakles
On Aristophanes's *Clouds* – Odysseus
On Aristophanes's *Knights* – Pirithous, Theseus
On Aristophanes's *Parliament of Women* – Theseus
On Aristophanes's *Peace* – Theseus
On Demosthenes – Aegeus
On Dionysius's *Description of the Earth* – Jason, Medea
On Euripides's *Alcestis* – Herakles, Nestor
On Euripides's *Andromache* – Helen, Paris
On Euripides's *Iphigenia in Aulis* – Helen, Paris
On Euripides's *Medea* – Aeetes, Aegeus, Aegisthus, Jason, Medea, Theseus
On Euripides's *Electra* – Agamemnon
On Euripides's *Knights* – Jason, Medea
On Euripides's *Orestes* – Acrisius, Agamemnon, Diomedes, Menelaus, Nauplius, Perseus, Prometheus

On Euripides's *Helen* – Nauplius
On Euripides's *Phoenician Women* – Cadmus
On Euripides's *Hecuba* – Danaides
On Homer's *Iliad* – Ajax the Lesser, Bellerophon, Cadmus, Cassandra, Nestor, Sisyphus, Teucer, Theseus
On Homer's *Odyssey* – Cassandra, Jason, Medea, Nestor, Odysseus
On Persius's *Saturae* – Dionysus
On Pindar's *Olympian Odes* – Arion, Dionysus, Herakles, Nestor, Phaethon, Prometheus
On Pindar's *Isthmian Odes* – Teucer
On Pindar's *Nemean Odes* – Admete, Adrastus, Diomedes, Herakles, Theseus
On Pindar's *Pythian Odes* – Aeetes, Danaides
On Sophocles's *Oedipus at Colonus* – Aegeus, Daedalus, Icarus
On Sophocles's *Ajax* – Sisyphus, Teucer
On Sophocles's *Philoctetes* – Odysseus, Sisyphus
On Statius's *Thebaid* – Sisyphus, Theseus
On Theocritus's *Idylls* – Dionysus, Epeius, Theseus

Seneca (c. 4 B.C.–A.D. 65)
Moral Essays – Helen
Medea – Jason, Medea
Hippolytus – Pirithous, Theseus
Phaedra – Theseus
The Mad Hercules – Herakles, Theseus
Agamemnon – Aegisthus, Agamemnon, Cassandra
Trojan Women – Agamemnon, Andromache, Odysseus
Thyestes – Aegisthus

Servius (4th–5th century A.D.)
On Virgil's *Aeneid* – Adrastus, Aegeus, Aeneas, Agamemnon, Andromache, Cadmus, Cassandra, Danaides, Dardanus, Diomedes, Helen, Herakles, Jason, Leto, Medea, Menelaus, Odysseus, Paris, Perseus, Pirithous, Sisyphus, Teucer, Theseus
On Virgil's *Georgics* – Herakles, Orpheus, Sisyphus
On Virgil's *Bucolics* – Dionysus, Prometheus

Silius Italicus (A.D. 26–101)
Verse – Jason, Medea, Odysseus

Simonides of Ceos (556–c. 468 B.C.)
Verse – Acrisius, Aegeus, Herakles, Perseus, Theseus

Solinus (c. A.D. 200)
    Collectanea Rerum Memorabilium – Phaethon

Sophocles (c. 496–406 B.C.)
    Ajax (451? B.C.) – Agamemnon, Ajax the Great, Menelaus, Nauplius, Odysseus, Sisyphus, Teucer
    Antigone (441 B.C.) – Adrastus
    Electra (409 B.C.) – Adrastus, Aegisthus, Agamemnon, Cassandra
    Oedipus Rex (409 B.C.) – Dionysus
    Philoctetes (409 B.C.) – Diomedes, Helen, Herakles, Menelaus, Odysseus, Paris
    Trachinian Women (409 B.C.) – Herakles
    Oedipus at Colonus (produced 401 B.C.) – Adrastus, Theseus
    Epigoni – Adrastus
    Eriphyle – Adrastus
    lost plays – Aeneas, Jason, Medea, Perseus
    Mysians – Auge
    Aleadai – Auge
    Odysseus – Odysseus
    The Deaf Satyrs – Orpheus
    Capture of Troy – Menelaus

Stasinus of Cyprus (8th century B.C.)
    Cypria – Achilles, Aeneas, Agamemnon, Cassandra, Diomedes, Helen, Menelaus, Nestor, Odysseus, Paris, Pirithous, Theseus

Statius (A.D. 45–96)
    Thebaid (A.D. 91) – Adrastus, Jason, Medea
    Achilleid (posthumous, A.D. 96) – Achilles

Stephanus Byzantium (5th–6th century A.D.)
    Thebe – Prometheus
    Bargasa – Herakles
    Zoster – Herakles
    Psophis – Herakles
    Olynthus – Herakles
    Philaedai – Ajax the Great
    Hydissos – Bellerophon, Jason, Medea
    Iope – Perseus
    Nedo – Nestor
    Atrax – Pirithous
    Arisbe – Dardanus, Helen, Paris
    Brisa – Dionysus

Stesichorus (6th century B.C.)
　Funeral Games of Peleas – Jason
　Helen – Agamemnon, Menelaus
　Recantation – Helen, Menelaus
　Iliu Persis – Aeneas, Agamemnon, Epeius
　Oresteia – Cassandra

Strabo (64 B.C.–A.D. 21)
　Historical Sketches – Aegeus, Alcaeus, Diomedes, Dionysus, Herakles,
　　Menelaus, Nestor, Orpheus, Pirithous, Prometheus, Sthenelus, Theseus
　Geography – Ajax the Lesser, Bellerophon, Canopus, Dardanus, Jason, Medea,
　　Menelaus, Nauplius, Palinurus, Perseus, Sisyphus

Suidas (10th century A.D.) – Arion, Odysseus
　Melite – Herakles
　Herophila – Helen, Paris

Tacitus (A.D. 55–117)
　Dialogue on Orators (c. A.D. 105) – Odysseus
　Annals (A.D. 117) – Aeetes, Jason, Leto, Medea

Tertullian (A.D. 165–220)
　Essays – Prometheus

Theocritus (300–260 B.C.)
　Poems – Dionysus, Odysseus
　Idylls – Cadmus, Helen, Herakles, Jason, Medea, Menelaus

Theognis (fl. 544–541 B.C.)
　Verse – Sisyphus

Theon (1st century B.C.)
　On Aratus's *Phenomena* – Dionysus, Nauplius

Theophilus (330–229 B.C.)
　Poems – Dionysus

Theophrastus (370–288 B.C.)
　History of Plants – Cadmus, Odysseus

Thucydides (fl. 430–399 B.C.)
　History (362 B.C.) – Dionysus, Herakles, Theseus

Tibullus (c. 54–c. 18 B.C.)
　Elegies (c. 26 B.C.) – Danaides, Dionysus

Timaeus (356–260 B.C.)
    History – Aeneas, Jason, Medea

Triclinius (14th century A.D.)
    On Sophocles's *Electra*

Tryphiodorus (5th century A.D.)
    Sack of Troy – Achilles, Aeneas, Andromache, Helen, Paris

Johannes Tzetzes (12th century A.D.)
    On Lycophron – Achilles, Admete, Adrastus, Aegeus, Aegisthus, Ajax the
        Great, Andromache, Bellerophon, Cassandra, Dardanus, Diomedes,
        Epeius, Helen, Herakles, Jason, Medea, Nauplius, Odysseus, Paris, Perseus,
        Pirithous, Prometheus, Sisyphus, Sthenelus, Teucer, Theseus
    Posthomerica – Sthenelus
    Chiliades – Aegeus, Daedalus, Icarus, Perseus, Phaethon, Pirithous, Theseus
    Hypothesis of Lycophron's Alexandra – Cassandra

Valerius Flaccus (died c. A.D. 95)
    Argonautica – Aeetes, Herakles, Jason, Leto, Medea, Nauplius

Valerius Maximus (1st century A.D.)
    Handbook – Orpheus

Varro (116–27 B.C.)
    Hebdomades – Aeneas
    On the Latin Language – Herakles

Virgil (70–19 B.C.)
    Bucolics (37 B.C.) – Dionysus, Phaethon
    Georgics (30 B.C.) – Dionysus, Herakles, Menelaus, Orpheus, Sisyphus
    Aeneid (posthumous, 18 B.C.) – Achilles, Acrisius, Aeneas, Agamemnon,
        Ajax the Lesser, Andromache, Bellerophon, Cassandra, Daedalus,
        Dardanus, Diomedes, Dionysus, Helen, Icarus, Menelaus, Orpheus,
        Palinurus, Paris, Phaethon, Pirithous, Sisyphus, Teucer, Theseus

Xanthus (7th century B.C.)
    Poems – Menelaus

Xenophon (c. 434–353 B.C.)
    Anabasis – Jason, Medea, Theseus
    Memoirs of Socrates – Herakles
    Hellenica – Herakles

Zenobius (?)

Proverbs – Herakles, Menelaus

Zenodotus of Ephesus (c. 325 B.C.)

Homeric Glossary – Achilles, Acrius, Adrastus, Aegisthus, Aeneas, Agamemnon, Ajax the Great, Ajax the Lesser, Andromache, Antigone, Bellerophon, Cadmus, Canopus, Cassandra, Dardanus, Diomedes, Dionysus, Epeius, Helen, Herakles, Jason, Leto, Medea, Menelaus, Nestor, Odysseus, Orpheus, Paris, Perseus, Pirithous, Sisyphus, Sthenelus, Teucer, Theseus

On Hesiod's *Theogeny* – Aeetes, Bellerophon, Cadmus, Dardanus, Dionysus, Herakles, Jason, Leto, Medea, Nestor, Orpheus, Perseus, Phaethon, Prometheus

Timeline of Ancient Works and Authors

2800–1050 B.C. – Bronze Age
    Dares of Phrygia (2000 B.C.) historian

1200–1125 B.C. – Destruction of Mycenae

1184 B.C. – Trojan War
    Homer (9th–8th centuries B.C.) epic poet

814 B.C. – Carthage Founded
    Agias of Troezen (8th century B.C.) epic poet
    Arctinus of Miletus (8th century B.C.) epic poet
    Cinaethon of Lacedaemon (8th century B.C.) epic poet
    Cyclic Poets (8th century B.C.) anonymous epic poets
    Eugammon of Cyrene (8th century B.C.) epic poet
    Lesches of Mytilene (8th century B.C.) epic poet
    Stasinus of Cyprus (8th century B.C.) epic poet
    Hesiod (8th–7th centuries B.C.) poet, moralist, mythographer, folklorist

776 B.C. – First Olympian Games

753 B.C. – Rome Founded
    Eumelus (fl. c. 730 B.C.) epic poet
    Alcaeus (7th century B.C.) lyric poet
    Sappho (7th century B.C.) lyric poet
    Xanthus (7th century B.C.) poet
    Carcinus (7th–6th century B.C.) tragic poet
    Mimnermus (fl. 632–629 B.C.) elegaic poet
    Arion (fl. 628–625 B.C.) dithyrambist

620?–560? B.C. – Aesop composes fables
    Thales (c. 600 B.C.) scientist, philosopher
    Epigenes (6th century B.C.) comic poet, astronomer, grammarian

Ibycus (6th century B.C.) epic and lyric poet
Stesichorus (6th century B.C.) lyric poet
Phrynichus (6th–5th century B.C.) lyric and tragic poet
Ptolemy Hephaestion (6th–5th century B.C.) critic, grammarian

582 B.C. – First Pythian Games

581 B.C. – First Isthmian Games

573 B.C. – First Nemean Games

c. 535 B.C. – Thespis invents drama

533 B.C. – First Drama Competition
Anacreon (fl. 550 B.C.) lyric and elegaic poet
Pherecydes (fl. 550 B.C.) historian, essayist, philosopher
Simonides (556–c. 468 B.C.) elegaic and lyric poet
Theognis (fl. 544–541 B.C.) poet, moralist
Aeschylus (524?–456 B.C.) tragedian
    The Persians (March 472 B.C.)
    Seven against Thebes (468 or 467 B.C.)
    The Suppliants (463 B.C.)
    The Oresteia (458 B.C.)
Onomacritus (c. 520 B.C.) epic poet
    Orphica (520 B.C.)
Pindar (518?–438? B.C.) odist and satirist
    Pythian Odes (446 B.C.)

509 B.C. – Roman Republic Founded
Hecataeus (c. 500 B.C.) historian and geographer
Acusilaus (5th century B.C.) historian
Amphis (5th century B.C.) comic playwright
Bacchylides (5th century B.C.) lyric poet
Hellanicus (5th century B.C.) mythographer and historian
Herodorus (5th century B.C.) logician
Ion of Chios (5th century B.C.) poet, hymnographer, tragedian, aphorist, critic
Panyasis (5th century B.C.) epic poet
Praxilla (5th century B.C.) lyric poet

490 B.C. – Battle of Marathon
Cratinos (484–419 B.C.) comedy, satire, mythological burlesque
Euripides (c. 484–c. 406 B.C.) tragedian
    Alcestis (438 B.C.)

Cyclops (438 B.C.)
Medea (431 B.C.)
Children of Herakles (c. 428 B.C.)
Hippolytus (428 B.C.)
Andromache (c. 427 B.C.)
Hecuba (425 B.C.)
The Mad Herakles (c. 422 B.C.)
Suppliants (421 B.C.)
Ion (c. 417 B.C.)
Trojan Woman (415 B.C.)
Electra (413 B.C.)
Iphigenia in Tauris (c. 413 B.C.)
Helen (412 B.C.)
Phoenician Maidens (c. 410 B.C.)
Orestes (408 B.C.)
Bacchanals (405 B.C.)
Iphigenia in Aulis (405 B.C.)
Gorgias (483–376 B.C.) philosopher and orator

486 B.C. – First Comedy Competition
Sophocles (c. 496–406 B.C.) tragedian
Ajax (451? B.C.)
Antigone (441 B.C.)
Electra (409 B.C.)
Oedipus Rex (409 B.C.)
Philoctetes (409 B.C.)
Trachiniae (409 B.C.)
Oedipus at Colonus (performed 401 B.C.)

460 B.C. – First Peloponnesian War
Lysias (458–380 B.C.) orator

450 B.C. – Law of the Twelve Tables Instituted
Aristophanes (c. 450–c. 385 B.C.) comic playwright
Knights (424 B.C.)
The Wasps (422 B.C.)
The Birds (414 B.C.)
Thesmophoriazusae (411 B.C.)
Frogs (405 B.C.)
Herodotus (fl. 450–428 B.C.) historian, sociologist, geographer
Isocrates (436–338 B.C.) orator

Xenophon (c. 434–353 B.C.) historian, biographer, memoirist, essayist, technical writer

431 B.C. – Second Peloponnesian War
Herodotus (fl. 450–428 B.C.) historian, geographer, folklorist
Thucidydes (fl. 430–399 B.C.) historian and social commentator
    History (362 B.C.)
Plato (428–347 B.C.) philosopher, critic, political analyst

404–371 B.C. – Spartan Era
Alcidamas (4th century B.C.) rhetorician and sophist
Dicaearchus (4th century B.C.) historian, politican commentator, biographer, drama critic, geographer
Aristotle (384–322 B.C.) teacher, philosopher, critic
Alexis (375–275 B.C.) poet and comic playwright
Theophrastus (370–288 B.C.) philosopher, sociologist, essayist, historian, scientist
Timaeus of Sicily (356–260 B.C.) historian
Clidemus (c. 350 B.C.) chronicler, mythographer, geographer
Duris the Samian (340–260 B.C.) arts critic and historian
Philochorus (fl. 340–306 B.C.) chronicler

336–323 B.C. – Alexander's Reign
Theophilus (330–229 B.C.) comic poet
Lycophron (c. 320 B.C.) grammarian, poet, satirist
Dyscolus (c. 316 B.C.) grammarian
Euhemerus (fl. 316 B.C.) travel commentator, mythographer, ethicist
Aratus (315–239 B.C.) didactic and elegaic poet, aphorist, scientist, hymnographer
Callimachus (305–241 B.C.) romantic poet, playwright, encyclopedist, satirist, cataloguer
Demon (c. 3rd century B.C.) chronicler and aphorist
Theocritus (300–260 B.C.) pastoral and romantic poet, aphorist
Conon (3rd century B.C.) mythographer
Diotimus (fl. 3rd century B.C.) aphorist
Fabius Pictor (3rd century B.C.) historian
Livius Andronicus (3rd century B.C.) translator, playwright, lyric and epic poet
Mnaseas (3rd century B.C.) geographer and social commentator
Apollonius of Rhodes (c. 300–225 B.C.) epic poet
    Argonautica (c. 260 B.C.)

Eratosthenes (c. 275–194 B.C.) literary critic, essayist, scientist, philosopher, chronicler

264–241 B.C. – First Punic War
Naevius (c. 264–261 B.C.) epic poet and mythographer

3rd century B.C. – Parian Marble
Plautus (c. 254–184 B.C.) comic playwright
  Pseudolus (191 B.C.)

240–84 B.C. – Republican Rome
Ennius (239–169 B.C.) epic and didactic poet, comic playwright, aphorist
  Annales (c. 170 B.C.)

218–202 B.C. – Second Punic War

195–159 B.C. – Terence writes comedies c.
Proclus (2nd or 1st century B.C.) cataloguer and anthologist
Apollodorus of Athens (c. 180–140 B.C.) mythographer, comic poet, etymologist
Moschus (c. 150 B.C.) pastoral poet, grammarian, and mythographer

149–146 B.C. – Third Punic War
Varro (116–27 B.C.) satirist, tragedian, chronicler, scientist, encyclopedist, anthologist

83 B.C.–A.D. 17 – Rome's Golden Age
Cicero (106–43 B.C.) orator, essayist, philosopher
  Against Atticus (68–44 B.C.)
  On Divination (60 B.C.)
  On the Duties of Office (44 B.C.)
  On Old Age (44 B.C.)
Bion (c. 100 B.C.) erotic and pastoral poet
Parthenius (c. 1st century B.C.) teacher and elegaic poet
Lucretius (96–55 B.C.) scientist and poet
  On the Nature of Things (60 B.C.)
Catullus (c. 84–c. 54 B.C.) lyric, satiric, and erotic poet
Didymus (c. 80–10 B.C.) critic, grammarian, mythographer, commentator
Virgil (70–19 B.C.) epic poet
  Bucolics or *Eclogues* (37 B.C.)
  Georgics (30 B.C.)
  Aeneid (posthumous, 18 B.C.)
Strabo (64 B.C.–A.D. 21) historian and geographer

Hyginus (64 B.C.– A.D. 17) mythographer, librarian, cataloguer, essayist, historian
Diodorus Siculus (fl. 60–21 B.C.) historian and cataloguer
    Library of History (21 B.C.)
Livy (c. 59 B.C.–A.D. 17) mythographer and historian
    From the Foundation of the City (c. A.D. 14)
Tibullus (c. 54–c. 18 B.C.) elegaic poet
    Elegies (c. 26 B.C.)
Horace (65–8 B.C.) lyric poet
    Satires II (30 B.C.)
    Odes (23 B.C.)
    Ars Poetica (20 B.C.)
    Carmina (19 B.C.)

44 B.C. – Julius Caesar Assassinated
Ovid (43 B.C.–A.D. 18) mythographer and elegaic poet
    Amores (22–15 B.C.)
    Heroides (15 B.C.)
    Art of Love (c. 1 B.C.)
    Remedies of Love (c. A.D. 2)
    Metamorphoses (A.D. 8)
    Tristia (A.D. 11)
    Fasti (posthumous, c. A.D. 18)
Dionysius of Halicarnassus (c. 30 B.C.) historian and rhetorician

27 B.C. – Roman Empire Begins
Juba (25 B.C.–A.D. 23) art critic and historian

14 B.C.–A.D. 117 – Rome's Silver Age
Seneca (c. 4 B.C.–A.D.65) tragedian, philosopher, essayist, satirist, aphorist
Apollonius of Tyana (1st century A.D.) aphorist and philosopher
Petronius (1st century A.D.) satirist, realist, novelist
Theon (1st century A.D.) drama critic and grammarian
Valerius Maximus (1st century A.D.) anthologist
Manilius (fl. 1st century A.D.) didactic poet
Pliny the Elder (A.D. 23–79) scientist, essayist, military historian and tactician
    Natural History (A.D. 77)
Silius Italicus (A.D. 26–101) epic poet
Josephus (A.D. 37–c. 100) historian, essayist, autobiographer
    History of the Jewish War (A.D. 76)

A.D. 40–61 – Paul Preaches Christianity
> Dio Chrysostomus (A.D. 40–112) philosopher and orator
> Plutarch (c. A.D. 45–c. 120) biographer, historian, philosopher, scientist, ethicist
> Valerius Flaccus (died c. A.D. 95) epic poet
> Statius (A.D. 45–96) epic poet
>> *Thebaid* (A.D. 91)
>> *Achilleid* (posthumous, A.D. 96)
> Tacitus (A.D. 55–117) historian, chronicler, biographer
>> *Dialogue on Orators* (c. A.D. 105)
>> *Annales* (A.D. 117)
> Epictetus (A.D. 55–135) stoic philosopher
> Juvenal (c. A.D. 60–c. 140) satirist and aphorist
>> *Satires* (c. A.D. 127)
> Arrian (A.D. 95–175) military tactician, historian, biographer
> Justin (c. A.D. 100–165) Christian apologist

A.D. 117–395 – Rome's Late Empire
> Antoninus Liberalis (2nd century A.D.) mythographer
> Athenagoras (2nd century A.D.) philosopher and Christian apologist
> Dictys Cretensis (2nd or 3rd century A.D.) diarist
> Dionysius Periegeta (2nd century A.D.) geographer and poet
> Pollux (2nd century A.D.) rhetorician and encyclopedist
> Zenobius (2nd century A.D.) anthologist
> Pausanias (fl. A.D. 150) geographer, historian, folklorist, mythologographer
> Polyaenus (c. A.D. 162) philosopher
> Tertullian (A.D. 165–220) Christian apologist and essayist
> Athenaeus (fl. A.D. 200) anthologist and encyclopedist
> Lucian (born A.D. 120) anthologist and commentator
> Aulus Gellius (c. A.D. 123–165) anthologist and encyclopedist
> Apuleius (c. A.D. 125–c. 171) translator, rhetorian, novelist
> Clement of Alexandria (b. A.D. 150) Christian commentator and apologist

A.D. 161 – First Germanic Invasion of Rome
> Tertullian (A.D. 165–220) Christian apologist, essayist, and satirist
> Aelian (A.D. 170–235) rhetorician, moralist, essayist, correspondent
> Philostratus (born A.D. 170) tragedian
> Solinus (c. A.D. 200) geographer and cataloguer
> Diogenes Laertius (3rd century A.D.) philosopher and anthologer
> Lactantius (A.D. 240–320) Christian apologist
> Eusebius (A.D. 260–340) chronicler and church historian
>> *Preparation for the Gospel* (A.D. 312)

Paeon the Amathusian (4th century A.D.) mathematician
Servius (4th century A.D.) grammarian and commentator

A.D. 306–337 – Constantine, the First Christian Emperor

c. A.D. 405 – St. Jerome's Vulgate
Macrobius (fl. A.D. 400) philosopher, grammarian, literary critic

A.D. 476 – Fall of Rome
Johannes Malalas (A.D. 491–578) chronicler and folklorist
Colluthus (5th century A.D.) epic poet
Hesychius (5th century A.D.) lexicographer and etymologist
Nonnus (5th century A.D.) epic poet
Tryphiodorus (5th century A.D.) epic poet
Stephanus Byzantium (5th–6th century A.D.) lexicographer
Quintus Smyrnaeus (6th ? century A.D.) epic poet
Isidore of Seville (A.D. 560–636) encyclopedist and Christian chronicler
Photius (9th century A.D.) anthologist and cataloguer
Suidas (10th century A.D.) lexicographer, grammarian, anthologist
Eustathius (12th century A.D.) scholar, commentator, historian, essayist
Johannes Tzetzes (12th century A.D.) scholar, critic, cataloguer

Bibliography

Allen, J. H., and J. B. Greenough, eds. *Selections from Ovid: Chiefly the Metamorphoses.* Boston: Ginn, 1891.

Anderson, Bernhard W. *Understanding the Old Testament.* 2d ed. Englewood Cliffs, New Jersey: Prentice-Hall, 1966.

Asimov, Isaac. *The Greeks: A Great Adventure.* Boston: Houghton Mifflin, 1965.

————. *Words from the Myths.* New York: Signet, 1969.

Aycock, Wendell M., and Theodore M. Klein, eds. *Classical Mythology in Twentieth-Century Thought and Literature.* Lubbock: Texas Tech Press, 1980.

Bell, Robert. *Dictionary of Classical Mythology.* Santa Barbara, California: ABC-CLIO, 1982.

————. *Place-Names in Classical Mythology.* Santa Barbara, California: ABC-CLIO, 1989.

————. *Women of Classical Mythology.* Santa Barbara, California: ABC-CLIO, 1991.

Biedermann, Hans. *Dictionary of Symbolism.* New York: Facts on File, 1992.

Blegen, Carl W. *The Palace of Nestor at Pylos in Western Messenia.* Princeton, New Jersey: Princeton University Press, 1973.

Bowder, Diana, ed. *Who Was Who in the Greek World.* New York: Washington Square Press, 1982.

————. *Who Was Who in the Roman World.* New York: Washington Square Press, 1980.

Bowra, C. M., et al. *Classical Greece.* Great Ages of Man Series. New York: Time, 1965.

Brooks, Nathan Covington, ed. *The Metamorphoses of Publius Ovidius Naso.* New York: A. S. Barnes and Burr, 1860.

Brown, Norman O. *Hermes the Thief: The Evolution of a Myth.* New York: Vintage, 1969.

Buck, Claire, ed. *The Bloomsbury Guide to Women's Literature.* New York: Prentice-Hall, 1992.

Bibliography

Budge, E. A. Wallis. *The Book of the Dead.* New Hyde Park, New York: University Books, 1960.

Bulfinch's Mythology. New York: Spring Books, 1969.

Calasso, Roberto. *The Marriage of Cadmus and Harmony.* New York: Alfred Knopf, 1993.

Carpenter, Rhys. *Folk Tale, Fiction and Saga in the Homeric Epics.* Berkeley: University of California Press, 1958.

Casson, Lionel. *The Ancient Mariners: Seafarers and Sea Fighters of the Mediterranean in Ancient Times.* Princeton, New Jersey: Princeton University Press, 1990.

Cavendish, Richard, ed. *Man, Myth & Magic.* New York: Marshall Cavendish, 1970.

Chase, Thomas. *The Works of Horace.* New York: Hinds, Noble & Eldredge, 1892.

Christ, Henry I. *Myths and Folklore.* New York: Oxford Book Company, 1968.

————. *Myths and Folklore.* New York: Amsco, 1989.

Cirlot, J. E. *A Dictionary of Symbols.* New York: Dorset Press, 1991.

Clark, R. T. Rundle. *Myth and Symbol in Ancient Egypt.* London: Thames and Hudson, 1959.

Cross, F. L., ed. *The Oxford Dictionary of the Christian Church.* London: Oxford University Press, 1957.

Devereux, Paul. *Secrets of Ancient and Sacred Places: The World's Mysterious Heritage.* London: Blandford, 1992.

Duff, J. Wight, and A. M. Duff. *A Literary History of Rome in the Golden Age.* London: Ernest Benn, 1960.

————. *A Literary History of Rome in the Silver Age.* London: Ernest Benn, 1964.

Durant, Will. *The Story of Civilization: The Life of Greece.* New York: Simon and Schuster, 1939.

Edwards, Paul, ed. *The Encyclopedia of Philosophy.* New York: Macmillan, 1973.

Eliade, Mircea, ed. *The Encyclopedia of Religion.* New York: Macmillan, 1987.

Ellis, Peter Berresford. *A Dictionary of Irish Mythology.* Oxford: Oxford University Press, 1991.

Evslin, Bernard. *Heroes, Gods and Monsters of the Greek Myths.* New York: Bantam, 1968.

Faraday, Winifred. *The Edda, Part 1 & 2.* New York: AMS Press, 1902.

Feder, Lillian. *The Meridian Handbook of Classical Mythology.* New York: New American Library, 1970.

Ferry, David. *Gilgamesh.* New York: Farrar, Straus and Giroux, 1992.

Fischer, Carl. *The Myth and Legend of Greece.* Dayton, Ohio: Pflaum, 1968.

Flaceliere, Robert. *A Literary History of Greece.* New York: Mentor, 1962.

Flaherty, Thomas H., et al., ed. *Wondrous Realms of the Aegean.* Alexandria, Virginia: Time-Life Books, 1993.

Frazer, Sir James George. *The Golden Bough.* New York: Macmillan, 1947.

Fuller, Edmund, ed. *Plutarch's Lives of the Noble Greeks.* New York: Dell, 1963.

Gill, Sam D., and Irene F. Sullivan. *Dictionary of Native American Mythology.* Santa Barbara, California: ABC-CLIO, 1992.

Godolphin, R. B. *The Latin Poets.* New York: Modern Library, 1949.

Grant, Michael. *Myths of the Greeks and Romans.* New York: Mentor, 1962.

———. *Ancient History Atlas.* New York: Sanford J. Durst, 1971.

Graves, Robert. Introduction to *New Larousse Encyclopedia of Mythology.* London: Prometheus Press, 1970.

Gregory, Richard, ed. *The Oxford Companion to the Mind.* New York: Oxford University Press, 1987.

Grene, David, and Richmond Lattimore, eds. *Greek Tragedies, Volumes 1-3.* Chicago: University of Chicago Press, 1960.

Grimal, Pierre. *Dictionary of Classical Mythology.* London: Penguin, 1990.

Guerber, H. A. *Myths of Greece and Rome.* New York: American Book, 1921.

Hadas, Moses. *Ancilla to Classical Reading.* New York: Columbia University Press, 1954.

———. Introduction to *Apollonius Rhodius's Argonautica.* Norwalk, Connecticut: Easton Press, 1988.

Hamilton, Edith. *The Greek Way.* New York: Mentor, 1942.

———. *Mythology.* Boston: Little, Brown, 1942.

Hammond Historical Atlas of the World. Maplewood, New Jersey, 1984.

Harrington, Karl Pomeroy. *Mediaeval Latin.* Boston: Allyn and Bacon, 1925.

Holy Bible. King James Version. New York: World Publishing, n.d.

Hooke, S. H. *Middle Eastern Mythology.* Baltimore, Maryland: Penguin Books, 1963.

Hopper, R. J. *The Early Greeks.* New York: Barnes and Noble, 1976.

Howatson, M. C., ed. *The Oxford Companion to Classical Literature.* New York: Oxford University Press, 1991.

Humphries, Rolfe, trans. "The Story of Daedalus and Icarus," *Arrangement in Literature.* America Reads Series.

451

Bibliography

Glenview, Illinois: Scott Foresman, 1982.

Ions, Veronica. *Egyptian Mythology.* London: Paul Hamlyn, 1968.

Jowett, Benjamin, trans. *Thucydides.* New York: Washington Square Press, 1970.

Jung, Carl G. *Man and His Symbols.* Garden City, New York: Doubleday, 1964.

Kelsey, Francis W. Introduction to *Selections from Ovid.* Boston: Allyn and Bacon, 1890.

Kitto, H. D. F. *The Greeks.* New York: Penguin, 1988.

Larrington, Carolyne. *The Feminist Companion to Mythology.* New York: Pandora, 1992.

Lattimore, Richmond, trans. *Hesiod.* Ann Arbor: University of Michigan Press, 1973.

———. *Iliad.* Chicago: University of Chicago Press, 1951.

———. *Odyssey.* New York: Harper & Row, 1965.

Lincoln, J. L. *Selections from the Poems of Ovid.* New York: Appleton, 1884.

Lurker, Manfred. *The Gods and Symbols of Ancient Egypt.* London: Thames and Hudson, 1974.

 McEvedy, Colin. *The Penguin Atlas of Ancient History.* London: Penguin, 1967.

MacKail, J. W., trans. *Virgil's Works: The Aeneid, Eclogues, Georgics.* New York: Modern Library, 1950.

MacKendrick, Paul. *The Mute Stones Speak: The Story of Archaeology in Italy.* New York: Mentor, 1960.

Manguel, Alberto, and Gianni Guadalupi. *The Dictionary of Imaginary Places.* San Diego: Harcourt Brace Jovanovich, 1980.

Mantinband, James H. *Dictionary of Greek Literature.* Paterson, New Jersey: Littlefield, Adams, 1963.

———. *Dictionary of Latin Literature.* Paterson, New Jersey: Littlefield, Adams, 1964.

Merrill, Elmer Truesdell, ed. *Catullus.* Cambridge, Massachusetts: Harvard University Press, 1893.

Mikolaycak, Charles. *Orpheus.* New York: Harcourt Brace Jovanovich, 1992.

Miller, Frank Justus, trans. *Ovid's Metamorphoses.* Loeb Classical Library. Cambridge, Massachusetts: Harvard University Press, 1984.

Miller, James E., Jr., et al., eds. *Literature of the Eastern World.* Glenview, Illinois: Scott, Foresman and Company, 1970.

More, Daisy, and John Bowman. *Aegean Rivals.* Empires Series. Boston: Boston Publishing, 1986.

Morford, Mark P. O., and Robert J. Lenardon. *Classical Mythology*. New York: Longman, 1977.

Moyer, Linda Lancione, and Burl Willes. *Undiscovered Islands of the Mediterranean*. Santa Fe: John Muir Publications, 1992.

Neal, Bill. *Gardener's Latin*. Chapel Hill, North Carolina: Algonquin Books, 1992.

Pelikan, Jaroslav, ed. *Sacred Writings: Buddhism*. New York: Quality Paperback, 1992.

————. *Sacred Writings: The Qur'an*. New York: Quality Paperback, 1992.

Perowne, Stewart. *Roman Mythology*. London: Paul Hamlyn, 1969.

Picard, Barbara Leonie. *Celtic Tales: Legends of Tall Warriors and Old Enchantments*. New York: Criterion Books, 1964.

Pierce, James Smith. *From Abacus to Zeus*. Englewood Cliffs, New Jersey: Prentice-Hall, 1991.

Pinsent, John. *Greek Mythology*. London: Paul Hamlyn, 1969.

Progoff, Ira. *The Symbolic and the Real*. New York: McGraw-Hill, 1964.

Radice, Betty. *Who's Who in the Ancient World*. New York: Penguin, 1984.

Radin, Paul. *The Trickster*. New York: Schocken Books, 1972.

Rawlinson, George, trans. *Herodotus's Persian Wars*. New York: Modern Library, 1942.

Rose, H. I. Introduction to *Hygini Fabulae*. Leyden, Holland: A. W. Sythoff, 1933.

————. *Gods and Heroes of the Greeks*. New York: Meridian, 1960.

————. *A Handbook of Greek Literature*. New York: E. P. Dutton, 1960.

Rosenberg, Donna. *World Mythology*. Lincolnwood, Illinois: Passport Books, 1992.

Rosenberg, Donna, and Sorelle Baker. *Mythology and You: Classical Mythology and Its Relevance to Today's World*. Lincolnwood, Illinois: National Textbook, 1984.

Seltman, Charles. *The Twelve Olympians*. New York: Crowell, 1962.

Severy, Merle, ed. *Greece and Rome: Builders of Our World*. Washington, DC: National Geographic, 1977.

Slater, Philip E. *The Glory of Hera: Greek Mythology and the Greek Family*. Boston: Beacon Press, 1968.

Smith, Eric. *A Dictionary of Classical Reference in English Poetry*. New York: Barnes and Noble, 1984.

Snodgrass, Mary Ellen. *Greek Classics*. Lincoln, Nebraska: Cliff Notes, 1988.

————. *Roman Classics*. Lincoln, Nebraska: Cliff Notes, 1988.

Bibliography

Tripp, Edward. *The Meridian Handbook of Classical Mythology.* New York: Meridian Books, 1970.

Van der Heyden, A. A. M., and H. H. Scullard, eds. *Atlas of the Classical World.* London: Nelson, 1959.

Wechsler, Herman J. *Gods and Goddesses in Art and Legend.* New York: Washington Square Press, 1961.

Wilkinson, Herbert. *Livy's Legends of Ancient Rome.* New York: Macmillan, 1906.

Wood, Michael. *In Search of the Trojan War.* London: British Broadcasting Corporation, 1985.

Illustration Credits

General Index

Because some names indicate the animistic personalities of rivers and other geographical locales (e.g., Ganges, Aegina, Hades, Asia, Nile, Tiber), I have placed them accordingly in the general index if they represent personae and in the geographical index if they represent places.

General Index

General Index

General Index

General Index

Geographic Index

Geographic Index

Bonifacio, 303
Bosporus, 91, 232–233, 313
Brasiae, 119
Britain, 61, 208
Brundisium, 162
Bulustra, Cape, 206
Buthoe, 122
Buthrotum, 56
Byzantium, 82

Cadistus, Mount, 258
Cadmeia, 123
Caicus River, 107–108
Calliste, 121
Calydon, 27, 65, 129, 159, 213, 261, 359, 400
Calymne, 141
Camelot, 191
Camicos, 141
Campania, 326
Canope, 127, 187
Caphareus, 87, 271
Capua, 61
Carchemish, 116
Caria, 115, 269
Carthaea, 180
Carthage, 57, 62
Caspian Sea, 367
Castalian Spring, 114, 121
Caucasus Mountains, 33, 209, 235, 354, 367, 369
Cecropis, 143
Cenaeum, Cape, 214
Ceos, 180, 282
Cephallenia, 288
Cephissus River, 74
Cerameicus, 91
Chaeroneia, 73
Chalcidice, 62
Chaonia, 97–98
Chemmis, 342
Chersonese, 79, 231, 291
Chimaera, Mount, 116
Chrysa, 288, 302
Cilicia, 95, 121, 354
Cinyras, 288
Cios River, 232
Circeo, Cape, 295, 303
Cirrha, 258
Cithaeron, Mount, 354
Cleonae, 202
Colchis, 35–36, 77, 204, 227–251, 278, 368
Colonus, 30, 369, 400
Corcyra, 239

Corfu, 299, 303
Corinth, 27–29, 33, 39, 41, 101, 111, 113, 115–116, 169, 202, 227–31, 241–243, 248–249, 275, 285, 354, 373, 375–376, 396, 402
Corsica, 303
Cortona, 105
Corythus, 156
Cos, 212, 335
Cranae, 185, 332
Crete, 35, 41, 56, 71, 77, 91, 119, 139, 141–142, 155, 172, 183, 205, 216, 240, 248, 263, 265–266, 269, 302, 332, 387, 397, 399, 401
Crimea, 73, 247
Cumae, 59, 140–141
Cyclades, 19, 56, 68, 87, 141, 177, 267, 288, 302
Cynthus, Mount, 255, 258, 354
Cyparissia, 278
Cyprus, 81, 95, 185, 265, 288, 389–390, 401
Cythaeron, Mount, 168, 201
Cythera, 56, 292

Damascus, 169
Danube River, 10, 36, 239, 244, 249
Dardanelles, 156
Dardania, 153, 155
Delos, 56, 68, 141–142, 253–255, 258, 263, 288, 302, 354, 375, 383, 400, 402
Delphi, 39, 41–42, 65, 97–98, 108, 114, 121, 134, 167, 189, 207, 211, 253–257, 261–263, 267, 288, 308
Dendra, 116
Dindymus, Mount, 231, 354
Diomeds, 162
Dodona, 56, 229
Dolops, 231
Dorium, 278
Dracanum, 165
Drepane, 56–57, 202, 239, 299,
Dreros, 258

Egypt, 119, 123, 127, 169, 187, 189–190, 209, 265, 332, 342, 389
Elaeus, 203
Eldorado, 246
Eleithyia, 302
Eleusis, 29, 77, 213, 387, 396
Eleuthera, 11
Elis, 10, 204–205, 277–278, 301, 375
Elymus, 62
England, 244, 402

Geographic Index

Malea, 266, 292, 302
Malta, 303
Mantua, 105
Marathon, 41–42, 91, 205, 359, 400–401, 403
Media, 243, 249
Mediterranean Sea, 114
Megara, 30, 39, 82, 399
Megaris, 39
Meles, river, 316
Memphis, 142
Messina, 239, 297–298, 303
Messenia, 59, 162, 275, 282, 287
Methymna, 11, 101
Midea, 345
Miletus, 387
Mimas, Mount, 354
Misenum, 323
Molorchia, 203
Morocco, 303
Mycenae, 45–47, 49, 65, 75, 81, 133, 195, 202, 261, 345
Mykonos, 87
Myrine, 231
Mysia, 5, 67, 79, 91, 98, 107–108, 153, 206, 288, 313, 389

Naples, 59, 141, 297
Naryx, 85
Nauplia, 107, 265, 269, 272
Navarino, 282
Naxos, 168, 171, 177, 399, 404
Nemea, 29
Neriton, Mount, 285
New Orleans, 172
Nile River, 127, 185, 190, 265, 332, 342
North Sea, 244
Numidia, 207
Nysa, Mount, 165, 171

Ocean, 244, 304
Oechalia, 210–211, 214, 287
Oeneus, 261
Oenoe, 93, 203
Oeta, Mount, 214–215, 354
Ogygia, 298, 303–304
Olenian Rock, 277
Olympia, 74, 223, 362, 367–368, 377
Olympus, Mount, 116, 121, 169, 171, 197, 206–207, 212, 216, 224, 253, 298, 311, 315–316, 347
Opus, 215
Orchomenus, 168, 201
Orthys, 354

Ortygia, 253–257, 258
Ossa, Mount, 240, 354

Paestum, 103, 124
Pagasae, 229, 247, 313
Palestine, 172
Palinuro, Cape, 326
Pambotis, Lake, 97
Pangaeum, Mount, 123
Panhaema, 171
Panopeus, 257
Paris, 245
Parnassus, Mount, 177, 287, 304, 315, 354, 375
Paros, 91, 93, 141, 206
Parthenius, Mount, 107–108
Patriae, 149
Peiresia, 230
Pelion, Mount, 10, 227, 361
Peloponnesus, 10, 17, 23, 27, 30, 45, 47, 56, 65, 75, 101, 168, 265, 287, 302, 373
Peneus River, 205, 355
Pergamus, 74
Pergamum, 56, 69, 98, 108
Periphlegethon River, 296
Phaestus, 258
Phalerum, 93
Phare, 266
Pharos, 129, 167, 187, 265
Phaselis, 116
Phasis, 33
Phasis River, 33
Pheneus, 212, 287
Pherae, 147
Philistia, 342
Phlegethon, 59
Phlegra, 212
Phloeum, 171
Phocis, 150
Phoenicia, 121, 265
Pholoe, Mount, 204
Phrygia, 79, 153, 167, 169, 257, 354
Phthia, 9, 97, 281, 305, 331
Pieria, 311, 316
Pileus, 278
Pillars of Herakles, 207, 220, 303
Pindus, Mount, 361
Planctus, 297
Pleuron, 114
Poeeessa, 282
Polyrrhenia, 71
Pompeii, 74, 103, 174, 218, 223, 347, 362
Pontus, 233

Geographic Index